MARKETING MANAGEMENT

Fred Selnes & Even J. Lanseng

MARKETING MANAGEMENT
A Customer-Centric Approach

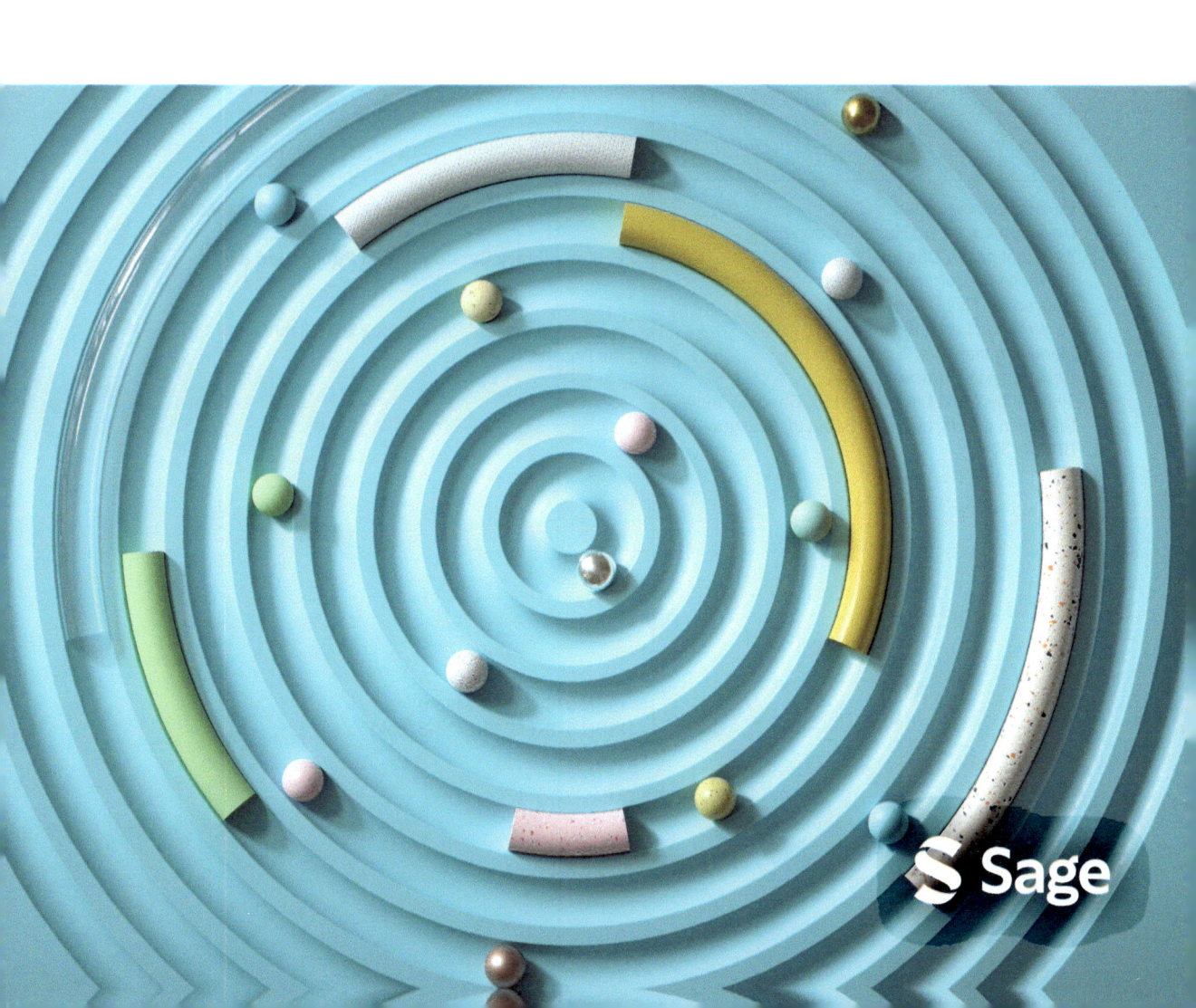

Sage

1 Oliver's Yard
55 City Road
London EC1Y 1SP

2455 Teller Road
Thousand Oaks
California 91320

Unit No 323–333, Third Floor, F-Block
International Trade Tower
Nehru Place, New Delhi – 110 019

8 Marina View Suite 43-053
Asia Square Tower 1
Singapore 018960

Editor: Matthew Waters
Development editor: Hannah Cooper
Assistant editor: Charlotte Hanson
Production editor: Imogen Roome
Copyeditor: Neil Dowden
Proofreader: Leigh Smithson
Marketing manager: Elena Asplen
Cover design: Francis Kenney
Typeset by: C&M Digitals (P) Ltd, Chennai, India
Printed in the UK by Bell & Bain Ltd, Glasgow
BB0347301

Library of Congress Control Number: 2024936862

British Library Cataloguing in Publication data

A catalogue record for this book is available from the British Library

ISBN 978-1-5296-2425-0
ISBN 978-1-5296-2424-3 (pbk)

Dedicated to
Line and Anette Selnes
Jonas, Mathias and Mia Lanseng

CONTENTS

ABOUT THE AUTHORS

Fred Selnes is a professor at BI Norwegian Business School. He holds a bachelor's degree in business administration from BI, a Master of Science degree in marketing from the Northwestern University and a doctoral degree from Norwegian School of Business Administration (NHH). He has published in leading journals such as the *Journal of Marketing*, *Journal of Service Research* and *Journal of Business Research*. Research interests include strategic marketing, customer relationship management and branding. In parallel with the academic work, he has been a leading management consultant in strategic marketing for more than a hundred companies across numerous industries. He has also started several companies, the latest being CPM Analytics located in Oslo. The company provides services in data engineering, modelling and analytics aimed at improving efficiency and effectiveness in sales, marketing, branding, distribution and customer service.

Even J. Lanseng is an associate professor at BI Norwegian Business School. He holds a doctoral degree from the Norwegian University of Life Sciences. He has published several articles in academic journals such as the *European Journal of Marketing*, *Journal of Service Management*, *Journal of Brand Management* and *Food Quality and Preference*. His research primarily focuses on consumer research, branding and marketing communication. He teaches marketing management, marketing communication and marketing analytics.

ONLINE RESOURCES

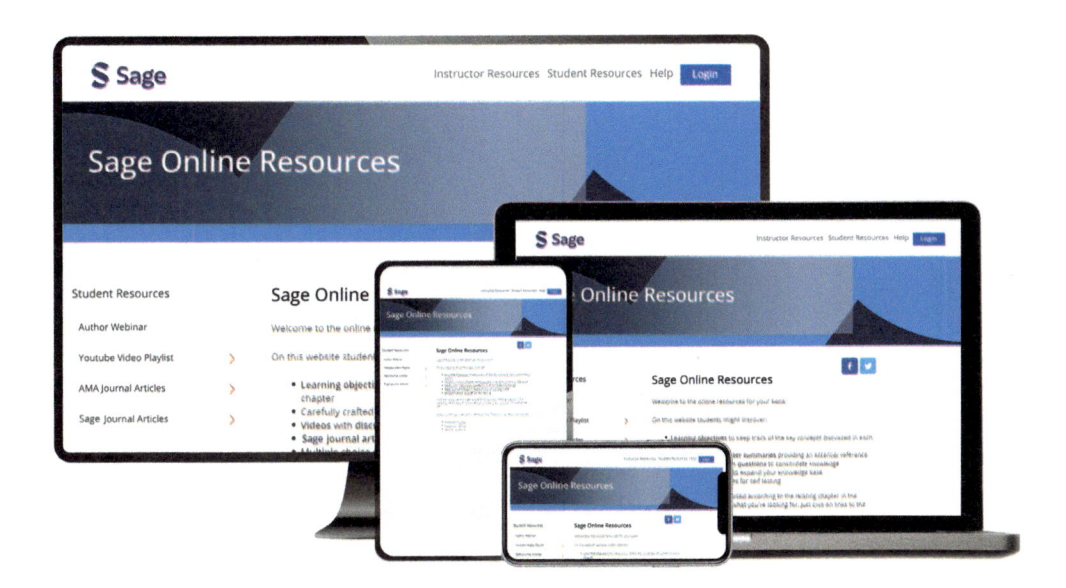

Marketing Management is supported by a wealth of online resources for both students and lecturers to aid study and support teaching, which are available at
https://study.sagepub.com/marketingmanagement

FOR LECTURERS

Teaching Guide outlining the key learning objectives covered in each chapter and providing you with suggested activities and cases to use in class or for assignments.

PowerPoint slides featuring figures and tables from the book, which can be downloaded and customized for use in your own presentations.

Resource pack containing many of the fantastic resources featured on the companion website are available for you to upload into your university's learning management system, allowing you to easily share the materials you feel are most relevant to your students.

PREFACE

Marketing Management: A Customer-Centric Approach offers a conceptual framework that delves into how businesses establish connections with their customers, ultimately creating mutual value. The success of a company is intricately linked to several factors: the quantity of customers it acquires, the durability of its customer relationships, and the profits or cash flow derived from individual customers in its portfolio. Equally important is the value experienced by customers, which is shaped by the fulfillment of their needs and their satisfaction with the company's market offers in terms of products and services.

The cornerstone of this book is the 'market-matrix', which serves as the primary organizing framework within the realm of marketing management. The market-matrix divides and apportions a company's revenues and profits among different product categories and customer segments. The core mission of marketing management is to secure and enhance revenues and profits within this market-matrix.

In cases where a company offers only one product category targeted at a single customer segment, the marketing management approach adheres to the traditional 4P marketing mix, coupled with a value proposition tailored to that specific segment. However, when a company extends its offerings to encompass multiple product categories and customer segments, the marketing management task becomes more intricate. The challenge is no longer just about crafting appealing value propositions for each segment but also about harnessing the company's resources to capitalize on synergies across various product categories and customer segments. Most companies today operate with multiple product categories and face several customer segments.

Derived from the market-matrix concept, it becomes evident that two vital domains of management within the realm of marketing management are product portfolio management and customer portfolio management. Moreover, brand management constitutes a third crucial facet for marketing management. Companies need to develop strategies and plans for how their brands can increase the value of their products and the value perception in customer segments. It is imperative that market-oriented activities are synchronized both internally and across product categories, customer segments, and brands. The foundational principles and reasoning behind these three management domains are expounded upon in Chapter 1.

Proficiency in marketing management necessitates a diverse set of competencies. Firstly, students pursuing marketing management should possess a firm grasp of the concept of markets, including their evolution influenced by competitive forces and various external factors. Secondly, students in the field of marketing management should establish a strong theoretical grounding to comprehend and analyze customer behavior, their purchase choices, and their interactions with brands over time. These essential theoretical foundations are expounded upon in Chapters 2 and 3.

Market communication plays a pivotal role in the realm of marketing management, and it's often associated with various communication endeavors such as advertising, email campaigns, social media engagement, packaging design, and interactions with sales representatives, among others. In our book, we've dedicated a whole chapter to market communication, where students can gain insights into the fundamental principles governing the dynamics of market communication. This chapter covers topics such as the mechanics of market communication, the capacity of communication to shape attitudes and preferences, the essence of creativity, distinctions among different communication channels, and how all of these factors tie into the management of investments in marketing communication and their impact on overall revenues and profits.

Efficiently overseeing a company's array of products is the primary objective of product category management, with the dual purpose of generating financial value for the company and enhancing the perceived value of the products for customers. A significant learning goal is to grasp how various product attributes and characteristics contribute to increasing the value perceived by customers, thereby elevating the overall appeal of the products. In parallel, it is essential for students to gain insight into the strategies employed by companies to communicate this value, ensure product availability at accessible points for customers, and guarantee the fulfillment of customer expectations and satisfaction. Chapter 5 is dedicated to delving into the management of the product portfolio, where these vital aspects are explored in detail.

The objective of customer portfolio management is to enhance the financial value of a company's customer base, primarily by augmenting the anticipated future cash flow. In our educational approach, students are instructed on methods to attain this goal, which encompasses activities such as acquiring new customers, retaining existing ones, and elevating the level of engagement with each individual customer. A key skillset in the field of marketing management involves the capability to identify, analyze, and strategically position a company's products and services within distinct market segments. Chapter 6 is dedicated to the exploration of customer portfolio management, where these essential principles are thoroughly examined.

Brands play a significant role in driving value. They employ various mechanisms to enable a company to command higher prices for their offerings, while simultaneously elevating the perceived value of those offerings among specific customer segments. A brand is defined as a distinct label, term, design, symbol, or another recognizable element that distinguishes the products or services of one provider from those of its rivals. It serves two primary functions: firstly, to establish the seller's identity, and secondly, to communicate its unique characteristics. These dual functions form the core of brand management, a subject thoroughly explored in Chapter 7.

We approach marketing management as a comprehensive set of actions and choices undertaken throughout an organization, all of which are centered on how customer value is defined, delivered, harnessed, and captured. When considering an organization, it operates as a continuous system engaged in activities that encompass acquiring new customers daily, safeguarding existing customers from switching to competitors, and optimizing the generation of cash flow from these customers. In this context, marketing management can be envisioned as the process of enhancing and securing this ongoing system, enabling it to seize market opportunities while averting potential threats. Consequently, strategic planning and the creation of a strategic marketing plan constitute pivotal learning objectives within this book, with the final Chapter 8 dedicated to this crucial topic.

The composition of this marketing management book resulted from several processes. Many years ago, like most academics in marketing, we followed the conventional path of creating textbooks centered around the traditional 4P marketing mix framework. This framework initially emerged during an era where the primary marketing objective was to generate volume to achieve economies of scale in industrial production. Profit was directly linked to volume and margin during that time.

However, as the economy evolved, the service sector grew larger, and companies shifted their focus towards customer satisfaction. Profit became more closely associated with retaining customers and sustaining cash flow over extended periods. Simultaneously, brands gained prominence as tools for global expansion and diversification into new product categories. Another significant transformation occurred with the advent of the World Wide Web and the Internet, fundamentally altering how customers accessed information, interacted with companies, and contributed to the rapid development of big data and machine learning.

Traditional textbooks attempted to incorporate these and other new developments by adding new chapters but adhering to the 4P marketing mix structure. Our experience in teaching marketing management revealed that students often felt lost and struggled to find a coherent thread throughout the book.

Another factor shaping our understanding of marketing management came from our interactions with numerous companies in various educational programs and consulting projects. One striking observation was that when the term 'marketing' was mentioned, managers often associated it with communication activities and the marketing department. In contrast, when the term 'customer' was used, managers linked it to the organization, not just a specific activity or department. Issues related to customers were quickly associated with revenues and the activities and costs related to acquiring, retaining, and developing customers. We think of this as the essence of a customer-centric approach to marketing.

We also observed that managers placed a high level of trust in our academic foundation in marketing when addressing various customer-related issues. We found it unfortunate that the label 'marketing' was frequently associated with marketing communication, overshadowing other important topics within the field. As educators, we believe in the importance of broadening perspectives, especially for managers, our academic peers in other business school disciplines, and the public, to understand the full scope of marketing. We believed that a wider perspective would generate more interest in our field and promote the dissemination of scientific knowledge.

We were fortunate to be part of BI Norwegian Business School when we initially developed our customer-centric approach to marketing management. BI has a history of innovation and has contributed significantly to business education in Norway across all levels. The school maintains strong connections with both the business community and the global network of scholars in the academic world.

Upon the introduction of our innovative textbook on marketing management (written in Norwegian), we witnessed a notable improvement in student ratings. No longer did students express grievances about marketing management being merely a compilation of models and concepts devoid of a coherent, unifying thread. Additionally, participants in our executive programs provided exceptionally positive feedback.

The pivotal moment in our journey came when Matthew Waters from Sage Publishing visited us. Initially, we were reluctant to consider producing the text in English due to the considerable undertaking it represented, coupled with concerns about potential resistance to altering the traditional approach to teaching marketing management among our colleagues in other business schools. However, discussions with our international academic peers indicated their interest in our approach if the text were available in English. Upon Matthew Waters' subsequent visit, he once again encouraged us to contemplate the prospect of creating a book for the global market. We embraced the idea and commenced the project, benefiting from invaluable assistance from Hannah Cooper, Sarah Turpie and others from this highly professional publisher.

Gratefully, our Norwegian publisher, Fagbokforlaget, led by Anders Nybø and Arno Vigmostad, exhibited tremendous enthusiasm and provided unwavering support throughout the endeavor.

Whether you are a student or an educator perusing this textbook, our hope is that we have successfully laid a solid and engaging foundation for comprehending marketing management. While we do not assert that this is the sole approach to learning marketing management, we hold absolute confidence that the traditional 4P marketing mix approach has become outdated and that the field necessitates a fresh perspective. Our aspiration is that we have sparked a discourse within business schools and their marketing departments, advocating the need to reconsider how marketing management is taught. In doing so, we aim to ensure that the valuable scientific contributions within the marketing discipline reach a broader and more appreciative audience.

1

INTRODUCTION TO MARKETING MANAGEMENT

This chapter

- defines marketing management;
- introduces the market-matrix as an organizing framework;
- presents the three management areas and the importance of coordination;
- explores the meaning of customer-centric marketing management;
- presents the key principles of the strategic marketing plan.

INTRODUCTION

Marketing management aims to convince potential customers to connect with a company's products and services, not just once, but to establish a lasting exchange relationship with a supplier (brand) that grows over time. The success of marketing is measured by the growth of the company's portfolio of valuable customers, which is reflected in the following:

- acquiring new customers and adding them to the portfolio;
- retaining more customers and increasing positive word of mouth;
- encouraging customers to expand their relationship with the supplier (brand) by purchasing more products and services.

Amazon is a highly successful company, with a significant growth in financial market value, and is also considered to be one of the strongest brands in the world as measured by brand value (Statista, 2023a). A brand is the name of a company (e.g. Apple) or a product (e.g. iPhone) used to identify a supplier and discriminate their products and services from competitors. The effectiveness of strong brands lies among others in their ability to attract and retain valuable customers more efficiently than their competitors:

- Strong brands attract and connect with more new customers. Amazon, for example, has been experiencing an annual growth rate of around 20% in terms of new customers. In a recent survey conducted in 2019, over 2,000 US customers participated, and 89% of them stated that they are more inclined to purchase products from Amazon over other ecommerce sites.
- Strong brands have higher customer retention rates because they excel at meeting customer expectations, leading to high levels of customer satisfaction and positive word of mouth. According to the American Customer Satisfaction Index, Amazon has a satisfaction score of over 80 on a scale of 0 to 100, making it one of the highest-scoring companies in the US (Statista, 2023b). In addition to this, strong brands such as Amazon are constantly innovating to improve and maintain their customer relationships, never resting on their laurels despite their success.
- Strong brands transform customer relationships into stronger and more valuable ones. Amazon, for instance, has converted a significant portion of its customer base into Amazon Prime subscribers, with over 200 million subscribers worldwide, 147 million of which are in the US (Business of Apps, 2023). Prime membership offers additional benefits such as free two-day shipping, music and video streaming. The Amazon mobile app also has a substantial monthly audience of almost 100 million customers. Furthermore, Amazon has successfully expanded its brand into a wide range of product categories and services beyond books, including electronics, clothing, shoes, jewellery, home and kitchen products, among others, creating a diversified and interconnected ecosystem of products and services. The ecosystem has also an important social dimension where their most loyal customers form communities for sharing information and services.

In nearly every market, a crucial aspect is the diversity among customers in their needs and responses to market-related actions. In the realm of marketing, the concept of 'need' can be seen as the perceived difference between the current state and the desired state. This disparity prompts customers to actively seek solutions to address the identified problem (Oliver, 1997). The recognition of a problem generates psychological tension, serving as a driving force for individuals to take action and resolve the issue at hand. Customer heterogeneity underscores the fact that people not only have different problem recognitions, indicating variations in the gap between current states and desires, but also differ in how their problem recognition evolves over time and how they are influenced by various market activities. To thrive in a market, companies such as Amazon must grasp the diverse nature of their customer base and tailor their offerings accordingly across different customer segments.

A second important phenomenon of a market is that companies usually offer more than one product category and that they have different competitors across categories. For example, Amazon will compete with bookstores for their book category while they will compete with another set of competitors in their electronics category. Notice that as customers connect through multiple product categories, their relationship with the company (brand) becomes stronger (i.e. more connectors).

To get a holistic view of the strategic marketing problem companies allocate revenues and costs in a market-matrix composed of their product categories and their customer segments.

In the following we will start by introducing some key principles for how grouping of products and customers can be done. How companies group their products and how they define their strategic segments of customers have huge implications for how they design and implement their strategic marketing. It follows from the market-matrix that companies need to manage both their product portfolio and their customer portfolio. We add brand management as the third management area.

To be effective in a market, companies need to coordinate and leverage potential synergies within and across the three marketing management areas. Marketing management is therefore a strategic issue addressed in the top management group and in the boardrooms. In the final chapter of the book, we will return to these questions and how companies develop and implement a strategic marketing plan.

GROUPING CUSTOMERS INTO SEGMENTS IN THE MARKET-MATRIX

Customer heterogeneity is a fundamental characteristic of markets, meaning that customers differ in terms of how they need and how they respond to marketing activities. To address this, marketers often group similar customers into *segments* and differentiate their offerings accordingly.

We differentiate between *macro-* and *micro*-segmentation variables. Each company must develop their own set of segmentation variables based on their understanding of the market and how they want to compete. Thus, there is no right or wrong way of segmentation, but there are effective ways of segmentation following a few principles. Macro-segmentation is strategic and involves how companies differentiate and tailor their products and activities to better create something that is valuable for customers in the segment and, through this, become more attractive than their competitors. For instance, a Scandinavian charter tour company identified three macro-segments – *Young Single*, *Family* and *55-Plus* – and used this segmentation scheme to differentiate, refine and innovate their products and value-creating activities. Given the investments and long-term commitment required, companies prefer to have few but highly distinct macro-segments.

Macro-segments refer to the strategic grouping of similar customers to differentiate and specialize a company's products and activities to better fit their specific needs and wants, which in turn makes the company more attractive than its competitors. On the other hand, micro-segments are used for tactical marketing activities, and each macro-segment can be further divided into a set of micro-segments. For instance, the Scandinavian charter tour company could differentiate its communication to the 55-Plus macro-segment by dividing it into age brackets (i.e. 55–60, 61–70 and 71 and older). Micro-segmentation variables can include the age of the relationship, the number of children, destination preferences, gender, geography, and more. Unlike macro-segments, there is no limit to the number of micro-segments as long as they increase the efficiency of marketing activities. Additionally, the composition of micro-segments can vary across macro-segments, as certain variables such as the number and age of children are only relevant in the Family segment, and not in the Young & Single and the 55-Plus segments. Whereas the macro-segmentation scheme should be constant over time due to the strategic investments, micro-segmentation variables are likely to be frequently updated and aligned with the tactical marketing activities.

By implementing a highly differentiated macro- and micro-segmentation strategy, companies can achieve greater effectiveness and efficiency in their marketing activities. However, as segmentation variables and differentiation increase, coordination complexity also increases. Therefore, companies must carefully select their segmentation model and balance the benefits of more fine-grained differentiation with the costs of coordination. With the advancement of digitalization and the availability of sophisticated data-management systems such as CRM, the coordination costs have decreased significantly, allowing companies to handle more complex micro-segmentation architectures. CRM stands for customer relationship management, and CRM systems are digital applications that store information about customers and use the data to differentiate and personalize communication through emails, text messaging, phone calls and service requests. Thus, while the number of strategic macro-segments are likely to remain few, the number of micro-segments will increase making marketing activities more relevant and personal through various digital applications.

GROUPING PRODUCTS INTO CATEGORIES IN THE MARKET-MATRIX

A second characteristic of markets is that we group products into different categories with different competitors. In most markets, products from different competitors have unique product characteristics and qualities, making it challenging to group them into competitive arenas. To overcome this, we group products into categories based on their similarities in fulfilling a customer's needs, where the different products are close substitutes. For instance, takeaway pizza and sushi restaurants are usually considered as close substitutes and should be grouped into the takeaway restaurant category. Similarly, Hennig-Olsen, a Norwegian ice-cream manufacturer, defined seven product categories based on this logic, as shown in Figure 1.1. These categories include Impulse, which contains single packaged ice-cream products consumed immediately after purchase; Multipack, which contains similar products to impulse but packed in boxes filled with 6–12 products; and Tubs, which contains boxes of ice cream in various flavours and is typically consumed as a dessert. The other product categories follow similar logic.

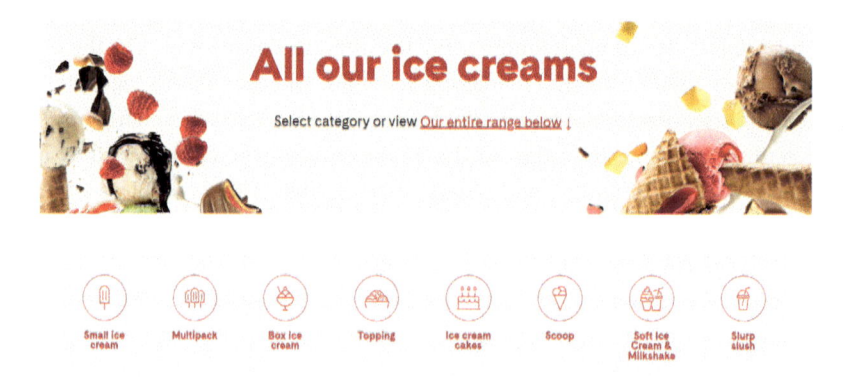

Figure 1.1   Hennig-Olsen product categories (https://www.hennig-olsen.no/en/)

Categorizing products is crucial as it determines the competitive landscape and the competitors of a company. For instance, in the Impulse category, the competing brands in Norway include Diplom Is, Drammens Is and Ben and Jerry's, while in the Tubs category, the competitors are Mövenpick, Ben and Jerry's and Diplom Is. Due to the different categories having different competitors, they also vary in terms of product innovation and competitive dynamics. For example, the Multipack category is highly price-competitive, while other categories have competitors that compete on non-price dimensions.

Recall that brand can be the name of a product (e.g. iPhone) or the name of a company (e.g. Apple). For some companies it will therefore make sense to categorize products as product brands. Thus, Apple may, for example, use iPhone, iPad, iMac, iPods, and so forth, to categorize their products.

A market-oriented approach to defining product categories prioritizes the needs of customers and the alternatives available to fulfil those needs. It is worth noting that if different companies have varying understandings of customers' needs, they will likely define product categories differently and, therefore, identify different competitors. A good illustration is Tine, a Scandinavian dairy company that had defined its primary product category as milk for several years and was satisfied with having the highest market share. However, sales of milk were decreasing despite population growth. To address this, Tine redefined its product category to 'Drinks for breakfast and lunch', realizing that juice, coffee and tea were close substitutes for milk. This led Tine to expand its product portfolio by adding juice products, which have now become a significant source of revenue (Tine, 2022).

BRANDS ACROSS CUSTOMER SEGMENTS AND PRODUCT CATEGORIES

A third fundamental characteristic of most markets is the presence of brands. A brand can be considered as a unit of information, stored in people's memories, which is represented by a name. People form associations with the name, which link the brand to other units of information which can be knowledge and emotions. When a brand name is recalled, a set of other units of knowledge and emotions is also activated through the links associated with the brand. For instance, when someone thinks about Mercedes, other thoughts may be activated, such as the association of Mercedes with Germany. Germany may, in turn, activate new associations linked to it, such as high-quality products. Thus, through the links of associations in memory, Mercedes may be connected to thoughts of high-quality products. As a result, what a person thinks about Germany can potentially affect their opinion about Mercedes, so positive thoughts about Germany are transferred to positive thoughts about Mercedes, and vice versa. This implies that the same product can be perceived as more or less attractive depending on what is associated with the brand. As a result, managing brand associations is a critical activity of marketing management.

The American Marketing Association offers a definition of a brand as 'a name, term, design, symbol, or any other feature that distinguishes one seller's goods or services from those of others' (AMA, 2023). Thus, the brand serves two primary purposes: identification (Who are you?) and differentiation (Why you?). For instance, Mercedes and BMW are both recognized as car manufacturers, but their distinctions can vary depending on the sets of associations held by different people, resulting in varying opinions about their differences. One individual might believe that Mercedes is distinct because it is typically driven by older people, while BMW is preferred by younger drivers. Another person might think that Mercedes is elegant, while BMW is the choice of people who want to appear rich but lack elegance. Brand managers at Mercedes and BMW systematically shape the associations people make with their brands in order to generate more positive opinions across customer segments and product categories.

Brands play a crucial role in the sale of products through independent retailers, establishing an exchange relationship between the company and these retailers (i.e. customers). The connection to end users is forged through a recognizable brand name, such as the manufacturer's name (e.g. Apple) or a product name (e.g. iPhone). The more appealing a brand is to consumers, the more likely they are to prefer retailers that carry that brand – a strategy known as a pull-strategy. Producers invest in creating compelling brands to attract customers to retailers offering their products. In certain industries, brands wield significant negotiating power with independent retailers.

To counterbalance supplier power, retailers focus on developing enticing chain brands and private labels (products branded by the retailer chain). Suppliers, or manufacturers, continually seek innovative ways to strengthen their connection with end users in order to maintain and enhance their market power. The era of digitalization has witnessed strategic initiatives like apps, concept stores, social media and customer clubs. Nike exemplifies how robust brands leverage digitalization to innovate in brand building, ensuring a sustained market presence within distribution networks (refer to Case Study 1.2 for further insights).

THE THREE MANAGEMENT AREAS IN MARKETING

A key strategic objective for a company is to bolster or enhance revenues and profits, ensuring they cover expenses, provide dividends to owners and establish a financial cushion for unforeseen circumstances. The market-matrix outlines the product categories and customer segments from which the company aims to derive its revenues and profits. At the core of the strategy lies the development of a plan with a series of actions designed to secure or increase future revenues and profits across the various product categories and customer segments outlined in the market-matrix. This linkage of marketing management to the overall company strategy involves overseeing a customer portfolio, a product portfolio and brands, as illustrated in Figure 1.2.

These three areas of management are highly interconnected, and the success of one area depends on how the other two areas are managed. To analyse marketing, the first step is to allocate the company's revenues and profits to the strategic product categories and customer segments in a matrix. It is important to note that a single customer from one segment may purchase products from one or more product categories, and a single product from a product category may be sold to customers in more than one segment. As most companies operate in multiple segments and product categories, marketing activities need to be coordinated across customer segments and product categories. Notice that the starting point for this framework is customers connected to the company through their purchases of products from the company. Another starting point could have been all customers in a segment of the market and then analysing the market share in these segments. This alternative approach makes less sense if customers' choices are influenced by their previous choices as is usually the case (Dwyer et al., 1987; Klemperer, 1987).

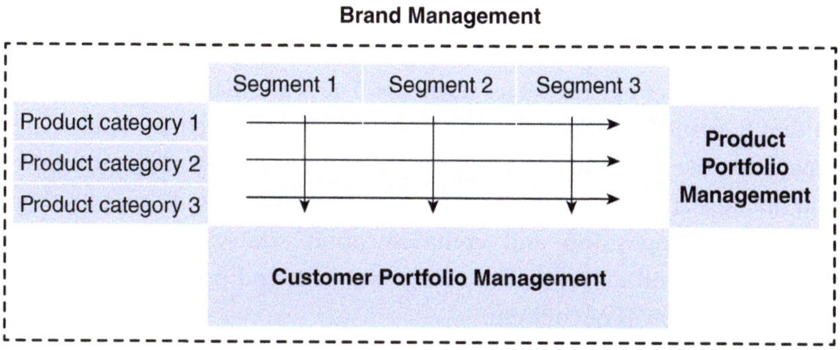

Brand Management

	Segment 1	Segment 2	Segment 3	
Product category 1				**Product Portfolio Management**
Product category 2				
Product category 3				
	Customer Portfolio Management			

Figure 1.2 The market-matrix and the three management areas in marketing

Case Study 1.1

The Charter Tour Company

The leisure, travel and tourism company mentioned earlier operates in three different product categories (Sun and Beach, Winter and City Weekends) across three main segments (Young & Single, Family and 55-Plus). The market-matrix with distribution of revenues across these categories and segments is presented in Figure 1.3. The Sun and Beach category generates the highest revenues, accounting for 67.3% of the total, while the Family segment generates the largest share of revenues, contributing 59.1% to the company's overall revenue. The Winter products are most popular among the Young & Single segment, and the City Weekend products are most popular among the 55-Plus segment.

	Young & Single	Family	55-Plus	
Sun and Beach	20	290	60	67.3%
Winter	80	20	20	21.8%
City Weekend	5	15	40	10.9%
	19.1%	59.1%	21.8%	100%

Figure 1.3 Market-matrix with distribution of revenues across product categories and customer segments

This example highlights the potential for growth within the existing customer portfolio. The Young & Single segment has room to grow by purchasing more of the Sun and Beach and City Weekend products. The Family segment has the potential to grow by purchasing more of the Winter and City Weekend products. Similarly, the 55-Plus segment could expand by purchasing more of the Winter and City Weekend products. It is also worth noting that the company has not been generating significant sales in either the Young & Single or the 55-Plus segments.

Companies can increase their revenues by tailoring their value propositions to meet the specific needs and desires of their target segments. The Scandinavian tour company initially promoted family-friendly features such as playgrounds, child clubs, family dinners and entertainment for their Sun and Beach products. However, they soon realized that these features did not appeal to the Young & Single or 55-Plus segments. As a result, they differentiated their value proposition and communication strategy for these segments by emphasizing comfort and luxury to the 55-Plus segment and promoting travel during off-peak weeks to avoid crowds of children.

The company also discovered that they had been offering discounts to attract the 55-Plus segment during the off-season, assuming that lower prices were the main incentive. However, they later learned that these customers preferred off-peak weeks because there were fewer children around, not because of the lower prices. Therefore, they concluded that discounts were an ineffective marketing tactic and that they could sell just as well without them, while also increasing profitability.

The aforementioned example also highlights the significance of aligning the management of customer segments and product categories to utilize the market-related resources of the product portfolio, customer portfolio and brands. A well-coordinated management of marketing resources is crucial to an overall marketing management strategy. In the following sections, we will first provide more details about the three management areas in marketing, and then discuss the significance of coordination to attain synergies for revenue and profit growth.

Customer Portfolio Management

The aim of managing a customer portfolio is to increase the value of the company's collection of customers. According to financial theory, the value of an object such as a company's stock, a plot of land or a machine is determined by the total cash it is expected to generate in the future. Similarly, the financial value of a customer portfolio is the sum of future cash flows it is predicted to bring in. This expected cash flow can be enhanced by adding more new customers, retaining existing customers and increasing the level of engagement with each customer. The process of customer portfolio management involves creating a strategy to increase the value of the portfolio and then executing the plan to capture the generated value. This is explored further in the case study of Nike below.

Case Study 1.2

Nike

To entice new customers, companies must take action to alter the typical behaviour of potential customers. For instance, Nike must change the way that customers view the desirability of their brand if they want to attract individuals who typically choose competitors like Adidas, Reebok or Asics. Adjustments in perceptions can arise from the introduction of new and improved product features, higher quality, more favourable brand associations, more attractive prices, positive recommendations and other factors that affect customers' views of desirability. Nike can invest in developing their products to make their running shoes lighter, with better shock absorption, more appealing design and other qualities that customers value. Beyond product development, Nike can also influence customer perceptions through advertising. By airing commercials on television, social media and other channels, they provide arguments as to why Nike is the best option. Nike can also shape perceptions through in-store activities at their network of retail locations. It is the responsibility of marketing to shape these perceptions so that the company's products are viewed as more attractive than those of their competitors.

Figure 1.4 Customers must choose from a wide selection of alternative brands and models

When creating a strategy to attract new customers, it is crucial to consider the differences across various customer segments. For example, the factors that make running shoes desirable may vary depending on factors such as customer ambitions, intended use, age and other

(Continued)

factors. Customers in the high-ambition segment are likely to be drawn to aspects like high performance, speed and weight, whereas those in the low-ambition segment may prioritize factors such as design and comfort. As illustrated in Figure 1.5, there are many different types of runners. To appeal to a broad range of customers, companies like Nike must differentiate and tailor their marketing activities to the specific needs and preferences of different customer segments. By doing so, they can become more attractive to customers in a wider range of segments.

Figure 1.5   Different types or segments of runners

In order to succeed in the competition for customers, companies must not only comprehend how new customers will respond to their latest offerings, but also anticipate how their competitors will react. Adidas, one of Nike's primary rivals, is also striving to develop better and more desirable running shoes and promote them with confidence. This means that Nike's actions may not necessarily attract new customers because Adidas (or any other competitor) may have taken actions that counteract the effects of Nike's efforts. Since the market is continuously evolving in terms of customer preferences and competitors' offerings, companies require a high level of analytical capabilities in order to anticipate how investments in marketing activities will perform.

In addition to attracting new customers, customer portfolio management also involves safeguarding existing customer relationships against competitors who may attempt to poach a company's customers. One effective defence strategy is to ensure customer satisfaction, as satisfied customers are less likely to defect to a competitor. Conversely, dissatisfied customers are more likely to switch to a competitor the next time they make a purchase. Therefore, a crucial defence strategy is to manage customer experiences with products and services in order to meet or exceed their expectations and ensure their satisfaction (Otto et al., 2020).

Figure 1.6 Competitors are always trying to outperform each other

This may involve various tactics, such as providing excellent customer service, offering high-quality products and services, and proactively addressing customer concerns and issues. By prioritizing customer satisfaction, companies can strengthen their existing customer base and reduce the risk of losing customers to competitors.

While customer satisfaction is important for maintaining customer relationships, it is not a guarantee of repeat business or customer loyalty. Ultimately, customers will choose the most attractive option available to them at the time of making a new purchase or contract renewal decision. As we have discussed, competitors are constantly innovating and improving their offerings, and even satisfied customers may switch to a competitor if they perceive their offerings to be more attractive. This phenomenon is not limited to any particular industry, as evidenced by the example of car manufacturers like BMW, Mercedes and Audi losing market share to Tesla due to their elegant, electric and smart-car technologies. However, as competing brands also develop similar technologies, the relative attractiveness of Tesla has decreased, resulting in a decline in their market share. In 2019, their share of all new cars sold in Norway was about 19%. However, as competitors gained momentum, their market share dropped to about 11% in both 2020 and 2021, and 12% in 2022 (Bilnytt, 2023). In order to defend existing customer relationships, companies must therefore continuously innovate and improve their offerings to stay ahead of the competition and remain attractive to customers.

Increasing perceived switching costs is an effective way for companies to defend against customers switching to competitors, in addition to customer satisfaction and relative attractiveness. There are several dimensions of switching costs identified in the literature (Burnham et al., 2003; Pick & Eisend, 2014). One is that switching leads to uncertainty and risk, and customers may prefer to stick with what they are familiar with. Another dimension is that switching requires effort to learn about the new company's products and services. Additionally, there may be monetary costs associated with switching, such as forfeiting rewards earned in loyalty programmes when customers switch to a new supplier. By imposing switching costs, companies can make it more difficult for customers to switch to a competitor, thereby defending their established customer relationships.

The third primary objective of customer portfolio management is to increase the cash flow from existing customers (Shapiro et al., 1987). This can be achieved by encouraging customers to purchase more frequently or in larger quantities, to buy products from different categories, or by reducing transaction costs. For example, Starbucks can increase the cash flow from a customer by encouraging them to visit their coffee shops more often, order more than just coffee, or use self-service systems like pre-ordering. Pre-order will reduce transaction costs because the ordering and payment is done electronically without using employees and thus saving labour costs. As companies gain more information about their customers through various digital applications, they will tend to use this information to cross-sell more products. With careful execution, customers tend to perceive such initiatives as positive (i.e. better value and lower prices) and contribute to more intimate and profitable relationships (Akçura & Srinivasan, 2005). Stronger relationships with customers can also create synergies and increase the attractiveness of a company's products and services, similar to how Apple's ecosystem of products and services has made its products more appealing to consumers than those of competitors, even if they have comparable features and quality. Converting relationships to capture more value has therefore become central in customer portfolio management (Johnson & Selnes, 2004; Selnes & Johnson, 2022).

Developing stronger relationships with customers is particularly crucial in business-to-business markets, where products and services tend to be more intricate. Customers seek solutions where a supplier's offering of products and services are deployed and integrated into the customers' organization of activities and systems (Tuli et al., 2007). Close collaboration between companies can result in mutual benefits and knowledge exchange, leading to more sustainable businesses. In these markets, companies also invest in relationship-specific resources and activities that enhance the value of their relationship, but also limit their ability to switch to alternative partners. Managing professional customer relationships in business-to-business markets differs significantly from managing relationships in consumer markets. However, the ongoing digitalization of products and consumer services provides companies with new opportunities to establish collaborative relationships following the principles seen in business-to-business markets.

Companies allocate resources towards marketing activities aimed at attracting new customers, reducing churn and strengthening customer relationships to increase their value. However, investing in such activities does not guarantee the desired outcomes. Many companies have experienced that their investments in CRM systems and loyalty programs have not provided the expected results (Rigby et al., 2002; Dorotic et al., 2012). The primary reason for such failures is often a lack of understanding of customer decision-making processes, leading to inadequate design and implementation of marketing strategies such as CRM systems, loyalty programmes, email marketing, advertising campaigns, etc. As a result, companies focus on building analytical capabilities to identify activities that generate the desired effects and invest accordingly.

Product Portfolio Management

The objective of product portfolio management is to achieve long-term growth and profitability by effectively managing the company's range of product categories. The initial step involves defining the positioning and value proposition for the company's products, i.e. determining why customers in various segments should select the company's products over those of competitors.

To make products more appealing, they must possess qualities and characteristics that customers perceive as more valuable and significant than other alternatives. It is important to note that customers vary in their preferences for these qualities and features, making it crucial for companies to identify and cater to their target customers' needs. For instance, in the charter tour industry, the Family segment values features related to activities for children, while the 55-Plus segment values comfort and luxury. Therefore, to appeal to both segments, the charter tour company will invest in hotel resorts that possess both sets of features to attract customers from both segments. Moreover, as the Family segment prefers to travel during school holidays, and the 55-Plus segment prefers to travel during non-holiday periods, the two segments complement each other in terms of capacity utilization, resulting in more profitable products than either segment can achieve independently.

Certain qualities and features can be appealing across various product categories. BMW, for instance, has recognized that combining driving performance with luxury is the key distinguishing characteristic for all their product categories, including sedans, SUVs, electric vehicles and convertibles. The BMW team strives to create the BMW experience in all their models. Regardless of which model a customer purchases from BMW, they can expect to enjoy the same core values that define the BMW brand.

Image 1.1   An example of a BMW car

Combining product categories into an ecosystem of products and services can also lead to attractive product qualities and features. Successful companies like Apple, Google and Amazon have developed solutions that create value across various product categories. For instance, Apple products offer common features that make them easy to use, regardless of the category of the product, such as mobile phones, personal computers, music players and TVs (see Figure 1.7).

Figure 1.7　The ecosystem or network of products and services connected with a brand

In certain markets, customers may perceive companies as having nearly identical products, while also perceiving significant differences in relational qualities. For instance, in the financial market, payment products, mortgages, savings accounts and pension plans have nearly identical features in all banks due to regulation and laws. However, banks differ in how they connect with their customers through personal relationships and digital services. By carefully designing these relationships, banks can differentiate themselves from their competitors and become more attractive.

In business-to-business markets, where competitors offer nearly identical products such as raw materials or transportation, companies have learned that differentiation can be achieved through the careful design of interaction activities in the value chain, such as logistics, quality control, engineering services and payment. Furthermore, relevant and value-adding relational qualities can vary across segments. Therefore, attractiveness can be created through relational features, and differentiation is not limited to product qualities alone.

Brand names can be utilized to create appealing product offerings, particularly for products where customers cannot easily distinguish true differences in quality. In such cases, customers tend to choose the supplier with the brand they trust the most. For instance, students may not be able to determine whether the theories and methods learned at a university are of high quality or not, but they may choose to trust the university's good reputation. Similarly, a patient may not know whether the prescribed treatment is the best, but they may trust the doctor's reputation. Brands can also provide symbols that add meaning beyond the product itself. For example, in the beer market, brands such as Carlsberg, Heineken and Corona have created attractive symbols associated with their brands. In blind taste tests where people fail to recognize the taste of their preferred brand, people still show a strong preference for their favourite brand, indicating that people consume symbols and not just the product itself. In the fashion industry, symbolic brands are particularly valuable, as customers use them to signal social status to others. Brands like Gucci have created an appealing symbolism associated with their brand that makes customers feel good and perhaps important in various social settings. It's worth noting that symbolic brands are typically found across different product categories. Gucci, for example, sells not only fashion clothes but also sunglasses, shoes, perfume, handbags, decor and many other products.

Once companies have established their value propositions, it is crucial to effectively communicate and deliver them to customers. The 'moment of truth' occurs when customers use the product and determine whether it meets their expectations. If the product meets or surpasses expectations, it generates a sense of satisfaction and positive attitudes towards future purchases. It is essential for companies to carefully define their value propositions to avoid making promises they cannot fulfil, while also setting ambitious goals to create attractive value propositions. Striking the right balance is both challenging and critical.

A crucial aspect of making products attractive is ensuring that they are available in the right places for customers to purchase them. This means making them accessible through physical stores or locations such as retailers, restaurants and other outlets. Additionally, having a strong digital presence is important, as companies can make their products easily discoverable through search engines like Google. Distribution partners can also play a significant role in making products available to customers. For instance, software providers such as Microsoft, SAP and Salesforce often work with value-added resellers and system integrators to connect with their customers. Many companies opt for a multi-channel approach to reach customers, such as how Apple sells its products through Apple Stores, concept stores, retailers and app providers.

Product portfolio management is the process of ensuring that a company's strategy is financially viable and that the quality of their offerings meets the expectations and needs of their customers, resulting in satisfaction and revenue growth. It involves defining, communicating and delivering attractive products while also making tough decisions to terminate or liquidate products that are no longer in demand. To achieve sustainable financial performance, product managers must balance short-term and long-term thinking, constantly innovating to meet evolving customer needs and adapt to changes in technology, market regulations and competition. Companies must stay ahead of these changes to take advantage of opportunities and avoid threats. Innovation is crucial to ensuring that products remain attractive in the future.

Brand Management

To effectively manage a brand, it is crucial to establish associations that position it as relevant and more appealing than its competitors (Keller et al., 2002). An important part of brand management is to secure that the brand is associated within the relevant product category. When consumers begin the process of purchasing a product, they need to identify potential brands to consider. As such, the brand's connection to the product category is of utmost importance.

Once the brand is activated in the consumers' memory, they will search for more information about the brand. They may first search internally by relying on their memory, but if more information is required, they will turn to external sources. Typically, the next step is to search for the brand name on search engines like Google. For example, when someone is looking for a pair of running shoes, they may consider Nike and Adidas. If Nike is the brand that comes to mind first, the person is likely to search for information about Nike first. If the information found on the Nike webpage is compelling and the shoes are appealing, the person is likely to make a purchase without considering other brands.

The likelihood of the consumer going back to search for other brands after identifying a good choice is often low. Therefore, the connection between the brand name and the product category has a significant impact on the likelihood that the brand will be chosen.

To position a brand effectively, it's essential to establish parity associations that qualify the brand for consideration within its relevant category. Brands that lack the necessary qualifications for a category may be excluded from consideration. However, what counts as a necessary qualifier may vary depending on individual preferences. For instance, some consumers may not consider McDonald's as a viable fast-food option due to their desire for healthier choices, and McDonald's not being associated with health (Eat This, Not That!, 2021). Similarly, Tesla may be disqualified by some because of negative associations with its leader, Elon Musk (Top Speed, 2023). In other cases, brands like H&M may not qualify due to perceptions of failing to uphold sustainability goals (Turn Around H&M, n.d.). Ultimately reasons for brand disqualification can be linked to product performance, individuals within the organization, ethical standards and other factors.

A brand must also create unique associations that make it different and more appealing than its competitors. For instance, some people view Volvo as a safe car, which makes it both distinctive and attractive. However, for others, safety is simply a basic requirement and not a unique selling point. Tesla was originally known for its electric engines, which made it more appealing than other luxury car brands like BMW or Mercedes. However, as electric engines become more commonplace, Tesla's competitive advantage in this area has diminished.

Brand associations are developed through learning from a variety of sources, with advertising being a crucial one through various media channels. As illustrated in Figure 1.8, Meta is presenting new technology associations in their advertising. With the shift in the media landscape from offline to online, investments in digital media have surpassed offline media, according to a PWC report (PWC, 2021). Brands are advertised where people spend most of their time – on the internet. Besides advertising, consumers also acquire knowledge about

Figure 1.8 Advertising is an important source for learning and developing brand associations

brands through other communication channels such as email. Over the years, email communication has emerged as one of the most significant channels for conveying brand-related information, with most emails containing links that lead the recipient to the brand's website, where they can continue the learning process.

Brand learning is not limited to advertising and other brand-related communication; it can also be influenced by personal experiences and word-of-mouth with the brand. These experiences can be with the brand's products, services, or any other touchpoints. Positive experiences can reinforce and amplify positive associations with the brand, thus increasing its attractiveness. For this reason, many companies collect data through surveys and other methods to monitor customer experiences and address any negative ones.

Hence, the pivotal strategic concerns in brand management involve positioning the brand effectively within pertinent product categories, ensuring it meets essential standards, and cultivating distinctive and attractive associations in the memories of the target audience (Keller et al., 2002).

COORDINATING MARKETING MANAGEMENT

The three management areas in marketing are interconnected and have a mutual impact on one another. Activities in an organization are interlinked, and it is important to understand how one activity depends on other activities, and how they can be reinforced to become more effective as a system of linked activities (Porter, 1996). For instance, the success of investments in developing new products relies on how well the new products meet the needs of existing customers and their relationship with the company, and how effective the brand is communicated to attract new customers to the new products. Even if Mercedes produces the best product in the world, it will not be a success if their existing customers do not approve of it, or if BMW and other brands' customers do not find it appealing. Strong customer relationships and attractive brands facilitate the sales of new products, as high-quality products create stronger customer relationships and more appealing brands. To achieve a high return on marketing investments, coordination is required between and within the three marketing management areas. Figure 1.9 highlights the activities that necessitate coordination.

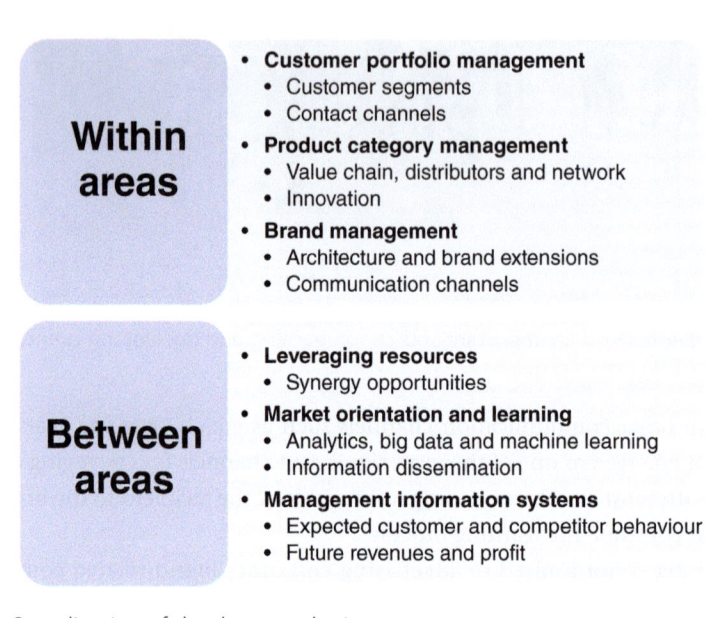

Figure 1.9   Coordination of the three marketing management areas

Coordination Within Customer Portfolio Management

Companies that operate in multiple segments need to ensure that their marketing activities are coordinated across those segments. For instance, the charter tour company mentioned earlier must coordinate its activities between the Young & Single, Family and 55-Plus segments. With a limited and fixed number of available rooms each week, they must avoid heavy promotion for the same week in all three segments. This can occur if there are different marketing managers for each of the segments who operate in isolation. They should coordinate and allocate their spending so that the total number of bookings does not exceed the limit. Spending more than necessary to fill up the rooms is simply a waste of resources.

Companies use various channels to interact and communicate with their customers, as shown in Figure 1.10. For the charter tour company these channels include catalogues, webpages, social media, emails, customer service calls, hotel rooms, aeroplanes, local tourist guides, and more. Customers expect that the information provided through these channels is consistent and accurate. They expect prices and availability to be the same across all channels, and they expect the channels to have the correct information about their reservations and orders. Customers also expect to be able to change their reservations or make requests through multiple channels, such as by phone or email. To meet these expectations and provide positive customer experiences, companies need to coordinate their contact and communication channels. CRM systems have been developed to help companies organize their customer dialogue and communication across different channels.

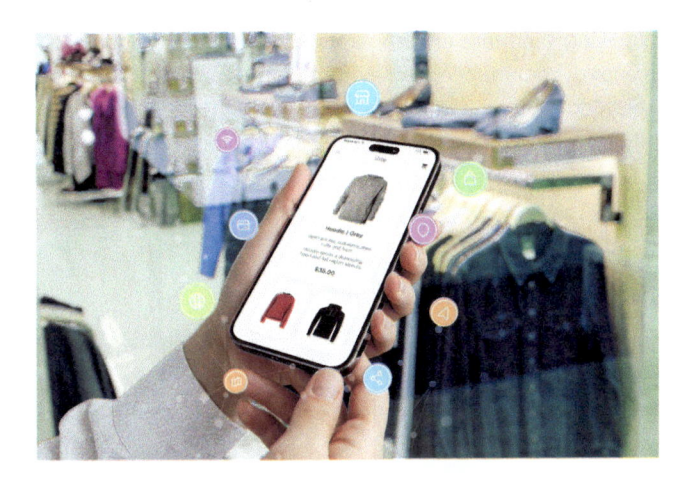

Figure 1.10 Customers interact and communicate with the company through multiple channels

Coordination Within Product Portfolio Management

Product managers play a critical role in balancing the profitability of a company with the quality of its products. To achieve this, they must consider the impact of every stage in the value chain, which includes procurement, logistics, operations, marketing, sales, outbound logistics and service (Porter, 1991). Secondary activities such as infrastructure, human resource management, technology development and procurement also impact on the value chain. Each activity contributes to the product's performance and adds costs. Therefore, it is vital for product managers to consider the entire value chain to ensure that each activity is optimized for quality and profitability. Quality is crucial because it affects the customer experience and satisfaction, which ultimately determines future sales. At the same time, cost-reduction measures can positively affect profitability but may result in negative customer experiences that harm future sales. Additionally, the activities of partners and distributors can affect both profitability and quality, making it crucial for product managers to coordinate and balance internal and external activities to find the ideal balance between costs and quality.

Case Study 1.3

Doro

To achieve product innovation success, companies must have a deep understanding of customer needs and competitive dynamics and be able to leverage technological opportunities. Doro AB is an electronics supplier that has successfully developed solutions for elderly and visually impaired individuals. For example, their phones have fewer and larger buttons, making them easier to operate for their target audience. Doro has also successfully expanded from mobile phones to tablets, smart watches and other accessories that are relevant to their customers. Coordination of innovation projects across various new and emerging product categories is critical for a company like Doro.

Image 1.2 A selection of accessible Doro phones

Coordination of Brand Management

To create a positive brand image and association with customers, companies need to ensure that their products, services and communication channels are consistent and aligned with each other. People form their perceptions and associations with a brand based on what they see, hear and experience, so companies try to manage this by carefully orchestrating how they present themselves to the public. This requires coordination and consistency across all touchpoints to create strong and desirable associations with the brand. This is explored further in the case study below about the Norwegian postal company and the brands Posten and Bring.

Case Study 1.4

Posten and Bring

The Norwegian postal company operates under two separate brands, Posten and Bring. The former is a national postal service, similar to the UK's Royal Mail and France's La

Poste, while the latter is a commercial transportation company competing with private firms in Northern Europe. The transformation of national postal services to a combination of public and commercial services has happened in other European countries as well. In Germany Deutsche Post became Deutsche Post DHL, and in Holland PPT Post became TNT Post and later PostNL. The strategy is a response to the digital transformation of distributing letters through mailboxes to sending letters digitally, which means that the costs of employees, machinery and buildings needed to be dramatically reduced and, if possible, transferred to new commercial transportation categories. The use of two brand names serves to convey a national public service with Posten and a commercial transportation company with Bring. Both brands have similar graphical designs to indicate a connection but are differentiated by colour: Posten is red and Bring is green. The aim is to create a positive association with one brand that transfers to the other. For instance, sponsoring the Norwegian women's handball team with Posten branding creates an association with both Posten and Bring. The dual-brand strategy also fosters a common culture among the 14,000 employees, who support and speak positively about both brands. Therefore, effective brand management requires coordinated communication and learning opportunities to strengthen both brands.

Image 1.3 Posten and Bring branding

Coordination Between the Three Management Areas

Companies aim to influence customer choice by enhancing the value in their customer relationships, creating more appealing products and establishing desirable brands. Managing these three areas of marketing can be challenging for companies that operate in multiple segments, with different product categories and brand names. The traditional 4-P marketing-mix approach referred to in many marketing textbooks is developed for companies operating with just one category, one customer segment and one brand. The 4-P marketing mix can be applied where there is no need for coordination and leveraging resources across product categories, customer segments and brands. The situation is, however, that most companies operate with multiple product categories in multiple segments where they leverage resources across product categories, customer segments and brands. In these situations, the traditional 4-P marketing-mix model is not very helpful. Therefore, effective coordination of the three marketing-management areas has a significant impact on a company's market success. Coordination is about:

- leveraging resources between the three areas;
- developing an organization-wide market-oriented learning;
- developing a holistic customer-centric market information system.

These three aspects of coordination will now each be examined in turn.

Leveraging Resources

Even though different product categories cater to different customer needs and face different levels of competition, they often share resources that can be used to create significant synergies. For example, when Tine, the dairy company mentioned earlier, introduced juice to their product portfolio, they were able to share resources such as packaging, logistics, sales and distribution systems between the two products. This allowed them to derive more value from the resources they already had at their disposal. The importance of volume is one of the fundamental principles in strategy referred to as economies of scale. Through specialization and accumulated usage of a production resource, companies achieve lower unit costs and competitive advantage (Marshall, 1890; Stigler, 1958). Economies of scale are achieved when lower unit costs are obtained as investments made in machinery, product development, procurement, administration, advertising and other areas can be shared among more units, resulting in lower unit costs.

Transforming a company's resources into sustainable competitive advantage is another key issue in business strategy (Barney, 1991; Peteraf, 1993). The rationale is that companies leverage their resources or, in other words, gain more value from what they have already invested in. This uniqueness enables the company to leverage or transform these resources into profits and revenues, thereby increasing their overall value. Strategic market-related resources such as products, customer relationships, brands and distribution partners become more valuable to a company when they possess unique qualities that are not available to their competitors (Srivastava et al., 1998).

Furthermore, resources can be leveraged not only within individual areas, but also across different areas. For example, a company can leverage its product portfolio by expanding into new customer segments or launching new brands. A case in point is the Swedish company SCA, now known as Essity AB, which is a major player in the global market for baby diapers under the Libero brand, boasting highly efficient production and logistics resources. By leveraging these capabilities, the company was able to expand into the more profitable and larger market for adult diapers under the Tena brand.

Deutsche Bank and many other banks globally have leveraged their customer relationships by expanding their product offerings. In addition to traditional bank products such as savings accounts and mortgages, they began offering insurance, investments and a wide range of financial products and services. By doing so, their sales representatives or financial advisors could add more value to their meetings with customers by presenting additional products.

Brand extensions have been a popular strategy for entering new product categories and customer segments among strong brands (Völckner and Sattler, 2006). Apple, for instance, expanded its product offerings from personal computers and music electronics (iPod) to mobile phones. Similarly, Amazon extended its initial product line of books to home appliances, jewellery, clothing and more. A company can use this strategy to leverage its sales force by offering a wider range of products.

Market Orientation and Learning

Companies gather, analyse and interpret data from various sources to better understand and predict customers and competitors, a process known as market orientation (Kohli & Jaworski, 1990; Jaworski & Kohli, 1993). This involves disseminating the information and insights gained from the data across the organization and responding accordingly. Research has shown that market-oriented companies are more successful in maintaining and growing their market positions and profitability (Kirca et al., 2005). In addition to understanding and predicting customer needs, companies must also anticipate how competition is developing, as competitors are constantly improving their offerings, reducing prices and improving their distribution, advertising and communication strategies to attract and retain customers.

The fundamental concept of market orientation is the collective knowledge and understanding of customers and markets throughout the organization, and how to utilize this knowledge to create appealing and profitable products and services. By exchanging information and insights between different departments, each party gains not only new information but also a fresh perspective on what they already knew. It is similar to adding a new piece to a puzzle: a previously unknown piece reveals the entire picture. Therefore, what product category managers learn from customer category managers and brand managers can enhance their comprehension of what makes their products appealing, and vice versa for the other managers and team members.

In the past, most companies gathered information through surveys and statistical sampling to understand what customers thought about their products and brands. However, this approach had limitations because there was no connection between the survey data and individuals' buying behaviour, which made it challenging to assess the effectiveness of market activities and learn about customers and competitors. But with the increasing availability of email addresses and the digitalization of customer interactions, companies can now collect rich data directly from customers that connect sentiment data, such as satisfaction and preferences, with actual behaviour data. This new data environment has grown tremendously and, with the emergence of big data, companies can now access new types of data, such as online search behaviour, at low costs (Wedel & Kannan, 2016). This new reality has also given rise to machine learning, which helps companies make sense of the data and better understand and predict customers and competitors (Shmueli, 2010). As a result, companies are now becoming substantially better informed about their customers and competitors, thanks to the rapid growth in digital data and analytical tools. This is frequently referred to as 'big data'. There are many conceptualizations of what big data is and how it is different from other data. For an excellent overview see Verhoef et al. (2021).

The advancement in digital tools has led to increased specialization in marketing functions, which may hinder cross-functional learning. Companies tend to create specialized teams for various functions such as CRM, email marketing, web design, loyalty programmes, customer service experiences, product innovation, sales and distribution, and public relations. However, each team may become too focused on their specific function and overlook the bigger picture of customer and competitor insights. Therefore, it is essential to organize learning in a way that promotes the sharing of market research and analytics across different organizational units.

Management Information Systems

A management information system (MIS) is a structured method of collecting, organizing and presenting data used for decision-making and for managing information in an organization. The traditional MIS is based on accounting data that shows revenue, costs and profits. However, this type of system has limitations for marketing purposes because it only provides backward-looking information. This is like driving a car by looking in the rear mirror and not out of the front window. In marketing we want information about how many new customers the company can expect to gain, how many customers the company can expect to continue their relationship with and how much cash flow these customers are expected to provide over the next periods. To make accurate predictions, companies need to collect data from multiple sources, including market activities, competitor behaviour, brand attractiveness, economic variables, season and weather changes, and other relevant factors. With the availability of big data and machine learning, companies can now develop new MIS that provides better insights and control over the future.

Figure 1.11   Stop looking in the rear mirror (historical behaviour) when driving forward (prediction)

The availability of richer data has enabled companies to make more precise decisions related to product category management, customer portfolio management and brand management, and to understand the interrelationships between the three areas. This includes making informed decisions about how investments in product development and other market-related activities will impact on customer relationships and brand attractiveness. By having this insight, managers can develop a strategic plan for future revenue and profit growth across product categories and customer segments, ultimately leading to a more customer-centric and effective strategic marketing plan.

CUSTOMER-CENTRIC MARKETING MANAGEMENT

Companies have varying perspectives on the role of marketing. The customer-centric approach focuses on growing the customer portfolio, with marketing being primarily responsible for attracting, retaining and nurturing strong and valuable relationships. Conversely, the product-centric approach to marketing aims to develop a portfolio of profitable products (for an excellent discussion on this topic, see Shah et al., 2006). This approach emphasizes sales volume to achieve economies of scale.

When customer heterogeneity increases, the difference between a customer- and product-centric approach becomes more apparent (Johnson & Selnes, 2004; Selnes & Johnson, 2022). In markets with high customer heterogeneity, customers have different needs and preferences, and they perceive competing alternatives as having different values. In such markets, a customer-centric approach to marketing is more appropriate, as the main goal is to attract, retain and develop strong and valuable customer relationships across different segments. This approach emphasizes creating relationship value beyond low prices and convenience. In contrast, a product-centric approach focused on sales volume is more suitable for markets with little or no customer heterogeneity, where customers have similar needs and perceive most competing alternatives as equal in terms of value. Examples of such markets include commodity markets such as electricity and gas stations.

When customer heterogeneity is high, companies tailor their value propositions and offerings to specific groups or segments of customers. For instance, airlines differentiate their offerings for private and business travellers. For the private segment, the value proposition is a low price, and the production activities are standardized to minimize costs. These customers have to queue and wait for requests such as reservations and baggage claims but benefit from lower prices. In contrast, for the business segment, the value proposition is high-quality service, and production activities are maximized to ensure service quality. These customers do not have to queue and are offered supplementary services like fast-track security control and VIP lounges. However, differentiation of production activities in the value-creation chain is limited to a few activities, with all production activities related to operating the aircraft remaining the same for both segments. This way, they achieve economies of scale on costly parts of the value chain, while remaining attractive to both segments.

The distinction between a customer-centric and a product-centric approach becomes particularly clear when companies diversify into new product categories. Combining multiple product categories can provide additional value for customers. IKEA, for example, has successfully expanded beyond furniture into categories such as mattresses, kitchen appliances, home textiles, lighting, and more. The value for customers lies in lower prices across a broader range of products and reduced shopping costs, as they can purchase multiple types of products in one visit. It's important to note that attractive products are still essential even with a customer-centric approach. Customers at IKEA expect both low prices and reasonably good-quality products.

Companies that adopt a product-centric approach run the risk of being myopic and not fully understanding market dynamics and customer needs (Levitt, 1960). This was demonstrated in the example of Facit, as explained further in the case study below.

Case Study 1.5

Facit

Facit was a Swedish typewriter company that faced severe problems in the mid-eighties when personal computers replaced traditional typewriters. Facit had invested heavily in building the largest and most sophisticated typewriter factory in the world, thinking that economies of scale from this investment would give them a huge cost advantage. However, when the market changed, they failed to understand the value they provided to their customers and the need to leverage their strategic resources. Facit's myopic approach misled them to believe that the factory was their main strategic resource that needed to be leveraged, rather than their customer relationships, brand and distribution partner network. They also failed to recognize that they were in the 'office writing market', not just the typewriter market. As a result, they missed the opportunity to become one of the key suppliers of personal computers and other office automation products. If they had, they could have avoided going out of business in 1998.

A product-centric approach can also lead to a bias towards creating value for the company rather than considering the needs and preferences of their customers. In the worst cases, companies may cut costs by offering low-quality products and poor customer service. While this may lead to short-term profitability through cost savings in production and innovation, in the long run these companies are likely to fail as customers become dissatisfied and look for better alternatives. When combined with a myopic focus on their existing products and failure to innovate in response to changing market and customer needs, a short-term cost focus can undermine the sustainability of a product-centric approach.

However, a sole emphasis on customer portfolio management can also result in short-term thinking and drive companies out of business. This was the case with newspapers and other media companies when their customers switched from print to digital channels. Having the best print newspaper with many satisfied and loyal customers would not help if customers preferred to consume news and other content digitally. Thus, a customer-centric approach requires a balanced focus on both customer portfolio management and product category management. Customers seek to establish relationships with companies that offer valuable and appealing products and services. As companies differentiate their value chain to segments and broaden their offerings to more categories, a customer-centric approach leverages a company's resources into additional products and customer relationships, resulting in a more sustainable and profitable growth. A customer-centric approach to strategic marketing is well aligned with the resource-based view introduced by Wernerfelt (1984), and although customers are not explicitly included as a resource in the strategy literature, a customer portfolio fits in very well with the criteria for treating this as a strategic resource (Barney, 1991).

A customer-centric approach to marketing places the growth in customer portfolio value as the top priority and the primary guide for managing future revenues and profits. However, sustainable market success also requires attractive and profitable products, so a balance between growth in customer portfolio value and growth in product category value must be maintained. The importance of brands is also high in certain markets such as luxury products, professional services and universities. To successfully implement a customer-centric approach to marketing, companies must establish and foster connections with their customers through attractive products, value-adding interactions and services, and highly regarded brands. A strategic marketing plan that prioritizes the customer's needs and desires is the starting point for achieving this goal.

STRATEGIC MARKETING PLAN

Every organization must have a well-thought-out strategy and plan to generate the necessary revenue for profitability and long-term viability. The strategic marketing plan specifies which market-related activities will be implemented and includes a budget that outlines how the strategic initiatives will translate into new revenues and profits over a period of three to five years. Additionally, an integral part of the plan is the establishment of key performance indicators that will be used to monitor and control the implementation of the initiatives.

The process of strategic marketing planning, as depicted in Figure 1.12, begins with a comprehensive analysis of the company's current situation. Marketing management can be seen as a system whereby the company has established a set of linked activities to attract, retain and leverage customer relationships. The objective of the strategic marketing plan is to improve this system of linked activities and make it more effective than in the past. The analysis starts with an assessment of revenues and profits across customer segments and product categories (i.e. market-matrix), an examination of market trends and competitors that may alter the competitive landscape and product attractiveness, changes in customer needs and behaviour, and a thorough audit of current marketing activities. The company aims to address two strategic questions in the process. The first question is: what opportunities exist to accelerate the growth of their customer portfolio value? The second question is: what are the risks of a significant decline in growth? These two questions assist the company in identifying the primary strategic challenges that the strategic marketing plan will strive to resolve.

Strategic marketing planning is a learning process that helps the organization develop a deeper understanding of how the market works and which market-related activities are likely to be most effective. Successful marketing management requires a deep understanding of relevant theories, rigorous analysis of information, and a clear focus on the causal relationships between market activities and customer responses. Guesswork should be informed by data and analysis, and it is essential to play the odds by making calculated decisions. As a senior marketing manager in the shampoo industry once said, 'Knowing what a person thinks and feels when taking a shower is not enough; we need to know how to convince them to choose our shampoo when shopping!'.

The significance of understanding customer behaviour and its impact on revenues and profits means that marketing is not just the responsibility of the marketing department. It is a shared responsibility of the board, the top management team and the entire organization.

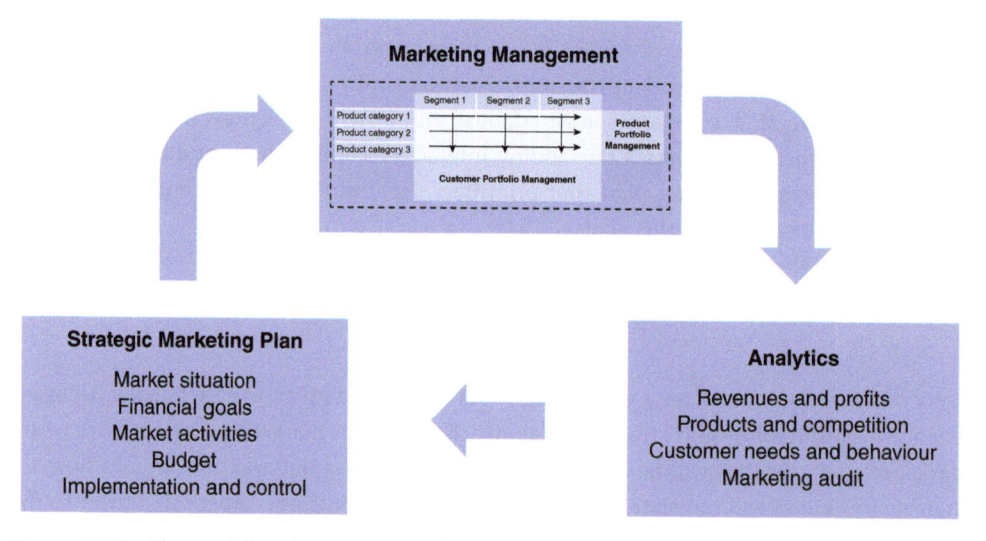

Figure 1.12 The workflow in strategic marketing planning

SUMMARY

To put it briefly, the aim of marketing is to persuade potential customers to opt for the company's products and services, not just on a one-time basis, but to continually choose and advocate the company's offerings, and broaden their relationship with the company by adding more products and services. In essence, marketing management involves implementing activities that establish connections between customers and the company, resulting in an increase in the company's portfolio of valuable customers. Marketing is considered successful when the value of the customer portfolio increases by:

- acquiring new customers and adding them to the portfolio;
- retaining more customers and increasing positive word of mouth;

- encouraging customers to expand their relationship with the supplier (brand) by purchasing more products and services.

The management of marketing involves the management of three key areas: customer segments, product categories and brands. These areas are interdependent and the success of one area is influenced by the management of the other two. To organize this interdependence, the market-matrix is introduced as a framework that defines strategic customer segments and product categories.

There are various approaches companies can take when it comes to the role of marketing. One is the customer-centric approach, which prioritizes the creation of customer portfolio growth. But to attract, retain and leverage their customer relationship, companies need to offer attractive products. They also need very attractive brands. Therefore, although the customer-centric approach places a primary focus on customer portfolio management, this must be balanced with product category and brand management.

The strategic marketing plans outline the necessary strategic initiatives that companies choose to undertake to capitalize on growth opportunities while also protecting their customer portfolio value, product categories and brands from potential threats.

END-OF-CHAPTER QUESTIONS

1 Examine the market-matrix in Figure 1.3. Make a list of market-related activities that may create synergies across product categories and customer segments. Discuss how these market-related activities should be coordinated among the three areas of marketing management.
2 What is the difference between marketing oriented and market oriented? Read Shapiro (1988) with the title 'What the hell is "market oriented"?'.
3 Interview a few people you know and ask them why they chose to buy a certain brand, whether they are satisfied with the brand and whether they think they will continue to buy the brand. Then ask them to identify a competitor to the brand and ask them what this competitor would have to do to make them change. Are there differences between products and services, and if so what are the most striking differences?
4 List all types of activities a company (i.e. a grocery retailer, a takeaway restaurant, a car manufacturer, and so forth) can do that will influence the number of customers they get, the share of customers that continue to buy from the company and don't switch to a competitor, and the number of products customers buy from this company. Discuss how these activities are likely to be organized in a company and how a top-management team will divide roles and responsibilities for these activities.

FURTHER READING

Barney, J. (1991). Firm resources and sustained competitive advantage. *Journal of Management*, 17(1), 99–120.

Feng, H., Morgan, N.A. & Rego, L.L. (2017). Firm capabilities and growth: The moderating role of market conditions. *Journal of the Academy of Marketing Science*, 45, 76–92.

Homburg, C., Theel, M. & Hohenberg, S. (2020). Marketing excellence: Nature, measurement, and investor valuations. *Journal of Marketing*, 84 (4), 1–22.

Kohli, A.K. & Jaworski, B.J. (1990). Market orientation: The construct, research propositions, and managerial implications. *Journal of Marketing*, 54(2), 1–18.

Shah, D., Rust, R.T., Parasuraman, A., Staelin, R. & Day, G.S. (2006). The path to customer centricity. *Journal of Service Research*, 9(2), 113–124.

2

COMPETITIVE DYNAMICS

This chapter

- explains the process of defining and analysing markets;
- delves into the impact of competitive dynamics on the market;
- presents and discusses PESTLE analysis;
- presents and discusses the competitive intensity in an industry;
- explores the theory of the product life cycle.

INTRODUCTION

A company must continuously strive to maintain and improve its market position in relation to its competitors due to evolving customer needs, innovations leading to new and superior products and services, increasing efficiency of market networks, and changing environmental conditions. The prevailing trend is that competitors are growing larger, more efficient, more global, more innovative and, hence, more competitive. Emerging technologies and innovative mindsets lead to novel products and fresh methods to market and sell them. The market networks transform as distribution systems become more interconnected, automated and streamlined, media channels become digitized and personalized, and payment services become more automated, secure and intelligent. In these rapidly changing environments, it is imperative for the company to possess a profound and accurate comprehension of the market and competitive dynamics to leverage opportunities and avoid threats. This chapter offers some conceptual frameworks, such as the market mechanism principle PESTLE and Porter's Five Forces model, to foster such an understanding. Key topics include supply and demand, forces driving shifts in supply and demand, competitive dynamics and competitive intensity, market structure and the notion of a product's life cycle.

ANALYSIS OF MARKETS

To analyse a market, it is important to first define it and identify which products, competitors and customers are included in the analysis. The term 'market' comes from the word 'marketplace', which originally referred to a physical location where independent traders such as farmers, artisans and merchants sold their products. In the traditional marketplace, sellers and buyers would come together and interact face to face. All products for sale were physically displayed, allowing buyers to inspect their quality and suppliers to closely monitor their competitors. Similar to flea markets, farm markets or garage sales today, there would often be multiple sellers and buyers present simultaneously. In today's world, marketplaces are less bound by physical locations than they were in the past. While a significant portion of goods are still sold by physical sellers or companies (as evidenced by the statistics found at https://www.statista.com/statistics/534123/e-commerce-share-of-retail-sales-worldwide/), competitors are no longer concentrated in one place. Instead, they are dispersed across various town centres, city streets, suburbs and shopping malls. Furthermore, the internet has given rise to geographic barriers being broken down, allowing companies from far-flung regions to compete with each other. This digital landscape has also facilitated the emergence of purely online businesses entering the market.

A market can be formally defined as a system that connects suppliers and customers, facilitating the buying and selling of products. In order to properly define a market, it is important to establish clear and precise boundaries, which specify the geographic area and the products and customers that are included in that particular market. An excellent discussion of market definitions can be found in Pindyck and Rubinfeld's textbook on microeconomics (2017, Chapter 1).

Case Study 2.1

Guadalajara Market

Figure 2.1   A traditional marketplace for fruit and vegetables in Guadalajara, Mexico

For effective market analysis, it is important to precisely define the boundaries of a market. Consider the example of the apple market in Guadalajara, Mexico. Defining the product category and geographic area is crucial. Should all types of apples be included, or only Red Delicious apples? Should the geographic area be limited to Guadalajara or include its suburbs and villages? To determine this, the principle of close substitutes must be applied, which means identifying products that customers consider as alternatives in a situation where they have options. Some customers may consider all types and colours of apples as close substitutes, while others may have a narrower range of substitutes such as red apples. Geographic boundaries also play a role, with some customers having a wider range of options including distant suppliers, while others may only shop with local suppliers in the physical marketplace in Guadalajara.

Defining close substitutes is a subjective task, and there is no clear right or wrong way to define a market. However, the way a market is defined plays a crucial role in how a company identifies its competitors, products and customers. Consequently, companies targeting the same customer base may define their markets differently based on their individual assessments. The success of a market definition will vary, but companies with in-depth knowledge of the market and its customers are likely to have a better understanding of how to define the market. This gives them a better chance of succeeding in the market and achieving better results.

The Fundamental Principles of a Market

After defining a market, it becomes possible to describe and analyse it. With information on the market size, price levels and growth, a company can form a well-reasoned and factual opinion on the market's future development, which helps in predicting the sales trends. Additionally, a company can use this market knowledge to determine how to improve its market position and make better decisions regarding the implementation of marketing activities.

Market analysis provides crucial information for making informed strategic decisions on product focus and customer targeting. Information such as market size, price level and growth provides insights into market attractiveness, with larger markets, strong growth and customers willing to pay high prices being particularly attractive. Companies should therefore invest in such markets, while avoiding those that do not meet these criteria. In summary, market analysis helps companies make sound decisions on which markets to focus on and how to prioritize their marketing efforts.

Details regarding the size, pricing and expansion of a market can indicate its level of desirability. Typically, larger markets (how large are the total sales), markets with substantial growth (how fast they change), and markets with customers who are willing to pay premium prices are more profitable, making them a worthwhile investment for companies. In essence, analysing the market offers vital information to help make informed strategic decisions about which products to focus on and which markets to prioritize, while avoiding less promising opportunities.

MARKETING MANAGEMENT

The market's scope is determined by the product category and geographic area. Nonetheless, the market's size is variable, and it fluctuates based on the number of customers and the quantity of their purchases within a given time frame, usually a year. As more people enter the market and increase their spending, the market expands. The customer base expands because of population growth in the market area and/or the introduction of new customer groups. The market mechanism is a theory that is primarily used to analyse pricing-level changes within a market. For a company, anticipating these changes is critical. If there is a projected price-level increase, investing in the market becomes lucrative, enabling the company to establish a strong presence in preparation for the upcoming price increase. Conversely, minimizing involvement in a market where prices are expected to decline is essential.

In line with the market mechanism, the pricing level in a market is determined by the relationship between demand (D) and supply (S). Figure 2.2 illustrates demand through the red line (D1), indicating that the quantity demanded (i.e. the total number of product units customers require) is a function of price. As the price decreases, more units are demanded in the market. For instance, if apartment prices in London were lower, more people would be interested in purchasing one. The demand curve (D) slopes downward, with the impact of a price reduction decreasing as the price falls.

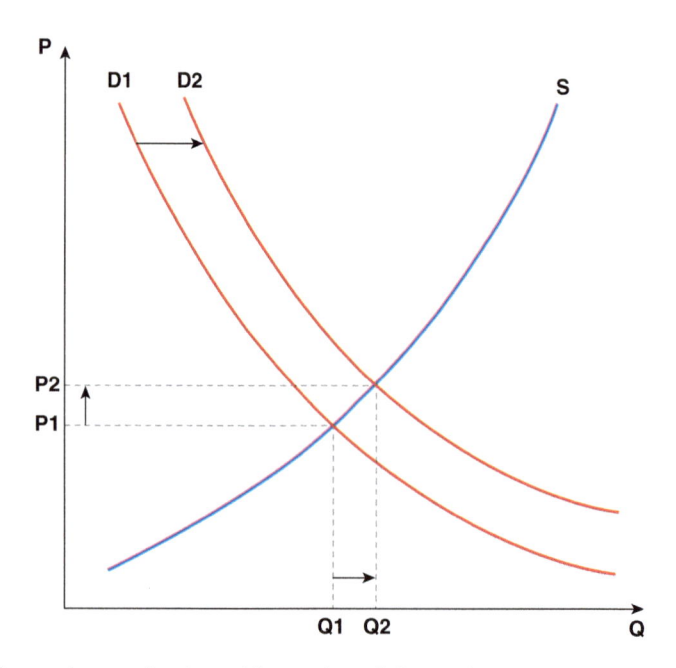

Figure 2.2 The market mechanism with supply and demand

The number of products sold is not solely determined by the quantity of products customers intend to buy, but also by how many products suppliers provide in the market. The blue line (S) in Figure 2.2 represents the number of products suppliers aim to sell overall. We observe that the higher the price, the more units suppliers aim to offer in the market. This is due to the increased attractiveness of selling products in a higher-priced market. For instance, if apartment prices in London rise, more people may choose to sell their flats, and more companies may want to construct new homes. The supply curve (S) slopes upward, indicating that the higher the price, the more companies are willing to invest and increase their production capacity.

In the market, a significant aspect is the movement of the price level towards a balance between supply and demand. According to the market mechanism, the price in the market will continue to fluctuate until the quantity supplied matches the quantity demanded. In case of a supply surplus (i.e. an excess of products for sale), prices are pushed down, whereas a supply deficit (i.e. a shortage of products for sale) increases prices. At equilibrium, there is neither a surplus to push prices down nor a deficit to push prices up. Figure 2.2 illustrates that the point of equilibrium is where the blue supply curve (S) intersects the red demand curve (D1). At this juncture, the price of the product is P1 and the quantity sold is Q1.

When the market price changes, it affects the size of the market since the demand and supply of the product category are influenced. According to the market mechanism theory, suppliers use information about the market price to modify the quantity they offer. The theory also necessitates that customers adjust their demand based on the market price. If the price increases, some customers will exit the market.

Anticipated shifts in demand and supply curves are crucial in market analysis. A shift in the demand curve can result from factors such as changes in customers' disposable income, fluctuations in the prices of similar product categories, or alterations in customer preferences and needs. In Figure 2.2, a positive shift in demand is shown as the demand curve shifts from D1 to D2. For example, if more customers prefer living in apartments than houses, they would be willing to pay more for apartments, resulting in a positive shift in demand. The new equilibrium is at the point where the supply curve S intersects with the demand curve D2, leading to a new price (P2) and a new quantity (Q2). As shown in Figure 2.2, suppliers will increase the total supply from Q1 to Q2 if the price increases from P1 to P2 by building more homes. A positive shift in the demand curve indicates that the product category is becoming more popular, causing both the price and the market size to increase. Conversely, when a product goes out of fashion or experiences a negative shift in demand, the price drops and the market shrinks. Companies should pay attention to the likelihood of negative shifts in the demand curve to make informed investment decisions. Failure to detect such negative shifts in a timely manner can result in irreversible investments. As illustrated in Case Study 2.2, LEGO is one company that experienced such a negative shift.

Case Study 2.2

LEGO

Predicting negative changes in demand can be difficult, leading companies to sometimes make serious mistakes. In 1994, Danish toy manufacturer LEGO, then Europe's largest toy producer, faced a negative shift in demand for their famous plastic bricks.

(Continued)

At the time, classic physical toys, such as LEGO bricks, dolls and board games, faced stiff competition from emerging electronic entertainment such as video games. LEGO and other toy companies competed for children's time and their parents' attention and money, but with video games becoming increasingly popular, children were growing up faster. As a result, many of the years that kids could have spent building with LEGO were lost, and so too was a large portion of LEGO's market share in the toys and games market. Adding to the company's troubles, most of their competitors were sourcing their products in low-cost countries, leading to strong price competition and reduced profit margins in a declining market.

LEGO responded to these challenges by implementing various innovation projects, some of which were successful in the market, but not all. However, these projects were costly, and one of them, known internally as Darwin, cost hundreds of millions of Danish crowns. In total, the innovations did not yield more revenue and higher profits, at least not in the short run. Between 1993 and 2002, LEGO lost 1.6 billion euros of economic value and was on track to default on its outstanding debt of 800 million euros by the end of 2003.

What ultimately turned things around for LEGO were licensing deals. The first deal was made in 1998 between LEGO and Lucasfilm, which gave LEGO a licence to develop, produce, and market products in the Star Wars universe. Later licensing agreements were made with Disney and Warner Bros. This allowed LEGO to sell a significant number of products year-round, not just during the Christmas season.

From a stable level of around 1 billion euros in annual sales between 2001 and 2006, including several years with negative profits, sales increased significantly in the following years. In 2023, LEGO's revenue amounted to approximately 8.8 billion euros, accompanied by a net profit of approximately 1.76 billion euros (Andersen, 2021; LEGO, 2024a, b).

A market is determined by the product category and geographic area it encompasses, and its size, price level and growth can be estimated based on these factors. One crucial reason for making such estimations is to forecast the market's future trajectory. As the case of LEGO demonstrates, changes in the demand and supply curve can significantly influence prices, competition and the market's overall economic viability.

It should be noted that that price is not the only determining factor in market exchanges. In the field of marketing, it is acknowledged that factors such as brandings, product varieties and customer perceptions affect supply and demand for products. Nevertheless, the analysis discussed above is valid for more aggregated product categories such as clothes, food or toys.

Drivers of Market Growth – PESTLE

The market experiences growth when there is an increase in customer interest in purchasing the products. As demonstrated in Figure 2.2, a positive shift in the demand curve results in both increased market volume and value. The growth of a market is influenced by significant underlying trends, and it is crucial to identify and assess these trends while analysing a market.

Various data sources can provide valuable information about these trends and enable us to make more accurate predictions about the future of the market. Systematic analysis of the PESTLE factors can help in identifying these underlying trends:

- political;
- economic;
- social;
- technology;
- legal;
- environment.

The PESTLE factors are factors in the macro-environment that impact on all actors in the market. It was originally developed by Aguilar (1967), who labelled it PEST; later the environmental (E) and legal (L) factors were added. Each of these factors will now be explored.

Political Trends

Political factors refer to how the government and other public institutions intervene in the economy and the market. Changes in political factors can have a significant impact on the growth and profitability of a market. For instance, there are considerable variations in the provision of public health, education and infrastructure services among different European countries. Politicians continuously debate the boundary between the private and public sectors in these industries. Moreover, even within a country, there can be disagreements among politicians on how these factors should be managed. Therefore, it is crucial for companies to anticipate changes in the political landscape regarding policy changes in industries that are important to them.

Another aspect to consider regarding political factors is market regulation and protection enforced by political institutions. For instance, the EU has imposed substantial taxes on processed food imports to safeguard their domestic processing industries. This, in turn, limits the capability of non-EU food manufacturers to export their processed food to European markets. It is crucial for food producers in these nations to anticipate whether these markets will open up, as it can lead to substantial prospects for new industrial activities.

A third factor to consider is the degree to which politicians support certain industries due to their importance to the national economy, either presently or in the future. During times of economic downturn, for instance, the French government provides financial support or subsidies to the French winemaking industry, which plays a vital role in the country's economy. However, such selective support schemes can create issues as they limit the ability of businesses in countries with lower labour costs to produce the same goods. Consequently, there is often international pressure to eliminate such arrangements. Businesses that are protected in this manner must therefore be particularly attuned to signals indicating that protection will be withdrawn. They must take the necessary steps to mitigate any resulting losses.

Yet another factor here is political risk which refers to the potential for political events or actions to have a negative impact on a country's business environment, which can affect the operations and profitability of companies operating within that country. The Brexit referendum in the United Kingdom is one such event. When the UK voted to leave the European Union in 2016, it created uncertainty and instability in the business environment. This decision led to concerns about potential changes in trade regulations and barriers between the UK and other EU member states, which had a significant impact on companies involved in cross-border trade and marketing activities. Another event was the hung parliament following the results of the Swedish election in 2018, which lead to a period of political uncertainty regarding potential shifts in taxation, industry regulations and subsidies while parties negotiated to form a coalition government.

Economic Trends

Most markets are impacted by the general economic conditions prevailing in society. Today's economy is influenced by several critical economic trends. One of the significant trends is the strong economic growth in Asia, particularly in China and India. Another trend is the growing inequality between the affluent population in Northern Europe and the poor population in Southern Europe. The third important trend is that an increasing number of countries are facing difficulties in meeting their pension and healthcare obligations due to a declining proportion of the income-generating population, leading to lower tax revenues in comparison to expenses. Such trends affect interest rates, tax policies and inflation, which may have significant direct or indirect consequences on the growth of several product markets.

During times of economic recession, countries often increase public spending to stimulate growth and counter the fall in value creation. This may include more investment in infrastructure, defence, culture, health and other items on the state budget. In prosperous times, public spending is typically reduced as increased spending not only creates growth in markets, but also leads to currency depreciation and increased inflation pressure, which can cause problems for multiple actors in the economy. For instance, the increased cost of imported goods can negatively impact consumers who rely on those products, while simultaneously providing a competitive advantage to exporting companies, as their goods become more attractively priced in foreign markets.

Another tool used by authorities to influence economic growth is the key interest rate. Lower interest rates reduce capital costs, which increases companies' and customers' ability and motivation to invest and spend money. However, there is a risk that increasing interest rates will lead to negative consequences, as households may struggle and demand for products and services may fall, which in turn would reduce the total value creation in the economy.

Social Trends

Social factors refer to changes in a population's demographic characteristics, such as population growth, age distribution, income, education, mobility, property ownership, employment, settlement patterns (e.g. urban vs rural) and other related variables. Population statistics provide a relevant indication of societal developments. Credit-Suisse's annual report, Global Watch, reveals that 1.1% of the world's population holds 45.8% of the total wealth in the world (see Figure 2.3). The statistics also demonstrate that the group holding between 100,000 and 1,000,000 dollars controls 39.4% of the world's total wealth, making up 12% of the world's population. Therefore, we can observe that only 13.1% of the world's population

(1.1 + 12%) controls 85.2% (45.8 + 39.4%) of the total global wealth. This group is expanding rapidly, leading to an increase in the luxury market's niche.

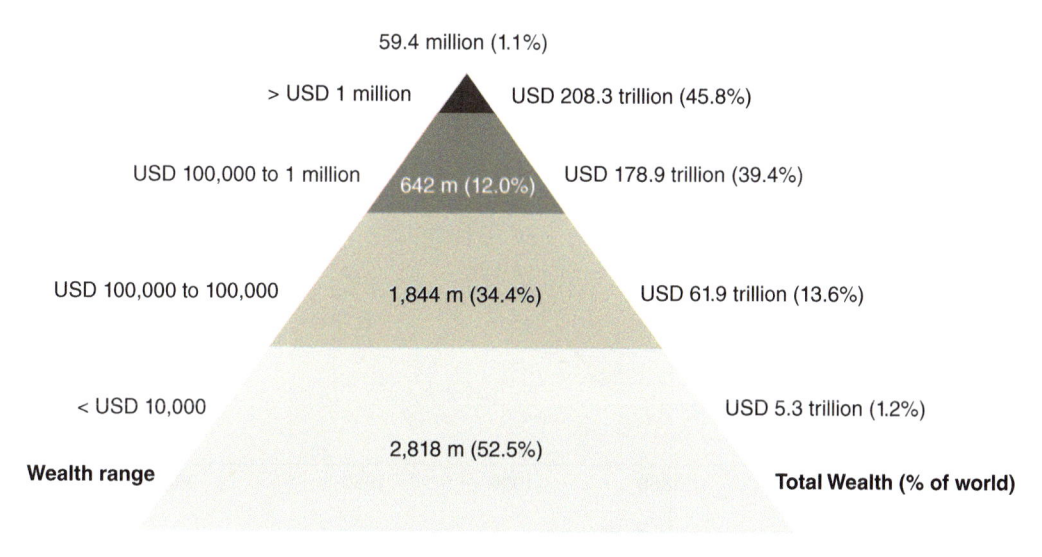

59.4 million (1.1%)

> USD 1 million — USD 208.3 trillion (45.8%)

USD 100,000 to 1 million — 642 m (12.0%) — USD 178.9 trillion (39.4%)

USD 100,000 to 100,000 — 1,844 m (34.4%) — USD 61.9 trillion (13.6%)

< USD 10,000 — USD 5.3 trillion (1.2%)

2,818 m (52.5%)

Wealth range — **Total Wealth (% of world)**

Number of adults (percent of world adults)

Figure 2.3 The distribution of global wealth (Credit Suisse, 2003)

Another significant trend is the rapid decline in the number of children born per woman, especially in large cities. Women living in urban areas are typically more educated, have active professional careers and tend to have fewer children. With more and more women attracted to cities, population growth is declining sharply. On the other hand, average life expectancy is increasing. For instance, a European citizen born in 2021 can expect to live up to 77 years, which is 30 years longer than a European born a century ago (as shown in Figure 2.4). In summary, it is expected that the world's population growth will slow down and eventually stabilize, although this will depend on the development of life expectancy. Such a shift will lead to significant changes in the basis for growth in many markets over the coming years.

A notable trend arising from declining birth rates and longer life expectancy is the ageing of the population, which will greatly affect the demand for specific products and services, such as healthcare, pharmaceuticals, retirement homes and elderly travel. As the wealth of the elderly population increases, particularly in affluent countries, there will be various intriguing developments in the market. The growth of several markets will be propelled by older consumers who possess different needs and standards for products and services compared to younger generations. Although life expectancy increases in all regions of the world, the age structure differs across regions. The median age (the 'midpoint' where half of the population has a lower age and the other half has a higher age than this point) varies considerably. The world median is around 30, North America 38, Europe 42, Oceania 32, Asia 32, Latin America 31, and Africa 19 (https://population.un.org/wpp/Download/).

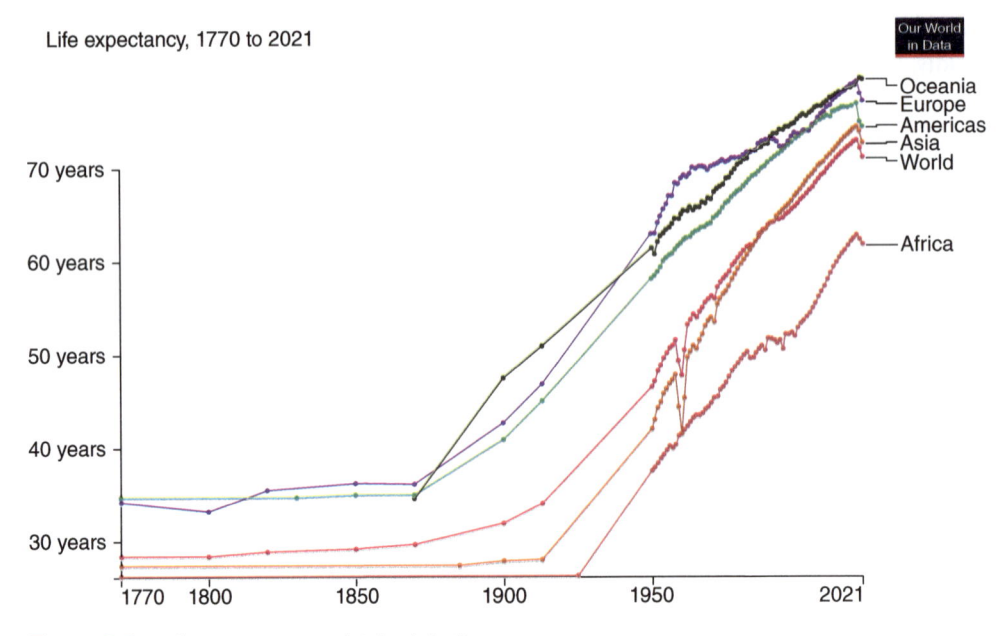

Figure 2.4   Life expectancy at birth globally

Technology Trends

Technological factors refer to the use and development of technology in new products or work processes, which can help to reduce costs, enhance quality and create new markets. An excellent illustration is the emergence of streaming services, which has significantly transformed the entertainment distribution market, particularly linear TV and the market for TV advertising. Traditional broadcasters like BBC, RTL and DR are facing competition from new global players such as Netflix and HBO. Similarly, electronic tablets and readers like the iPad and Kindle have revolutionized the book and newspaper industry. Consumers can purchase books and newspapers online directly from publishers or newsagents, rendering traditional bookstores and other retailers obsolete. Consequently, the markets for books and newspapers have undergone a complete overhaul in terms of competition.

New payment technologies are enabling customers to register and pay for their purchases without the assistance of traditional cashiers. As a result, many stores will soon no longer require the services of cashiers. This will lead to cost reductions, making products more affordable. Moreover, electronic payments will provide companies with greater insights into customers' purchasing behaviour, leading to more effective marketing. The advent of new payment technologies is thus creating entirely new competitive environments and forms of competition.

The current global economy invests more in research and development than ever before, resulting in a constant flow of new and improved products and services. This trend is particularly noticeable in the healthcare industry, where it is predicted that innovative technology, such as new treatment methods and drugs, will contribute to a 30–50% expansion of the healthcare market within the next decade. Illnesses that are currently incurable may become curable in the near future, leading to new demand. The impact of technological advancements is likely the most significant factor affecting growth in most markets.

Legal Trends

Legal factors encompass various laws that impact both the demand and supply sides of the market. Changes in legislation can introduce new standards for product quality, distribution channels and sales methods. They can also impose limitations on the use of products.

In many European countries, smoking in public spaces such as restaurants and railway stations, as well as mobile-phone use in cars, has been prohibited by law. Legislators can also enforce regulations that mandate the purchase of specific products. For instance, many European countries require homes to be equipped with smoke detectors and fire extinguishers. An alternative to legally banning a product can be to incentivise or allow for alternatives. In the case of smoking, less harmful alternatives exist – nicotine pouches and vaping. While banning smoking aims to eliminate the harmful effects of tobacco smoke and reduce overall tobacco consumption, nicotine pouches offer a potentially safer alternative for nicotine delivery and can aid in harm-reduction efforts and smoking cessation. Currently, the regulation of nicotine pouches versus tobacco varies from country to country within Europe, with some regulating nicotine pouches on a par with tobacco products and others treating it as a regular consumer product (https://tobaccotactics.org/article/nicotine-pouches).

The implementation of GDPR (General Data Protection Regulation) in the EU is one of the most significant legal changes in recent years. The regulation aims to safeguard individuals' privacy by preventing the misuse of their personal data. It is designed to install trust in individuals that the information they provide to companies will be used in a way that benefits both the individuals and reputable companies. Regulations like the GDPR are becoming increasingly important as markets become more digitized. The GDPR is a set of regulations designed to protect the privacy of individuals and has been introduced in the EU. It applies to all companies worldwide operating in the EU, regardless of whether they are located within the EU or not. Even large digital companies like Facebook, Google, Amazon and Apple must comply with the GDPR, and face fines of up to 20 million euros or 4% of global turnover. These are significant fines, and as a result major players in the market are making sure they comply with the GDPR.

Environment Trends

Environmental factors encompass weather, climate and climate change. Temperature fluctuations can impact various industries such as agriculture, tourism and transportation. As environmental consciousness continues to grow, customers are increasingly demanding locally produced goods to reduce the carbon footprint. This creates new demands on market players who need to take action. Food producers, for instance, must disclose not only the nutritional value of their products but also their environmental impact.

The awareness of sustainability and the urgent need for reducing the world's energy consumption and other factors affecting the planet's sustainability is rapidly increasing. Consumers are now changing their consumption patterns to contribute to lower emissions, and many are willing to pay a premium for products with a lower carbon footprint. As a response to these new needs and demands, several companies have successfully developed new technologies and products. Tesla, a car manufacturer, is an excellent example of a company that capitalized on this emerging trend and is currently at the forefront of developing innovative transportation products. In 2022, Tesla was the highest-valued car manufacturer globally, surpassing other well-known brands such as Toyota, Porsche, Volkswagen and GM by a significant margin (https://companiesmarketcap.com/automakers/largest-automakers-by-market-cap/, accessed 29 June 2023).

Image 2.1   Tesla founder Elon Musk

The market for electric vehicles has experienced significant growth and is anticipated to continue in the coming years. The growth is driven by a combination of technological and environmental factors. Specifically, new battery technology is expected to revolutionize the market by providing smaller and more efficient batteries with larger capacity, which will result in electric vehicles having the same range as petrol-powered cars. Additionally, the market is influenced by political factors, as policymakers are keen to promote environmentally friendly policies, such as incentivizing electric vehicle usage through tax breaks and subsidies.

Environmental considerations can have both positive and negative consequences in various markets. On the one hand, they create opportunities for businesses that offer sustainable products and cater to the growing demand for environmentally friendly products. On the other hand, they have negative consequences for some industries, such as the aviation industry, which is expected to experience a decline due to concerns over carbon emissions. Similarly, industries that rely heavily on importing products from distant manufacturers may also be impacted negatively as consumers increasingly demand locally produced goods to reduce the carbon footprint of transportation.

Image 2.2   GDPR

Several PESTLE factors have gained renewed attention since the United Nations' launch of 17 goals aimed at contributing to sustainable development worldwide by 2030. These sustainability goals include 'decent work and economic growth', 'innovation and infrastructure', 'responsible consumption and production' and 'climate action'. The political factor is brought to the forefront as local governments incorporate the sustainability goals into their policies. It is reasonable to assume that customers are highly aware of these sustainability goals and that this awareness will increase the significance of PESTLE factors. Some companies incorporate these goals into their strategy. H&M is actively working towards the UN's sustainability goals by collaborating with organizations like the World Wide Fund for Nature (WWF) to minimize water usage and protect freshwater sources in countries where their fashion items are produced, through policy advocacy and training (https://www2.hm.com/en_us/sustainability-at-hm/our-work/clean-up.html).

Image 2.3   UN's sustainability goals

Case Study 2.3

The Vital Fitness Club

PESTLE Interpretation

The Vital fitness club chain conducted a PESTLE analysis and assessed the potential impact of each factor on their market. Table 2.1 illustrates their findings. According to their analysis, the most significant political factor affecting the fitness club market is the concern among politicians about the rising prevalence of health issues such as obesity, muscle pain and depression. This has led to increased health budgets and a decline in the number of people in the workforce due to health problems, making these issues both social and financial problems. To address this, politicians have discussed subsidizing gym memberships through tax breaks or state-subsidized doctors' prescriptions. Such subsidies would have a strongly positive effect on the growth of the fitness centre market. Vital also identified important trends among economic, social and technological factors, as well as significant trends among environmental and legal factors. Additionally, the potential for future pandemics like COVID-19 could have significant negative economic consequences.

Table 2.1   PESTLE analysis for a fitness club

Factor	Finding	Consequent
Political	Governments are increasingly concerned about increasing degrees of obesity, muscular pain and depression in the society.	Public subsidies of fitness clubs may be implemented.
Economic	Fiscal policy to stimulate economic growth.	Positive effect of increase in general income and welfare levels. More people are motivated to spend money on fitness club membership.
Social	Ageing, but physically more active population – particularly in the 55+ group.	New customer segments are entering the market, which will stimulate and maintain high growth levels.
Technological	Developments of apps and other technologies that monitor physical performance and help users to optimize exercising.	Growth in sales of fitness gadgets. Opportunity for collection and analysis of new types of data.
Legal	GDPR	Important to handle personal data according to legal requirements. Personal data must be protected.
Environmental	Pandemics like COVID-19 can occur also in the future.	Lockdown of fitness clubs for longer periods.

The data required for performing a PESTLE analysis is largely available in various publicly accessible publications online. National statistical offices, such as the Official Office of Statistics (UK), Destatis (Germany) or Insee (France), provide extensive information about crucial development trends. In addition, organizations such as the OECD (Organisation for Economic Co-operation and Development), Eurostat (the EU's statistical office), research institutions, universities and business interest organizations have a wealth of information available. Both the library service at universities and online search engines provide easy access to vast amounts of relevant information. However, the primary challenge is often not the lack of data about trends, but rather interpreting the effects of the trends on market growth and other market dynamics.

Analysing Market Dynamics

The market analysis and planning process requires answering key questions that help define the market and understand its dynamics. Accurately defining the market is crucial for obtaining reliable information about its size, growth potential and profitability. It is important to identify the driving forces behind changes in market size and prices, including the underlying mechanisms that affect supply and demand. The PESTLE framework is a useful tool for systematically analysing these driving forces and identifying significant trends that could impact the market.

Table 2.2 Analysis of the market

Analysis of the market
How is the market defined with regard to product category and geography?
How large is the market, and what characterizes the development over the last five years?
How fast is the market changing, and what characterizes the changes over the last five years?
What is the price level in the market, and how has this developed over the last five years?
What are the most important (PESTLE) trends and drivers of growth in the market, and how will these affect the growth and dynamics of the market in coming years?

COMPETITIVE DYNAMICS

In a market economy, companies aim to increase their market share in order to boost their profits. This is because having a larger market share can lead to lower unit costs due to fixed costs being spread across a greater number of units sold. Additionally, the company with the largest market share typically has more bargaining power and can negotiate better purchasing conditions, resulting in further cost savings. Therefore, increasing market share often leads to greater profitability, ceteris paribus. However, competition is a key feature of a market economy and it is crucial to analyse how companies compete with each other.

One common way to gain market share is by lowering prices, as this can attract more customers and increase market share. For instance, a farmer selling apples may reduce their prices to sell more apples. However, this pricing strategy can have two major drawbacks. Firstly, the farmer with lower prices may end up with lower profits per apple sold, and there is a risk of selling at a loss if costs are not covered. Secondly, if other farmers in the market observe the price reduction, they may lower their prices as well to avoid losing sales, which can lead to a reduction in profitability for everyone in the market. Lowering prices is not a viable competitive strategy unless the company has a lower cost structure than its competitors. A cost advantage can be used to increase market share by lowering prices, or by following competitors who lower their prices.

Developing a better product than competitors' is another way for a company to gain market share. Developing better products and charging higher prices can be a viable strategy in many markets since customers are typically willing to pay more for products that offer greater benefits. For example, a farmer may advertise that his or her apples taste better and therefore cost more. One of the challenges with the strategy of developing better products and charging higher prices is that customers in the marketplace may doubt that the company actually has better products and suspect that the company is using the claim only to justify the higher price. The second challenge with the strategy of developing better products and charging higher prices is that customers may not be willing to pay a premium for higher quality, even if they believe the farmer's claim. Thus, in order to compete on quality, companies must convince customers that they actually have a better product.

In certain cases, there can be advantages to driving market growth in order to expand the overall market size, as exemplified by Tesla's efforts in transitioning from combustion engines to electric vehicles (EVs). The rationale is that it is preferable to capture a relatively larger market share within a smaller market rather than obtaining a relatively smaller share in a larger market. This strategy allows for greater potential for growth and market influence.

A fourth strategy to gain market share is to 'control' the market. For example, a group of farmers in a marketplace can join forces to squeeze out other farmers and increase their own market share. However, this strategy is illegal in most countries due to cartel laws that prohibit such cooperation. Additionally, competitors who are pushed out may find ways to retain market access and innovate new and better products with sustainable benefits.

The story of Dong's transition into Ørsted shows how a company can succeed despite facing a similar challenge. Established in Denmark in 1972, Dong Energy transformed itself from an energy company depending on oil, gas and coal to become a leading offshore wind developer known as Ørsted from 2017. Due to increasing concerns about climate change in the society, and the shift towards renewable energy sources, Ørsted made a strategic decision to transition from being a fossil energy company to a renewable energy leader. The transition involved divesting from their fossil activities and investing in offshore wind energy. They innovated and developed cutting-edge wind turbine technologies, improving their efficiency and reducing the cost of offshore wind energy production. The company's strategic shift towards renewable energy and sustainability paid off. Today, Ørsted is one of the world's largest offshore wind developers and a leading provider of green energy solutions. They have successfully positioned themselves as a key player in the global transition to clean energy, retaining and expanding their market access (Voldsgaard & Rüdiger, 2022).

Competitive Intensity

The functioning of the market is based on the premise that prices fluctuate in response to changes in the supply and demand of goods and services. However, prices are not solely influenced by supply and demand. Competitors also have a pricing strategy, leading to different companies charging different prices. Despite this, all companies strive to maintain high prices to achieve better margins and profitability. The level of competition among market players, known as competitive intensity, determines the pressure on prices. Companies aim to both increase prices and gain a larger market share, creating a fundamental dynamic. Therefore, when analysing markets, it is crucial to evaluate the level of competitive intensity and the likelihood of any changes that may increase it.

The level of competition in a market can have a negative impact on the price level and, ultimately, profitability. Thus, it is crucial to comprehend the factors that drive competition. Professor Michael E. Porter has created a model that analyses competitive intensity in an industry (Porter, 1980, 1985). According to his model, competitive intensity is influenced by five forces:

- competition among current competitors;
- the possibility of substitutes emerging in the market;
- the likelihood of new competitors entering the market;
- the bargaining power of suppliers;
- the bargaining power of customers.

Analysing these five competitive forces can provide valuable insight into the competitive dynamics at play in a market. When there are changes in one or more of these forces, companies must determine whether these changes are likely to impact on the competitive intensity of the market and therefore the price level.

Rivalry Among Existing Competitors

Competition among existing competitors is determined by their pricing strategies, promotional campaigns and other price-offensive activities. Intense price competition is common in markets with low growth, high fixed costs in comparison to variable costs, minimal differences between products and low customer-switching costs. The airline industry is an example of such a market, with high fixed costs and low variable costs, making it profitable for airlines to offer low prices to fill seats. Commodity markets also face intense price competition, particularly in times of low demand. The pharmaceutical markets are an example of the opposite, namely markets with little price competition. Even after the patent has expired, prices remain high as customers tend to trust well-known pharmaceutical products over generic drugs.

Substitutes can be a threat to a market in two ways: by affecting relative prices or by introducing new technology and innovation. Fish and chicken, for example, are substitutes that offer more favourable nutritional content than red meat, and many customers find them equally attractive. As a result, lower prices for chicken pose a significant threat to the price level in the fish market, and vice versa. New technology and innovation can also pose threats. Video-conferencing tools like Zoom, for instance, make it possible for businesspeople to limit travel, which threatens the air and hotel markets. Similarly, email has dramatically reduced the need for express mail services, thereby increasing price competition in this market.

Threats of Substitutes

Substitutes can be a threat to a market in two ways: by affecting relative prices or by introducing new technology and innovation. Fish and chicken, for example, are substitutes that offer more favourable nutritional content than red meat, and many customers find them equally attractive. As a result, lower prices for chicken pose a significant threat to the price level in the fish market, and vice versa. New technology and innovation can also pose threats. Video-conferencing tools like Zoom, for instance, make it possible for businesspeople to limit travel, which threatens the air and hotel markets. Similarly, email has dramatically reduced the need for express mail services, thereby increasing price competition in this market.

Threats from New Competitors

Industries that have high prices and profit margins tend to attract new competitors, especially when the capital requirements and economies of scale are low. However, in industries that require high capital investments and have significant economies of scale, such as automated manufacturing, new entrants have a hard time competing since production costs are much higher for them. For instance, in the cheese production industry, the cost of investing in machinery is significant, and small-scale producers have to pay the same amount for machinery as large-scale producers but can't make use of it because of their smaller output. Conversely, in industries with low capital requirements and economies of scale, like a pizza restaurant, new entrants face fewer cost-disadvantages and are more likely to succeed. For instance, a start-up pizza restaurant incurs similar costs to an established large pizza chain in renting premises, hiring employees and kitchen appliances. Thus, small businesses do not have a cost disadvantage compared to large ones. Therefore, it is less likely for markets with large capital requirements and high economies of scale to experience intense price competition from new entrants.

An additional illustration is how new technology can alter the requirement for significant investments in infrastructure. For instance, opening a physical store involves costly investments in renting a prime location (such as a shopping centre), designing the store interior and hiring staff to serve customers during opening hours. Conversely, launching an online store incurs low capital requirements. Hence, several new retailers have entered numerous markets, and companies such as Alibaba have leveraged this to establish themselves across various product categories, selling goods globally.

In numerous markets, access to distribution systems represents a crucial barrier to entry because a handful of players usually control such systems. For instance, in Norway, three ownership groups manage the distribution system for grocery products. These groups leverage their power to regulate which producers are granted access to distribute their products and at what price. Existing manufacturers continually face pressure to lower prices, which restricts their profitability. Furthermore, new manufacturers are prohibited from entering the market unless they can present retail chains with a significantly improved profit margin. As a result, a new entrant in the grocery market must not only convince consumers to select their product but also persuade individual grocery chains that their stores will boost profits. This approach curtails competitive dynamics, and grocery prices tend to remain relatively high.

Suppliers' Bargaining Power

The bargaining power of suppliers can significantly impact competitive intensity when suppliers are more concentrated than buyers, switching suppliers involves high costs, suppliers offer highly differentiated products, few substitutes are available and volume is of little significance to suppliers.

Numerous fashion retailers are small, independent shops that are typically owned and operated by fashion enthusiasts. These retailers possess limited bargaining power in comparison to the larger fashion brands and are generally required to conform to the suppliers' stipulations. This situation leads to the unsurprising result that fashion apparel is more lucrative for manufacturers than for retailers. To bolster their bargaining power, fashion retailers have established chain stores and improved their margins by procuring goods in larger quantities. Moreover, these chain stores create clothing collections under their own name, which makes them less reliant on suppliers. In response to the advent of chain stores, many suppliers have developed concept stores and online stores, thus enabling direct communication and distribution to customers.

CATL, a Chinese manufacturer of lithium-ion batteries for electric vehicles, is an example of technology-driven product differentiation. Their battery cells offer higher energy capacity, improved efficiency and longer lifespan compared to traditional batteries, providing an advantage in terms of driving range and overall performance of EVs. Their ongoing innovations, including its new battery-swap solution branded EVOGO, allow them to stay ahead of their competitors and maintain a technological edge. By consistently improving their products, CATL attracts and retains customers, enhancing their bargaining power in negotiation with automotive manufacturers who gain access to cutting-edge battery solutions that enhance their EV offerings (https://www.fitchratings.com/research/corporate-finance/catl-aims-to-trailblaze-chinas-battery-swapping-market-13-02-2022; https://time.com/6217992/china-electric-vehicle-catl/).

Customers' Bargaining Power

When customers are concentrated and represent significant volumes, switching costs are low, competitors offer undifferentiated products, brands are weak and substitutes are available, customers have substantial bargaining power. In several business-to-business markets, a few customers often possess considerable bargaining power. As a result, prices in the market are typically reduced. When a market consists of a few large customers, prices and profits are often low. Consequently, a company should be wary if customers in the market form larger units by joining forces. In the airline industry, a small number of major airlines known as 'flag carriers', including British Airways, Lufthansa, Air France-KLM and SAS, have significant bargaining power due to their size, market dominance and the volume of aircraft purchases they make. These airlines often place substantial orders for new aircraft to expand their fleets or replace older planes. The sheer scale of these orders gives them significant leverage when negotiating with aircraft manufacturers. Moreover, by requesting offers from multiple manufacturers, airlines can compare offers and negotiate more advantageous terms based on the competitive environment. When a few key players are responsible for a substantial portion of the demand, they can demand lower prices, favourable contract terms or customized aircraft configurations.

Analysing Competitive Intensity

When analysing the competitive forces in a market, it is crucial to link the analysis to one's own market and position within it. Not all factors carry equal weight, and the importance of each factor may change over time. We will now look again at the example of the Vital fitness club, who conducted their own analysis of competitive intensity.

Case Study 2.4

The Vital Fitness Club
Analysis of Competitive Intensity

Vital, a fitness club, conducted an analysis of competitive intensity, which revealed that the most significant threat was the increasing number of smaller players offering low prices to attract new customers. This aggressive pricing strategy can prompt larger players to do the same, leading to reduced profitability in the market.

The growing interest in outdoor activities, such as running, cycling and skiing, is also a threat that can slow down growth in the fitness club market and intensify price competition. These are serious challenges that Vital must address through a well-planned strategy. None of the other three competitive forces were found to have a significant impact on future competitive intensity in the fitness club market.

Table 2.3 Analysis of the five competitive forces for a fitness club company

Factor	Finding	Consequence
Competitive rivalry	Smaller fitness clubs use price aggressively to attract new customers.	Can also drive large players to price aggressively and increase their use of promotional campaigns.
Substitutes	The most serious threat is that customers prefer outdoor exercise – trends indicate that jogging, cycling and skiing are becoming increasingly popular. These activities also cost far less than fitness clubs.	Reduced market size through loss of customers to substitute, combined with diminished basis for recruiting new customers. Reduced market size forces competitors to price more aggressively.
New entrants	The high profitability of the industry attracts new competitors. So far, only small companies have entered, but there is a risk that companies with larger financial resources will follow.	No threats for the time being.
Supplier power	Suppliers are small and fragmented, and they have little bargaining power. Expected to continue.	No threats for the time being.
Customer power	Customers are few in number and fragmented. Excepted to continue.	No threats for the time being.

Market Structure

The configuration of a market with respect to the number of competitors, obstacles to entry and product differentiation can also impact on the nature of competition. A market with numerous competitors, low entry barriers and limited product differentiation results in intense competition among rivals who frequently use price promotions to attract customers. A commonly used measure to assess the level of concentration or competitiveness within an industry or market is the Herfindahl–Hirschman Index (HHI). It is calculated by summing the squares of the market shares of all firms or participants within the industry. The formula for calculating the HHI is as follows: $HHI = (s1^2 + s2^2 + s3^2 + \ldots + sn^2)$, where s1, s2, s3, …, sn represent the market shares of individual firms within the market (United States Department of Justice, 2018). The index ranges from 0 to 10,000, with higher values indicating greater market concentration. Markets with lower numbers on this index exhibit intense competition, which is accompanied by lower prices, higher advertising costs, decreased profit margins and diminished profitability, as compared with markets with higher numbers on the index.

To withstand competitive pressure, companies can employ various strategic actions. One strategy is to merge with competitors, reducing the number of competitors in the market and alleviating some of the competitive pressure. Another approach is to invest heavily in production technology and distribution systems to achieve cost-effectiveness, thereby creating a competitive advantage that can withstand price competition and make it more difficult for new players to enter the market. A third strategy is to invest heavily in technology and innovation to develop superior products that are harder for competitors to copy, making the company more resistant to price competition. These strategic actions can alter the market structure, and the company's analysis of the market should therefore focus on how competitive dynamics evolve and change the nature of competition. There are four types of market structures: perfect competition, monopolistic competition, oligopoly and monopoly, each with its own characteristics, as shown in Table 2.4.

Table 2.4 Characteristics of different market structures

Market Structure	Number of Suppliers	Number of Customers	Supplier Entry Barriers	Product Differentiation
Perfect competition	Many	Many	Low	No
Monopolistic competition	Many	Many	Low	Yes
Oligopoly	Few	Many	High	Yes/No
Monopoly	One	Many	High	No

Adapted from https://businessoer.com/competing-in-a-free-market/

Perfect Competition

Perfect competition refers to a market structure where many suppliers offer similar products with no significant differentiation, and there are no barriers to entry. While there are very few markets that meet these strict criteria, some markets come closer to perfect competition than others. In markets with perfect competition, no single player can determine the price level, and since the products are undifferentiated, prices tend to be similar across suppliers.

Due to the limited profitability in perfect competition markets, companies in these markets must constantly seek new ways to differentiate themselves from their competitors. This differentiation can take place through investment in production technology to reduce costs or in product development to justify higher prices. As competitors innovate and differentiate, the market structure changes accordingly. The constant pressure to innovate and differentiate is what makes the perfect competition market dynamic.

One example is the emergence of mobile payment solutions like Apple Pay, Google Pay, Samsung Pay, Vipps (Norway), MobilePay (Denmark) and Swish (Sweden). While these products serve the common goal of providing mobile payment, they use different technologies that distinguish them in terms of compatibility, convenience and the range of payment methods supported. These distinctions result in variations in the user experience and the acceptance of payments across different retail environments.

A company may also emphasize features like packaging, purity or convenience. Consider the market for bottled water. Appealing and distinctive bottle designs and labels help the products stand out on store shelves, many suppliers emphasize the pure water source origin of their product, and products are made widely available to customers through multiple retail outlets, online platforms and convenience stores.

Monopolistic Competition

Monopolistic competition refers to a market structure where there are numerous suppliers and customers, but the suppliers sell differentiated products. These products are substitutes, but with distinct features and brand names. Since the products are differentiated, suppliers can charge higher prices if customers see added value in the differences. For example, a restaurant can become more popular than other restaurants by offering an attractive menu. Customers visit the restaurant and accept higher prices because the food is particularly good. In the short run, suppliers in monopolistic competition markets can achieve higher profits than their competitors. A popular restaurant will earn more profit than its competitors because it sells more at better prices. However, competitors are likely to copy the successful innovator and possibly offer even more attractive menus, possibly at lower prices. A competitive advantage in monopolistic markets is easily copied, leading to suppressed profits in the long run, resulting in companies earning the same as their other competitors.

To attain a sustainable advantage, a company must create activities and resources that are difficult to replicate, which means developing barriers against imitation. For instance, if a restaurant succeeds in creating a recipe that competitors cannot replicate, it can secure its position. The Big Mac's hamburger sauce is a prime example of such a recipe. Alternatively, a company can establish a strong brand name that cannot be easily duplicated. Although several of Danone's dairy products are nearly identical to those of its competitors in terms of product attributes, the Danone brand's standing among consumers often leads them to choose Danone's products over those of its competitors. If market players can create such barriers against imitation, the market structure will shift towards oligopoly.

Oligopoly

Oligopoly is a commonly observed market structure where a small number of dominant suppliers control the market, typically consisting of three or four large players that together hold a significant market share ranging from 70% to 90%. A discussion of market leaders' competitive strategies and their impact on profitability can be found in Uslay et al. (2010). Due to the limited number of players in the market, the actions of one supplier significantly affect and are influenced by the decisions of others. In such a scenario, strategic decisions must be made considering the potential response from competitors. For instance, if one of the large banks in an oligopoly market lowers the mortgage interest rate to attract customers, the other banks will quickly follow suit. Conversely, if one bank increases the interest rate, customers may switch to the competitors. Hence, price changes in oligopolies are often small and gradual. Oligopolies can have differentiated products, such as cars, or homogeneous products, such as banks. Since competitors in an oligopoly market closely monitor each other, they tend to quickly replicate successful innovations, which makes the market structure relatively stable over time. The grocery markets in the Scandinavian countries can all be considered oligopolies. Each of these markets is dominated by a small number of major players who control much of the market share. In Norway, the three grocery chains

NorgesGruppen, Coop Norge and Rema together hold more than 95% of the market. The HHI for the grocery market is higher than 2,500 in all the Scandinavian countries, which is considered concentrated, but lower than for duopoly (HHI = 5,000) and monopoly (HHI = 10,000) (https://www.regjeringen.no/globalassets/departementene/nfd/dokumenter/rapporter/sifo-dagligvarerapport-korrigert-ver.pdf).

Monopoly

A monopoly occurs when a single company has control over market access for a product, resulting in no competition and the ability to set high prices and earn very high profits. However, most countries have laws in place to regulate monopolies, as they stifle innovation and typically lead to products of lower quality at higher prices. The USA and the EU have strict regulations to prevent mergers and the abuse of monopoly power, with the former famously claiming that Microsoft abused its monopoly power in the Intel-based PC market by bundling its own browser, Internet Explorer, with the Windows operating system. As a result of the case, Microsoft was ordered to share its programming interface with third-party companies.

When analysing market structure, companies should attempt to predict future competition and changes in the market structure, as all markets are subject to dynamic changes.

Competitor Intelligence

Knowing your competitors' plans is crucial in market analysis as it can help a company develop effective countermeasures to reduce or eliminate their impact. This is particularly important in oligopoly markets where there are only a few competitors with a large market share, and their actions strongly influence each other. By anticipating their competitors' behaviour, a company can stay ahead of the game. For example, if a competitor is planning to launch a product with unique features, the company can neutralize its impact by developing a similar product.

Obtaining information about competitors is relatively straightforward, as there are various sources available, including electronic databases and the internet. Additionally, suppliers, customers, industry experts and former employees of competitors can provide valuable information. Analysing competitors requires a similar approach to military intelligence work, where information is not obtained directly but indirectly through triangulation. In other words, analysing multiple sources of information allows companies to make educated guesses about their competitors' plans. This process is similar to a puzzle, where small pieces of information are put together to create a complete picture. By combining different pieces of information, companies can gain a better understanding of their competitors' strategies and plans.

The primary objective of conducting a competitor analysis is to anticipate their most likely moves. By identifying their market challenges, we can make an educated guess on their next moves. We can also determine their market objectives and the strategies they will use to attain them. Through analysis, we can estimate the impact of these actions on the market, as well as their influence on our company and the competitive landscape (refer to Figure 2.6).

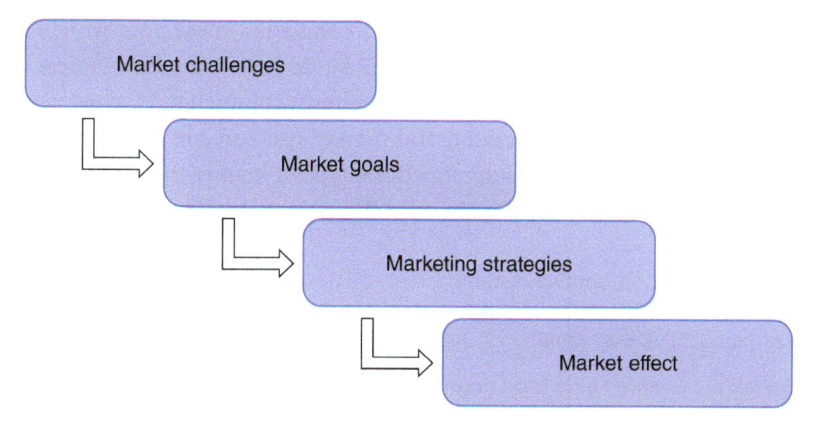

Figure 2.5 Important question in competitor intelligence

Through the analysis of changes in sales revenue and profits, it is possible to determine whether a competitor is content with their current market position. In the case of negative developments, it is important to investigate the underlying cause. For instance, a competitor may have lost customers due to poor customer service. In such a scenario, the competitor is likely to make improved customer service a marketing objective and develop strategies accordingly. If successful, this would make it harder to attract customers from this competitor.

Understanding how competitors perceive their own success and the strategies they attribute it to is crucial in competitor analysis. For instance, a competitor who has achieved higher-than-average sales growth may attribute their success to investments in advertising. This insight can help companies hypothesize that the competitor is likely to set even higher goals and increase their advertising expenditure to maintain their market position.

To begin competitor analysis, one must develop a set of hypotheses regarding their market problems, goals and marketing strategies. The collection of information and data will then either support or reject these hypotheses. For instance, if we learn that a competitor is laying off their head of customer service, it may be an indicator that they have plans for significant improvements in customer service. Similarly, if a competitor invites advertising agencies to compete for a new contract, it may indicate that they are reconsidering their current advertising strategy.

Once we have identified and verified our competitors' marketing strategies, it becomes crucial to evaluate their potential impact on the market and competitive landscape. For example, if our research suggests that a competitor is planning to significantly boost their advertising efforts, we need to consider how the market will respond. Will this advertising increase results in an overall growth of sales within the market? This situation occurs in markets where there is minimal differentiation between competitors' products, such as milk. In such cases, the competitor's advertising increase will have a positive impact on the market by boosting sales volume, but our market share will remain unaffected. On the other hand, will the advertising increase influence customers' choices and, as a result, impact our relative market share? If so, our company must take corrective actions, such as increasing our advertising spending, to counteract this effect.

Table 2.5 highlights the critical enquiries that companies must pose while conducting competitor analysis. To gain comprehensive insights into how competitive forces impact on future market growth and pricing levels, companies must comprehend the mechanisms that drive changes. The nature of competition and market structure are evident in competitive dynamics. Thus, companies must comprehend the type of market they operate in and evaluate whether there will be any modifications in the market structure.

Table 2.5 Analysis of competitive dynamics

Analysis of competitive dynamics
How do the five competitive forces shape competitive intensity?
How will the structure of the market evolve in the short and long term?
Will political legislation influence the competitive dynamics?
What is the strategy of the individual competitors, what are their likely actions and how will this affect competition in the market?

PRODUCT LIFE CYCLE

The product life cycle (PLC) is a vital concept in marketing that explains the evolution of new product categories (i.e. emerging markets), their progression, and the attributes of the markets and competitive environment during their lifespan. According to this theory, product sales go through four distinct phases (as illustrated in Figure 2.7):

- introduction;
- growth;
- maturity;
- decline.

New product categories such as mobile phones, MP3 players, pads, GPS systems and electric bicycles are all prime examples of products that follow the pattern predicted by the PLC theory. During the introduction phase, sales volumes are low and growth is sluggish. The growth phase sees a rapid increase in sales volume until growth plateaus during the maturity phase. Finally, after a period, sales begin to decline, leading to the decline phase (Levitt, 1965).

The PLC theory also outlines a categorization of customer segments that adopt the product (Rogers, 1962; Bass, 1969). According to the theory, a new innovation is first embraced by a select group of innovators. These innovators possess extensive knowledge and interest in the product category and are continuously seeking new information. They enjoy exploring novel ideas and seek inspiration and information beyond their primary social groups. The innovators introduce the new products to their social circles, and subsequently other members start following suit. One example is that of the first customers to buy the Tesla

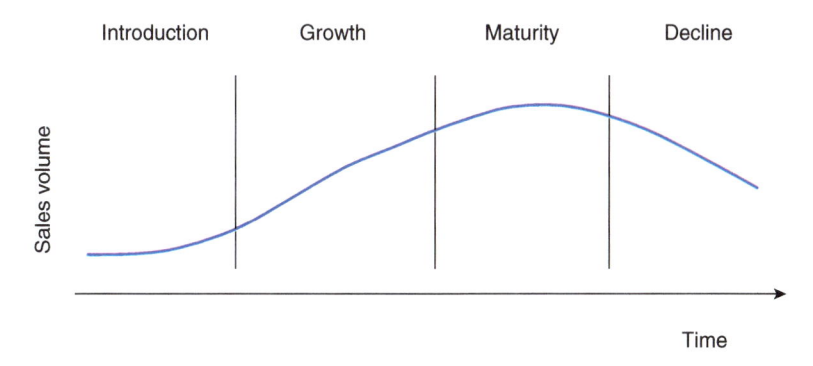

Figure 2.6   Sales volume in the four phases of the PLC

Roadster, launched in 2008. The Tesla Roadster was an all-electric sports car at a time when electric cars were still a relatively new concept, and the market was dominated by traditional fossil-powered vehicles. The Tesla Roadster appealed to innovators who were likely intrigued by its innovation, environmental sustainability and high-performance capabilities. These early adopters saw the potential of electric cars and were willing to take the leap to test this emerging technology.

Within the group, some are more inclined to adopt the new product than others. These early followers are referred to as early adopters. The early adopters are typically opinion leaders who utilize the new product to establish their position as influencers within the group. The majority and laggard groups are generally sceptical of anything new and take a long time to adopt the product, waiting until it proves to be useful and user-friendly.

Introduction Phase

In the introduction phase of the product life cycle, there are only a few innovative and usually smaller companies involved. The process of developing new products is gradual and often involves contributions from various entrepreneurs with different ideas. Newly established companies tend to collaborate with research universities, research institutions and larger well-established companies to form different types of networks. It is common for larger companies to take over once the entrepreneurs succeed and the product has survived in the market, which fuels growth as they provide the required capital and expertise.

In this stage, strategies include informing innovator customers, creating awareness among early adopters, distributing product samples and building a selective distribution system. Prices and costs are usually high, and heavy investments are made not only in product and production development but also in other aspects of marketing. Due to these investments, profits are low at this stage of the product life cycle.

The introduction stage spans from the first launch of the product until it experiences a breakthrough in the market. Research has shown that the average length of the introduction stage used to be around ten years before the product achieved a breakthrough (Golder & Tellis, 2004). Although this average has reduced to five years or less, it still remains a long period (several good examples of fast-growing new solutions can be found in Gladwell, 2000). The speed at which larger companies are willing to invest in new product categories and whether they are willing to do this before knowing whether the product will be successful impacts how long it takes for a product to achieve its market breakthrough. For instance, car manufacturers were initially hesitant to invest in the commercialization of electric cars until Tesla began to take significant market shares.

Growth Phase

In the growth phase, the product becomes more widely adopted by the early majority and demand increases rapidly. This is facilitated by suppliers who have developed better production technology, leading to economies of scale that give early players a cost advantage. Product differentiation is usually low in this phase, as the focus is on building mass distribution and advertising to create brand awareness and preference. Differentiation aims to capture emerging new segments but is mostly limited to functional properties and design elements. Prices gradually decrease to reach new market segments.

For durable consumer goods, the growth phase typically lasts around eight years with an annual growth rate of 45% (Golder & Tellis, 2004). As sales growth accelerates and economies of scale kick in, companies experience increasing profits in the growth phase.

Maturity Phase

During the maturity phase, which typically lasts about five years, the annual sales growth rate levels off at around 15% (Golder & Tellis, 2004). At this point, competitors begin to differentiate their products to a greater degree and develop more efficient production and marketing methods. While product differentiation increases, the overall investment in product development decreases relative to sales. As a result, companies tend to achieve their highest profits in the early years of the maturation stage. However, as sales level off, many businesses experience excess capacity and begin to lower their prices, which intensifies competition. Some companies respond by focusing on specific segments and strategic product differentiation, leading to a more fragmented market and some competitors succeeding in developing distinctive products.

Decline Phase

The stage of decline is anticipated to take place when around half of the market's customers have embraced the new product, the competition has diminished, and profits have decreased. During the decline phase, a typical marketing tactic is to curtail investments, eliminate products with low sales, concentrate distribution in fewer outlets and minimize advertising efforts. Prices tend to decrease during this stage, compelling companies to cut costs to maintain profitability. Even well-established brands confront price competition in declining markets.

Analysing PLC

The product life cycle (PLC) concept aids in comprehending how new markets emerge and develop, as well as how competitive dynamics function at different developmental stages (see Shanker et al., 1999). Each stage of the cycle is marked by distinct differences in market structures. At the introduction stage, monopoly prevails as early entrants try to safeguard their ideas through patents, but competitors often find ways to replicate them, leading to a more monopolistic market structure. Monopolistic competition is most common during the growth stage. In the maturation and decline stages, oligopolistic competition is the norm. It's crucial to note that market evolution in the maturity and decline stages varies significantly, more so than what the PLC suggests. The PLC assumes that customers only use a single product exemplar and does not account for product replacement. For example, most customers buy more than one mobile phone in their lifetime and replace it after a few years. As customers begin to replace their products once or multiple times, sales may start to grow again in both the maturity and decline stages.

In addition, companies endeavour to create fresh and innovative iterations of the initial product concept during the maturation and decline stages. There are numerous approaches to developing new products during these stages (see Nadeau & Casselman, 2008). The product alternatives become more distinctive, enticing customers to purchase not just one, but multiple variants. For instance, customers may acquire multiple mobile phones for various purposes, such as one for work, one for use in the car and another for outdoor activities. This type of fragmentation may even lead to the formation of new sub-markets within the original product category. As an example, the former mainframes have evolved into several new product categories, including PCs and servers.

The product life cycle (PLC) theory lacks a precise definition of what constitutes a new product category or market (see Day, 1981). However, some suggest that a new product category is characterized by a clear departure from current market practices, and it typically emerges when there is a significant transformation in the product's technology or function or when it is adopted by a completely new customer group. Using this definition, the advent of modern coffee shops, exemplified by Starbucks, can be classified as a new product category and market. Although coffee has been sold in cafés and restaurants for a long time, the coffee bars represented a distinct departure from the conventional way of selling coffee. Digital cameras can also be classified as a new product category since they replaced traditional film technology with new digital technology, providing innovative uses such as digital image processing. As customers shifted from old film cameras to new digital ones, a new market emerged, and its evolution has followed the product life cycle.

Analysing markets and competitive dynamics using the PLC theory can help companies gain a deeper understanding of the underlying dynamics and the likely future development of the markets. This analysis can provide insight into the current stage of the market and an assessment of the likelihood of the market entering a new stage in the near future. For example, if the market has experienced rapid growth for several years, it may soon enter a more mature stage with different competitive dynamics. In such cases, companies should identify new growth categories that can replace the current product category. Specifically, the company can search for growth markets that can effectively use their existing resources and capacity. Table 2.6 highlights the key questions that companies must ask as part of their PLC analysis.

Table 2.6   Analysis of PLC

Analysis of PLC
In which stage of the PLC is the market now?
Will the market enter a new stage, and if so, when and how will this happen?
Are there any emerging markets that can substitute products in our market?
Are there any rapidly growing markets our company should invest in?

While models such as the competitive forces and the PLC theory are widely used concepts in marketing, they have received some objections regarding their managerial usefulness in real world situations. For example, critics assert against the PLC that the theory fails to provide specific guidelines or actionable insights for managers to implement during each stage of the product life cycle (Iveson et al., 2022). It lacks the necessary depth and granularity to guide practical decision-making in marketing strategies and resource allocation.

SUMMARY

A company must continuously improve its market position due to evolving customer needs, innovations, market network efficiency and changing conditions.

A market connects suppliers and customers for buying and selling products. Clear boundaries, including geography, products, customers and competitors, are necessary. This allows for analysis of market size, price levels, growth and sales trends. This knowledge helps a company improve its market position and marketing activities.

Shifts in demand and supply curves are important in market analysis. Changes in factors like customers' income, prices of similar products or preferences can cause positive or negative shifts in the demand curve, affecting price and market size.

Market growth is influenced by important trends that need to be identified and assessed during analysis. Analysing PESTLE factors (political, economic, social, technological, legal and environmental) helps identify these trends.

Competitive intensity creates competitive dynamics and determines pricing pressure. Michael E. Porter's model analyses competitive intensity in an industry using five forces: current competitor competition, emerging substitute products, new entrants, supplier and customers.

Market analysis should focus on the evolution of competitive dynamics and the four market structures: perfect competition, monopolistic competition, oligopoly and monopoly.

Knowing competitors' plans is crucial in market analysis. It helps develop countermeasures and is particularly important in oligopoly markets with few dominant competitors who strongly influence each other. Anticipating competitors' behaviour keeps the company ahead.

The product life cycle (PLC) explains the evolution of emerging markets through four phases (introduction, growth, maturity and decline) and segments of customers with different adoption sensitivity. Innovators introduce the product to their social circles, followed by early adopters as opinion leaders. Majority and laggard groups take longer to adopt the product.

END-OF-CHAPTER QUESTIONS

1 Define the market for ice cream. Identify the market's key competitors and calculate the market size and development over the past three to five years. How has the price level in the market evolved over the years? What factors have caused these changes?

2 Use the PESTLE framework to discuss possible changes in supply and demand in the ice cream market. How do you think the market will develop in terms of volume and prices?

3 Use the five forces framework to analyse the competitive dynamics in the ice-cream market. What are the main reasons why intense price competition is prevented in this market?

4 How would you describe the market structure in the ice-cream market? Is it a monopoly, monopolistic, oligopolistic or perfect competition market? If all competitors were to merge, the market would become a monopoly. How would this affect prices and profits in the market? Why do competition authorities believe that such monopolies must be prevented?

FURTHER READING

Levitt, T. (1965). Exploit the product life cycle. *Harvard Business Review*, 43(6), 84–94.

Pindyck, R.S. & Rubinfeld, D.L. (2017). *Microeconomics*. Pearson Prentice Hall.

Porter, M. (1985). *Competitive Advantage: Creating and Sustaining Superior Performance*. The Free Press.

Uslay, C., Altintig, Z.A. & Winsor, R.D. (2010). An empirical examination of the "rule of three": Strategy implications for top management, marketers, and investors. *Journal of Marketing*, 74(2), 20–39. DOI:10.1509/jmkg.74.2.20

3

CUSTOMER BEHAVIOUR

This chapter

- presents the customer's decision journey;
- discusses the customer's mental and behavioural stages in this journey, including:

  - problem recognition
  - information search
  - evaluation of alternatives
  - purchase and choice
  - usage;

- discusses customer decisions from the perspective of Behavioural Decision Theory;
- presents the most important characteristic of business customers.

INTRODUCTION

An effective marketing strategy requires a comprehensive understanding of customers' needs and their impact on purchasing behaviour. Analysing customer behaviour involves studying why customers make specific choices and how marketing influences their decision-making process. This analysis begins with identifying the underlying needs that drive choices in relevant product categories and predicting how these needs will evolve in the future. The assumption is that customers are rational decision-makers who gather information about available options and select products that best meet their needs. However, this does not imply that customers always make optimal choices or only purchase products they truly need. Rather, customers try to satisfy their needs through their choices and seek information to facilitate their decisions. Therefore, the company's primary goal is to provide excellent products, promote them through effective marketing communication and deliver what customers expect in order to achieve satisfaction.

The chapter commences by introducing the customer decision journey, which provides a framework for analysing the decision-making process's different stages. Because it is not always easy to observe that customers are going through something resembling a journey prior to making a purchase, we also present a behavioural decision theoretical perspective on customer decisions. Following that, the chapter highlights the critical characteristics of professional customers who act on behalf of organizations. In contrast to consumer markets, professional customers organize their purchases differently, and their needs' structure varies. Nonetheless, many of the fundamental principles of customer behaviour apply to professional customers as well. Just like in consumer markets, professional customers are also drawn to excellent products and effective marketing communication.

THE CUSTOMER DECISION JOURNEY

To understand the consumers' decision-making it is fruitful to look at the journey customers undertake from the conception of a problem to the problem being solved. The customer journey is defined as the process the customer goes through, across all stages and touchpoints with an organization, comprising the customer experience (Court et al., 2009; Edelman & Singer, 2015; Lemon & Verhoef, 2016). To develop market offers that provide value for customers, the company must understand customer behaviour. Specifically, the company must understand customers' experiences and decisions throughout their entire purchase journey. At each stage of the journey, there are multiple touchpoints between the company and the customer at which value can be delivered or co-created as well as perceived by customer, like social media, websites, physical stores, customer service, among others. These touchpoints elicit cognitive and emotional responses from the customers (Tueanrat et al., 2021), which may be taken as indicators of value creation. Similar touchpoints exist between the customer and competing companies and to some extent between customers and third parties (e.g. retail). In addition to company–customer touchpoints, there are customer–customer touchpoints. Throughout the journey, customers experience external touchpoints online as well as offline, including other customers, influencers and product reviewers. These touchpoints create both opportunities and challenges for the company's value creation with the customer (Lemon & Verhoef, 2016).

Consistent with the customer-centric perspective of this book, the journey is seen from the customer's viewpoint, rather than from the company's or its products' points of view. Although the company views the journey from the customer's point of view, it need not be reactive. The company can actively shape the path by adjusting technologies, process and organizational structures to enhance value and thereby gain a competitive edge (Edelman & Singer, 2015). By proactively defining a customer's problem by sending a customized mail explaining energy cost reduction, providing references from other customers effectively reducing the consideration set to one and streamlining the evaluation phase online, the solar panel provider Sungevity put the customer directly into the loyalty loop (Edelman & Singer, 2015).

In this chapter, a generic journey consisting of five stages is used: problem recognition, information search, evaluation, purchase decision, and usage. In a given context, different and alternative stages might be more useful. For example, in channel management, problem definition, search, purchase and aftersales have been identified as decision stages (Neslin et al., 2006). The primary objective of the customer journey is therefore to comprehend the customer's viewpoint, responses and interactions at each stage, with the aim of delivering a seamless and gratifying experience, hence increasing value for both customer and company.

The first stage in the journey is recognizing a need, which leads to motivation to satisfy that need. This is called problem recognition. However, simply being aware of the need may not be enough to generate sufficient motivation to proceed. If motivation is present, the next stages involve gathering information, evaluating alternatives, choosing the best option and, finally, using the product. The process is illustrated in Figure 3.1 and is iterative, meaning that the customer may go back to earlier stages as they gain more knowledge about the relevant product. For example, during the evaluation of alternatives, the customer may realize that they lack information about one of the options and may return to gather more information. Moreover, because there are myriad touchpoints across the journey, and some are likely to be more influential than others, the journey may not start with problem recognition. The presence of influential peers in a store or service environment can encourage a customer who may not initially have any recognized problem to try a product or service.

The duration and complexity of the decision journey depend on multiple factors, such as the customer, product type, buying context or situation. One journey may take only a few milliseconds, from problem recognition to purchase decision, while another may last for several years. Furthermore, the journey does not end with the purchase decision. The customer continues to use the product, gaining experience and knowledge that will shape their future buying decisions.

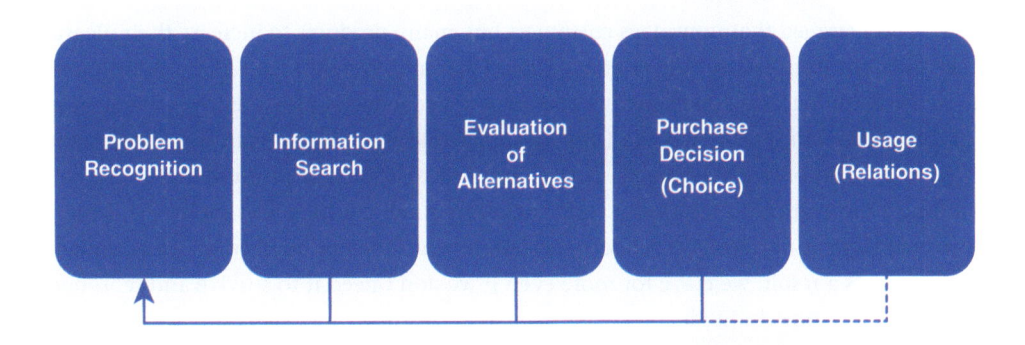

Figure 3.1 The customer decision journey[1]

---

[1]The model is a revised version of the one found in Kotler & Keller (2015). In the literature, there are several models of the customer buying process (see Howard & Sheth, 1969; Engel et al., 1994; Schiffman & Kanuk, 2007).

Problem Recognition

The journey is likely to start out with a problem being recognized, which occurs when there is a significant gap between the current state and the desired state, prompting the customer to seek a solution. For instance, a person may realize that there is no milk in the refrigerator, prompting them to start the buying process to acquire some milk. Recognition of a problem can result from either an internal or external influence. External influences could be an advertisement, an empty fridge or the milk shelves in a store. An ad constitutes an important touchpoint for value creation by forming beliefs and elicit emotions. Internal influences could be thoughts about the contents of the fridge, consideration of ingredients needed for cooking or a feeling of thirst. Problem recognition creates psychological tension, which motivates the person to act and solve the problem. Solving the problem removes the tension. The solution to the problem may not always be straightforward, as it may involve more complicated considerations. For example, recognizing that one's car is old may prompt them to consider buying a new one. However, if a new car is too expensive, they may remove the mental tension by convincing themselves that the car is still safe and in good condition. It is worth noting that not all product-related problem recognitions result in purchases.

The recognition of needs and wants should be distinguished as two different types of problem recognition.[2] A need is a situation where customers feel a lack (deficit) of something and have the desire to return to a neutral mental state (as shown in Figure 3.2). In the milk example, the customer experiences discomfort at the thought of not having milk and initiates a process to alleviate this negative feeling. Most biological drives such as thirst, hunger and fear are feelings of lack that motivate us to return to a neutral state. On the other hand, a want is a type of problem recognition where the customer desires a surplus. For instance, a customer who wants a new car desires the pleasurable feeling associated with owning a new car.

It has been argued that nowadays customers buy many products to increase their pleasure rather than out of necessity (Vieira et al.; 2018; Dhar and Wetenbroch, 2000). Additionally, due to the abundance of goods, people may experience reduced pleasure from them. In her book *Dopamine Nation* (2021), Anna Lembke argues that the human brain was not designed to live in a world of overabundance. It was designed to approach pleasure and avoid pain, including a motivation to seek more stuff, including food, clothing and shelter. This mechanism is still operating in today's modern societies in which people do have an overabundance of products. As a result, we crave for more even if we don't need it to survive and reproduce. As an example, some individuals have grown so accustomed to having a modern car that they may feel a sense of deficiency when their car begins to age, even if it still functions properly. In such cases, the desire for a new car may stem more from a need to maintain a certain lifestyle than from a genuine desire for pleasure.

Understanding the motivation behind the buying process is crucial from a marketing standpoint. When a customer recognizes a problem, it generates a state of tension that motivates them to take action to remove it, either by satisfying a want or repairing a deficiency.

---

[2]The argument that we should distinguish between a negative drive to fulfil needs and a positive drive to realize wishes is based on the analysis in Oliver (1997).

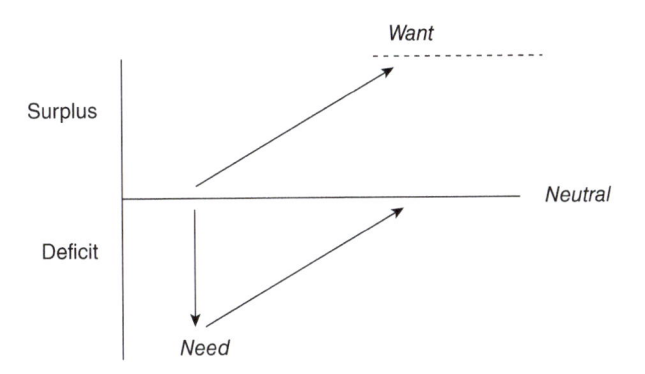

Figure 3.2 Problem recognition may be a need to restore neutrality or a want to create a surplus

The problem phase of the buying process involves not only recognizing a problem, but also structuring it and devising ways to solve it. This includes identifying and defining goals and considering what actions will alleviate the tension. If the problem is a familiar one, the solution is likely already stored in the customer's memory. For example, the customer knows exactly what to do when they run out of milk. However, if the problem is new, it may require careful consideration and information search to arrive at a solution. In the case of an 'aged car', most people would need to restructure the problem before proceeding with their buying process.

The goals that are activated during the problem recognition phase are indicative of what customers need and want. These goals can be at different levels of abstraction and can be interconnected. For instance, a product-specific goal like the goal of purchasing a gym membership may be linked to more general goals such as living a healthier life, looking good, feeling good and losing weight (Bagozzi & Dholakia, 1999). These general goals, in turn, may be linked to other product-specific goals such as purchasing only certain types of food products. To understand the various and interconnected goals of customers, it is crucial for companies to identify the different product categories that may be involved in the buying process.

Psychologists have devoted significant attention to understanding what motivates human behaviour. One of the early theorists in this area was Sigmund Freud, who posited that subconscious needs, particularly biological and sexual needs, drive people's behaviour and shape their personalities (Freud et al., 1953). Although Freud's theories were considered controversial during his own time and have since been challenged, his ideas about the power of the unconscious mind have had a significant influence on subsequent theories in the field of motivational psychology.

Abraham Maslow (1943) expanded upon Freud's ideas and developed the theory of a hierarchy of needs as shown in Figure 3.3. This theory suggests that our needs are structured in a hierarchy, ranging from basic to less basic needs. The fulfilment of more basic needs is required before higher-level needs can be activated. For instance, if an individual's basic needs such as food and shelter are not met over time, they may lose interest in other aspects of life. Maslow's hierarchy of needs suggests that after the lowest physiological needs have been satisfied, motivation is dominated by the need for safety and security at the next level.

This need extends beyond physical security and encompasses areas such as control over one's life, such as savings, routines, education and work. The third level addresses the need for belonging to social groups and communities, including love and friendship. The fourth level focuses on the need for status, including esteem and recognition from others, as well as self-respect, including inner-directed aspects like achievement, strength and self-confidence. The fifth and final level concerns people's need for realizing their potential, also known as self-actualization. According to Maslow, very few people reach this level.

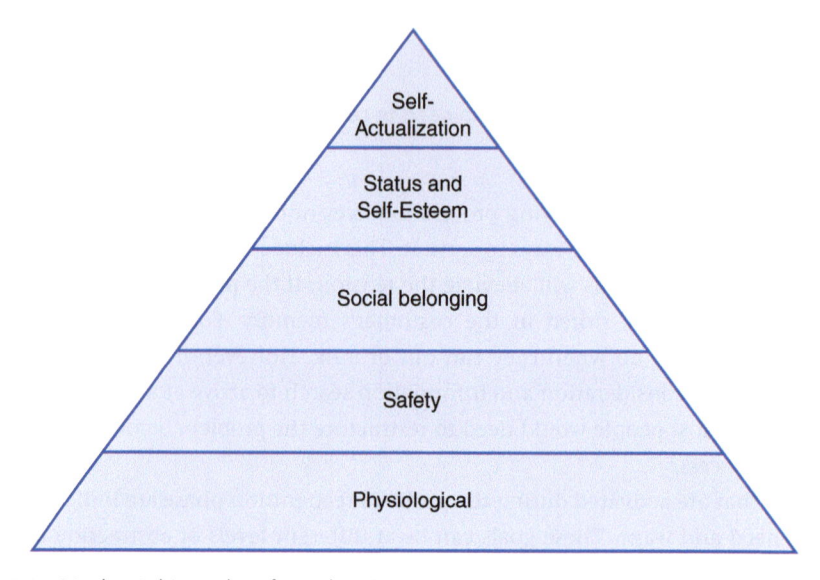

Figure 3.3 Maslow's hierarchy of needs (1943)

Maslow's hierarchy of needs offers a valuable framework for understanding customer motivation. The theory suggests that certain needs may remain dormant until others are fulfilled, and that human behaviour, including consumer behaviour, is influenced by a mix of various types of needs. However, not all scholars agree that lower-level needs must be satisfied before higher-level needs can be activated. Instead, it is more commonly believed that human behaviour is determined by a combination of needs that exist to varying degrees depending on the context and time. Since Maslow introduced his ideas, numerous theories have emerged in the psychology literature that attempt to explain motivation and behaviour.

Building on Herzberg's two-factor motivation theory (1966), Richard Oliver proposed that product properties align with different levels of needs as per motivational theories (Oliver, 1997). At the lowest level, hygiene factors only prevent dissatisfaction when present, such as fresh milk or punctual trains, but do not generate additional satisfaction. Hygiene factors are seen as necessary by customers but do not evoke extra satisfaction. However, missing hygiene factors, such as stale milk or delayed trains, cause dissatisfaction. At the higher level, properties are considered desirable by customers and follow the 'more is better' principle, which creates motivation and increases pleasure. For example, better-tasting milk or more comfortable trains motivates customers to buy such products. Thus, companies need to understand which product properties are viewed as necessities versus those that are seen as motivational and desirable.

To gain insight into the problem recognition phase and identify customer–company, customer–customer and third-party touchpoints, companies must ask the essential questions listed in Table 3.1. In addition to analysing goals, needs and key properties, they must also consider whether customers can be categorized into segments based on their diverse goals and needs, and which product properties are associated with goal-fulfilment. For instance, personal trainers may be the most important property for some fitness centre customers, while others may prioritize the fitness centre's location and operating hours.

There are numerous methods and sources that companies can employ to obtain answers to these questions. These include market research, customer interviews, discussions with salespeople and front-line staff, analyses of social media and blogs, reviews of articles and information from the internet, and interviews with industry experts.

Table 3.1 Analysis of problem recognition

Analysis of problem recognition
What product-specific goals are the customers looking for?
What overall goals underly the product-specific goals?
What deficiencies and wants motivate customers to shop?
What are the most important properties that drive customer choice?
Are there segments that have different goals and different needs?
Are there customer segments that emphasize different properties?

Information Search

The phase that follows problem recognition is information search, during which customers seek information to help resolve the problem. The search for information starts automatically once the problem has been recognized. Initially, the customer refers to the knowledge they have stored in their long-term memory about the product category. This stored knowledge plays a crucial role in controlling the search process. However, if the stored knowledge is inadequate, the customer will seek information from external sources. The search for information includes:

- determining which product properties are relevant;
- how these properties create utility;
- what alternatives are available;
- the strengths and weaknesses of the alternatives;
- where reliable sources of information can be found.

These external sources constitute potential touchpoints for creating customer value. Nevertheless, customers use both internal and external sources of information during the search process.

To begin the information search phase, customers evaluate whether their existing knowledge about the product category is relevant to the problem at hand. For instance, someone in the market for a new mobile phone might question the relevance of their prior knowledge, given the major changes that have occurred in the category. In such cases, the customer will seek information to learn more about the new functions, uses and technologies in the mobile-phone market. This learning process during information search can lead to a redefinition of the initial problem and the product-specific goal (for studies of information search, see Bettman, 1979a and 1979b; Brucks, 1985; Selnes & Troye, 1989). As a result, customers may move back and forth between the problem-recognition stage and information gathering.

The customer's next step is to determine how various product properties contribute to utility and how to interpret product-related information. The customer needs to have a clear understanding of their minimum and maximum property requirements. For example, some car buyers may require a minimum of 100 horsepower, but they may not want more than 200 horsepower. Additionally, the customer may consider whether the relationship between property levels and utility is linear or not. If an increase from 100 to 150 horsepower yields the same increase in utility as an increase from 150 to 200 horsepower, the relationship is linear. Conversely, if the increase in utility value is greater from 100 to 150 horsepower than from 150 to 200 horsepower, the relationship is not linear. Moreover, the customer must understand the relationship between different product properties. For instance, a faster car consumes more energy than a slower car. If the customer wants a fast and fuel-efficient car, she needs to strike a balance and find the solution that provides the highest overall utility. Identifying the touchpoints the consumer searches, such as expert car reviews, and using these to educate customers about product property interrelationships is a means for value creation.

Customers' knowledge of a product category and their understanding of how different properties are connected and provide utility can influence their information search behaviour. Customers with more expertise in a product category are likely to search for more information than those with less expertise, as they have more specific questions they want answered. However, they may also be able to process information more easily and quickly than those with less expertise. Therefore, product expertise does not necessarily lead to spending more time and effort on information search (Selnes & Troye, 1989).

Product expertise can also impact on which attributes are considered important by the customer. For example, a wine expert is likely to focus on the wine's inherent quality and various sensory aspects, while a less knowledgeable customer may rely on extrinsic cues such as price, bottle design and country of origin to make their purchasing decision.

The vast amount of available information makes it impossible for customers to search for and evaluate all the properties of all the alternatives. To simplify the search process, customers often rely on mental shortcuts called heuristics to obtain information about a smaller set of alternatives. Initially, the customer assesses whether known alternatives can solve the problem, and only if they cannot, they look for new alternatives. Motivation to search for new options arises when the customer is dissatisfied with known alternatives or desires variety. Some customers value variety for its own sake and enjoy trying new things, while those with high product expertise find it effortless to consider multiple options.

The primary source of information for nearly all product categories and buying situations is online search. The internet allows for easy access to vast amounts of information at a low cost. However, some types of information cannot be effectively conveyed digitally due to technical limitations. For instance, it's impossible to communicate the texture of a dress's fabric through the internet. In such cases, customers have to look for information from other sources. Usually, the search process begins online before visiting a physical store to gather complete information. More about multichannel search can be found in Kumar & Venkatesan (2005).

The amount of effort that customers put into information search has been extensively researched in marketing literature. Surprisingly, the findings indicate that most people do not seek much information, even for expensive or high-risk products (Punj & Staelin, 1983; Srinivasan & Ratchford, 1991). This does not necessarily imply that they are reckless, but rather they rely on methods other than systematic analysis of information to learn more about their options. The most common approach is to ask for advice from someone they trust, such as friends, family, acquaintances or even salespeople (Biong & Selnes, 1995; Price & Arnould, 1999). Social media has made it easy to obtain such advice within a few minutes. Also, online product reviews made by other customers are a valuable source of easy-to-understand information. Platforms such as Tripadvisor have become central for tourism because they provide a simple way to enter and retrieve information about hotels, restaurants and points of interest. Scientific studies have shown that online product reviews are crucial for a company's sales (see Zhu & Zhang, 2010; Floyd et al., 2014). Consequently, product reviews are obvious touchpoints for the company to consider.

Table 3.2 lists essential enquiries that a company must pose to gain insights into customers' information search behaviour. It is crucial to determine what type of information customers are seeking, which sources and channels they use for their search, and how they discuss brands and suppliers among themselves. It is particularly critical to monitor what customers are saying about the company and its brands on social media platforms. Positive and negative information can have a significant impact in social media since it influences customers' decision-making and reaches a vast audience.

Table 3.2 Analysis of information search

Analysis of information search
What information about product properties is stored in the customer's memory?
Which choice options are stored in the customer's memory?
What information is stored about these options?
Are customers actively seeking information? Why? When? Where?
Which sources are reliable providers of information? What do these sources think and what are their opinions?
Are there significant differences between segments in terms of knowledge and information search?

Evaluation of Alternatives

To proceed with the decision-making process, the evaluation phase aims to identify brands that are relevant and capable of solving the problem. This requires the customer to gain an overview of brands and products that could be the solution, and to be aware of any alternatives that should be avoided, for any general or particular reasons. As the customer has to make a choice, the different brands must be assessed and ranked accordingly. For example, if there are two appealing mobile phones, the customer must choose between them. Therefore, the evaluation phase is concerned with reviewing and ranking the different brands before making the final decision.

The process of selecting an alternative can be thought of as a way of sorting through all possible options and ultimately choosing one. Figure 3.4 illustrates how this process involves the creation of several sets, including the awareness set, consideration set and choice set. During the information search phase, the awareness set is established and serves as the basis for evaluating alternatives. Initially, the customer's memory contains the alternatives they are aware of. However, through information search, more alternatives can be added to the awareness set, which is a subset of all available options. It is worth noting that many brands might go unnoticed if customers are unaware of their presence in the market, highlighting the importance of brand awareness. Developing a strong brand that is recognized as a key member in relevant product categories for solving the customer's problem – one that many customers discuss and that is associated with frequently occurring situations, well-known individuals, countries or other prominent entities – serves as a way to establish a touchpoint in the consumer's awareness set. In the evaluation phase, the consideration set, a subset of the awareness set, is examined. Finally, the evaluation process culminates in the identification of a set of suitable brands, referred to as the choice set.

The composition of the consideration set is not fixed and can vary during the evaluation process. As a result, customers may assess different sets of alternatives based on their specific product goals and situation. For example, a particular brand of bicycles might be included in a consideration set when purchasing for personal use, but the same brand may not be considered if buying the bike as a gift. Thus, the decision rule and range of potential alternatives for the consideration set are influenced by the context or situation at hand. Consequently, customers may consider different sets of options depending on their product objectives and circumstances.

To identify the most appropriate alternatives for their final choice set, customers adopt diverse information-processing methods. For instance, assuming customers have information about three coffee shops, they can evaluate each shop based on four properties, also known as attributes, as indicated in Table 3.3. Each attribute has a corresponding importance or weight, reflecting its contribution to overall utility. For example, taste has a weight of 40%, meaning that 40% of the utility provided by a coffee shop is dependent on taste. As shown in Table 3.3, taste is the most crucial attribute, and coffee-shop brands with high scores on this attribute have a greater likelihood of being selected.

Furthermore, each alternative is evaluated based on the customer's perception of attribute quality, i.e. how well it performs on each of the four attributes. In the case of our coffee-shop example, each alternative receives a rating on a scale of 0 to 10, where 0 represents very poor quality, and 10 indicates excellent quality. Brand A, for instance, has a taste score of 7, which

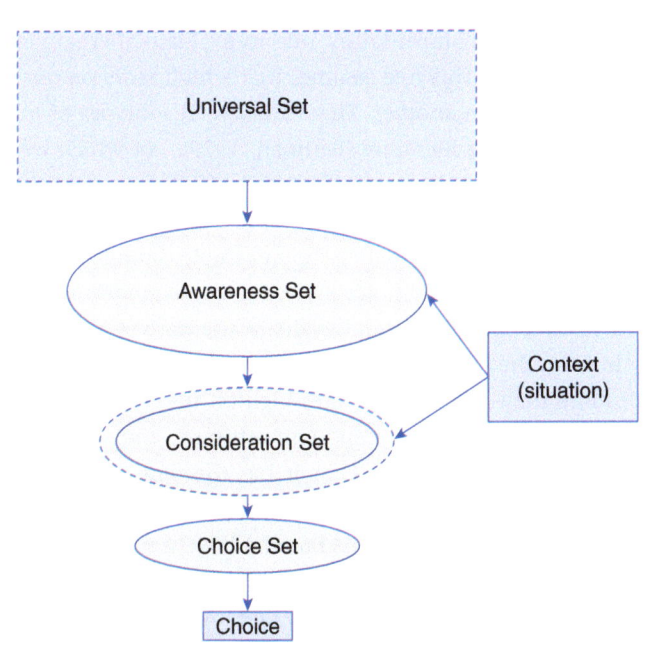

Figure 3.4   Formation of consideration and choice set (Shocker et al., 1991; based on Oliver, 1997)

is the same as brand B and one point lower than brand C. Additionally, only Brand A has a loyalty card.

When customers employ a compensatory decision rule to process attribute information, they evaluate alternatives based on the total sum of the weighted scores of all individual attributes. Each attribute's score is multiplied by its weight and the results are added together. This rule allows for low scores on one attribute to be compensated by high scores on other attributes, hence the term 'compensatory'. In the example shown in Table 3.3, the compensatory rule is applied to determine the total utility for each alternative. Brand A is evaluated as better than both competitors using this rule: the bonus card score compensates for the low scores on taste, atmosphere and waiting time. The total utility score for brand A is 7.0, while the competitors score 5.6. The ranking of alternatives is determined based on their total utility value.

Table 3.3   Information customers have about three coffee shops

Attribute	Utility Weight	Brand A	Brand B	Brand C
Taste	40%	7.0	7.0	8.0
Atmosphere	20%	6.0	8.0	6.0
Waiting time	20%	8.0	6.0	6.0
Loyalty card	20%	7.0	0.0	0.0
Sum utility	100%	7.0	5.6	5.6

When customers use a non-compensatory rule to evaluate alternatives, the ranking of options can differ significantly. This rule assumes that a high score on one attribute cannot compensate for a lower score on another. There are several subtypes of non-compensatory rules discussed in the marketing literature (Bettman, 1979a), of which we will discuss two particularly relevant ones: conjunctive and lexicographic. In conjunctive rules, customers establish a minimum acceptable score for one or more attributes. For instance, if customers set a minimum taste score of 8 in the coffee-shop example, Brand A would not make it to the choice set as it falls below the threshold. In lexicographic models, customers rank attributes based on their relative importance and evaluate alternatives accordingly. If an option scores sufficiently high on the most important attribute, it is chosen without considering the other attributes. If more than one option scores high on the most important attribute, the process is repeated for the second most important attribute, and so on. In the coffee-shop example, customers would choose Brand C as it has the best taste. However, if Brand A improves its taste score to 8, it will be evaluated based on the next important attribute, i.e. atmosphere, waiting time and loyalty card. As Brand A largely outperforms Brand C on these attributes, customers will prefer Brand A.

In the market, various customer segments may employ distinct evaluation rules, making it unclear how a brand's performance on one attribute will translate into customer choice and overall market share. As a result, companies should conduct market analysis to identify which rule their brand is most likely subject to. Specifically, they should determine if customers have minimum thresholds for one or more attributes.

Customers may revisit the information search phase during the evaluation stage if they require more information on one or more alternatives. For instance, if the customer ends up with two equally appealing options in the choice set, additional information search might reveal subtle differences. This additional search may also take the customer back to the problem-recognition stage to refine or redefine the problem.

The evaluation phase is a time-consuming and laborious process. It would be impractical to go through this process every time we purchase a cup of coffee. As purchases are repeated, the customer relies on the outcome of the previous evaluation. These general evaluations are often stored in customers' perceptions and attitudes towards the brand. Therefore, it is crucial to comprehend the role of brand attitudes, and how they impact on evaluation and choice.

In fact, customers often tend to stray away from these more or less rational decision rules, either because they are too burdensome or time-consuming to apply. As a result, determining the chosen product based solely on understanding the specific decision rule becomes challenging. However, these deviations from rationality can still be predicted, as highlighted by Ariely (2008). Instead, customers rely on shortcuts called heuristics, which will be discussed further, later in this chapter.

Alternatives that are considered for the consideration set may not necessarily have similar attributes (Ratneshwar et al., 1996). As previously discussed in the problem-recognition section, customers' goals may not be product-specific but rather general, which means they are not tied to one specific product category. For instance, if the goal is to buy a gift for a friend, the consideration set may include flowers, theatre tickets, wine, a spa stay or books. Even though these options are all regarded as gifts, they possess varying product characteristics (a wine cannot be long-stemmed nor written by a Nobel laureate in literature). The implication of the customer's general and non-product-specific goals is that companies must manage competition from brands in several product categories. Therefore, product development that focuses on enhancing product attributes may not be successful if the attribute is not critical in the customer's decision. Instead, through marketing communication, a company can position an existing product closer to the customer's goals that unify various product categories (such as the ideal gift). Clearly, a critical touchpoint for shaping beliefs and eliciting emotions, which subsequently impact the customer's perception of value, involves enhancing attributes that are considered important by the customer segment.

Table 3.4 lists essential enquiries that companies should consider when analysing the evaluation phase. Customer evaluations play a significant role in their ultimate purchase decisions. Companies can leverage this understanding to devise marketing strategies that position their brands during the evaluation phase.

Table 3.4 Analysis of the evaluation of alternatives

Analysis of the evaluation of alternatives
Which alternatives are evaluated?
Which attributes are used in the evaluation?
Which processing rules are used for evaluation?
What evaluations of the alternatives are stored in memory?
Are there important differences between the segments?

Case Study 3.1

Jeans Purchase

In 2023, the global jeans market was worth 68 billion dollars, and the forecast is that this figure will rise to 95 billion dollars by 2030, meaning 3.3 billion pairs of jeans. Possible drivers of this growth include changed consumer trends and preferences and continuous product innovation. It is projected that 30% of jean sales will take place through online channels in 2030. On average, women own seven pairs of jeans and men own six pairs.

The jeans market is an old and established one, with companies behind leading brands like Levis, Lee and Wrangler dating back more than a hundred years. Today, there are a plethora of jeans brands on the market, in addition to the old ones. Among the better-known ones are 7 for All Mindkind, True Religion, Rock & Republic, Antikk Denim, Diesel, Miss Sixty, Replay, Nudi, Acne and Evisu. Additionally, many designer brands have also ventured into jeans, such as DKNY, Dolce & Gabbana and Calvin Klein.

(Continued)

Jeans, which were previously work attire, have now become a status symbol and a part of people's identity. Jeans have also become a garment that is accepted in almost any situation, from everyday life and work to nightclubs and parties.[3]

Questions

When making a jeans purchase, which attributes do you find relevant to consider:

durability, comfort, fit, style, fabric, design, stitching, ease-of-maintenance, country of origin, influencer endorsement, sustainability, store image or brand?

When judging the jeans' quality, how do you do it, by vision or touch?

Can you infer the quality from any of the attributes? Which attributes: fabric or store image?

Are any attributes more dominant than others?

Do you have any idea which decision rule you are using? A compensatory or non-compensatory one?

Purchase Decision and Choice

The evaluation phase ultimately results in the customer's intention to choose one of the options. For instance, in the case of a coffee shop, a customer may decide to purchase from brand A during their lunch break. Once the customer has identified their preferred option, they need to determine the time, quantity, location and payment method for the purchase. To analyse actual purchase decisions, it can be helpful to categorize them into three different decision types:

- high-frequency purchases;
- low-frequency purchases;
- contract purchases.

High-Frequency Purchases

High-frequency purchases involve typical consumer products that are purchased regularly, such as petrol, milk and shampoo. Customers develop a routine-based buying behaviour for such purchases. In the example of the coffee shop, a customer may decide to have lunch at coffee shop A and then visit the place daily without considering any alternatives. High-frequency

---

[3]www.fashionunited.uk/news/business/infographic-data-from-the-denim-industry/20160926 21896; www.statista.com/statistics/1368005/global-units-of-denim-jeans-market/: https://www.grandviewresearch.com/industry-analysis/denim-jeans-market; https://www.statista.com/statistics/734419/global-denim-jeans-market-retail-sales-value/

purchases are characterized by the repetition of the same brand choice as long as it is considered the best option. Alternatively, high-frequency purchases can involve repeated purchases from a small set of brands, either because they are practical or affordable, or as a result of a need for variety.

During high-frequency purchases, customers transition from choosing to using a brand. The purchasing process becomes automated, and the customer selects the same brand every time they need to solve a problem without much cognitive effort. For instance, when buying groceries, a customer may return to the same store they usually use without much thought. As long as customers do not experience any problems or discover better options, they will continue with this buying pattern.

However, occasionally customers may try out new brands due to the unavailability of their preferred brand, dissatisfaction with it, or an advertisement encouraging them to try something new. Trying out a new brand can lead to a reassessment of the existing choice set as customers have a broader basis for evaluation. Positive new experiences may even prompt them to switch to another brand.

Low-Frequency Purchases

Low-frequency purchases refer to products that are purchased less frequently, such as flights, restaurants, painkillers, skis, trainers and cars. The key difference between high- and low-frequency purchases is that customers repeat some or all of the purchasing process each time due to the time between purchases. Infrequent flyers, for example, will evaluate offers from various airlines by checking availability, prices and more. However, since they have purchased these products before, they already have some knowledge of the process and do not need to start from scratch.

Incentives, such as loyalty programmes, can encourage repeat purchases in the airline industry. Customers may also choose to buy from the same brand because it is familiar and requires less thought. However, if there is a change in needs or surrounding conditions, customers may reconsider their choices rather than repeat past behaviour.

Customers who are buying a durable product for the first time follow a different pattern because they lack experience with the product category. They need to learn which criteria and attributes are important in the category and what options are available. First-time purchases are often seen as high-risk decisions, and customers may seek more information, recommendations from trusted sources, or supplier guarantees to reduce uncertainty. When all else is equal, first-time buyers are more likely to choose well-known brands that offer greater certainty.

Contractual Purchases

A contractual purchase involves a formal agreement between a customer and a supplier, typically for products or services that require membership or subscription, such as financial services, fitness centres, electricity and telephone subscriptions. The key difference between contractual and repeated purchases is that contractual purchases are based on a payment plan that may include initial fees, fixed or regular fees, or variable fees. The difference between recurring and contract-based purchases is discussed in Bolton & Lemon (1999).

Contractual purchases involve mutual obligations between the buyer and seller. The buyer agrees to pay over an extended period, and the seller agrees to deliver over the same period, creating risks for both parties. To mitigate these risks, both parties can sign a written agreement that defines and accepts sanctions for breaches, such as resolving disputes through the court system. However, relying solely on legally binding agreements can be costly, so parties often choose to base the contract on mutual trust. For a discussion of the relationship between legal contracts and relational norms (trust), see MacNeil (1980).

Another difference with contractual purchases is that customers must actively terminate the relationship to switch to another supplier, process referred to as churn (the proportion of contractual customers who leave the company during a given period). For example, to change mobile-service providers, a customer must first cancel their existing contract. Compared to non-contractual purchases, changing suppliers requires more effort.

Table 3.5 lists essential enquiries that companies should consider when analysing the product decision and choice stage. Companies typically encounter a mix of different purchase types among their customers, ranging from regular buyers to occasional buyers, and those with contractual agreements in the corporate market. It is also essential to understand the growth dynamics of the market, including the number of new customers entering at different stages of a product's life cycle. As the market matures, customers tend to become more knowledgeable, and competition becomes more price sensitive. Companies must identify the factors that motivate customers to switch brands and how their marketing activities relate to these factors. Additionally, companies should have a comprehensive understanding of how purchase decisions differ across various customer segments.

Table 3.5 Analysis of the purchase decision

Analysis of the purchase decision
Are purchases characterized as high-frequency, low-frequency or contract purchase?
What characterizes the purchases of first-time buyers?
What characterizes processes where customers change brands or suppliers?
How do established relationships create value for customers, and how do these affect customers' choices?
Are there significant differences between segments?

The Use of the Product and the Cultivation of Relationships

The customer journey does not end with the decision to buy. Once the customer starts using the product, a relationship is established between the customer and the brand. Some crucial factors that come into play during this phase are:

- relationship development;
- satisfaction;
- equity;
- cognitive dissonance;

- Word of mouth
- complaint behaviour.

As the customer has now acquired a product from the company and will interact with it regularly through usage, this stage of the customer journey encompasses several significant touchpoints. Usage, support, regular servicing and eventual maintenance are among the prominent touchpoints that shape the customer's experience and influence their perception of value.

Relationship Development

After the customer makes the purchase decision, the buying process does not end. Instead, a relationship starts to form between the customer and the brand as the customers begins to use the product. Similar to the development of a relationship between a doctor and a patient, the interaction between the customer and the brand leads to familiarity and better understanding of each other. This relationship creates a barrier to switching to another brand, as it requires time and effort to rebuild the relationship. The degree of organization of the relationship can vary from informal and sporadic to formal and systematic, such as through loyalty programmes. The company can also form a relationship with customers by utilizing tribes of consumer (Cova & Cova, 2002). An outdoor apparel company that specializes in sustainable and eco-friendly products can identify a community of outdoor enthusiasts who are passionate about sustainability and the environment (the tribe) and position its brand here by being present in social media groups where tribe members also meet.

The formation of a relationship between a customer and a brand can have a significant impact on future buying decisions, as previous choices can influence current decisions. As illustrated in Figure 3.5, a customer's purchase decision at a given time is not only influenced by the available alternatives, but also by the choice made in the previous time period. Therefore, it is important for companies to provide competitive offers, even if they have established relationships with their customers. Customers always have the freedom to choose, and competitors are always vying to attract new customers.

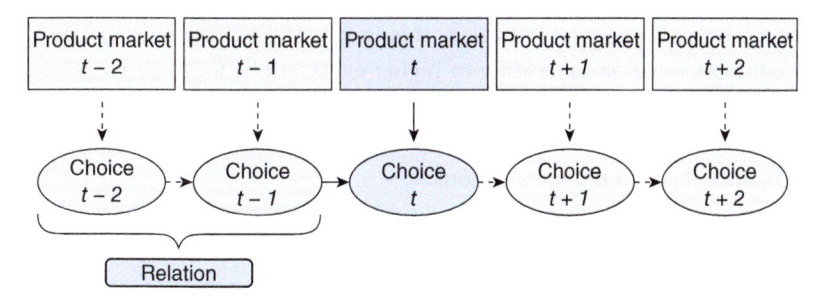

Figure 3.5 How relationship formation affects future choices

The development of the customer–brand relationship can also be facilitated through brand adaptation, whereby the customer adjusts their buying behaviour to take further advantage of the brand's benefits. This adaptation involves the customer making various investments in the relationship with the brand, such as joining a customer club, downloading an app or participating in customer training. An opportunity to create additional touchpoints and deliver enhanced value is to persuade customers to purchase brands from other product categories offered by the company. In the case of contractual purchases, buyers often adapt their behaviour to the seller's systems and procedures, as seen with bank customers adapting their payment behaviour to the functionality of online banking. As customers adapt their purchasing behaviour to the brand, they begin to expect to receive more from the brand, including saving time or receiving better service.

Satisfaction

Satisfaction can be described as the feeling of pleasure derived from the fulfilment of a need, desire or goal through consumption. It is based on the customer's perception of how consumption measures up against their standard of pleasure versus displeasure, which is often shaped by their expectations (Oliver, 1980). Negative disconfirmation occurs when the customer's experiences fall short of their expectations, while positive disconfirmation occurs when their experiences exceed their expectations (Oliver, 1980; Oliver & Winer 1987).

There are multiple theories attempting to explain the formation of satisfaction. One is cognitive dissonance theory (discussed later in this chapter) which proposes a tendency of consumers to justify decisions afterwards and therefore also adjust their satisfaction upwards even if experiences are not very good. For example, to reduce or avoided cognitive dissonance, a consumer will place more satisfaction in a chosen than in an unchosen product. Hence, the relative satisfaction with two products is influenced by dissonance (Cummings & Venkatesan, 1976). A customer who chooses a fancy hair salon for her wedding styling, and later discovers that the same styling can be obtained for 30% less at a newly opened basic salon, may tend to heighten her satisfaction with her styling and experience to counteract the negative feelings of dissonance.

The role of expectations in the buying process is highlighted in Figure 3.6. Customers tend to choose the brand that aligns with their highest expectations. When the actual quality of the product matches their expectations, customers are satisfied and their expectations are confirmed. If the actual quality exceeds their expectations, customers become delighted and their satisfaction increases, leading to higher expectations for future purchases. On the other hand, if the actual quality falls below their expectations, customers not only become dissatisfied but also lower their expectations. These updated expectations are stored in memory and influence future purchase decisions.

Additionally, expectations can also impact the perceived quality of products, as shown in Figure 3.6. Customers with high expectations may evaluate the quality of products more positively due to the assimilation theory, which suggests that people tend to assimilate their quality assessments with their existing expectations (Sherif & Hovland, 1961). For example, members of a fitness club who have high expectations of personal trainers being highly qualified are likely to evaluate the trainers better than they actually are. Conversely, if customers have low expectations of a personal trainer's qualifications, they are likely to evaluate them worse than they actually are. Understanding how expectations are updated during product usage is crucial in effective marketing management.

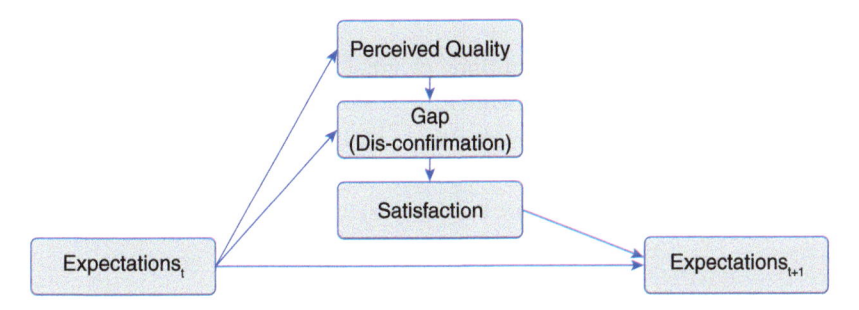

Figure 3.6 Dynamic update of expectations through use of a product or a brand (adapted from Oliver, 1980)

Customer Equity

Equity refers to customers' perception of fairness (Adams, 1963; Bolton & Lemon, 1999).[4] Customers strongly believe that companies should act in a fair manner, and when they experience injustice, they react negatively. Instances of injustice include unfair pricing, poor service, cheating and deception, among others. These reactions stem from customers' development of norms or standards regarding acceptable and unacceptable behaviour from companies. While customers understand that businesses need to generate profits, they also have expectations about how these profits should be attained. For example, customers deem it unreasonable when a company raises prices solely to maximize profits. However, they consider price increases reasonable if they are driven by increased costs.

Customers hold specific expectations regarding business conduct. If a purchased product breaks shortly after the purchase, most customers anticipate the seller to either replace the item or provide a refund. This expectation is rooted in their perception of fairness, regardless of their legal rights. There are three types of justice that can be distinguished: distributive justice, procedural justice and relational justice. Distributive justice refers to a reasonable correlation between what customers contribute and what they receive, such as receiving a level of service commensurate with the price paid. Procedural justice relates to decisions and conflict resolution, encompassing customers' experiences with a company's procedures and choices. For instance, customers expect equal treatment and to wait in line for their turn. A touchpoint that potentially has a negative impact on value is when customers hear or see

---

[4] Customer equity can also refer to the financial or economic value of a customer over the lifetime of the company–customer relationship (see the discussion of customer portfolio value in Chapter 5). Customer equity therefore has two different meanings in the marketing literature – one related to fairness and another related to financial value. It is usually clear from the context which meaning is being referred to.

stories of others receiving preferential treatment. If a VIP customer is allowed to bypass the queue, it can be perceived as highly unfair and elicit strong negative reactions. Relational justice pertains to how a company communicates information and discloses outcomes, encompassing the extent to which customers affected by a decision are treated with dignity and respect.

The memories of customers' perceptions of unfairness have a lasting impact on their future behaviour as consumers. Consequently, customers might choose to steer clear of brands that they perceive as unfair, even if those brands offer products of superior quality. Therefore, when evaluating customers' experiences after a purchase, it is vital to assess whether they feel they have been treated unfairly.

Cognitive Dissonance

Cognitive dissonance refers to a state of mental unease that arises from inconsistency (see Festinger, 1957). When a customer selects a particular brand, they may experience cognitive dissonance when considering the alternatives that were not chosen. This dissonance is more likely to occur in situations where the decision is irreversible, such as purchasing a new car; when the decision is significant and engaging, like choosing a university; and when the customer must choose between options that all have distinct advantages and disadvantages, such as deciding on whether to spend your bonus salary on a holiday trip or a new sofa.

Customers adopt various strategies to alleviate cognitive dissonance. One approach involves seeking information that confirms the correctness of their decision. For instance, a customer may reach out to the seller to receive reassurance that their choice was the right one. Another strategy involves denying negative thoughts. This concept is exemplified in Aesop's fable 'The Fox and the Grapes', where a fox spots some grapes hanging high on a tree. Unable to reach them, the fox convinces itself that the grapes probably wouldn't have been enjoyable anyway. In this fable, denial is employed to reduce the dissonance arising from desiring something that is unattainable. The fox concludes, against logic, that it was foolish to exert effort for a bunch of sour grapes that were not worth longing for.

Word of Mouth

Word-of-mouth recommendations play a crucial role when customers have chosen and are using a brand, significantly impacting on a company's ability to attract new customers. Particularly for new products, positive recommendations can have a more profound effect than any form of mass media advertising (see Trusov et al., 2009; Floyd et al., 2014; Watson et al., 2018). In a broad sense, a recommendation encompasses any informal communication among customers regarding the ownership or use of a specific product or brand, or the qualities of the providers. Due to the perception of recommendations as more credible and trustworthy than information directly from companies, they hold significant influence in the purchasing process. Many individuals find it valuable to explore other customers' experiences, making recommendations via social media (i.e. influencers) a faster and more comprehensive alternative to traditional interpersonal channels, given the multitude of members and information-exchange opportunities. Social media influencer is a significant source of word of mouth. An influencer is an individual who utilizes their online presence on platforms such as Instagram, YouTube, X, Facebook or TikTok to sway their followers' opinions, behaviours or purchasing decisions. They exert influence through their professional content and competence in social media; their fame, expertise and identification with customers; and their unique access to certain audiences (Campbell & Farell, 2020). Dutch make-up artist and beauty vlogger Nikkie de Jager has achieved a significant source of word of mouth in the realm of beauty. She possesses a high level of expertise, creativity and talent in make-up application, shows her true personality, discusses real-life issues, and is known to be upfront and honest with her audience; she reaches 12 million followers around the world (https://www.businessinsider.com/who-is-nikkietutorials-beauty-youtuber-2020-1).

Online reviews, including rating systems, are another common starting point for consumers seeking information about product quality.

Word of mouth is clearly a challenging touchpoint for the company to manage and create consumer value from. However, the company can adopt a proactive approach by creating shareable content for social media or engaging with influencers.

Complaint Behaviour

The way customers express their dissatisfaction when a product fails, and how the supplier responds to those complaints, hold immense importance for overall satisfaction and future behaviour. It's important to note that not all instances of product failure result in complaints. Some customers may choose not to complain due to the perception that the company will not address their concerns or because they find the complaint process too cumbersome. Instead, these dissatisfied customers tend to voice their concerns by sharing their negative experiences with others and/or exit by discontinuing their purchases from that particular company.

Because the complaint touchpoint obviously can be a source of negative beliefs and emotions, many companies actively encourage their customers to voice their concerns in the event of product failures. By proactively addressing complaints and providing effective solutions, these companies aim to prevent dissatisfied customers from spreading negative feedback about their products, or even exit. Not only does active encouragement of complaints reduce exist and voice, it can foster positive relationships with the customer and thereby build loyalty.

Research indicates that effective handling of customers who have encountered failures, along with their strong negative emotions and reactions, requires front-line employees to accurately interpret the problem. Correct interpretation involves actively listening to customers, understanding their concerns, expressing genuine regret or apology, and offering appropriate compensation. Merely offering compensation without demonstrating understanding or expressing regret often yields no impact or, worse, a negative effect (see Andreassen, 1999; Smith & Bolton, 2002).

To thoroughly analyse the product usage stage, companies should carefully consider the essential factors listed in Table 3.6. Through consistent and methodical evaluations of customer satisfaction, companies can gauge their performance in this pivotal area. Notably, customer satisfaction is generally independent of the specific product category or market, allowing companies to compare themselves with others. National customer satisfaction indices, like the American Customer Satisfaction Index in the USA, exemplify tools that facilitate such comparisons.

Table 3.6   Analysis of user experiences

Analysis of user experiences
Are the customers' wants and expectations met, and are the customers satisfied with their choices?
Do the customers perceive the supplier to be unfair, and if so, why?
Do customers experience cognitive dissonance after purchase, and if so, why?
What do customers tell others about their experiences, and through which channels does this happen?
Do the customers have complaints, and if so, how do they perceive their complaints are being handled?

Case Study 3.2

Volta

Image 3.1   Electric car charger symbol

Fictitious electric car dealership Volta decide to map their customers' journey. For Volta, the customer journey refers to the series of touchpoints that a customer goes through to reach their final goal – in this case, owning or leasing an electric car. The dealership began by identifying the different touchpoints that customers have with the dealership, from the initial interest in electric cars to the actual purchase or lease of one, and further usage. Some of the touchpoints that the dealership identified included:

> Customers recognizing they have a problem to solve, possibly through advertising in social media or increased awareness of their possessions' contribution to emissions of greenhouse gasses.

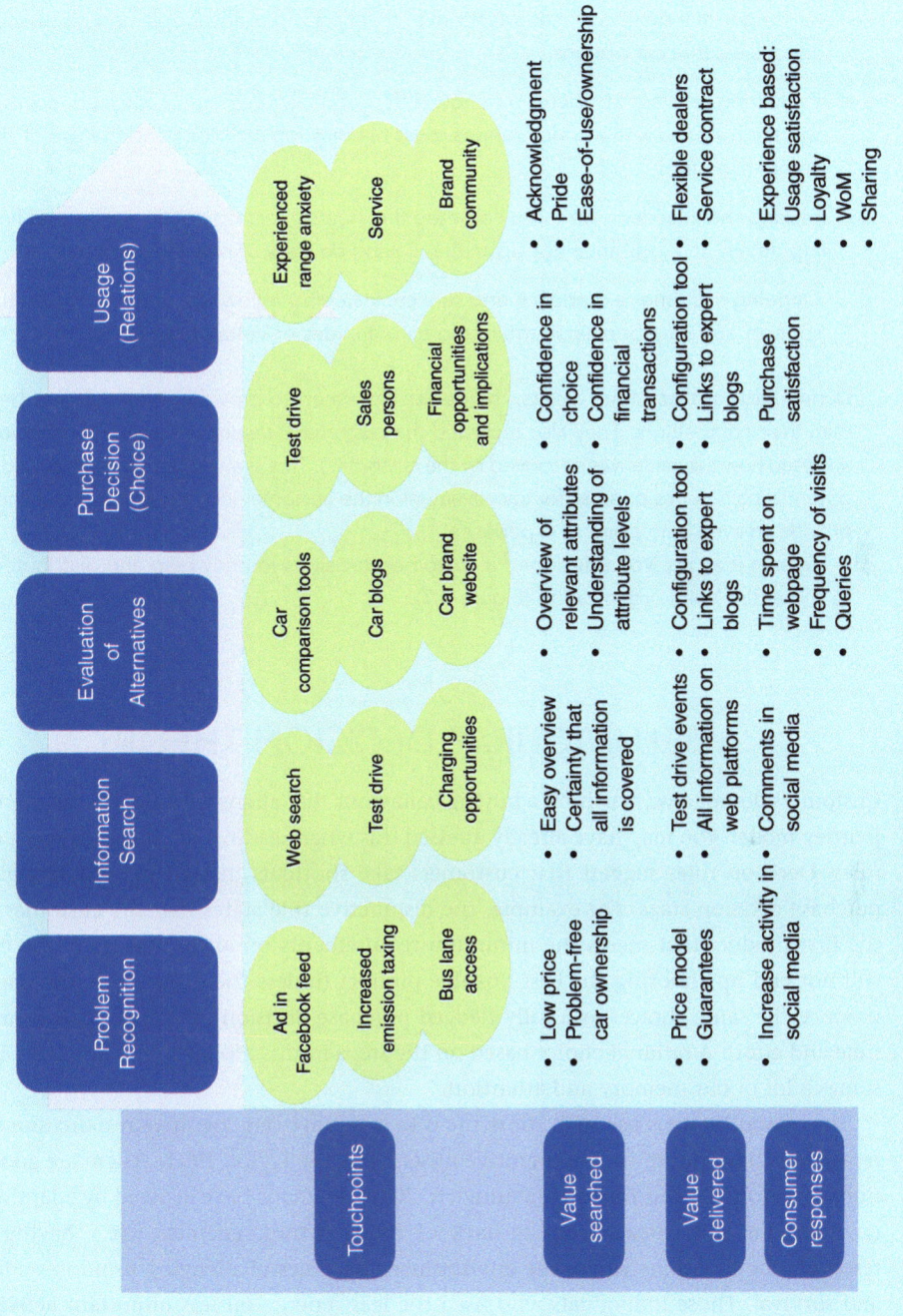

Figure 3.7 Customer decision journey map of Volta customers

	Problem Recognition	Information Search	Evaluation of Alternatives	Purchase Decision (Choice)	Usage (Relations)
Touchpoints	Ad in Facebook feed Increased emission taxing Bus lane access	Web search Test drive Charging opportunities	Car comparison tools Car blogs Car brand website	Test drive Sales persons Financial opportunities and implications	Experienced range anxiety Service Brand community
Value searched	• Low price • Problem-free car ownership	• Easy overview • Certainty that all information is covered	• Overview of relevant attributes • Understanding of attribute levels	• Confidence in choice • Confidence in financial transactions	• Acknowledgment • Pride • Ease-of-use/ownership
Value delivered	• Price model • Guarantees	• Test drive events • All information on web platforms	• Configuration tool • Links to expert blogs	• Configuration tool • Links to expert blogs	• Flexible dealers • Service contract
Consumer responses	• Increase activity in social media	• Comments in social media	• Time spent on webpage • Frequency of visits • Queries	• Purchase satisfaction	• Experience based: Usage satisfaction • Loyalty • WoM • Sharing

(Continued)

Becoming aware of the dealership's brand and offerings, possibly through advertising referrals, or online search, and rumoured test drives.

Arriving at the dealership for a test drive, meeting with salespeople and discussing the various electric car options.

Evaluating relevant attributes and how different dealerships and car brands score on the attributes as well as price ranges, possibly through car blogs and the use of online comparison tools.

Making the final decision to buy or lease the electric car, after having reviewed financing details and insurance opportunities. Taking delivery of new electric car.

Ongoing customer experience and service, including follow-up, ongoing maintenance, support and membership in the brand communities of Volta's brands.

During each of these touchpoints, the dealership aimed to provide better value or benefits than their competitors. They also recorded the customers' response to each touchpoint and analysed how the value was perceived by the customers. This allowed the dealership to identify potential pain points or areas for improvement in the customer journey, and make changes to provide an even better overall experience.

To sum it all up, Volta designed a customer decisions journey map and distributed this to the entire Volta organization (Figure 3.7).

BEHAVIOURAL DECISION THEORY

Customers do not always exhibit a buying behaviour that aligns with the customers' decision journey model. You may have already guessed this when reading about the different decision rules. Decision rules suggest that customers take shortcuts instead of completing the full purchase decision-stage. For example, the disjunctive rule states that the customer chooses the first product that meets the minimum requirements on attributes. Here, the customer will not end up choosing the best possible product (unless the disjunctive rule happens to produce the same choices as a fully fledged purchase decision), but instead will save some time and effort. A rational choice based on the steps in this model comes at a cost, as it consumes a lot of our memory and attention.

The reason humans use such shortcuts is that we save our cognitive resources or, as some researchers have put it, we are cognitive misers (Fiske & Taylor, 1991). There are good evolutionary reasons for this frugality (Stanovich, 2020). Humans have evolved by adapting to the environment and threats from it (lack of food, viruses, enemies, etc.). Saving mental resources for situations where the environment becomes challenging promotes adaptation and survival. Those individuals who used the least energy on less important activities and the most energy on more urgent activities survived and could pass on their genes to the next generations.

Therefore, what customers actually do often deviates from what the decision journey model or similar models, such as theories of rational choice in economics, assume. These theories assume that the customer is fairly rational and gathers information with the goal of making the best possible decision. The field known as behavioural decision theory focuses on decisions that deviate from the decisions that would have been made if customers had followed such a rational model. Behavioural decision theory scholar and Nobel laureate in economics Daniel Kahneman concludes that people make decisions mainly in two different ways. Either we use an automatic, intuitive and less energy-demanding way called System 1, or we use a deliberative, logical and energy-demanding way called System 2. System 1 is faster than System 2 and is the default choice between the two (Kahneman, 2003, 2011). When our thinking is less deliberative and we use fewer cognitive resources, the choices we make will be more influenced by context and other peripheral factors. The decision journey model falls under System 2, which means that in most cases customers will not complete this journey in its entirety.

Within System 1, customers think in terms of heuristics or mental shortcuts to make decisions. A heuristic is 'a strategy that ignores part of the information, with the goal of making decisions more quickly, frugally, and/or accurately than more complex methods' (Gigerenzer & Gaissmaier, 2011, p. 454). Which heuristic is used is determined by the specific decision problem and its context (Saad, 2015). This means that in some situations, one heuristic is used, while in other situations, different heuristics are employed. We will look at some of the more prominent ones (Slovic et al., 1977).

Representativeness heuristic: This is the tendency to assess the probability of something based on how similar or representative it is of a particular category or group. Or stated differently, how similar this something is to something we already know. For example, if you have experienced poor service at hairdresser Shortcut in your home country and come across Shortcut when travelling in another country, you are likely to think that if you enter here, you will experience poor service again. The latter is in fact similar to the former. In reality, there are many more problem-free hairdresser experiences than bad ones, so it is unlikely that you will experience poor service if you visit Shortcut abroad.

Availability heuristic: This is a tendency to give more weight to information in the form of events and examples that are easily accessible from memory or the environment than to more relevant but less accessible information. We tend to assess the likelihood of an event based on how easily it comes to mind as more probable than a less accessible event. For example, imagine you are trying to decide whether to spend your vacation in Greece or Spain. You recently saw a news report with live footage of wildfires on the Greek island of Rhodes and in the areas around Athens. As a result, you perceive Greece as a risky holiday destination compared with Spain. In this case, the availability heuristic plays a role because your decision is influenced by how easily you can remember the information about the wildfires. However, it may well be that there are just as many wildfires in Spain, but it has been longer since you read about them or the images were not as vivid.

Anchoring and adjustment heuristic: This heuristic is a tendency to start a decision with a strong reliance on an initial reference point (anchor) and adjust this point based on subsequent information. The initial anchor can have a significant impact on the final decision. An example of this heuristic can be found in price perception. If you see a product with a high price, you may assume it is of high quality and compare subsequent information about the same product against this high-quality standard. Therefore, when you later discover negative customer reviews about the same product, this information will adjust your perception of quality to some extent but not enough to completely change your perception of the product's quality. It is important to note that anchors can be arbitrary and still have a significant influence on the decision. Research has shown that when participants think about the last two digits in their social security number before being asked how much they are willing to pay for a new toaster, it leads to willingness-to-pay figures that are related to this arbitrary anchor. Participants with low numbers had significantly lower willingness-to-pay than those with high numbers (Simonson & Drolet, 2004).

Confirmation heuristic: This is the tendency to search for or interpret information in a way that confirms one's existing beliefs or hypotheses. If you have formed an opinion that products from a particular country have low quality, you will interpret the experience of products from this country as bad, more or less independent of objective facts.

These heuristics can help us with quick and efficient mental processes, but they can also lead to errors and systematic deviations in thinking and decision-making, known as biases. One of these biases is the status quo bias. Customers have a tendency to want to remain in their current state (status quo), which means continuing to buy the brand they are currently using or have tried before, rather than leaving this state and trying a new brand.

Both the anchoring and adjustment heuristic and the availability heuristic can explain this bias in favour of the status quo (Samuelson & Zeckhauser, 1988). If one anchors on certain information and then adjusts new information towards this anchor, this will favour the choice of the status quo because it is this option that is the anchor. The information one has about the status quo through experience will weigh more than new information about the new brand, which will only be used to adjust the information about the status quo, not to reject it. Using the availability heuristic will also lead to a preference for the status quo because the information customers have about this option is very accessible compared to the information regarding a new brand.

Framing is another notion from behavioural decision theory that testifies to the influence of context on our perception, evaluation and choices. Framing refers to the way these variables are 'framed' by context. In a famous experiment (Tversky & Kahneman, 1981), one treatment for a deadly disease was preferred over an alternative treatment by 72% of participants when this treatment emphasized the number of lives saved, but only 22% when the treatment emphasized the number of lives lost, even though the proportion of deaths and survivals was identical with the alternative treatment in both cases. Evidently, framing effects concerns marketing. If you walked into an unfamiliar clothing brand store with moderately priced items on Bond Street in London, Avenue des Champs-Élysées in Paris or Kurfürstendamm in Berlin, you would perceive the prices as lower than if you visited the same store in a shopping centre outside of these cities. Similarly, a package of ground beef is likely to be perceived as healthier if it is labelled '90% fat-free' compared to a package labelled '10% fat'.

Because context influences our evaluations and choices and varies, few or no choices are made on neutral ground. They are always biased in one direction or another. Sometimes this leads us to make choices that are not good for us in various areas, including health, environment, personal finances and careers. For example, many people procrastinate or skip exercise, even though they know it is detrimental to their health, or they fail to pay off their credit card balance in full, even though they know it results in interest charges. If marketers and policymakers have insight into these biases, different choice situations can be designed in a way that nudges customers in a direction that is better for them and society (Thaler & Sunstein, 2008). The Norwegian hotel chain Strawberry uses nudging to reduce food waste among its guests.

On a global scale, about 1.3 billion tons of food is wasted every year from grocery stores, households, restaurants and hotels (https://www.theworldcounts.com/challenges/people-and-poverty/hunger-and-obesity/food-waste-statistics). It is estimated that approximately 9% of all food waste comes from hotels and the tourism industry (Tostivint et al., 2016). This has negative consequences for both people and the environment, including unnecessary CO_2 emissions.

To reduce this type of waste, researchers have used the nudging method in hotels (Kallbekken & Sælen, 2013). The research on nudging suggests that it is possible to change people's choices in a direction that reduces these negative consequences. By making small changes in the choice situations people face in their lives, they can be nudged in the desired direction. Some researchers wanted to test if it was possible to influence guests' choices by making small changes in the plate size on buffets and thus reduce food waste from hotels.

The researchers initially assumed that reducing plate size could be an effective nudge. The idea is that the same portion of food is perceived as smaller when served on a large plate and larger when served on a small plate. This is an optical illusion (Delboeuf illusion, 1865) that stems from the contrast between the circle that represents the food and the circle that represents the plate. When the circle of food is almost the same size as the circle of the plate (with a small plate), they are perceived as the same circles (a pair of circles), and the food is perceived to be more than it actually is. Guests assimilate the food and the plate. Conversely, the same circle of food is perceived as far away and separate from the large plate (with a large plate), and the food is perceived to be smaller than it actually is. Guests contrast the food and the plate. The result is that people unconsciously tend to compensate by taking larger portions on large plates and smaller portions on small plates (Van Ittersum & Wansink, 2012).

The researchers conducted an experiment in the restaurants of 52 hotels in the Nordic Choice (now Strawberry) hotel chain to test these assumptions. In seven of the hotels, the researchers reduced the size of the plates used for breakfast and lunch buffets from a diameter of 24 centimetres to 21 centimetres. In seven other hotels, the researchers put up a sign that said: 'Welcome back! Again! And again! Visit our buffet many times. It's

(Continued)

better than taking a lot at once.' In the remaining 38 hotels, none of the interventions were implemented, and these served as a control group.

All three groups of hotels recorded and reported how much food was wasted throughout the two-and-a-half-month study period.

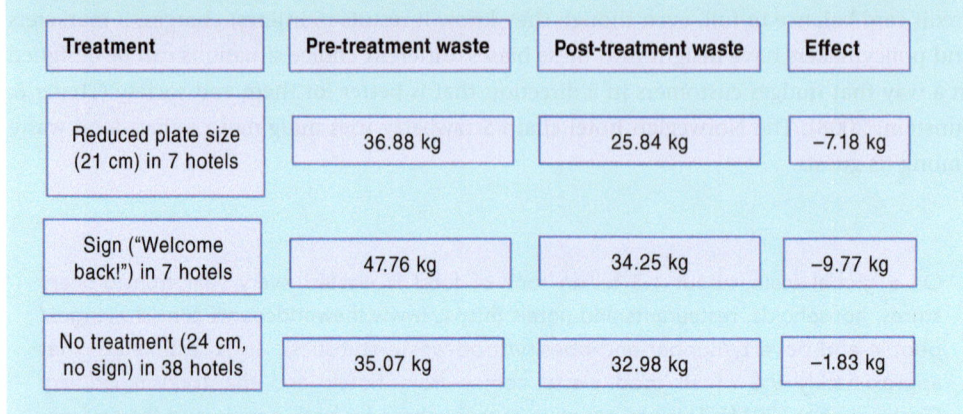

Treatment	Pre-treatment waste	Post-treatment waste	Effect
Reduced plate size (21 cm) in 7 hotels	36.88 kg	25.84 kg	−7.18 kg
Sign ("Welcome back!") in 7 hotels	47.76 kg	34.25 kg	−9.77 kg
No treatment (24 cm, no sign) in 38 hotels	35.07 kg	32.98 kg	−1.83 kg

Figure 3.8   The numbers pre- and post-treatment are observed values, while the effect is estimated values (from a regression model), where the researchers controlled for potentially confounding factors, including differences between the hotels that existed before the treatments and the number of guests at the hotels. Therefore, the effect is not equal to the difference between the observed pre- and post-values. The results in percentages were obtained by dividing the estimated effect value by the observed before value (from Kallbekken & Sælen, 2013)

The results showed that reducing plate size led to a 19.5% reduction in food waste, while the sign led to a 20.5% reduction. This demonstrates that small changes in the choice situation can have a significant impact and help reduce food waste.

Another question that might have come up when you read about the decision journey is: How do I know which attributes to use and how to weigh them? And if this is vague for you, then it's also vague for the customer. If the attributes and utility weights are not fixed, their use will vary from situation to situation (time of day, location, who we are with, our mood, etc.). This will lead to changes in our preferences (which brand is preferred over others) so that the choice may be coffee bar B instead of coffee bars A and C in one situation, while in the next situation it could be C instead of A and B). The attributes and utility weights will typically not be fixed because we do not have clear opinions about everything that exists. For example, we do not know how to value one attribute over another (Is the coffee's taste twice as important as the store's atmosphere?), and we also don't know if this valuation will remain after we have chosen the brand and started using it (Payne et al., 1992). Therefore, customers operate with what is called constructed preferences (Payne et al., 1992; Slovic, 1995). The preference for a particular brand of coffee shops is determined more or less on the spot because choice situations are where we begin (need) to assess the importance and value of different attributes (construct a preference).

When customers use resource-saving shortcuts and the context is constantly changing, it may seem unnecessary to use the decision journey model. Does not this model provide an insufficient description of human decision behaviour? Presumably, but the fact that considerable deviations from the decision journey model can be observed, does not mean that the model has been replaced by a new model.

Science usually evolves through the use of thesis, antithesis and synthesis (Fichte & Breazeale, 1993). The thesis of the decision journey model and other models for rational decisions and choices has been challenged by an antithesis named behavioural decision theory. This theory argues that decisions are made with limited cognitive resources and under significant influence from the context in which they are made. However, it remains to be seen whether a synthesis of elements from the decision journey model and elements from behavioural decision theory can provide the most accurate model. Rational models likely have something to offer in a synthesis with heuristic-based decision-making (Kivetz et al., 2008).

Several experiments that have found evidence of heuristic use have disfavoured the decision journey model. These experiments have forced the influence of context by, for example, excluding customers' absolute attribute values from the experiments (Simonson, 2008; Simonson & Rosen, 2014). Absolute value refers to the value that is best for the customer or that closely aligns with their ideal preference. For example, many people prefer clothes that feel comfortable to wear, a preference that likely applies generally to all types of clothing. Comfortable is an absolute or ideal value on the attribute of fabric. In order for the customer to be aware of this ideal value, they must have broad experience with available alternatives in the market. This can be achieved through personal experience or through extensive online and social media information. Today, one can find this ideal value because one can gather information from so many experts and users online, some of whom will share your preferences (Simonson & Rosen, 2014). These sources of information are not present in experiments. Instead, participants choose one alternative among several others that are presented to them. Thus, they are forced to make relative evaluations. For example, they may choose the garment with the best-known brand name or the most colour alternatives. These attribute values are likely less relevant than comfort, but experiment participants still have to make a decision based on them. Therefore, the choice of clothing in a normal situation with access to the internet and relevant information sources will be different from that in an experiment.

Think back to the example of the anchoring and adjustment heuristic, where the irrelevant information about the last two digits of the social security number determined people's willingness to pay for toasters. When participants were asked to state how much they were willing to pay for a toaster without any idea of the market price due to lack of experience in buying the product, they necessarily had to base their willingness to pay on something else. And in such a situation, that something else is the information readily available from the context, such as the social security number they were already thinking about. However, if participants had a lot of experience buying toasters, the effect of the social security number would be less pronounced (Simonson, 2008).

As we mentioned, heuristic-based decisions often lead to bias towards one of the alternatives. One such bias closely related to the status quo bias, the endowment effect, is that the value of an object one owns or possesses is perceived to be higher than the value of an identical object one does not own but can acquire. The endowment effect is assumed to be a result of irrational human loss aversion. But when some researchers checked whether this effect persisted when they slightly changed how the experimenters worded their instructions to the participants, they discovered something interesting (Plott & Zeiler, 2007). If participants perceive the object they are endowed with as a gift from the experimenters by saying 'Here you go, you can have this …', then the objective similarity between what they possess and what they can acquire ceases. And then we are not talking about bias anymore, but a comparison between apples and oranges. It is not irrational to prefer apples over oranges. When researchers changed the wording to make it clear that it was not a gift (the distributed product was randomly chosen), the endowment effect disappeared.

More generally, we can assume that if the experimental situation included more elements from the decision journey model, such as the customers' own problem recognition, a complete consideration set and all relevant attribute values, the customers would be more resistant to contextual influence, think less in terms of heuristics and exhibit less bias.

CUSTOMER BEHAVIOUR IN BUSINESS MARKETS

While private customers purchase products to fulfil their personal needs, professional customers acquire products to meet the requirements of an organization. We commonly refer to private customers as the consumer market and professional customers as the business market. Despite the consumer market typically receiving more attention, the economic value of the business market is significantly greater. Given the importance of the customer journey in the business market and the notable differences in customer behaviour between the consumer and business markets, it is worthwhile to briefly explore some of the key characteristics of professional customers.

The primary distinction between private customers and professional customers lies in the fact that professional customers represent organizations, thereby purchasing based on the organization's needs rather than individual preferences. However, it is important to note that organizations are comprised of individuals, and marketing efforts are directed towards these individuals. Many of the principles that apply to individual buying behaviour in the consumer market are also applicable to the individuals representing organizations (i.e. professional customers). Nonetheless, due to the representation of organizations, there are certain differences that come into play.

Customer Needs in Business Markets

To comprehend the needs of customers in business markets, companies need to grasp the objectives and operational methods of the organizations they are dealing with.

There are two main types of organizations: commercial organizations, which prioritize profit for their owners or shareholders; and non-commercial organizations, which pursue goals other than profit. Commercial organizations aim to generate profit for their owners, while non-profit organizations lack owners and utilize any profits to advance their specific objectives. Within non-profit organizations, a distinction can be made between those driven by idealistic purposes, such as private universities, charities, sports associations, trade unions and interest groups, often with a board elected by their members. The other category encompasses non-commercial organizations that serve public purposes, including state and municipal entities, as well as public services such as schools, hospitals, transportation and infrastructure. These organizations are managed through the political system.

Every organization operates through a production system, known as its value chain, which transforms input factors into tangible outcomes or products (Porter, 1985, 1996; Stabell & Fjeldstad, 1998).[5] In Figure 3.9, the value chain is divided into two categories: primary activities and support activities. The primary activities encompass the production and delivery of products to distributors, end customers and consumers. On the other hand, support activities provide assistance to the primary activities. Each activity within the value chain contributes value to the final product but also incurs costs. The remaining revenue after deducting all costs is referred to as the margin, illustrated on the right-hand side of Figure 3.9.

Companies strive to enhance their margins by reducing costs associated with the value chain activities. They aim to optimize the cost-efficiency of these activities as much as possible. For instance, they may negotiate lower prices with suppliers to minimize procurement expenses for materials and parts. To enhance cost-efficiency in production, companies may implement automation and seek ways to reduce labour costs, such as relocating production to countries with lower wages. Similarly, cost-reduction efforts extend to all other activities within the value chain.

The effectiveness of the value chain relies on the creation of value and the associated costs. All organizations work towards generating more value at lower costs, focusing on individual activities as well as the collective system of activities. Consequently, the effectiveness of the value chain is not solely determined by the efficiency of each individual activity but also by the effectiveness of the entire system of activities. For example, the value chain's effectiveness depends on how well the marketing function communicates customer needs to the production function and how suitable the products produced align with marketing and sales requirements.

---

[5]The value chain concept is widely known, but was first described in Porter (1985). Porter later emphasized the importance of analysing how the activities are included in the company's general value creation (Porter, 1991, 1996). Other definitions of value chains can be found in Stabell & Fjeldstad (1998).

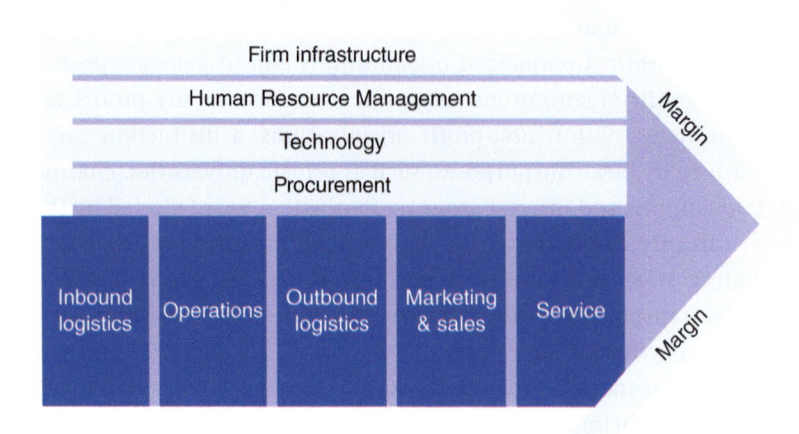

Figure 3.9   A framework for analysing needs in the business market – activities in the value chain

---

Case Study 3.3

IBM

In order to comprehend the specific products and services needed by professional customers, it is crucial to possess knowledge regarding their value chain and cost structure. Let's consider the example of IBM, which offers IT solutions aimed at helping companies reduce their energy costs. By analysing the value chain activities of their professional customers, IBM can tailor their offerings more precisely to meet their specific needs. For instance, when dealing with a wholesaler customer, IBM's solutions would likely be relevant in addressing energy costs associated with the logistics part of the value chain. On the other hand, for a hotel customer, energy costs are closely tied to the hotel's operations. IBM's website has more information about the company's solutions for various parts of the value chains in various industries (www.ibm.com).

Figure 3.10 presents a model that enables companies to analyse the importance of their supply within a business customer's overall value chain. The model is characterized by two dimensions. The horizontal axis represents the complexity of the supply, indicating whether the supplied product is simple or intricate to acquire. Suppliers in the market may differentiate themselves based on functionality, technological level, logistics system and other factors. On the other hand, the vertical axis represents the importance of the supply, which considers factors such as the proportion of costs allocated to the supplied product, its value-added contribution, profitability profile and more. These dimensions give rise to four distinct purchasing strategies.

Addressing the needs of business customers in the lower-left quadrant of Figure 3.10 (non-critical) entails providing straightforward concepts and cost-reducing solutions. Customers in this quadrant prioritize simplicity and affordability. In the upper-left quadrant (leverage), customers place significant emphasis on obtaining the lowest possible price. They evaluate multiple suppliers in the market and choose the one offering the most competitive price.

When deliveries are considered bottlenecked, customers accept relying on a single supplier while ensuring their independence. Contingency plans are developed as safeguards against any potential issues with the primary supplier. Conversely, for strategic deliveries, customers establish a close working relationship with a main supplier. This partnership often involves mutual investments to ensure efficient deliveries in terms of both price and quality. Customized products tailored to the specific needs of these customers are frequently developed in this quadrant. Customers in this category consider not only prices but also the quality and expertise offered by suppliers.

In business markets, customer needs tend to be more diverse and fragmented compared to consumer markets. This can be attributed to various factors, such as differences in customer goals, organization of value chain activities, company size, product categories and geographical factors. As a result, analysing and understanding customer needs in business markets is significantly more complex than in most consumer markets.

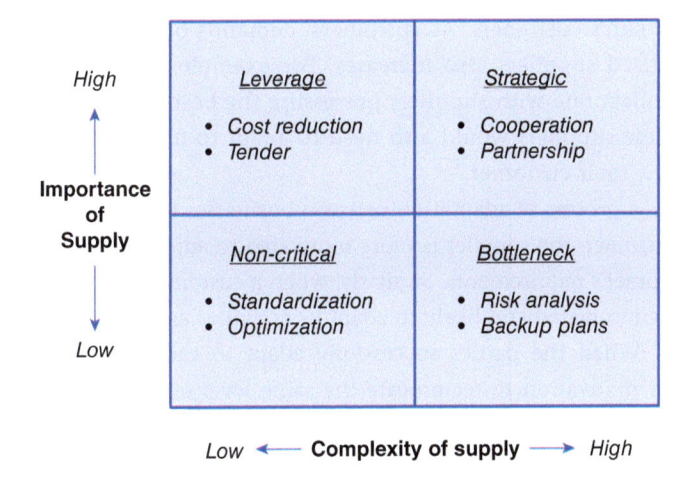

Figure 3.10 Kraljic's framework for classifying purchasing strategies (after Kraljic, 1983)

Relationships and Networks

Another key differentiation between consumer and business markets lies in the significance of relationships and networks. In the realm of business, suppliers and customers often develop interdependent bonds that encompass various dimensions such as personal connections, structural integration, financial ties, or a combination of these factors. These relationships frequently extend beyond individual pairs and form part of a broader network involving suppliers, customers, stakeholders and vital resources. To comprehensively grasp customer behaviour in the business market, it is essential to examine and analyse these intricate relationships (Ford, 2002).

Over time, interpersonal connections emerge among individuals collaborating on behalf of organizations, thus adding a social dimension to customer behaviour. The strength of these connections may range from casual acquaintanceships to strong friendships (see Wathne et al., 2001). As the relationship strengthens, so do the expectations and requirements to fulfil each other's needs. The influence of interpersonal ties on decision-making varies depending on several factors. For instance, these ties may have little impact if a competitor can provide a significantly lower price. However, connections between suppliers and key decision-makers within the customer's organization facilitate information exchange and conflict resolution (Biong & Selnes, 1995). Therefore, understanding the social aspects of the relationship holds great importance.

Structural ties develop as customers and suppliers adjust their respective activities and resources to align with one another. Over time, they acquire knowledge about individuals, competencies, technologies, procedures, and more (see, for example, Dwyer et al., 1987 and Hallén et al., 1991 on adaptations; Tuli et al., 2007 on selling solutions). Collaborating companies also engage in joint activities and establish shared processes for ordering, distribution and product development, involving employees from both sides. For instance, a supplier of orange juice may tailor their product to suit the preferences of a supermarket chain's customers. As customers' demands become more specialized, the need for specialized suppliers also increases. For example, a hybrid car manufacturer would closely collaborate with suppliers possessing the best product parts and resources in this field. These suppliers would also need to adapt to meet the requirements of the car manufacturer, their customer.

In Figure 3.11, a process of adaptation between businesses is illustrated. When a supplier depends on a customer, the supplier is more motivated to adjust its activities and resources to meet the customer's requirements. Similarly, when a customer depends on a supplier, the customer is more motivated and likely to adapt its activities and resources to align with the supplier's needs. When the parties successfully adapt to each other, it builds trust and strengthens their motivation to reciprocate the same level of responsiveness. This mutual adaptation fosters a cooperative environment and facilitates joint development between customers and suppliers.

Over time, as suppliers and customers engage in structural adjustment, they develop lasting connections. However, the value of these ties lies in the customer's continued utilization of the same supplier. If the customer switches to a different supplier, the benefits derived from the relational ties are lost, and the customer must establish similar relationships with new suppliers. This phenomenon is referred to as idiosyncratic or transaction-specific investments (Williamson, 1985; Heide & John, 1988, 1990; Heide & Weiss, 1995). Consequently, these ties also serve as barriers to exit, as customers face challenges in severing connections and transitioning to alternative suppliers.

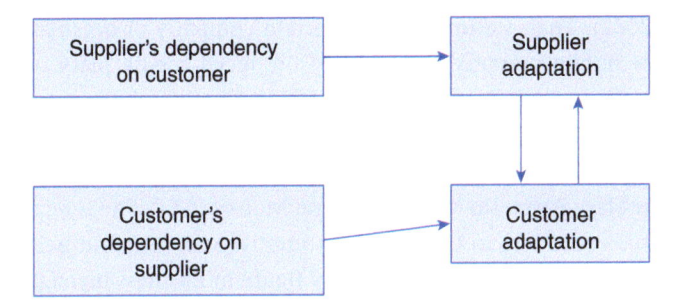

Figure 3.11 Process for mutual dependence and adaptation between companies (Hallén et al., 1991)

Not all interactions between customers and suppliers will evolve into closer collaborative relationships. Some customers intentionally maintain a certain distance from their suppliers, and vice versa. When examining purchasing behaviour in business markets, it becomes crucial to comprehend customers' strategies regarding the establishment of structural ties with suppliers. See the case study below about Johanson's ownership of the Evergood coffee brand (see http://www.evergood.no)

Case Study 3.4

Evergood Coffee

Financial ties refer to ownership arrangements that govern transactions between customers and suppliers. A notable example can be observed in one of Norway's prominent grocery wholesalers, which possesses its own coffee brand: Evergood. The wholesaler's ownership and control over a vast distribution network mitigate the risks associated with investments in coffee production and marketing. Initially, the wholesaler's decision to invest in coffee stemmed from a desire to offer the market high-quality coffee. During and after the Second World War, when the quality of coffee was generally low, Norwegian coffee consumers were willing to pay a premium for superior coffee. Recognizing this opportunity, the wholesaler invested in coffee production and marketing.

In subsequent years, the same wholesaler acquired a grocery distribution system, thereby gaining control over the distribution of its coffee brand. Consequently, the stores within the network are compelled to procure coffee exclusively from this supplier. Similar arrangements can be found in numerous large industries. When analysing buying behaviour, it becomes vital to understand how such financial ties influence decision-making processes.

Within business-to-business networks, though, leaders play a role. These individuals can be likened to social media influencers in the business-to-consumer market. However, unlike external independent influencers, thought leaders are typically integral parts of a company, such as chief executive officers (CEOs), or closely associated partners, like consultants

(Neuhaus et al., 2022). Their stature within a certain company or organization, their competence and their public presence, particularly on social media platforms, substantially contribute to their influence (Neuhaus et al., 2022). Thought leaders leverage platforms such as LinkedIn to share their deep and specialized knowledge, unique insights and forward-thinking perspectives with their followers (Barry & Gironda, 2018).

One example is Mary Barra, the CEO of General Motors (GM). She is recognized as one of the most influential executives in the global automotive industry, and her leadership experience and decisions have made her an authority figure in business management, especially in manufacturing and technology enterprises. She shares insights about strategic planning, leadership and the future of the automotive industry.

Thought leaders add value both to their companies and to their customers. Their deep insight and expertise increase their company's credibility. They also play a role in consumers' decision-making processes, as many customers look to thought leaders for their invaluable advice and insights when considering purchases.

Buying Centre

Professional customers exhibit a systematic method of acquiring goods or services. The purchasing journey begins when a staff member within the organization recognizes a problem that can be resolved by making a product purchase. In the case of one-time purchases, an impromptu project team is assembled to address the procurement matter. On the other hand, recurring purchases are handled within the established organizational framework, with designated employees responsible for procurement as part of their job responsibilities. In both scenarios, the buying process involves multiple individuals within the organization, collectively forming a purchasing unit. These individuals can assume any of the six distinct purchasing roles listed below (Webster & Wind, 1972; Bonoma, 1982):

- Initiator: The person who suggests the purchase of a product or service.
- Influencer: The individual who seeks to sway others in the group when it comes to the outcome of the decision. This person gathers information and attempts to influence the criteria for the purchase decision.
- User: The actual end user of the product.
- Decision-maker: The individual who holds the formal authority to make the final decision regarding which product to purchase.
- Purchaser: The person who possesses the formal authority to choose suppliers and establish contracts.
- Gatekeeper: The individual who controls the flow of information within the buying centre. This person determines who can access certain information and denies access to others.

The level of formality within the purchasing centre may vary. While influencers and gatekeepers play significant roles, individuals with these responsibilities may not necessarily be formal members of the buying centre. Additionally, some roles may be fulfilled by multiple individuals. For instance, there may be multiple influencers and gatekeepers striving to regulate the information flow. Furthermore, a single person can assume multiple roles within the buying centre. For example, the purchaser could also be an influencer and gatekeeper. It is probable that each person in the buying centre will possess their own distinct perceptions, goals and attitudes shaped by their experiences, personality, role within the buying centre and the organization as a whole. The individuals within the purchasing centre hold diverse formal positions within the organizational hierarchy. Top management typically becomes more involved in particularly significant purchases, while initiators and influencers are commonly middle managers rather than top-level executives (see Grønhaug, 1976).

Consider the following scenario in which a fashion retailer is looking to increase the product portfolio it offers its customers:

Initiator: The fashion buyer at ABC Fashion Retail noticed a growing demand for designer handbags among customers and initiated the idea of expanding their handbag collection to cater to this trend.

Influencer: The store manager, fashion influencers and fashion magazine editors were all influencers in the buying decision. They provided recommendations, shared insights on popular designer handbag brands and styles, and highlighted the potential market appeal and profitability of adding new handbags to the store's inventory.

User: The sales associates and visual merchandisers were the users of the handbags. They provided feedback on current trends, customer preferences and the suitability of various designer handbags for display and promotion. Their input helped in selecting handbags that resonated with the store's target audience.

Decision-maker: The decision-maker was the CEO. She, along with the fashion buyer, evaluated different designer handbag brands, considered factors such as brand reputation, quality, pricing and potential profit margins, and made the final decision on which handbag brands to stock.

Purchaser: The procurement team, in collaboration with the finance department, was responsible for purchasing the designer handbags. They negotiated with suppliers, reviewed pricing, handled ordering and logistics, and ensured that the purchase aligned with the company's budget and financial guidelines.

Gatekeeper: The corporate communication department acted as the gatekeeper, ensuring that the selected handbag brands aligned with the store's overall ethics and sustainability policy. They reviewed the brand owners' ethics and sustainability certifications and carbon footprint record.

When companies develop strategies to influence the buying centre of their customers, it is imperative to initiate the process by creating a comprehensive profile of the various individuals involved. This profile should not only encompass the individuals within the customer's organization but also consider the broader network in which they operate. Understanding the interconnectedness of this network with the supplier's organization and its connections to key stakeholders in other organizations, such as other suppliers and consultants, is essential. By mapping these relationships and connections, companies can gain invaluable insights that allow them to shape their influence strategies effectively (see Johnston & Bonoma, 1981).

In order to devise a successful sales strategy, it is crucial for a company to have a thorough understanding of the internal dynamics and influences among the members of the buying centre. Typically, individuals within the buying centre tend to prefer softer forms of influence, such as information exchange and recommendations, over coercive tactics or promises based on formal power. Recognizing these preferences and dynamics empowers the company to tailor its approach accordingly and employ strategies that effectively align with the preferences of the buying centre (see Venkatesh et al., 1995).

To conduct a comprehensive analysis of customer behaviour in business markets, companies should carefully consider the essential factors outlined in Table 3.7. Understanding customers' overarching objectives and how they influence their purchasing behaviour is crucial. If there are significant differences in the buying process between commercial and non-commercial customers within a business organization, these distinctions should be reflected in the segmentation model. However, it is possible that no substantial differences exist, making the commercial/non-commercial variable unsuitable for segmentation. For example, the purchasing process for photocopiers may be similar in both commercial and non-commercial organizations, requiring the application of alternative segmentation variables.

Analysing Customer Behaviour in Business Markets

When analysing customer behaviour in a business market, the company should ask itself the questions presented in Table 3.7.

First, the company must find out what the overall goals of the customer are, and the role they play in the customer's behaviour. In order to effectively cater to the diverse value creation methods of customers, companies must have a deep understanding of their value chains. Additionally, comprehending how customers' cost structure impacts on value creation is vital. In the aviation industry, for instance, the marginal cost of an additional passenger is negligible while other costs remain high. Therefore, an airline's profitability is highly dependent on capacity utilization. Price differentiation is used to manage capacity utilization due to the price sensitivity of aviation services. Offering software that enables airlines to implement precise pricing and increase profits would be highly valuable to customers.

Furthermore, companies need to recognize that customers employ different purchasing strategies based on the type of delivery offered. Some customers prefer to maintain a certain distance from their suppliers for certain deliveries, while seeking closer cooperation for others. Similarly, customers may have distinct strategies for each product offered by the same company.

Segmenting professional customers is more challenging than segmenting private customers. Analysing each segment in terms of buying centre dynamics and relational ties provides valuable insights into business market purchases. Additionally, there are significant variations in the value represented by different customers. Often, a small number of customers contribute a substantial portion of total revenue, while numerous customers make up the remainder. In such cases, it is advisable to treat the few large customers individually rather than as a segment. The remaining customers can then be segmented based on their value creation approach and the most suitable approach for engaging with them.

Table 3.7　Analysis of professional customers in the business market

Analysis of professional customers in the business market
What are the overall goals of the customers' organizations?
What are the most important characteristics of the customers' value chain and cost structure?
How do customers assess the importance and complexity of supply?
How can customers be segmented by type of value creation?
What characterizes relationships and purchasing centres in different segments?
What characterizes the type of collaboration and the presence of relational ties?

SUMMARY

To thoroughly analyse customer behaviour, it is essential for companies to have a comprehensive understanding of their customers' needs and the impact of these needs on purchasing behaviour. This involves studying the reasons behind customers' specific choices and how marketing efforts influence their decision journey.

The decision journey begins with problem recognition, which occurs when customers identify a significant gap between their current state and the desired state, motivating them to seek a solution. Problem recognition can be categorized into two types: needs and wants. Needs arise when customers feel a lack of something and desire to return to a neutral mental state, while wants involve a desire for pleasure. During the problem phase, customers not only recognize a problem but also structure it and devise ways to solve it by identifying goals and considering appropriate actions.

Following problem recognition, the information search phase involves customers seeking information to help resolve the problem. Initially, customers rely on the knowledge stored in their long-term memory about the product category. However, if their stored knowledge is insufficient, they seek information from external sources. This information search process includes determining relevant product properties, understanding how these properties create utility, exploring available alternatives, evaluating their strengths and weaknesses, and identifying reliable sources of information. Both internal and external sources are utilized during the search process.

In the evaluation phase, customers aim to identify brands that are relevant and capable of solving the problem. This involves gaining an overview of brands and products that could serve as a solution and being aware of alternatives to avoid. Customers assess and rank different brands based on their preferences. The evaluation can be conducted using compensatory or non-compensatory decision rules. Compensatory decision rules involve evaluating alternatives based on the total weighted scores of individual attributes, while non-compensatory rules do not allow high scores in one attribute to compensate for lower scores in others. Non-compensatory rules can be further classified into conjunctive and lexicographic models.

Actual purchase decisions can be categorized into three types: high frequency, low frequency and contract purchases. High-frequency purchases involve regularly used consumer products, and customers develop routine-based buying behaviour for these items. Low-frequency purchases differ from high-frequency purchases in that customers repeat some or all of the purchasing process each time due to the time between purchases. Contract purchases are based on payment plans and may involve initial fees, fixed or regular fees, or variable fees.

The decision journey extends beyond the decision to buy. Once the customer starts using the product, a relationship is established between the customer and the brand. This phase involves relationship development, satisfaction, equity, cognitive dissonance, word of mouth and complaint behaviour as key factors.

As customers, we do not always exhibit a purchasing behaviour that is consistent with the decision journey model. We are predisposed to be frugal with our mental resources and use them for the most important decisions. Therefore, customers often rely on shortcuts (heuristics) and are also susceptible to the influence of contextual variables in decision-making (framing).

When it comes to professional customers, they acquire products to meet organizational needs rather than personal preferences. Understanding the value chain and cost structure of professional customers is crucial to identify their specific product and service requirements. In business markets, relationships and networks play a significant role. Suppliers and customers often develop interdependent bonds encompassing personal connections, structural integration, financial ties, or a combination of these factors.

The buying process involves multiple individuals within the organization, forming a purchasing unit. These individuals assume various purchasing roles, including initiators, influencers, users, decision-makers, purchasers and gatekeepers. Initiators suggest the purchase, influencers seek to sway the decision, users are the end users of the product, decision-makers hold formal authority, purchasers have the authority to choose suppliers and establish contracts, and gatekeepers control the flow of information within the buying centre, determining access to information for others.

END-OF-CHAPTER QUESTIONS

1   Interview two individuals and ask them to describe the buying process for a product they frequently purchase (such as beer, petrol or chocolate), for a product they occasionally purchase (such as running shoes, bicycles or plane tickets), and for a

contract purchase (such as gym membership, a bank account or insurance). Ask both individuals to specify their product-specific and overarching goals, key product characteristics and their significance, and how they seek information. Analyse similarities and differences between the two individuals and the different types of purchases.

2   Test the routines for complaint handling in a random store. Go back to the store with a product you just bought. Tell them something is wrong with the product, but that you have lost the receipt. Pretend to be angry about the product's defect and that this is not the first time you have experienced a malfunction. Analyse how the store handles the case. What could have been done better? Remember to end by telling the employee in the store that it was just a test. Ask if they can explain more about the store's service procedures.

3   See Shocker et al. (1991), 'Consideration set influences on consumer decision-making and choice: Issues, models, and suggestions'. Interview a person who has just purchased a new bike, skis, TV or similar (low-frequency purchase) and ask if they can mention the brands in their awareness set (at the beginning of the buying process), in the original consideration set, and in the final choice set. Also, ask the person to tell you which rules of information processing they used to eliminate options from the consideration set. Do you recognize any of the non-compensatory rules we have described in this chapter?

FURTHER READING

Edelman, D. & Singer, M. (2015). Competing on customer journeys. *Harvard Business Review*, 93(November), 88–100.

Lemon, K.N. & Verhoef, P.C. (2016). Understanding customer experience throughout the customer journey. *Journal of Marketing*, 80(6), 69–96.

Mahoney, M. (2001). The subconscious mind of the consumer (and how to reach it). Retrieved from https://hbswk.hbs.edu/item/the-subconscious-mind-of-the-consumer-and-how-to-reach-it.

Oliver, R.L. (1997). *Satisfaction: A Behavioral Perspective on the Consumer*. New York: Irwin/McGraw Hill.

Shocker, A.D., Ben-Akiva, M., Boccara, B. & Negungadi, P. (1991). Consideration set influences on consumer decision-making and choice: Issues, models, and suggestions. *Marketing Letters* 2(3), 181–197. https://doi.org/10.1007/BF02404071.

4

MARKETING COMMUNICATION

This chapter

- discusses the role of marketing communication;
- explains how marketing communication works;
- explains communication goals and target groups;
- discusses messages and creativity;
- discusses message placement in communication channels;
- discusses budgeting marketing communication investments;
- discusses monitoring and control with marketing communication.

INTRODUCTION

Marketing communication involves effectively conveying the company's value proposition to persuade customers to purchase its products and brands. This activity holds significant importance, as without communication with the market, the company's products and brands would struggle to survive. Having clear objectives for marketing communication is crucial. These objectives can include creating awareness of a new product, strengthening an established brand, or motivating customers to continue choosing the company's offerings. Setting objectives is essential for assessing the success of marketing communication efforts.

To assess the success of a recruitment campaign, let's consider an example where a company invests 20,000 euros and attracts 1,000 new customers.[1] The company's objective is to determine whether this communication effort was successful and financially viable. In order to evaluate its profitability, the company needs to compare the expected cash flow, which is the revenue generated minus the costs incurred, from these 1,000 new customers with the initial investment of 20,000 euros.

---

[1] For an excellent discussion of how to evaluate investments in acquisition see Reinartz et al. (2005).

To make this assessment, the company must estimate the size of the expected annual cash flow and determine how long these new customers are likely to continue their affiliation with the company. By analysing factors such as average customer spending, retention rates, and customer lifetime value, the company can gauge the financial impact of these newly acquired customers. If the expected cash flow from the 1,000 customers surpasses the initial investment of 20,000 euros, the campaign can be considered successful and profitable.

Clearly defining objectives and accurately assessing the impact of marketing communication efforts are vital for developing effective strategies. By setting specific goals and conducting comprehensive financial evaluations, companies can make well-informed decisions and optimize their marketing communication initiatives for long-term success.

To establish suitable objectives and determine how to achieve them, it is essential for companies to understand how marketing communication influences customers. This entails gaining insight into how customers receive, process and respond to the company's messages. Moreover, companies need to make informed choices regarding their target audience, message content and design, available communication channels (such as radio, sports events, social media), and tools (such as advertising, sponsorship, influencers) to ensure effective communication. Intelligent allocation of resources, including budget, is critical in maximizing the impact of marketing communication efforts. Finally, measuring the actual outcomes and comparing them against the desired effects is crucial. All of these steps necessitate a comprehensive understanding of how customers perceive, process and respond to communication.

By following this approach, companies can enhance their marketing communication strategies, achieve their goals and establish long-lasting connections with their target audience.

This chapter will explore how customers, and in particular targeted customers, receive, process and respond to communication about a company's offerings. Additionally, it will outline the steps that the company must take to develop and execute effective marketing communication, guided by insights into how this communication is expected to resonate with customers.

HOW DOES MARKETING COMMUNICATION WORK?

By the term 'how', we refer to the different ways consumers process marketing messages, and what effects this has. We also consider what determines whether the message produces effects other than those initially planned. These mechanisms primarily operate within the realm of psychology. The impact of the message is also influenced by competitive communications, such as messages conveyed by rival brands. Furthermore, contextual variables such as social relationships, economic factors and culture can significantly influence the reception and interpretation of a message. For instance, if a message is shared within an online community, it can have a higher impact due to the influence of personal recommendations and trust among friends or family members. If a message is tailored to the general economic circumstances or purchasing power of the audience, it is more likely to resonate with customers.

Adapting the message to align with cultural sensitivities and preferences will also enhance its effectiveness and avoid unintended negative consequences.

Many of the same variables that influence consumer behaviour in general, as discussed in Chapter 3, also shape how customers engage with marketing communication. This encompasses how they receive a message, how they interpret it, and how they respond to it. Numerous theories and models exist that examine the workings of marketing communication, and we will examine the most pertinent ones in detail.

Hierarchy of Effects Models

The hierarchy of effects models have a lengthy and extensive history, tracing back to the late 19th century (Barry & Howard, 1990). These models aim to elucidate how the target audience processes and responds to marketing communication, shaping their purchasing behaviour. These models operate under the assumption that the target audience follows a sequential and structured pattern of response when exposed to marketing communication. The process comprises three stages: cognitive response (thinking process), affective response (emotional response) and conative response (action). During the cognitive stage, customers perceive and form assumptions or beliefs about the product or brand and its attributes. For example, upon seeing an advertisement highlighting the advantages of a regular bicycle over an e-bike, customers may assume that a regular bike is more environmentally friendly because it doesn't require a battery for production and charging. In the affective stage, customers develop emotions associated with the product. In this case, the customer may develop a liking for the bike due to its environmental friendliness. Finally, in the conative stage, customers form intentions and take actions directed towards the product, such as planning to purchase a bicycle within the year. Each of these steps is necessary but not sufficient for progression to the next step.

In Figure 4.1, we have presented three prominent hierarchy of effects models: AIDA, DAGMAR and Lavidge & Steiner. The AIDA model suggests a process that starts with attention, then moves to interest, desire and finally action (Strong, 1925). To persuade the target audience through advertising, they must first become aware of the product or brand, followed by developing an interest in the advertised content. Subsequently, the advertising should evoke a desire to purchase or consume the product by demonstrating how it fulfils a specific need, such as quenching thirst, enhancing status or reducing waiting time. The ultimate goal of advertising is to prompt a purchase (action) and generate revenue for the company. The DAGMAR model, Defining Advertising Goals for Measured Advertising Results, encompasses the steps of awareness, comprehension, conviction and action (Colley, 1961). This model emphasizes the value of marketing communication beyond mere sales generation, recognizing the significance of its impact on message awareness and comprehension. The Lavidge & Steiner model proposes that customers progress from awareness, knowledge, liking, preference, conviction, to purchase (Lavidge & Steiner, 1961). This model highlights that advertising's long-term effects are achieved by guiding the target audience through these various steps.

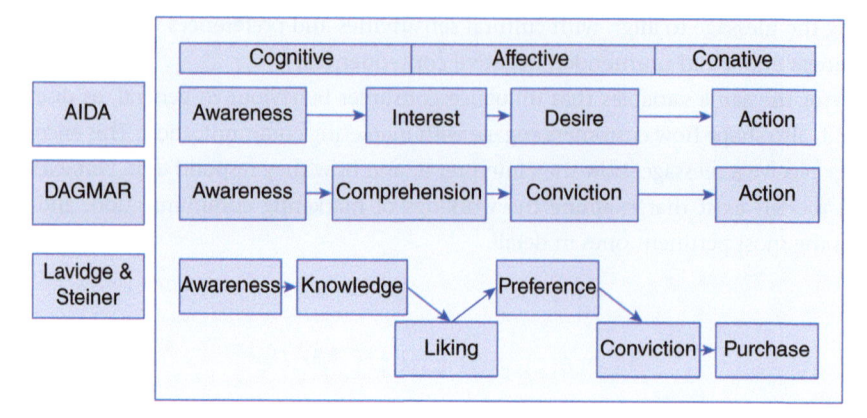

Figure 4.1   The three dimensions of the hierarchy of effects models: AIDA, DAGMAR and Lavidge & Steiner

Hierarchy of effects models have been utilized by practitioners such as brand owners, media agencies and advertising agencies for campaign planning, as well as by marketing researchers to gain insights into customer responses to these campaigns. Sociologists and psychologists also study and employ hierarchy of effects models. The existence of numerous developed models indicates substantial support among researchers for the perspectives they offer on how a target audience processes, responds to and is influenced by marketing communication.

One of the key insights from these models is that marketing communication impacts not only sales but also customers' thoughts and emotions. Therefore, in order for a company to assess the effectiveness of its marketing communication, it must measure its impact on various variables beyond sales. These variables include awareness, conviction and the audience's perception of the communicated value proposition. Although hierarchy of effects models are widely used by professional communicators, they do have limitations and shortcomings.

While the models suggest a sequential progression through the steps, empirical evidence does not consistently support this notion. Target audiences often move through the steps in a different order than the typical think–feel–act sequence. Krugman (1965, 1966) highlighted that target audiences may not always be actively engaged in processing a message but instead act as passive recipients. In such cases, the target audience is unlikely to adhere to the original order of the effect hierarchy. Additionally, many models focus solely on the purchase or trial stage and overlook the post-purchase or consumption phase (Egan, 2007).

Moreover, researchers have put forth arguments stating that preferences are not solely based on cognition but can also be influenced by affect alone (Zajonc, 1980). Experimental evidence demonstrates that affective responses can occur independently of cognition and even precede it in time. When encountering something new, the initial response of an organism often tends to be affective. For instance, one can develop a liking or disliking for the design of a summer dress without considering whether it is new, old, retro or borrowed from another culture. In such cases, the target group may undergo fewer steps than what the hierarchy of effects models suggest.

In certain situations, preferences can be solely based on awareness. The target group may prefer a product simply because they have been exposed to it and find it familiar, known as the mere exposure effect (Zajonc, 1968). Customers tend to favour products they are familiar with, even if they possess limited knowledge about them. This preference forms without customers progressing through the knowledge and liking steps outlined in hierarchy of effects models.

The review above of the hierarchy of effects model shows that the effect of marketing communication can be hard to understand and predict. In the following we will address how marketing communication can be used for attitude formation and change, and in building expectations.

Persuasion and Attitude Change

As previously mentioned, marketing communication aims to persuade customers to choose products and brands offered by the company. To this end, the company must cultivate customers' attitudes. Our attitudes guide our behaviour by influencing our preferences and choices, allowing us to navigate through daily life without extensively deliberating on each decision. For instance, when we need to go grocery shopping, we naturally gravitate towards stores we already hold positive attitudes towards, without extensively evaluating alternative options. Thus, attitudes simplify our daily routines. One notable characteristic of attitudes is their resistance to change once they are established. Individuals are hesitant to process information that challenges their existing attitudes, but they are more receptive to information that aligns with their attitudes. Consequently, marketing communication faces the task of both persuading customers to shift from negative to positive attitudes and reinforcing existing positive attitudes. Effective persuasive marketing communication can have long-lasting effects since individuals tend to be resistant to attitude change once they are formed.

Attitudes are closely intertwined with our knowledge, emotions and behavioural patterns. This relationship is known as the tripartite model of attitudes, which suggests that attitudes manifest in three ways: cognitively, affectively and behaviourally.[2] Notably, these dimensions align with the steps outlined in the hierarchy of effects models depicted in Figure 4.1. Additionally, it has been proposed that these attitude manifestations may vary across different contexts (Hogg & Vaughan, 2005). An individual may hold a positive attitude towards purchasing a specific brand in one situation but hold a negative attitude in another situation. For instance, a customer may prefer a convenience store under time pressure but opt for a supermarket with a larger selection when time is not a constraint. Marketing communication endeavours to influence attitudes by providing new information to alter customers' cognition, delivering affective stimuli to modify their emotions, and employing incentives (e.g. promotions) to change learned behaviour.

---

[2]The tripartite model was first introduced by Rosenberg & Hovland (1960).

The elaboration likelihood model (ELM), depicted in Figure 4.2, is widely recognized and utilized to understand how marketing communication can effectively persuade customers, even when they allocate limited cognitive resources (Petty & Cacioppo, 1986b; MacInnis & Jaworski, 1989). Persuasion aims to shape or alter people's attitudes, and the ELM elucidates how attitudes are influenced by a message through one of two thought processes or routes.

In one route outlined by the ELM, individuals are persuaded through careful and in-depth processing, known as elaboration, of the message's central arguments. Central arguments typically emphasize the core attributes of a product and the benefits it offers to customers. For instance, in an advertisement for an electric car, information about its superior range would be a central argument. This route, where customers critically evaluate the message, is referred to as the central route. In this route, recipients actively engage with the message, dedicating time and effort to its processing. Three prerequisites must be met for a message to be processed through the central route (Petty & Cacioppo, 1986b, 123–205). Firstly, the recipient must possess motivation, meaning the message is directly relevant to them. If the message lacks direct relevance, the motivation to process it will be limited, and recipients are likely to disregard the entire message. Secondly, the recipient must have the ability to process the message. If the recipient struggles to comprehend the message, the ability to process it in a central manner is absent. Lastly, the recipient must have the opportunity to process the message. The opportunity to process is influenced by external factors beyond the recipient's control, such as time constraints, message length, the number of arguments presented and distracting thoughts triggered by competing messages (Batra & Ray, 1986).

Consider an individual who has the intention to purchase a mountain bike for both exercise and gaining a competitive advantage in racing. When this person comes across an advertisement for a new bicycle, their extensive expertise acquired through years of training, riding and maintenance enables them to evaluate the message effectively, especially when it highlights features like a 'dropper post remote' and '160 mm fork travel'. If the processing of the advertisement evokes positive thoughts, such as recognizing the superiority of the bike's features in comparison to its competitors, the central route of persuasion will have a strong and influential impact. This can be attributed to the fact that individuals tend to have a high level of confidence in their own thoughts when they have engaged in careful and thorough processing. Moreover, attitudes formed through the central route tend to be relatively enduring as the information from the message becomes integrated into long-term memory.

The alternative route, known as the peripheral route, involves individuals processing a message without engaging in significant cognitive processing. Most advertising messages are processed through this route. When employing the peripheral route, recipients may lack the necessary motivation, ability or opportunity to thoroughly assess the message. Consequently, recipients do not form a clear stance regarding their agreement or disagreement with the advertised message. Instead, other factors such as pictures and sounds can significantly influence the persuasiveness of the message. In the context of our bicycle example, a customer with lower motivation and expertise, exposed to multiple competing messages, may be persuaded if they come across the advertisement on a social media platform they follow where they notice that many people like the ad. Although positive attitudes can be formed through the peripheral route, these attitudes are less enduring and more susceptible to influence from counterarguments compared to attitudes formed through the central route. Thus, the peripheral route is a weaker form of persuasion than the central route. The ELM supports the notion that customers often allocate minimal cognitive effort when processing a message, and as a result companies should not expect their messages to be thoroughly considered.[3]

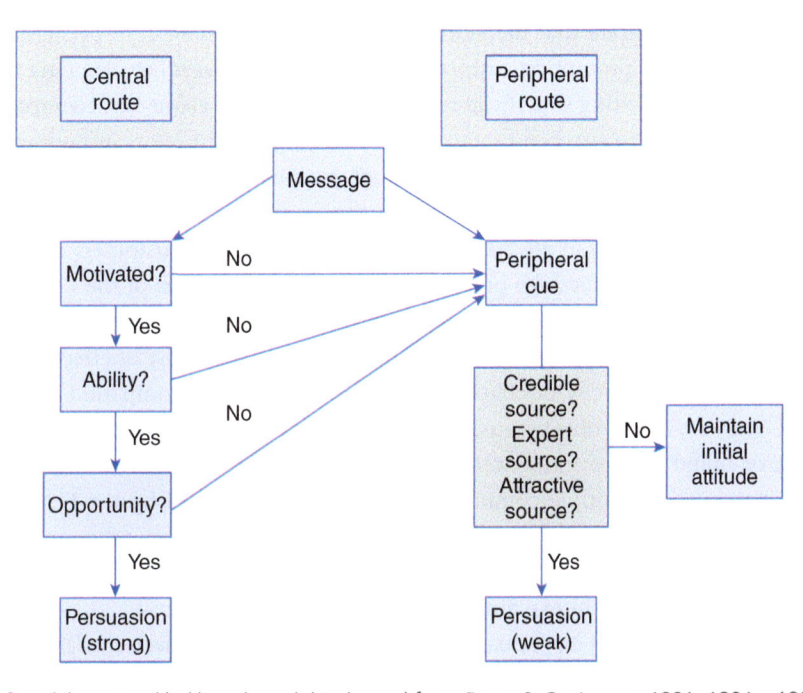

Figure 4.2 Elaboration likelihood model (adapted from Petty & Cacioppo, 1981, 1986a, 1986b)

Another model that aligns with the ELM is Nobel laureate Kahneman's (2003) framework of two systems of thinking: System 1 and System 2. Kahneman's extensive research led him to identify two distinct modes or systems through which humans make decisions. These systems closely parallel the two routes proposed by the ELM. The first system, known as System 1, operates intuitively and automatically, requiring minimal effort. It functions as the default mode of thinking and is frequently utilized in decision-making processes. System 1 enables quick and effortless responses without conscious deliberation. In contrast, the second system, referred to as System 2, involves deliberate initiation. It operates at a slower pace and demands significantly greater cognitive resources compared to System 1. System 2 is activated when conscious effort and careful thinking are required to make decisions. Just as the ELM distinguishes between the central route and peripheral route, Kahneman's two systems of thinking offer insights into how individuals navigate decision-making processes.

---

[3]This perspective is also supported by other models, such as Chaiken's (1980) heuristic-systematic model of information processing, which proposes two routes of information processing: the systematic route (corresponding to the ELM's central route) and the heuristic route (corresponding to the ELM's peripheral route).

System 1 corresponds to the peripheral route, where automatic and intuitive processing predominates, while System 2 aligns with the central route, involving conscious and effortful cognitive processing.

In order to persuade customers to purchase its products and brands, the company needs to shape the attitudes of its customers by delivering specific messages. The models discussed in this section demonstrate that marketing communication can achieve persuasion in two distinct ways: either by prompting customers to thoroughly process key elements within the message itself, or by eliciting superficial responses to peripheral elements accompanying the message. Generally, recipients tend to avoid investing significant effort in message process-ing, leading persuasion to occur primarily through peripheral message elements.

The notion that marketing communication can operate through this peripheral route complements the hierarchy of effects models, which assume that customers allocate cogni-tive resources and time to message processing. However, a limitation of the ELM is its focus on demonstrating how marketing communication leads to persuasion without fully address-ing its impact on the intermediate variables outlined in the hierarchy of effects models.

In summary, the hierarchy of effects models and the ELM are compatible and mutually beneficial. They are compatible because both types of models illustrate how attitudes towards a product or brand can be influenced. They complement each other as the hierarchy of effects models specify multiple communication objectives omitted by the ELM, while the ELM emphasizes that marketing communication can be effective even when message recip-ients exhibit limited cognitive engagement. However, it's important to note that both model categories have limitations in explaining the process of purchase.

The ELM primarily focuses on persuasion, whereas the hierarchy of effects models do not exten-sively elaborate on the transition from attitude to purchase. To gain a comprehensive understanding of how attitudes influence purchase and adoption, as well as the consequences of attitudes on information processing during these stages, we will now delve into a related concept: expectations.

Attitudes and Expectations

Put simply, attitude theories propose that a person's attitude towards an object is influenced by their expectations and evaluation of the object's attributes. Consequently, behaviour, such as purchasing a product or brand, is a result of the expectations individuals hold for the object.[4] Simultaneously, these expectations serve as a standard or reference frame that influ-ences how the usage experience is perceived. When a company employs marketing communication to generate high expectations for a brand or product, it is crucial for these expectations to align with the customers' experience when they begin using the product or brand. Failure to meet these expectations can lead to customer dissatisfaction, discontinued purchases and negative word of mouth.

---

[4]This relationship between attitude and behaviour is referred to as the Theory of Reasoned Action (TRA) and the Theory of Planned Behaviour (TPB). See Fishbein & Ajzen (1975); Ajzen & Fishbein (1980); Ajzen (1985).

According to the adaptation-level theory, a stimulus, such as a product attribute, is always perceived in relation to an adapted standard and not in isolation. For instance, if a pair of running shoes is *expected* to have excellent cushioning, it is likely to also be *perceived* as having excellent cushioning. Thus, the evaluation of the product, once it is tested, will closely align with the consumer's attitude. As the customer adopts the product, their perception of an attribute will increasingly rely on their own experiences. However, even after experiencing the value proposition, the initial expectation continues to exist. It becomes adjusted based on the customer's own experiences and serves as an adapted standard against which the value proposition is evaluated (Oliver, 1980). Throughout the hierarchy of effects, the expectation evolves as customers progress. During the awareness stage, limited information is available, and expectations are malleable and easily influenced. As customers reach the interest stage, expectations become more well-founded and defined. After purchase and during adoption, expectations are primarily shaped by personal experiences and gradually become less significant as experience becomes the primary reference point.

Having high expectations increases the likelihood of customers choosing a product, and these expectations also shape the customers' own experience of the value proposition in a positive direction during trial and adoption. The company can play a role in creating these expectations among customers through its marketing communication efforts.

How Marketing Communication Works – an Integrated Model

As discussed earlier, the combination of hierarchy of effects models and the ELM offers several advantages that make them complementary, and these advantages can be integrated into a single model. A key insight from hierarchy of effects models is that marketing communication has long-term effects beyond short-term sales increases. Various responses can be elicited from target group members, all of which are vital for the long-term success of the company's products and brands. These responses may not always follow a fixed sequence and can occur independently of each other. Therefore, it is necessary to have a flexible model that accommodates variations in the order and number of responses.

From the ELM and similar models, we have gained an understanding that the target group often lacks motivation to process a message and, as a result, does not allocate much mental capacity to it. Attitude formation and persuasion can occur through two routes: a peripheral route, where the message is superficially processed, and a central route, where message processing is more elaborate. Expectations, which form the cognitive component of attitudes, are influenced both before and after product trial. Before the trial, marketing communication plays a significant role in shaping attitudes, while personal experience becomes the primary influencer after the trial and during adaptation. Figure 4.3 illustrates this integrated model, capturing the interplay between marketing communication, attitude formation and expectations.

The integrated model depicted in Figure 4.3 encompasses four distinct routes of message processing that can lead to persuasion and influence behaviour. The specific route taken depends on the situation at hand. Even for the same product and message, two customers in different contexts may process the information differently. One customer may be rushing to

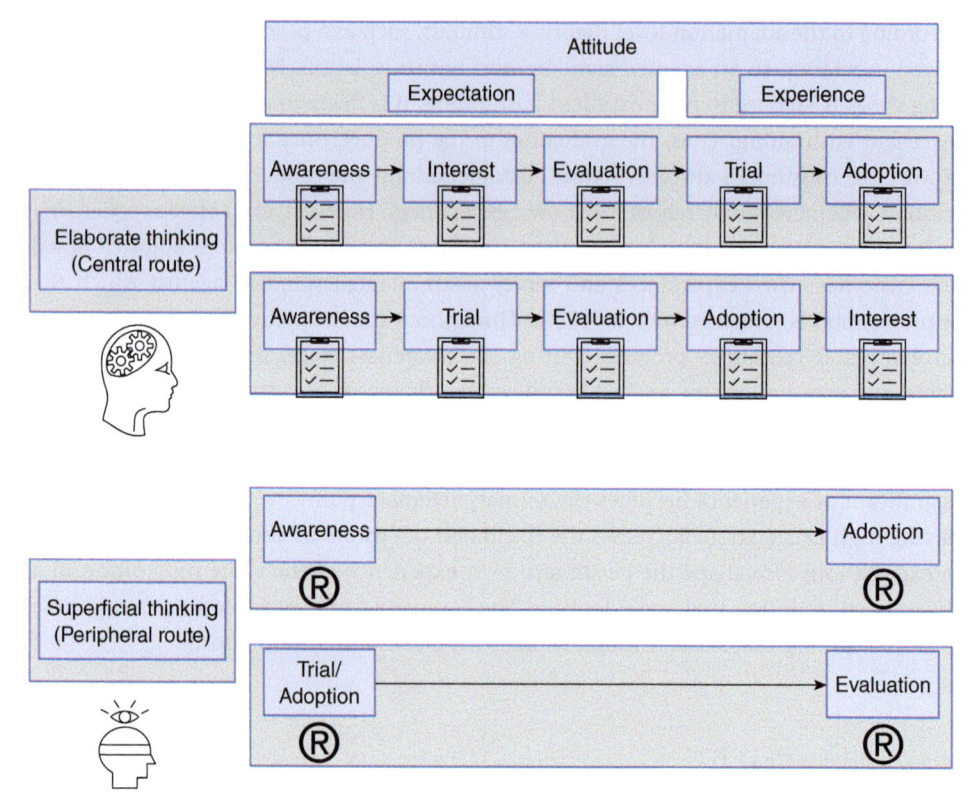

Figure 4.3　An integrated overview of how marketing communication works. Message processing – a function of the target group's cognitive effort, expectations, experience, response stage and response order. The 'shopping list' symbolizes that the target group processes the message's central element and R symbolizes that the target group processes more peripheral elements

catch a bus on her way home from work, while the other customer may be on vacation with more time and the opportunity to consider her family's opinion.

The chosen route of message processing can also be influenced by the customer's individual factors, such as product expertise, position in the response hierarchy (including prior experience with the product), personality, lifestyle, life situation, and more. For example, a customer with low product expertise or less familiarity with a yoga mat might take a peripheral route of message processing. This customer may rely on peripheral cues, such as the brand name or endorsements from influencers, to form their attitude towards the product.

Additionally, the nature of the product itself may typically demand a specific route of processing (for example, expensive products may require a more thorough evaluation of product attributes and competitor comparisons compared to cheaper products). However, it's important to note that the product itself doesn't inherently dictate a specific processing route.

Instead, the situation can be seen as a combination of the context (immediate surroundings), the individual customer and the product itself.

These diverse situations suggest the presence of sub-segments within the target group that should be communicated to in different ways. To illustrate the integrated model, let's consider a few case study examples.

Case Study 4.1

Car Purchase (route 1)

Let's consider a car purchase situation. One day, Mia discovers that she needs to replace her current car. Her children have been constantly talking about the importance of sustainability, and Mia has grown tired of hearing about it. Although she has limited knowledge about electric cars, she has come across various advertisements and social media posts showcasing Volkswagen's ID.3 and ID.4 models. This exposure, combined with her children's emphasis on sustainability, piques Mia's interest in the largest model, the ID.4, as it seems suitable for her family's needs.

Motivated by this interest, Mia visits Volkswagen's website to gather more information. As she explores the details, she discovers exciting features such as augmented reality in the windshield and a panoramic roof. She also learns that the car's battery capacity is satisfactory, and she finds its design quite appealing. Mia takes the time to compare the ID.4 with similar-sized cars from other brands. After careful consideration and evaluation, Mia forms a highly positive attitude towards the ID.4, viewing it as an excellent car choice.

Simultaneously, Mia begins to develop certain expectations. She expects the car to be enjoyable to drive, provide a sense of safety and satisfy her children's preferences. That evening, while scrolling through her Facebook feed, Mia comes across another advertisement for the ID.4, shared by an old schoolmate. Intrigued, she clicks on the ad, which leads her to a dealership's website. Without hesitation, she schedules a test drive.

Two days later, Mia visits the dealership and experiences the car first-hand. To her delight, it lives up to her expectations. Upon returning home, she immediately grabs one of her children's tablets and navigates to the dealer's website. There, she customizes her order by selecting the desired colour, accessories and extra features. Finally, Mia confidently clicks on 'order'.

A month later, Mia receives a call from the salesperson she met during the test drive, informing her that she can now complete the payment and pick up her new car. In the following months, Mia thoroughly enjoys driving the car, familiarizes herself with nearby charging stations and learns to optimize her driving style to maximize battery life. She even contemplates, 'I will keep this car for a long time, and my next one will also be a Volkswagen'.

Case Study 4.2

Car Purchase (route 2)

Let's now consider another car purchase example. Ali finds himself sitting in a ski lift with a colleague who incessantly talks about cars. The colleague shares that he recently ordered an ID.4 online without even trying it out beforehand. Intrigued by this, Ali realizes that he lives near a dealership and decides to visit it on his way home from the gym the following week. At the dealership, Ali expresses his interest and enquires about how to arrange a test drive. To his surprise, the salesperson informs him that they currently have a car available for immediate testing.

Excited by the opportunity, Ali hops into the car and embarks on a half-hour test drive. The experience is exhilarating, and Ali discovers a multitude of impressive features. It becomes evident to him that this car is among the best he has ever driven. When Ali returns from the test drive, the salesperson informs him about a special offer that will expire in a couple of weeks. The offer includes additional equipment and free service for three years if he places an order now. Furthermore, the salesperson assures Ali that he can cancel the order within the two-week period if he has any regrets.

Considering his colleague's experience of ordering the car without a test drive, and given the reputable brand and dealership, Ali contemplates, 'If he can do it, why can't I?'. Feeling confident, Ali makes the decision to order the car right then and there. In the following days, Ali reflects more on the car's attributes and realizes that its size and comfort are perfectly suited for his family. Additionally, he acknowledges that it has been several years since his last car purchase and recognizes the environmental benefits of owning an electric car.

As time goes on, Ali's attitude towards the car becomes exceedingly positive. He does not experience any regrets about the purchase, and if the car lives up to its performance during longer trips with greater battery demands, Ali expects it to satisfy him for a long time. When he finally receives the car a month later, he and his family extensively utilize it, solidifying Ali's belief that it was a fantastic purchase. Moreover, as he continues using the car, his interest in electric cars deepens. He becomes curious about their range, new battery technologies, and other related aspects.

Case Study 4.3

Coffee Shop (route 3)

Let's consider another type of product and situation: purchasing coffee. Sarah has recently relocated to the city to pursue her studies. Near her bus stop, she notices two coffee shops: one is a well-known Starbucks, while the other bears a name unfamiliar to her. Coming from a small village without a Starbucks, Sarah has never had the opportunity to taste her favourite coffee, a flat white, from this renowned chain. Given Starbucks' global presence and its popularity, Sarah holds high expectations for the quality of their coffee beverages. Additionally, she generally feels more positive towards things she is familiar with rather than the unknown. Taking these factors into account, Sarah decides to choose Starbucks.

To her delight, the coffee drink at Starbucks exceeds her expectations – it is truly delicious. From that day on, as she commutes to the university, Sarah makes it a routine to stop by Starbucks and indulge in their coffee.

Case Study 4.4

Coffee Shop (route 4)

Now let's explore another coffee-shop scenario involving Victor. After spending several years living in various European cities, where he had the opportunity to visit numerous coffee shops, Victor returns to his hometown in Iceland. During one of his leisurely walks, he stumbles upon a coffee shop he has never heard of before – BrentCoffee. Intrigued, Victor decides to give it a try and orders an espresso. To his delight, the espresso at BrentCoffee surpasses his expectations, leaving a lasting impression on him.

Victor's positive experience with BrentCoffee leads to a strong inclination towards the coffee shop. He expects that future visits will provide equally enjoyable coffee experiences. As a result, Victor incorporates a stop at BrentCoffee into his regular walks, ensuring that he can continue savouring the exceptional espresso they serve. Over the following weeks and months, Victor often reflects on the quality of the espresso at BrentCoffee compared to the ones he had across various European cities. Eventually, he concludes that it ranks among the top five espressos he has ever tasted.

As demonstrated by the case study examples, the message conveyed to the target group ('buy an electric car', 'try our coffee') plays a significant role in shaping attitudes and creating expectations. At each stage of the hierarchy, customers respond to the message differently based on their motivation, ability and opportunity to process it, whether through the central or peripheral route.

When the target group is highly motivated to evaluate the message, they will consider core attributes such as battery capacity, comfort and spaciousness. Conversely, if group members lack motivation, they may rely on superficial cues like the reputation of a brand, such as Starbucks being world famous. Additionally, customers will vary in the sequence and number of response steps they undertake when engaging with the message.

The existence of different routes within the target group implies that the company needs to tailor its message to various subgroups. Therefore, many companies use a combination of customer journey and personas (i.e. stereotypical customer type) to develop marketing communication strategies to different customer segments and situations. While Figure 4.3 depicts four possible routes, it is important to acknowledge that alternative routes with fewer or more responses, as well as different response orders, can also be envisioned.

The integrated model presented here bears resemblance to the customer decision journey discussed in Chapter 3. Both models propose that customers go through various stages in a sequential order when making a purchase. Some of these stages also exhibit similarities between the two models, such as evaluation.

One distinction between the models lies in the focus of the decision journey. The decision journey centres around the customer's thoughts and actions regarding the purchase of products and brands, while the integrated communication model pertains to the customer's processing and responses to marketing communications related to these products and brands. Since purchasing products involves not only processing marketing communication but also other activities, such as evaluating competing brands, we can conclude that the decision journey encompasses a broader scope than the integrated marketing communication model.

Another difference is that in the decision journey, the customer is typically an active agent. They identify a purchase problem and actively seek information to address it. In contrast, the communication model does not assume such proactive initiatives on the part of the customer. The customer processes and responds to a given message when and if they come across it, with varying levels of effort. As a result, there is a possibility in the communication model that the customer may never encounter the message if it is not part of their problem recognition or information search. Nonetheless, the communicated product can still be chosen indirectly if the customer finds it worthwhile to compare it to another product for which they have seen an advertisement. Depending on the relative utilities of the two products, the communicated but unnoticed product may end up being selected as the preferred alternative.

EFFECTIVE MARKETING COMMUNICATION

Effective marketing communication plays a pivotal role in successful marketing management. As previously mentioned, the impact of investing in marketing communication on customer behaviour is multifaceted and requires meticulous planning. In the following section, we will outline the steps involved in this planning process, as depicted in Figure 4.4.

Goal and Target Group

The significance of marketing communication within the broader marketing strategy is to define its range and subsequently establish the goals to be accomplished through investments in this area. As discussed in Chapters 5, 6 and 7, marketing communication plays a pivotal role in each of these domains. For instance, marketing communication is instrumental in

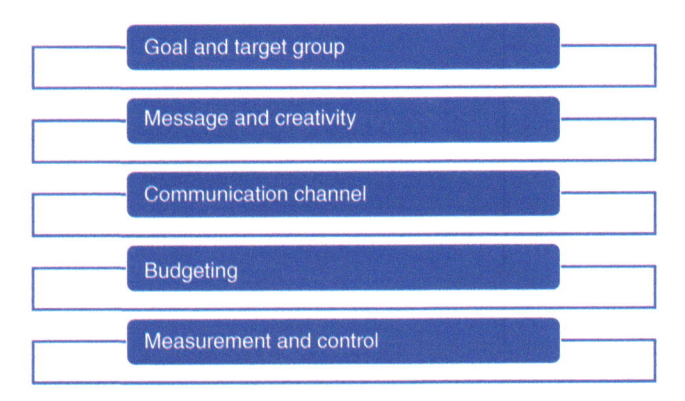

Figure 4.4   Steps in developing effective marketing communication

acquiring new customers by effectively reaching and engaging with them. It also plays a crucial role in communicating the value propositions associated with various product categories. Moreover, marketing communication is essential in cultivating brand familiarity and shaping brand associations. Consequently, a company typically sets multiple goals for its marketing communication investments, necessitating the coordination of various marketing communication plans.

The customer base is not uniform, and an essential part of the planning process involves identifying specific groups within this diversity. These groups are referred to as target groups, and the goal is to create a set of messages and communication channels that effectively reach these specific targets. For instance, using the response hierarchy illustrated in Figure 4.3, target groups can be established to generate awareness, interest, positive evaluation, trial and adoption.

If a coffee bar focuses on the target group 'people commuting to work', it should design a message that highlights product features or other attributes that cater to the needs of this group, such as prepayment and minimizing wait times, rather than focusing on organic beans or participating in barista competitions. Simultaneously, customers within this target group will vary in their expectations and attitudes. In other words, different target groups correspond to different stages in the response hierarchy. Some customers may have just started a new job and are unfamiliar with the coffee shop and its offerings, while others might be highly interested but struggle with punctuality and have yet to find time for a visit. There are also those who have tried the coffee once and are considering whether to become regulars, as well as loyal customers who have been visiting for years. These distinct groups represent different target audiences and should receive the message of 'minimal queuing', for example, in slightly different ways. The awareness group needs to be enticed to develop an interest, which can be achieved by communicating the convenience of enjoying coffee on their propane bus, e-scooter, or highlighting the time and money saved by avoiding long queues. For target group members who have already visited the café, a message like 'Wasn't the coffee even better than expected?' would be more suitable.

Message

The objective of communication is to convert the desired communication goal into a message that can be effectively conveyed to the target group. Therefore, the company needs to determine what it wants to communicate, which is known as a message strategy. A message strategy represents the company's strongest claim about its value proposition. For example, a message strategy could be, 'We provide the most technologically advanced heart rate monitor available in the market'.

Creating a persuasive message requires the company to empathize with the target group. The message should resonate with customers and address their specific needs. However, customers may not perceive the product in the same way as the company due to the 'developer's curse'. While the company may focus on product features, technology and services, customers view these aspects through their own needs and perspectives. Therefore, the company must adopt a customer-centric approach to design the message, ensuring it communicates the value proposition in a way that satisfies the customers' perceived needs.

Different customers may have varied requirements for the product. Some may prioritize the practical need for warm winter underwear, while others seek comfortable and non-itchy options for hedonic reasons. There could also be customers who see the underwear as a symbol of their commitment to intense workouts. Thus, the company must consider these diverse customer needs when crafting the message.

Additionally, the company should account for other factors that can influence how customers perceive the message. Company characteristics, such as reputation or past incidents, can impact on the message's reception. Customers may also have preconceived ideas that shape their interpretation of the message. Moreover, customers have varying abilities and opportunities to process the message effectively.

Furthermore, the message exists within a context filled with 'noise'. This context comprises competitors' messages and other everyday life information that customers encounter. If the company's message revolves around being the provider of the 'most comfortable underwear', they can expect similar messages from competitors. Even if the company were the only one with such a message, numerous other commercial and non-commercial messages would still vie for customers' attention, potentially diverting their focus in different directions.

In summary, effective communication involves developing a message strategy that aligns with customer needs and perceptions. It requires considering company characteristics, managing contextual noise, and ensuring a clear and focused message without overwhelming customers with multiple sub-messages.

Creativity and Creative Appeals

In marketing communication, creativity plays a crucial role (MacInnis & Park, 1991). By incorporating creative elements into marketing communications, the company can boost the recipient's motivation, ability and opportunity to effectively process the intended message. The image provided below showcases an instance of creativity in marketing communication for Colgate toothpaste. Can you identify the creative element in this image?

Image 4.1 Creativity in toothpaste advertising

Message creativity refers to how the company presents the intended message. The message itself represents what the company wants to convey. For instance, the same message can be delivered in a factual and informative manner, or it can be infused with humour and entertainment. When asked about creativity, individuals may provide various definitions. Some may describe it as being innovative, thinking outside the box, finding new paths to the goal, breaking conventions, or doing the unexpected.

Given these definitions, creativity can be viewed in terms of *analogical reasoning*. In developing creative advertising, creativity refers to the use of analogies or comparisons to draw connections between two unrelated concepts or ideas. It involves finding similarities between the features, benefits or qualities of one object or event and applying them to another unrelated object or event. This technique helps create unique and unexpected associations.

The academic literature echoes these sentiments and the notion of analogical reasoning, while adding further nuances.

According to the literature, the creativity of marketing communication is determined by two key factors: divergence and relevance (Smith et al., 2007, 2008). Divergence pertains to whether the communication is original, different and uncommon. It aligns with concepts like being innovative, thinking outside the box and drawing analogies. On the other hand, relevance focuses on whether the communication is personally meaningful, useful or valuable to the message recipient. In other words, it addresses whether the communication holds personal significance for the recipient.

For a creative marketing communication element to effectively persuade customers, it must possess both originality and relevance. It should not only be unique and different but also resonate with the customers' needs and interests. By combining these aspects, companies can create persuasive marketing communications that capture the attention and engagement of their target audience.

The concept of divergence encompasses five sub-dimensions:

Originality: Communication that incorporates elements that are uncommon, surprising or deviate from the expected and commonplace.

Flexibility: Communication that presents different ideas or shifts perspectives, allowing for alternative viewpoints.

Elaboration: Communication that includes unexpected details or expands upon and refines basic ideas, making them more intricate, complex or sophisticated.

Synthesis: Communication that combines, connects or merges typically unrelated objects or ideas, creating new and unique associations.

Artistic value: Communication that features artistic verbal expressions or visually appealing colours and shapes.

The relevance concept consists of two sub-dimensions:

Ad-to-consumer relevance: The marketing communication incorporates elements that are important or useful for the customers, addressing their specific needs or interests.

Brand-to-consumer relevance: The brand being communicated possesses elements that are relevant or useful to customers, offering value and meeting their expectations (Smith et al., 2008).

A study has highlighted the significance of creativity across all stages of the response hierarchy (Smith et al., 2008). It also revealed an interaction effect between divergence and relevance on customers' responses. This implies that marketing communication that is solely creative in terms of divergent elements has a lesser impact compared to communication that incorporates both divergent and relevant elements. The study identified two mechanisms that explain how divergent marketing communication influences customers' information processing: the contrast effect and the customers' need for certainty (Smith & Yang, 2004).

The contrast effect: Divergent marketing communication stands out amidst the overall communication in the surrounding environment. As humans, we are sensitive to changes or contrasts in our environment rather than to monotonous and unchanging stimuli. For instance, when scrolling through a Facebook feed, numerous colourful ads may go unnoticed, but a black and white ad is more likely to grab attention. Our brain directs cognitive resources towards stimuli that stand out, facilitating further processing. This phenomenon is referred to as the contrast effect. By incorporating sufficiently divergent elements, marketing communication can create a response in customers due to this contrast.

The need for certainty: Divergent elements in marketing communication also increase the motivation to process the message. Divergent elements are often unusual and may carry a sense of ambiguity. As humans, we have a fundamental need for certainty. Consequently, we direct cognitive resources towards divergent marketing communication in order to gain certainty about its meaning. For example, you may have paid attention to and utilized cognitive resources on advertisements featuring the logo of the UK fashion retailer French Connection (FCUK).

By understanding these mechanisms, marketers can leverage divergent elements in their marketing communication to capture attention, engage customers and address their need for certainty, thus enhancing the effectiveness of their messaging.

Our inherent need for certainty implies that divergent communication increases the likelihood of message processing through the central route, as compared to non-divergent communication. If a company desires central processing of not just the advertisement but also the brand itself and intends to target a specific stage in the response hierarchy, the design of divergent elements becomes crucial. For instance, if the company aims to influence brand strength or product preference, the divergent elements should be carefully crafted to highlight the unique attributes of the product. Case Study 4.5 below illustrates how divergency highlights a core attribute.

Case Study 4.5

Blåkläder

Blåkläder, a work clothing brand, provides an example of divergent communication that effectively emphasizes the durability of its clothes through humorous comparisons with various other objects. In their radio commercials, they juxtapose Blåkläder with a robot mower, beer, bitcoin and shopping list to underscore the physical toughness of their clothing. As an example, when comparing Blåkläder to a shopping list, the commercial may sound like this:

> If Blåkläder was a shopping list, it would not be a pink sticky note reading 'milk and bread and kisses and hugs'. Nah! That shopping list would be a giant mafia-type debt collector who followed you around the store with a raging pit bull on a leash and shouted the items into your ear with a megaphone. If you picked any diet products, you would have to deal with the pit bull. And, if you or even dared to look in the direction of the gluten-free shelf, you'd lose your kneecaps faster than you could say wholemeal pancakes.
>
> (Blåkläder – the toughest workwear on the market)

If customers lack the motivation, ability or opportunity to process a message centrally, or if the divergent elements fail to increase motivation, they can still be processed through the peripheral route. In these cases, persuasion can occur through the transfer of feelings from the divergent elements. For instance, customers' fascination with an advertisement itself can be transferred to a positive attitude towards the product being promoted. The original and

(Continued)

humorous ads from Blåkläder has the ability to put us in a good mood, even if we don't consciously consider key product attributes like durability, functionality and comfort.

When communication is both original and personally relevant to the customer, it increases the customer's motivation to process the message, thereby enhancing the likelihood of central processing. Elements that are both novel and relevant provide customers with a fresh perspective (divergence) on how to approach things, which is also beneficial and valuable to them personally (relevance). This prompts a more thoughtful consideration of the message (Smith & Yang, 2004; Smith et al., 2008).

Relevance can be established by linking the brand to a situation that customers have personal knowledge of. In the example of Blåkläder, making an analogy to outdoor activities or hunting, rather than a shopping list, can be more relevant for certain customer segments because they can identify with it. For these segments, these new associations can result in a more active processing of the message than when Blåkläder is compared to a shopping list, which may be less relevant to them.

Creative elements can also enhance the recipient's ability to process the message. Customers are likely to be more receptive to repeated exposure to creative marketing communication compared to non-creative communication, as novel elements take longer to become tiresome. When customers are repeatedly exposed to the same old elements, they may lose motivation to process the message (wear out effect) or even become irritated, leading to a dislike of the communication (Smith & Yang, 2004; Smith et al., 2008).

This acceptance of creativity enables the company to expose customers to the same communication multiple times without it becoming stale. By repeating the communication, the time span during which customers are exposed to the message increases, providing them with more opportunities to process it.

When designing creative communication, the company has various appeals to choose from. Going back to the teachings of the Greek philosopher Aristotle and his work on rhetoric (see Aristotle, 2010), we find three main categories of rhetorical appeals: logos, pathos and ethos. In this context, we can refer to them as rational appeals (logos), emotional appeals (pathos) and source effects (ethos). Rational appeals primarily elicit a cognitive response, emotional appeals are more effective in evoking emotional responses, while source effects can elicit both types of responses.

Rational Appeals

Rational appeals are persuasive techniques that rely on empirical facts, logic, arguments or reasoning. They are typically informative in nature and emphasize the attributes of products and the benefits they offer to customers. A meta-study conducted across multiple countries examined the information content of advertisements and found that the most commonly used information includes product performance, availability, components, price, quality, special offers, guarantee, packaging and taste, among other factors (Abernethy & Franke, 1996).

Product demonstration: Product demonstration is a rational appeal that involves showcasing a product's appearance, features, functions, usability and the benefits it provides to customers. By demonstrating a product, the company can address customers' uncertainties and alleviate any anxiety they may have about using the product incorrectly. An example of this can be seen in a Facebook video by Tupperware, a home products brand, where they effectively showcase their food storage boxes in various sizes, colours and designs. The video demonstrates that the products are user-friendly, easy to clean and suitable for storing a wide range of food items, thereby highlighting their usefulness and versatility.

Problem solving: This type of appeal effectively demonstrates how a product can address and solve the customer's problem. A common example is that of the before-and-after advertisements for wrinkle cream, which often feature a split face. One side of the face displays wrinkles and an aged appearance, representing the condition before the cream is applied. In contrast, the other side of the face appears youthful and smooth, showcasing the desired outcome after using the cream. This visual representation effectively communicates the product's ability to transform and improve the customer's skin, emphasizing the positive results it can achieve.

Testimonials: When customers encounter a new or unfamiliar product or brand, they often seek validation and assurance regarding its quality. Testimonials play a crucial role in meeting this need by providing statements or recommendations from ordinary individuals or experts. For instance, when a new brand is endorsed as superior to well-established brands, it serves as a testimony. The use of an ordinary person as a reference point creates relatability for the customer, making the advertising more relevant. An everyday consumer showcasing their shiny white teeth serves as a credible witness, reinforcing the effectiveness of the toothpaste and its ability to deliver the desired results.

Comparison: Comparative marketing communication involves contrasting a brand with a competitor, highlighting the communicated brand's superiority over the competitor, particularly in terms of specific attributes. This comparison can take a direct or indirect approach. For instance, an advertisement stating that the brand emerged as the 'best in test' makes a direct comparison, while an advertisement indicating that the brand is the sole organically produced product in its category employs an indirect comparison. Comparative advertising has been shown to elicit higher levels of cognitive activity in recipients compared to non-comparative advertising, indicating a greater likelihood of processing the message through a central route (Chattopadhyay, 1998).

Emotional Appeals

Emotional appeals aim to evoke consumers' emotions as a means of effectively conveying the message to the target audience. These appeals often rely on non-verbal elements such as images, videos, sound and lighting, and may even incorporate sensory experiences like smell or taste.

Humour: Humour is employed to elicit laughter, create a positive mood or generate a sense of well-being among customers. It is a commonly utilized appeal in marketing communication, with some estimates suggesting that humour is present in up to half of all advertisements (Beard, 2005). Humour has the ability to capture attention, making humorous communication more likely to be processed further and potentially influencing persuasion and purchase decisions. One of the reasons why humour can impact on persuasion and purchase is its memorability (Cline & Kellaris, 2007). Assuming that the customer accepts or enjoys the humour, it tends to put them in a positive mood. Humans naturally associate experiences with the mood they are in during those experiences. Consequently, when they encounter a similar mood later on, those associated experiences, including the advertised brand, come to mind (Bower et al. 1981). If this mood arises during a decision-making situation, the advertised brand is likely to be considered. However, one drawback of humour is that it can dominate attention, potentially overshadowing the message itself and hindering brand recall. An example of humour in advertising is an ad for the French coffee brand Grand'Mère, where a son reveals to his mother that she is going to be a grandmother by pointing to the brand logo while they share a cup of coffee.

Fear: Fear appeals are designed to instil a sense of fear by presenting a threat. The underlying assumption is that a threat to the customer's well-being will generate fear, leading them to purchase the advertised brand. For a fear appeal to be effective, the brand must offer a clear solution to address the identified threat. The threat can range from something as minor as bad breath, which can be eliminated by using the promoted chewing gum, to more serious concerns such as the risk of contracting a life-threatening disease without using sunscreen. Certain threats, known as drives, are so significant that they motivate us to take actions that ensure our survival and reproduction, such as hunger, thirst and fear of death (Hovland et al., 1953). These types of threats can be highly persuasive.

Threats can extend beyond physical risks and encompass social or financial aspects as well. For example, the fear of becoming an outdated employee without executive education represents a social threat, while the risk of a poor retirement due to insufficient pension savings represents a financial threat. Fear appeals are commonly employed by public authorities in campaigns aimed at influencing attitudes and behaviours, such as discouraging drinking in front of children, promoting adherence to speed limits, preventing environmental pollution or advocating for condom use.

An example of a fear appeal can be seen in a print advertisement by WWF, featuring a depiction of a mutant human fish accompanied by the statement 'stop climate change before it changes you'. This ad is likely to evoke fear regarding the consequences of human-induced climate change and prompt individuals to reflect on how they can modify their behaviour to prevent such outcomes.

Eroticism: Erotic appeals utilize elements such as nudity, provocatively dressed individuals, seductive expressions or movements, and sexual suggestions to capture attention (Belch et al., 1987). An example of this is a Super Bowl advertisement by the fast-food chain Carl's Jr., featuring model Kate Upton straddling in the back seat of a car at a drive-in movie theatre while enjoying a cheeseburger from Carl's Jr. Another instance of an erotic appeal is actor and former football player Isaiah Mustafa posing shirtless and addressing female customers, proclaiming that although their men do not look like him, they can smell like him if they switch to Old Spice body wash.

The primary effect of eroticism in advertising is attention-grabbing. For an appeal to qualify as erotic, it must elicit an erotic response (Reichert & Ramirez, 2000). Research has indicated that in addition to attracting attention, erotic appeals evoke arousal. However, studies have also revealed that erotic appeals generate fewer cognitive thoughts and less thorough message processing compared to non-erotic appeals (Reichert et al., 2001). Therefore, it appears that erotic appeals do not primarily operate through cognition and deep thinking but rather through emotions and a peripheral route to persuasion. Similar to humour, erotic appeals can divert attention from the brand (Wirtz et al., 2018). Nonetheless, eroticism is not inherently a peripheral element and can be processed through the central route if it directly relates to the product (Kahle & Homer, 1985), as seen in various beauty product advertisements.

It is worth noting that excessive and irrelevant erotic appeals are often perceived negatively. Advertisements like the cheeseburger commercial from Carl's Jr. can be seen as examples of erotic appeals with little or no relevance to the product being advertised. On the other hand, the use of the same model posing on the beach wearing sandals in an advertisement for the shoe brand Sam Edelman can be considered relevant. Research has identified a gender difference in the acceptance of erotic appeals, with women responding negatively to ads and brands when the erotic appeal lacks relevance, while men tend to have a relatively positive response regardless of relevance (Putrevu, 2008).

Depending on their design, erotic appeals may also conflict with the United Nations' sustainability goals of promoting 'equality between the sexes'.

Music: Music used in marketing communication can encompass pre-existing or specially created tunes, songs, voices, sound logos (jingles) and product-related sounds (such as the sound of crunching chips). One example of a sound logo is McDonald's iconic 'I'm lovin' it', recorded by Justin Timberlake. Music is a widely employed appeal in marketing communication, with a study of TV commercials in the United States revealing that over 80% of them incorporated music (Allan, 2008). Music is typically considered a peripheral element in marketing communication, as it influences our emotions and, consequently, our attitudes (i.e. liking) towards the communication itself, such as the advertisement. These attitudes can then transfer to attitudes towards the brand, contributing to persuasion and purchase decisions (Stout & Leckenby, 1988). Music can also influence purchasing behaviour in another way. It functions as a form of information that creates a specific mood and often evokes strong, positive attitudes and associated emotions in individuals. Initially, the music may not have an explicit connection to any brand. However, through repeated pairing of a particular piece of music with a specific brand in marketing communication, customers develop associations between the music and the brand in their memory. Once this music–brand link is established, the emotions associated with the music can elicit positive feelings when customers consider the brand in a decision-making situation, even in the absence of the music itself (Gorn, 1982; Knoeferle & Spence, 2021).

Research has indicated that music has the greatest impact on attitudes towards the brand when customers are expected to have little involvement or investment in the decision (MacInnis & Park, 1991).

Sensory appeals: In recent times, marketers have increasingly focused on how marketing communication can engage multiple senses – hearing, smell, taste, sight and touch – and how these interactions can influence customers' responses to the communication (Knoeferle & Spence, 2021). An interesting example is Dunkin' Donuts, which implemented an appealing coffee aroma that was released aboard buses in Seoul, South Korea, every time Dunkin' Donuts' audio logo played on the buses' radio (Garber, 2012).

Research has demonstrated that products that are communicated through both visual and auditory channels are more easily and quickly recognized by customers in subsequent encounters, such as when they see the products on store shelves, compared to products that are only presented visually (Knoeferle & Spence, 2021). This enhanced recognition could be attributed to the activation of a greater number of brain regions when multiple senses are engaged. A study revealed that marketing communication can shape customers' expectations, which, in turn, influence their sensory perception of food products. Customers who were exposed to advertisements for chewing gum, popcorn and crisps that mentioned multiple senses (e.g. taste, smell, and texture) reported that these products tasted better compared with customers who saw advertisements that only mentioned taste. The reason behind this phenomenon is that the sense of taste involves all five of our senses, and when more senses are mentioned, it evokes more thoughts and expectations related to taste in customers' memory. Assuming these thoughts and expectations are positive, communication that highlights more senses can trigger a greater number of positive thoughts, potentially influencing the perceived taste of the products, compared with advertisements that mention fewer senses (Elder & Krishna, 2010).

Warmness: Warmth can be described as a gentle, positive and transient sensation that is closely associated with feelings of love, family or friendship. It generates a mild sense of excitement, which is more moderate compared with emotions like fear (Aaker et al., 1986). An example of a warmth appeal is Budweiser's 'Puppy Love' commercial created for the Super Bowl. This advertisement tells a heart-warming story about the strong bond between a puppy and a horse on a farm. When the puppy is taken away, the horse and his horse friends race to stop the car and bring the puppy back to the farm. The ad concludes with the puppy and the horse playing together, emphasizing their friendship as 'best buds' (https://adage.com/videos/budweiser-puppy-love/218).

Warmth elicits physiological responses in individuals. One study demonstrated that advertisements employing warmth appeals, including one from McDonald's, temporarily increased participants' skin conductance, indicating heightened emotional arousal (Aaker et al., 1986). Moreover, warmth was found to foster a positive attitude towards the advertisement and increase the likelihood of purchasing the brand. Presumably, warmth functions as a peripheral element that engenders a favourable response to the advertisement, which then transfers to the attitude towards the brand.

However, companies should exercise caution when employing warmth appeals. According to research in social psychology, humans have an inherent tendency to categorize both people and brands as either warm or competent (Fiske et al., 2002; Peter & Ponzi, 2018). Warmth and competence seem to be inversely related, meaning that if a brand is perceived as warm, it is often seen as less competent, and vice versa.

Nostalgia: The term 'nostalgia' has its roots in the Greek language, where it signifies a 'homecoming' (Persvold, 2018). In contemporary usage, nostalgia refers to a yearning or longing for the past, whether it be a specific period in one's personal life, such as childhood, or a broader sense of past times, like the 1980s. Within the realm of marketing, nostalgia is defined as a fondness for objects or experiences that were more prevalent during one's younger years (Holbrook, 1993). A memorable scene from the *Mad Men* TV series exemplifies the relevance of nostalgia to marketing communication. Ad executive Don Draper delivers a ground-breaking pitch for the Kodak Carousel, a slide projector, in a profoundly emotional and unforgettable manner. Utilizing the power of the Carousel, Don takes the audience of Kodak executives on an evocative journey by sharing a carefully curated collection of nostalgic photographs from his own childhood and personal experiences. Don's pitch communicates the significance of emotional connections, the value of treasured memories and the essence of capturing life's little moments. He effectively conveys that the Carousel rises above mere technological functionality, instead serving as a vessel that captures cherished memories and allows for a retreat into the embrace of nostalgia (https://www.youtube.com/watch?v=suRD-UFpsHus).

An instance of employing nostalgic appeal can be observed in some of Adidas shoe and other collection items, with retro designs similar to the original items from the previous century (https://unsplash.com/photos/red-and-white-adidas-low-top-sneakers-7irKimCkk6g).

According to a study, the inclusion of nostalgic elements in advertising was found to generate favourable attitudes towards both the advertisement itself and the brand being promoted (Muehling & Sprott, 2004). Interestingly, the study revealed that a significant portion of the thoughts evoked by nostalgic advertising focused on friends, neighbours and past experiences rather than specific aspects of the brand and its benefits. This suggests that nostalgia operates through a peripheral route to persuasion. Recipients develop a positive emotional response to the advertisement, which then influences their evaluation of the brand.

Source Effects

In addition to rational and emotional appeals, marketing communication can also use the source effect as a means of persuasion. The source effect refers to the phenomenon where the message's source influences its persuasiveness. Various properties of the source can impact on how the message is perceived, and it can elicit both rational and emotional responses from the target audience. Examples of sources include the company or brand itself, the company's owner, employees, distribution channels, spokespersons, existing customers or reviewers. Each source possesses distinct characteristics or qualities that contribute to its persuasive effect. Credibility, expertise and attractiveness are commonly recognized properties of the source that influence persuasion (Hovland et al., 1953; Chaiken, 1980; Petty et al., 1981; Ohanian, 1990). According to the Elaboration Likelihood Model (ELM), in situations where message elaboration is low, source characteristics serve as cues for a simple decision-making process of accepting or rejecting the message. In high elaboration situations, however, source characteristics play a lesser role (Petty et al., 1981). Nonetheless, source characteristics can still influence persuasion through the central route by framing the message's central

Image 4.2   Adidas Campus, in original design

arguments. Customers, for instance, may expect expert opinions to carry validity. If an expert expresses a similar opinion to the customer's own beliefs, it reinforces the customer's confidence in their assessment of the central arguments (Tormala et al., 2006). Companies often leverage celebrities, attractive individuals, experts and influencers in their marketing communications, as they tap into the persuasive power of source effects.

Creativity in Social Media Communication

In traditional media, the company engages with a target group who behave relatively passively, despite actively processing the message. In contrast, social media platforms offer an interactive and engaging environment that encourages content sharing. The target group becomes more active, and the interactive experience they create through their engagement differs from appeals directed at a passive audience. This interactive experience can be described as four-dimensional. It engages the senses, such as sight; evokes emotions; facilitates physical activity, such as recommending and sharing content; and stimulates curiosity, problem-solving, creativity, or other mental cognitive activities (Brakus et al., 2009; Tuten, 2020). To leverage the potential of social media in capturing the attention of customers and encouraging message processing, the creative elements employed must trigger one or several of these dimensions. Furthermore, in addition to harnessing social media's capacity to activate the target group, the company should capitalize on the fact that members of the target group themselves will share content and reach other (target) groups through social media.

Sensory dimension: To capture the sensory dimension, it is crucial for the creative elements to actively engage the customers' senses, including sight, hearing and potentially one or two other senses. This can be achieved through the use of videos, music, images and even virtual reality. Taco Bell, an American company known for its global presence in offering Mexican food, effectively utilizes visual representations of their products through photos and videos to create impactful impressions.

Image 4.3   Taco Bell

Emotional dimension: To evoke emotional responses from customers, the creative components must shape their perception of whether the message is enjoyable or unpleasant. Various emotions can be elicited, including feelings of joy, sorrow, sentimentality, nostalgia, inspiration, and more. In the YouTube video titled 'Lifebuoy' by Tryg, a Norwegian insurance company, an elderly gentleman arrives at the beach with his dog and notices that the life-saving buoy provided by Tryg is missing. He assumes that a group of young people has taken it for recreational purposes and becomes angry. However, a surprising turn of events occurs when the man realizes that the youngsters have actually used the lifebuoy to rescue another individual from drowning.

Image 4.4 The video 'Lifebuoy' triggers emotions

Behavioural dimension: In order to encourage customers to become brand advocates, actively recommending and promoting the brand through word of mouth or online reviews, the company must facilitate such behavioural activities. This can be achieved by establishing direct contact between brand representatives (employees, influencers, salespeople) and customers. Additionally, customers should be provided with opportunities to create or co-create content through competitions or participation in an online community. The company should also consider rewarding customers for their engagement. Furthermore, it is crucial for the company to consider the devices customers will utilize during their interactions, such as PCs, phones or tablets.

To celebrate its centenary, the manufacturer of Oreo biscuits launched a campaign called 'Daily Twist'. The campaign's name is derived from the way Oreo enthusiasts enjoy the cookie – by twisting, licking and dunking it. Each day, for a hundred days, content was created based on a significant news event occurring on that particular day (e.g. Elvis Week, the release of a new Apple phone, Bastille Day). This timely approach resulted in the campaign gaining significant attention, being widely shared and discussed. Moreover, it sparked numerous ideas and discussions among customers on platforms like Facebook, X and Pinterest (Elliott, 2012).

Cognitive dimension: In order to elicit cognitive engagement and foster customer commitment, the creative components need to stimulate curiosity, problem-solving abilities, creativity and other cognitive activities. These activities can include competitions where customers contribute creative ideas for the brand, participate in quizzes, or follow influencers on social media.

Zenni Optical, an American online eyewear store, executed a content marketing campaign titled 'You've been framed'. This campaign was disseminated through various channels such as the store's homepage, newsletters, fashion and lifestyle influencers, optics influencers and Facebook. As part of the campaign, Zenni engaged with customers through a quiz consisting of nine questions related to face shape, clothing patterns, preferred season, preferred decade, and more. Based on their responses, customers were provided with personalized recommendations for the most suitable spectacle frames (REQ Marketing, 2015).

Communication Channels

The company establishes communication with customers through various communication channels, including TV, newspapers and the internet. By communication channel, we mean anywhere the message is placed to reach the customers, in particular the target groups. Channels include both media (e.g. TV, internet) and more specific tools (e.g. sponsorship, social media) as well as combinations of media and tools. These channels can be either owned by the company itself, such as their homepage and online store, or purchased from other media outlets, like mass media. Mass media encompasses platforms like TV, radio, newspapers, magazines, websites, social media and billboards, along with other channels that are frequented by or connected to customers.

Digital Media Channels

The advent of digitalization has significantly transformed the advertising landscape, revolutionizing how brands connect with their target audience. It is assumed that digital advertising accounts for more than 50% of the global advertising spending.[5] Digital platforms offer advanced targeting capabilities, allowing advertisers to reach specific segments of their audience based on demographics, interests, behaviours and online activities. This precise targeting enables personalized and relevant advertising messages, unlike traditional media where companies pay for broad audience exposure.

In digital channels, companies leverage programmatic buying, where they bid on opportunities to reach their target audience. This approach ensures that ad spending is focused on the intended audience and maximizing efficiency. By optimizing the frequency of ad displays based on customer information, companies can avoid excessive exposure to individuals unlikely to respond positively. This results in more relevant advertising experiences, tailored to the preferences and needs of different customer segments.

Real-time tracking is a key feature of digital advertising, allowing advertisers to monitor metrics like impressions, clicks and conversions. This data-driven approach enables campaign optimization and informed decision-making. Additionally, by linking digital advertising to websites, brands can leverage interactivity, creating engaging and memorable ad experiences that foster deeper connections with their audience.

Digital advertising also capitalizes on the widespread use of smartphones, utilizing location data, push notifications and mobile-specific formats to deliver personalized and contextually relevant experiences. However, it's worth noting that traditional media channels such as TV, radio and print still maintain significant ad spend. Yet the shift towards digital advertising continues to accelerate due to the growth of online audiences, precise targeting capabilities and robust analytics for measuring campaign performance.

---

[5]Statistics are not precise but see https://www.oberlo.com/statistics/digital-ad-spend.

It is important to acknowledge that digitalization has also presented challenges, including the rise of ad-blocking software and the development of banner blindness, where individuals overlook or disregard advertising content due to ingrained search behaviours (e.g. Gordon et al., 2021).

In summary, digitalization has profoundly impacted on advertising, offering advanced targeting, real-time tracking, interactive experiences and personalized messaging. While traditional media channels still hold value, the digital shift is driven by its ability to reach specific audiences efficiently and provide data-driven insights for optimizing campaigns.

Advertising in Bought Media Channels

According to the American Marketing Association, advertising is defined as 'the placement of announcements and messages in time or space by business firms, nonprofit organizations, government agencies, and individuals who seek to inform and/or persuade members of a particular target market or audience regarding their goods, services, organizations or ideas' (https://marketing-dictionary.org/a/advertising/). Advertising involves payment for its placement. Its purpose is to capture consumers' attention and direct it towards the company and its brands by providing information that can generate a positive attitude towards them.[6] It's important to note that capturing consumers' attention towards a brand does not necessarily mean directly asking them to purchase it. The main objective of advertising is to cultivate a favourable attitude towards a brand, increasing the likelihood that consumers will choose this particular brand over others. We will now explore this further in a case study about advertising on Google.

Case Study 4.6

Google Ads

Google Ads is the largest digital advertising platform globally. According to Statista, Google's share of the global search ad market is consistently above 90% (Statista, 2023). This dominance stems from Google's position as the most widely used search engine, making it an essential channel for advertisers to reach potential customers who are actively searching for information or products. Google Ads empowers businesses to create and manage campaigns across Google properties like the search engine, YouTube and partner sites. By strategically placing ads in search results, businesses can reach potential customers precisely when they express intent, boosting conversion rates. Google Ads offers advanced targeting features, enabling advertisers to reach specific audiences based on location, language, interests and demographics. This precision targeting maximizes the likelihood of generating valuable leads and conversions. Moreover, companies can monitor ad performance in real time, gaining immediate insights into advertising effectiveness and website traffic conversion.

---

[6]From Latin: *advertere*; ad = towards, *vertere* = turn (Percy & Rosenbaum-Elliott, 2021).

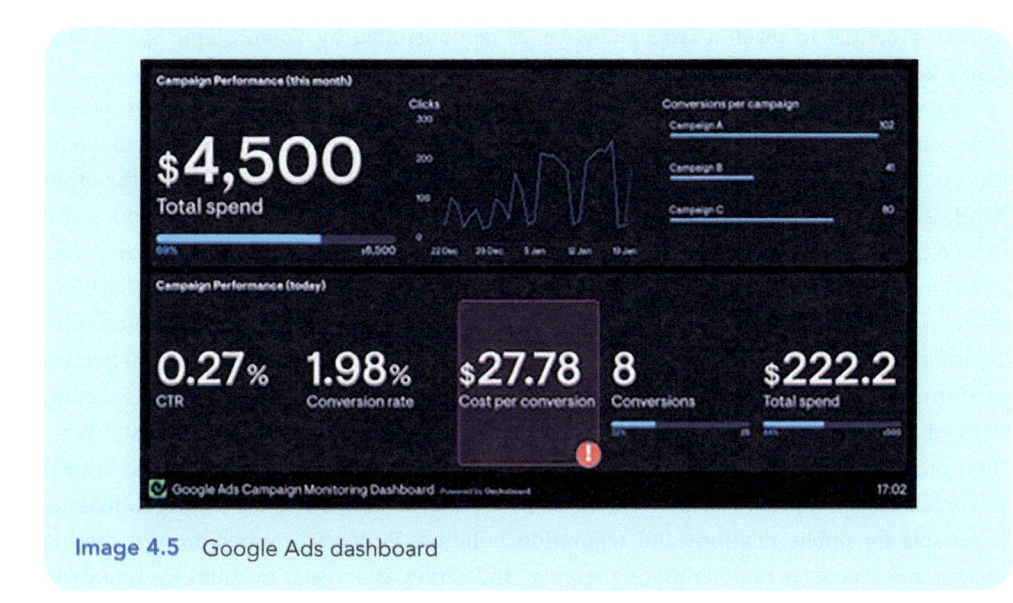

Image 4.5   Google Ads dashboard

Social Media Advertising

Social media platforms are online communication channels that facilitate interaction among members of a social network. These networks consist of users and groups who share and engage with various types of content such as news, updates, text, stories, photos, videos and music. As of 2024, more than 5 billion people worldwide use social media.[7] These platforms are utilized not only by individuals to connect with one another but also by various professional entities, including media companies, news broadcasters, authorities, businesses, politicians, celebrities, influencers and public institutions.

There are numerous social media platforms available, and below we will discuss some of the most common ones. The rise of these platforms has transformed the advertising landscape by providing brands with direct access to billions of active users. In terms of market share, Facebook and its subsidiary, Instagram, are estimated to hold around 20% of the global digital advertising market.

Brand building in social media has been found to revolve around three main strategies (Wien & Tafesse, 2017). The first strategy involves building brand communities, where passionate consumers gather around a particular brand. This sense of community fosters brand loyalty and is often observed in iconic motor brands and sports teams (Muniz & O'Guinn, 2001; McAlexander et al., 2002). The second strategy focuses on developing strong relationships between consumers and the brand (Fournier, 1998). Brands can engage with their followers, share information and receive feedback on platforms like Facebook. The third strategy aims to generate viral spread of messages through stimulating word-of-mouth among consumers (Wien and Tafesse, 2017). Memorable content that resonates with users

[7]Statista https://www.statista.com/statistics/617136/digital-population-worldwide/

has the potential to reach a large audience, as demonstrated by Volvo's 'Epic Split' video (Chai, 2013; Digital Synopsis, n.d.).

Facebook is a leading platform for businesses, with 90% of social media marketers world-wide using it to promote their businesses (Statista, 2023). With over 3 billion users globally, Facebook offers a wide reach across different age groups and genders. Snapchat, on the other hand, is an app-based platform known for its ephemeral content. It has 635 million active users worldwide and is particularly popular among younger demographics. Instagram, with 2 billion users globally, focuses on visual content and is well-suited for brands in fashion, makeup and well-being industries. YouTube, the second most popular social medium with 2.5 billion users, allows for the upload, viewing and sharing of videos, making it an effective platform for brand awareness and educational content (Tuten & Solomon, 2018). LinkedIn, tailored for businesses and professionals, provides a platform for companies to showcase their products and brands, advertise events, and nurture customer relationships. X, known as a microblogging platform, allows users to post and interact with short messages, making it suitable for public relations and reputation building. Pinterest, centred around sharing images and videos, is popular among women and serves as a visual medium for brands to inspire and engage their audience. TikTok, with over 1 billion active users, is a platform focused on short video clips, primarily appealing to younger demographics.

Each social media platform has its own unique characteristics and user demographics, allowing brands to tailor their strategies accordingly. It is important for businesses to under-stand their target audience and select the platforms that align with their objectives and brand identity.

Advertising Through Influencers

An influencer can be described as an individual who possesses the power to sway others, often through various social media platforms. When a company leverages an influencer's ability to reach potential customers, it is known as influencer marketing. Depending on the specific social channels they utilize, influencers may be referred to as bloggers (or vloggers), YouTubers, Instagrammers or Snapchatters. Individuals who regularly follow and pay atten-tion to an influencer's content are called followers. These followers are often inspired by the influencer and their attitudes and behaviours towards market offerings can be influenced by them. In this role, the influencer acts as an opinion leader. As an opinion leader, the influ-encer can shape the opinions of their followers through their own messages or, when collaborating with a company, by conveying the company's message.

Long before 'influencer' became a widely recognized concept, Katz and Lazarsfeld put forth the theory of opinion leaders, suggesting that messages from a company reach the public through opinion leaders who interpret and disseminate the message within their network (Katz & Lazarsfeld, 1955). An individual can become an opinion leader by virtue of personal involvement, product knowledge, and by standing out as unique and different in the public eye (Chan & Misra, 1990). These qualities make influencers an excellent catalyst for word-of-mouth marketing (WOMM). Influencers can initially be celebrities known to the public for their accomplishments or fame, such as world-class athletes or celebrated movie stars. On the other hand, some influencers gain prominence solely through their social media presence and lack initial public recognition. Consequently, influencers are typically categorized into two groups: macro-influencers and micro-influencers (Hatton, 2018). Macro-influencers are well-known celebrities who can reach a large follower base, while micro-influencers are relatively unknown individuals without an extensive following. For instance, at the beginning of 2024, Ariana Grande and Cristiano Ronaldo had the two most followed Instagram accounts, representing macro-influencers (Statista, 2024b). Conversely, Nikkie de Jager, a Dutch make-up artist, exemplifies a micro-influencer who gained fame through YouTube. The pre-existing recognition and broad connections of macro-influencers make them valuable brand ambassadors for companies. They often influence customers through their attractiveness or expertise in a particular field.

Micro-influencers, on the other hand, employ different tactics to influence their followers. One approach involves being transparent about their own lives and showcasing themselves as 'real people' with relatable challenges (Senft, 2008). Generally, micro-influencers establish a sense of closeness with their followers. Four types of closeness have been identified: commercial proximity, interactive proximity, reciprocal closeness and revealing closeness.

Commercial proximity occurs when influencers utilize their personal lives strategically to foster a sense of closeness with followers. Interactive proximity arises when influencers engage with their followers face to face through various social media interactions. When the influencers then engage, by liking, replying and commenting on follower responses, mutual closeness akin to friendship, referred to as reciprocal closeness, emerges. Revealing closeness is formed when influencers share intimate and lesser-known experiences from their lives, making followers feel special (Abidin, 2015). The use of influencers, who the company has limited control over, carries inherent risks. An example of this is PewDiePie, one of the world's most popular YouTube influencers, who has faced backlash for publishing videos with content that could be interpreted as anti-Semitic. As a result, on of his major collaborators, Walt Disney, severed ties with him (Winkler et al., 2017).

Advertising Through Sponsorship

Sponsorship refers to the provision of payment, whether monetary or in the form of other resources, to an entity, such as sports events, cultural activities, organizations, charitable causes, teams or individuals, in exchange for access to the associated commercial opportunities (Marketing Accountability Standards Board, 2020). By aligning with these entities, also known as sponsees or sponsor objects, companies promote themselves and their brands. The objective is to establish a connection between the company/brand and the sponsor object so that when consumers think of the object (e.g. the Olympics), they also associate it with the company/brand (e.g. Coca-Cola). Typically, sponsorship takes the form of a simple message, such as a logo, brand name or company name, displayed on the sponsor object. For example, the TeamViewer logo can appear on the jerseys of Manchester United players. Unlike an advertising campaign, which is typically managed by the marketing department, sponsorship is often overseen by top management within the company.

Various theories can explain how sponsorship works and influences consumer judgements and decisions (Cornwell et al., 2005; Olson & Thjømøe, 2009, 2011). One theory is the mere exposure effect, which suggests that when a brand name is repeatedly exposed through its presence at the sponsor object over an extended period, it leads to an increased preference for the brand without customers going through the intermediate steps in the response hierarchy. The mere exposure effect is often attributed to familiarity, as frequent exposure to a brand name makes it more familiar, and people tend to prefer familiar things over unfamiliar ones. Another explanation focuses on the concept of congruence between the sponsor and sponsor object. If there is a strong match between them, the sponsor is more likely to be remembered and considered by customers in purchase situations. For example, consumers are likely to remember Nike training clothes better than Qatar Airways when both brands appear on the jerseys of Paris Saint-Germain players. A third explanation suggests that the sponsorship's image can be transferred to the sponsor's brand through sponsorship. In this way, a company like Qatar Airways can benefit from the positive image associated with French football.

However, because a sponsor object is not directly controlled by the company, sponsorship offers less control over the message compared to advertising, for example. This lack of control became evident for well-known companies such as Anheuser-Busch, Oakley, Radio Shack and Nike when Lance Armstrong was charged with and eventually admitted to doping.

Advertising Through Product Placement

Product placement refers to the strategic inclusion of a company's products or brands in various forms of media, such as TV shows, films and creative works, in exchange for payment or compensation (Wiles & Danielova, 2009). This placement can be either direct, where the product is integrated into the action, or indirect, where it may be mentioned or referenced. Examples include Ray-Ban featuring its sunglasses on Tom Cruise in the *Top Gun* films, Daniel Craig consuming Heineken in the James Bond movie *Skyfall* and participants on *Love Island* using Samsung phones for texting. Products and brands can be incorporated into the plot or editorial and artistic content. However, when a brand appears as a natural part of the storyline or content, it is not considered product placement. Product placement is not a recent phenomenon, as early as the 1950s, viewers could see Humphrey Bogart enjoying Gordon's gin on his riverboat in the renowned film *The African Queen*. Today, product placements extend beyond TV and film to encompass music, musicals, games, literature, blogs and other arenas. For instance, the liqueur brand Grand Marnier appeared in Avicii's music video 'Lay me down', Nike showcased its shoes in the popular game Fortnite and author William Boyd featured the Land Rover in his short story 'The vanishing game'. When planning product placement, companies need to consider where to position the product and how well it aligns with the overall vision of the movie, music or game. Research has indicated that brands that are not organically integrated into the plot are better remembered but less favoured compared with brands that seamlessly fit within the storyline. This effect occurs because brands that feel out of place make consumers pause and contemplate, leading to a negative perception of the brand (Russell, 2002).

Communication in Owned Communication Channels

Companies engage in communication with their customers using various channels such as emails, SMS, letters and personal sales. With the advancement of customer relationship management (CRM), automated communication has emerged as a crucial channel for many companies. Unlike advertising, where media costs vary and are campaign-specific, direct communication costs are primarily fixed and involve investments in technology, personnel and the acquisition of contact information. These investments include CRM software, sales teams, content specialists, customer clubs and loyalty programmes aimed at obtaining email addresses, phone numbers and other relevant customer data.

Consequently, the marginal cost of communicating through owned channels is significantly lower compared to advertising through external channels that are purchased. Another key distinction between advertising in bought media channels and communication through owned channels lies in the sequencing of communication. Advertising is often campaign-driven, with a defined start and end, whereas communication through owned channels consists of repetitive communication programmes triggered by events in the customer relationships. In Chapter 5, 'Customer Portfolio Management', you can find examples of customer communication programmes.

Communication in Earned Communication Channels

In addition to buying media space or using their owned communication channels, companies can *earn* distribution of their message. Earned communication channels refer to the channels through which companies receive exposure and communication without directly paying for it. Unlike paid advertising or owned channels, earned channels rely on organic and unpaid efforts from external sources such as customers, influencers, journalists or the general public. These channels typically involve word of mouth, online reviews, social media mentions, press coverage, viral content and recommendations from satisfied customers.

Examples of word of mouth (WOM) occur in various situations.[8] For instance, a customer might share a picture on Instagram while trying on a new dress at Zara's fitting room, a restaurant guest might recommend a newly discovered vegetarian burger joint on TripAdvisor during their lunch experience, or a fellow student might engage in a conversation about their new athletics shoes. WOM happens when consumers voluntarily discuss or share information about a product or service with others, without any commercial influence. The effectiveness of WOM is often attributed to the credibility of the source. A message from a trustworthy and credible individual holds more persuasive power than one from an unreliable source (Ohanian, 1990). Moreover, WOM frequently occurs among friends or acquaintances, further enhancing the persuasiveness of the communicated message (Bearden & Etzel, 1982). However, it's important to note that WOM can also have a negative impact. For instance, if a friend warns about a product that requires frequent repairs, such negative WOM can significantly affect persuasion. In other words, companies cannot solely rely on positive messages when leveraging WOM;

---

[8]See also word-of-mouth customer programmes in Chapter 5.

they need to address both positive and negative experiences to effectively navigate WOM channels.

Public relations (PR) focuses on obtaining media coverage for a product or brand and can be classified as earned communication. PR serves the purpose of influencing customers as well as communicating with various stakeholder groups such as authorities, the local community, shareholders, investors and banks. Although companies typically don't directly pay for media coverage, marketers invest significant time in planning and ensuring that PR presents the company, its products and its brands in a positive light. Positive PR can have a substantial impact on customer responses for most products. Marketers can expedite their progress through the response hierarchy by distributing press releases to the media. A notable example is Apple, which often issues press releases when launching new products and subsequently garners substantial free publicity from the media (Lessin, 2013). In comparison with advertising, PR offers several advantages. PR is perceived as more objective, cost-effective and well-suited for managing crises. However, a disadvantage of PR is that the message becomes more challenging to control compared to advertising or other forms of communication.

Earned communication channels are valuable because they often carry more credibility and authenticity than paid or owned channels. Positive experiences and recommendations from others can significantly impact on a company's reputation and brand perception. However, companies have limited control over earned channels since they rely on external entities to initiate and amplify the communication.

To effectively leverage earned communication channels, companies can focus on delivering exceptional products or services, fostering positive customer experiences, engaging with their audience on social media, implementing influencer marketing strategies, and maintaining strong relationships with the media and industry influencers. By nurturing these relationships and providing value, companies can increase their chances of earning positive exposure and communication through these channels.

Integrated Marketing Communication

To maximize the effectiveness of marketing communication, it is crucial to integrate communications across various channels. The American Marketing Association defines integrated marketing communication as the cohesive combination of marketing communications activities, techniques and media aimed at delivering a coordinated message to a target market, achieving a common objective, or set of objectives with a powerful or synergistic effect (Marketing Accountability Standards Board, 2020). This requires the company to take a holistic approach to their communication channels and tools, ensuring that the message conveyed to the target audience appears coordinated and unified, also known as seamless.

By achieving integration, the company can harness synergy effects, where the combined impact of using multiple channels together is greater than the sum of their individual effects when used separately and uncoordinated. In other words, integrated marketing communication allows the company to achieve synergy effects while preventing the various channels from undermining each other's effectiveness. For example, Nespresso's exclusive concept stores, which sell their coffee machines and capsules, reinforce the impression of exclusivity portrayed in newspaper, magazine and social media ads. However, selling Nespresso products in regular stores could undermine this synergy effect.

Integrated marketing communication goes beyond recognizing the interrelationship of various channels. The company must also plan the roles of these channels and actively connect them to fulfil their intended purposes. To realize integrated and effective communication, the company needs to understand the strengths and weaknesses of different channels in achieving communication goals, whether through central or peripheral message processing. Mass media channels like TV, radio and newspapers have high reach and frequency, making them ideal for creating awareness. Advertising, with its flexibility in appealing to both rational and emotional aspects, is suitable for generating a positive brand attitude. However, in-store marketing is better suited for triggering brand trial due to its proximity to the customer's decision-making situation.

Furthermore, different channels have varying characteristics that make them more or less conducive to facilitating thorough message processing. Channels that allow customers to spend time and immerse themselves, such as social media or sponsorships, are advantageous for central route processing when persuasive messages require deeper engagement. For example, an instructional video showcasing how to apply make-up foundation with MakeUp Mecca's products can enhance the target audience's ability to process the message centrally. Sponsoring a football team followed by the target audience throughout the season offers high exposure frequency, providing an opportunity for central message processing.

While some channels, like the company's owned channels and bought advertising, are within the company's control, earned media attention such as word of mouth, independent influencers or media coverage are not. These external factors can potentially disrupt the seamless brand impression. As part of an integrated marketing communication plan, it is essential to monitor media for negative publicity or distorted messages and have a plan in place to respond effectively.

Budgeting

Companies allocate resources to marketing communication activities with the objective of boosting sales. Determining the appropriate budget requires understanding the relationship between these activities and sales responsiveness. However, quantifying this relationship can be a complex and challenging task, as exemplified by John Wanamaker, a department store pioneer and prominent marketer once remarked, 'Half the money I spend on advertising is wasted; the problem is I don't know which half'.[9] While the authenticity of the quote may be debated, it highlights an important concern. Companies need some level of understanding regarding how their communication efforts impact sales, revenues and profits.

[9]Britannica: https://www.britannica.com/biography/John-Wanamaker; B2B Marketing: https://www.b2bmarketing.net/en-gb/resources/blog/half-money-ispend-advertising-wasted-trouble-i-dont-know-which-half.

The sales response to advertising is typically considered non-linear, implying that the impact of communication diminishes over time. In many markets, a minimum level of communication may be necessary before any noticeable effect is observed. Furthermore, a common assumption is that the response function follows an S-shaped curve (Figure 4.5). Initially, the effect of advertising is relatively low at lower levels, then it increases after surpassing a certain threshold, before eventually reaching a plateau at another threshold level. This concept of the advertising response function is further explored in Chapter 6, 'Product Category Management'.

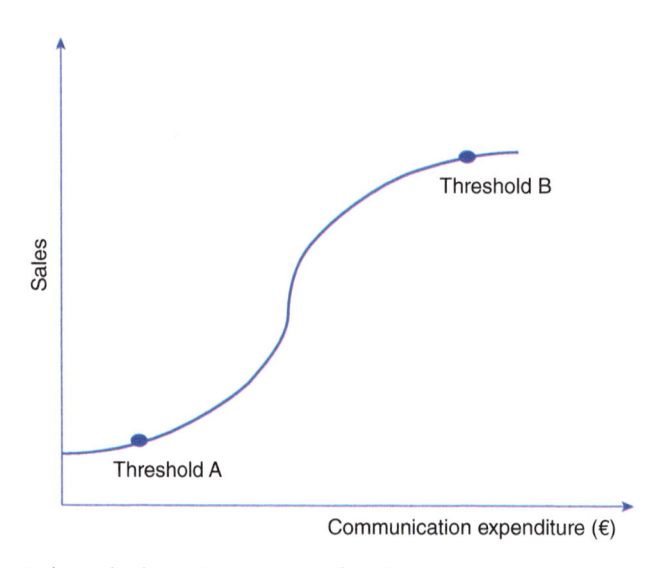

Figure 4.5 The S-shaped advertising response function

Determining the size and allocation of the marketing communications budget involves various principles and methods. These budgeting approaches can be broadly classified into two categories: rule-of-thumb-based methods and analytical and data-driven methods (Piercy, 1987). We will now examine each of these methods in turn.

Methods Based on Rules of Thumb

If a company lacks the necessary data or resources to determine the optimal size and distribution of the communication budget, there are several decision rules that can be used as alternatives. These rules are easy to understand and implement.

One simple method for determining the budget size is to increase it every year by a percentage greater than or equal to the inflation rate. This ensures that the budget keeps up with rising costs. Another relatively straightforward method is to allocate the budget to customer segments in proportion to their size. This ensures that resources are distributed based on the potential reach and impact of each segment.

Alternatively, you can base the budget size on a percentage of sales. This can be done for specific products, product categories, brands or the entire product portfolio. However, this method may result in over- or under-investment in marketing communication, as it does not consider other factors that influence sales performance.

A third method is to allocate the budget as a percentage of profits. This approach allows for distribution across products and brands based on their individual profit contributions. Products with higher profit percentages receive more budget, assuming they have performed well and can sustain their success. Conversely, products with lower profits may receive more budget to support their growth and increase future profits.

Another method is to set the budget equal to historical levels, replicating the budget from the previous year in terms of size and distribution. This approach assumes that if there have been no significant changes in the environment, customer preferences or competitive land-scape, the past budget will continue to be effective.

The competitive parity method involves setting the budget to match that of competitors. This method ensures that the company maintains a similar share of voice in the market, which is related to market share for sales. However, it assumes that competitors have set their budgets optimally and that they are similar to your own company. For small businesses com-peting against larger companies, this method may require a disproportionately large share of their sales to be allocated to communication, which may not be financially viable.

It is important to note that all these methods rely on an anchor (such as inflation, sales, profit, previous years or competitors). The company should closely monitor the impact of their spending on sales and adjust the anchor if needed to achieve the desired outcomes (Palmatier & Sridhar, 2021). Other methods, such as the affordability method, involve invest-ing remaining resources in communication after covering all other necessary costs (de Pelsmacker et al., 2018). This method may be used when budget constraints are tight. However, it is not aligned with strategic positioning as it does not consider specific goals or objectives.

A major limitation of these methods is their inability to shed light on the specific impact of individual communication activities on sales. For instance, if sales increase by 10% in a particular year and the company allocated 3% of sales to advertising, it remains uncertain whether alternative communication activities could have generated even greater sales growth. Similarly, the company cannot determine whether the same sales increase could have been attained with a lower budget allocation, such as 1% of sales.

Analytical Methods

Instead of relying on rule-of-thumb methods, companies can employ more analytical and data-driven approaches to budgeting. These methods include field experiments, ends–means thinking and statistical response models.

Field Experiment

In a controlled field experiment, the company selects a specific communication activity, such as search engine optimization, to assess. The experiment involves systematically adjusting the spending level in different product categories (or customer segments), tracking the effects on sales, website visits, or other relevant metrics. For example, the company may increase spending by different percentages in various product categories and observe the corresponding changes in sales. This allows the company to determine the optimal spending level for achieving desired outcomes. The company must also form an expectation about when (e.g. in which weeks or months) the effect will occur. By analysing the results, the company gains insights into the effectiveness of the communication activity and can make informed decisions about budget allocation. Imagine that PepsiCo, a company spending 3.5 billion dollars worldwide on advertising (Statista, 2024a), wanted to refine its allocation of spending on digital ads. PepsiCo then partnered with a digital advertising platform and randomly selected different geographic regions to receive varying levels of digital ad exposure. By comparing sales from the different regions, PepsiCo was able to determine the optimal spending level that generated the highest impact on sales.

Objective-Task Method

The objective-task method involves defining communication goals, such as increasing brand awareness, and identifying the resources required to achieve these goals. The company assesses different communication measures (e.g. advertising, social media, direct sales) and estimates the necessary investments to implement them effectively. This method requires strategic planning, investment analysis and historical data on the company's marketing communication performance. The budget can be evaluated regularly to optimize resource allocation and enhance efficiency. However, estimating the impact on profitability from various communication tools and tactics can be challenging with this method (de Pelsmacker et al., 2018). Also, the level of resources necessary to reach the desired level of brand awareness might be so large that the company simply does not have the financial strength to achieve it.

Response Modelling

With the increasing availability of data and improved data analysis capabilities, companies can utilize response modelling to explore the impact of communication efforts on business success. By analysing previous periods' data on resource utilization and corresponding outcomes, the company can establish a response model that illustrates the relationship between communication spending and desired results. This model helps determine the optimal level of spending that maximizes return on sales or identifies potential cost reductions without compromising results. The response model provides valuable insights into the shape of the relationship between spending and outcomes, the specific impact of different communication activities, and the influence of environmental factors and competitors' efforts (Palmatier & Sridhar, 2017). This allows the company to fine-tune its communication strategy and make data-driven budgeting decisions.

Overall, these analytical methods provide companies with a more informed and data-driven approach to budgeting their marketing communications, enabling them to optimize resource allocation and achieve desired outcomes.

Measurement and Control

Measurement and control are essential components of marketing communication to evaluate effectiveness, make informed decisions and optimize outcomes. Establishing key performance indicators (KPIs) is vital for measuring the effectiveness of communication efforts. These KPIs encompass metrics such as brand awareness, brand perception, reach, engagement, conversion rates, sales, return on investment (ROI) and customer lifetime value (CLV).

Implementing tracking mechanisms and leveraging analytics tools enable the collection and analysis of relevant data related to advertising campaigns. This includes monitoring website traffic, social media interactions, ad impressions, click-through rates, conversion tracking and other pertinent metrics. Analytics platforms like Google Analytics or social media insights provide valuable insights into audience behaviour and the performance of marketing campaigns.

Market research, such as surveys, focus groups, or customer interviews, can provide valuable feedback on the effectiveness of advertising. It helps assess consumer attitudes, perception and recall of advertising messages. Market research also uncovers insights about target audience preferences, competitor strategies and market trends, thereby informing future advertising efforts.

Regular analysis of spending patterns, cost per acquisition (CPA) and ROI aids in optimizing budget allocation across different channels, campaigns and target segments. By adjusting budgets based on performance insights, companies can focus investments on the most effective channels and tactics.

Monitoring how customers move through the response hierarchy is important for some companies. Trial, a key response in this hierarchy, is directly linked to the company's product and brand sales. By observing actual sales to distributors, subsequent sales by distributors to customers and sales through the company's own online store, companies can measure the impact of marketing communication on sales in terms of units sold and monetary value. Market-share figures in various product categories can be obtained from market analysis agencies like Nielsen for grocery trade companies.

To measure the effect of marketing communication on adoption, companies can examine changes in brand loyalty after customers are exposed to communication. Brand loyalty can be captured through behavioural indicators such as repurchase or attitudinal indicators such as customer identification with the brand, sharing opinions with others, investing time in the brand or monitoring its performance in the market. Surveys, social media activity observation, online community engagement and customer club activity can help capture brand loyalty.

To understand why trial and adoption have changed, companies must analyse changes in awareness, interest and evaluation. Awareness can be measured by assessing changes in brand recognition and recall through surveys. Brand interest can be determined by examining customer curiosity and willingness to learn more about the brand, through either survey questions or observing online search behaviour (Machleit et al., 1990). Evaluation can be captured by measuring variables such as brand image, brand attitude, brand preference and purchase intention through survey questions. Brand image relates to the characteristics and benefits consumers associate with the brand, brand attitude reflects an overall positive or negative evaluation, brand preference indicates favourability compared to competing brands, and purchase intention measures the likelihood of purchasing the brand within a specific period.

By implementing effective measurement and control practices, companies can gain comprehensive insights into the impact and effectiveness of their marketing communication efforts. These insights enable data-driven decision-making, campaign optimization and resource allocation to achieve desired outcomes.

SUMMARY

In summary, marketing communication is essential for conveying a company's value proposition and persuading customers to choose its products and brands in the marketplace. Setting clear objectives and assessing the impact of marketing communication efforts are vital for effective strategies.

Effective marketing communication requires an understanding of how the communicated message is processed. The hierarchy of effects models explain how the target audience processes marketing communication, progressing through cognitive, affective and conative stages. Attitudes influence behaviour and are resistant to change once formed. The elaboration likelihood model (ELM) explores how attitudes are influenced through central and peripheral processing routes. Expectations and evaluation of product attributes shape attitudes and behaviour. These expectations also serve as a standard or reference frame that shapes how the usage experience is perceived.

Marketing communication's importance lies in defining scope and goals, and acquiring new customers. It conveys value propositions, builds brand familiarity and shapes brand associations. Consequently, a company must set goals for its communication and define which customers to address with it.

Creativity helps getting the communicated message across. Creativity in marketing communication depends on divergence and relevance. Successful marketing communication must combine both.

Communication occurs through various channels, bought, owned or earned with digitalization offering targeted, real-time, interactive and personalized options. Integration across channels ensures a unified message, leveraging synergy effects.

Companies must allocate resources to marketing communication activities in order for them to have any effect. Budget allocation requires an understanding of the link between communication and sales responsiveness. Analytical approaches enhance budgeting decisions through field experiments and statistical models.

Measurement and control are integral aspects of marketing communication that allow for the evaluation of effectiveness, informed decision-making and outcome optimization. Measurement and control use KPIs like brand awareness, perception, reach, engagement, conversion rates, sales, ROI and CLV. These insights drive data-driven decisions, campaign optimization and resource allocation for desired outcomes.

END-OF-CHAPTER QUESTIONS

1 Chose some advertisements from a newspaper, a magazine or a website for a brand. Analyse how you personally process these advertisements. Have your perceptions of the brands changed during the processing?

2 Now look at the same advertisements. What creative elements do you find? In what way are these elements divergent? For which target audiences are these creative elements relevant? Do you think these advertisements will succeed in changing your attitude towards the advertised brand?

3 Based on the same advertisements, what communication goals do you think the company or advertising agency had in mind when they created these advertisements?

- Put aside the advertisements. When or in what situations is it appropriate to have awareness as a goal? When or in what situations is it appropriate to have product or brand adoption as a communication goal?
- Now, look at the advertisements again. Do you think the company/advertising agency did a good job regarding achieving the assumed objective?

4 Imagine that your favourite café is facing increased competition from a newly established international coffee chain. Your beloved café is losing customers every week. The owner turns to you and asks how the café can stop this decline. The owner knows that you are very skilled in marketing and especially marketing communication. You quickly decide that the message should be something like 'continue being a customer, don't switch to the international coffee chain'. You also decide to develop three alternative proposals for how this message should be conveyed – one option that uses rational appeals, one that uses emotional appeals and one that uses source effects. What do these three proposals look like?

5 You did such a great job for your favourite café that the international coffee chain decides to hire you when you finish your studies. Your first task is to revitalize the chain's marketing communication. Currently, the marketing communication consists of a website and a Facebook group, and occasionally a banner ad. One of the goals of revitalization is to attract customers from competitors, including independent cafés and other larger chains. You are asked to evaluate the advantages and disadvantages of sponsorship, word of mouth and influencers, and then select two of these communication channels. You are also asked to assess which media are appropriate. Naturally, in this context, you must also consider how marketing communication through the various communication and media channels you choose should appear integrated. What are your assessments?

6 The resources a company can allocate to marketing communication are limited. Imagine that you work for the international fashion chain XYZ and are responsible for

marketing communication in your home country. Last year, XYZ spent 5 million euros on marketing communication in your country, which was 5% of the previous year's profit. XYZ has a membership club where the company can collect data about customers' purchases, demographics and product reviews.

- What resource allocation method (how much money should be spent on marketing communication and how it should be distributed among segments and target groups) does XYZ appear to be using? Which method or methods would you use to assess whether this spending was effective or not? How would you utilize information from the membership club in connection with these methods?

FURTHER READING

Barry, T.E. & Howard, D.J. (1990). A review and critique of the hierarchy of effects in advertising. *International Journal of Advertising*, 9(2), 121–135.

ELM model: https://www.youtube.com/watch?v=heE8m-bReDM

Smith, R.E., MacKenzie, S.B., Yang, X., Buchholz, L.M. & Darley, W.K. (2007). Modeling the determinants and effects of creativity in advertising. *Marketing Science*, 26(6), 819–833.

Tuten, T.L. (2020). *Social Media Marketing*. Sage.

5

CUSTOMER PORTFOLIO MANAGEMENT

This chapter

- explores customer portfolio value;
- presents the key elements in a customer portfolio strategy;
- presents the principles of segmentation;
- introduces key elements in a customer data base and in customer analytics;
- presents fundamental principles for crafting customer value propositions;
- introduces the management of customer experiences;
- examines customer programmes for acquiring, capitalizing on, converting and safeguarding customers.

INTRODUCTION

The strategy for growing the value of a company's customer portfolio involves a plan for increasing the expected cash flow from current and future customers. Figure 5.1 provides a framework for developing this strategy. Since customers vary in their relationship with the supplier (brand), needs, and responses to stimuli, a good starting point is to group customers into segments. This requires the development of customer databases and related customer analytics. The next step is to define value propositions for each segment of customers. Customer experience management is also critical to ensure that customers' expectations are met and that they are satisfied providing the foundation for closer and more collaborative relationships. Customer programmes are designed to acquire new customers, defend existing relationships, convert them into stronger ones, and leverage current relationships to create more value.

Customer portfolio management aims to increase the financial value of a company's customer portfolio by increasing the expected future cash flow. This is achieved by adding new customers to the portfolio, retaining more existing customers, and increasing the level of engagement with each customer. The first step in customer portfolio management is to identify the current value of the customer portfolio and create a plan that outlines how the

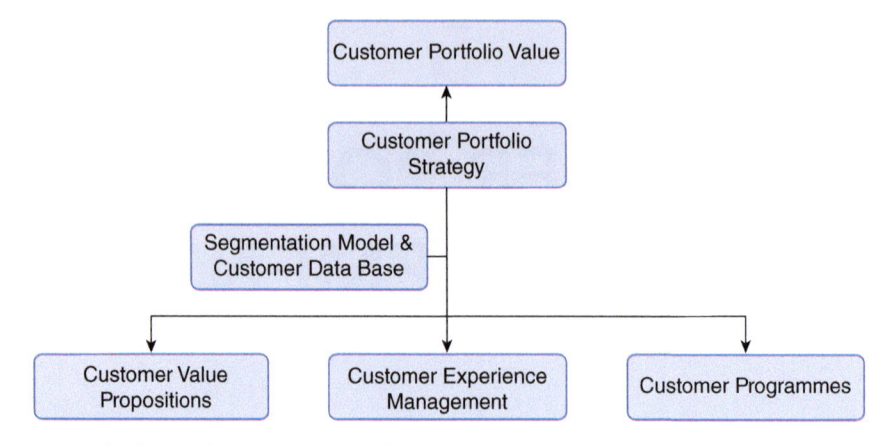

Figure 5.1 The layout for customer portfolio strategy

portfolio's value will grow. The next step is to implement the plan and capture the value created.

CUSTOMER PORTFOLIO VALUE

The value of a customer lies in his or hers expected future cash flow. We calculate this number by multiplying the probability that the customer will continue to be a customer in the next periods with the expected cash flow or surplus this customer is likely to give the company in these periods. We discount the amount in every period with a discount rate and sum the discounted amounts. The sum is the net present value of a customer which in the marketing literature is referred to as customer lifetime value (Berger & Nasr, 1998). Notice that the customer lifetime value (CLV) is different from the historical profitability of a customer. This means that profitable customers in the past are not necessarily valuable customers in the future, and that unprofitable customers in the past may become valuable customers in the future (Kumar, 2018).

At the strategic level we want to estimate the value of the entire portfolio of customers (Johnson & Selnes, 2004; Selnes & Johnson, 2022). Future cash flow considers not only existing customers but also potential new customers who are likely to be acquired in the future, while subtracting customers who are likely to leave the company. The expected increase in cash flow of existing customers is also included, which is determined by the success of selling more products to them and reducing the costs of serving them. While historical purchase behaviour and profitability can be calculated using accounting data, predicting future expected cash flow involves statistical prediction models with data from several sources in addition to accounting data (i.e. customer analytics).

Increasing the number of customers will lead to lower unit costs as fixed costs are shared across a larger volume, resulting in a lower cost per customer. This makes even low cash-flow customers important as they contribute to lower unit costs. For instance, the cost of an advertising campaign on TV remains the same regardless of the number of customers the company has. Similarly, IT systems, administration, machinery, and other similar costs can be shared between more customers, reducing the cost per customer. A larger volume can also create economies of scale in production, leading to a lower cost of products. Additionally, many weak relationships are valuable as they create a larger pool of potential customers that can be converted into stronger and more valuable relationships.

To calculate cash flow, we need to subtract transaction costs from revenues. Transaction costs can be directly related to the number of products sold to a customer, known as direct variable product unit costs, or indirectly related to other activities related to producing and selling the product, known as indirect transaction costs. Direct variable costs include the costs of producing a unit, such as input materials and labour in manufacturing, or the procurement costs that retailers pay to a manufacturer for a product. Variable selling costs, such as the commission paid to a distributor or sales representative for each product they sell, are also considered direct variable costs.

For instance, if a customer pays 100 euros for the products they buy (sales revenues), we subtract the procurement costs of the products, the sales and distribution costs, and any other costs directly or indirectly associated with the purchases made by the customer. Assuming that the procurement costs for the products are 50 euros, sales and distribution costs are 30 euros, and other costs connected to the transactions are 10 euros, the cash flow is 10 euros (100–50–30–10).

In order to accurately estimate cash flow from a customer, we need to allocate costs related to transactions with that customer. Direct costs are easy to allocate since they vary directly with the transactions, but indirect costs are more complex and require approximations that may not be entirely accurate. Activity-based costing is the standard method used to allocate indirect costs (Cooper & Kaplan, 1991). This involves assessing each activity in the value chain (such as procurement, production, sales, advertising, distribution, customer service and administration) and determining how they relate to each transaction with a customer.

For example, consider a retailer chain that spends 10 million euros annually on advertising. Assume that 50% of this is used to recruit new customers and that the other 50% is invested in reducing customer defection. Let us further assume that the 5 million euros spent on advertising for new customers has resulted in 10,000 new customers, which means that every new customer costs the company 500 euros. Similarly, the other 5 million euros spent on retention efforts translates to a cost of 50 euros per existing customer, given that the company has 100,000 customers.

There are, however, significant assumptions involved in the allocation of advertising investment to individual customers in the example provided above. The major fallible assumption is that all customers are equal and respond equally to advertising and retention programmes (and other marketing activities). It is rare that all new customers come to a company solely because of advertising. New customers may come because they were actively searching for this type of product, or because the company was recommended by someone. To allocate advertising costs correctly, we must first determine the additional effect of advertising on the acquisition of new customers, for which various statistical techniques are available.

Assuming that the statistical methods used in the example determined that 8,000 of the 10,000 new customers would have come without the help of advertising, the 5 million invested in advertising for recruiting new customers must be divided by 2,000 and not 10,000. Thus, the average advertising cost for acquiring a new customer is 2,500 euros and not 500 euros. Next, we must allocate these costs to those customers that were acquired through advertising and not to those new customers who came for other reasons. To do this, we need to know the characteristics (i.e. customer profiles) that discriminate the two groups (those recruited without and those recruited with advertising). Characteristics can be demographics (i.e. age, gender, address, etc.), behavioural (e.g. search behaviour on the company website), or other factors. There are statistical techniques that can help us find such characteristics that discriminate between those who are recruited with advertising and those who are not. By the same logic, we need to estimate how much advertising reduces defection or churn and the characteristics of those customers affected by advertising.

By identifying the most valuable customers more precisely and understanding their characteristics, companies can develop more effective marketing strategies that are targeted and differentiated. In the example above, if the primary difference between the 2,000 customers acquired through advertising and the remaining 8,000 was the distance from their homes to the store, the retailer can stop advertising to those who live less than five minutes away from the store and target only those who live further away. The close customers will come anyway even without advertising. This allows the retailer to reduce advertising costs by targeting only those who live more than five minutes away. With more accurate information about the effectiveness of marketing activities, companies can eliminate investments in activities that have little or no effect.

To progress, we must transition from calculating past cash flow to forecasting CLV for both new and existing customers. Predicting the likelihood of the customer's activity not just in the next period (i.e. a week, a month or a year) but also in the following periods is necessary. The predictions are dynamically updated for each customer as the probabilities will change as a function of time itself as well as with events that occur. Each company must decide the appropriate time horizon for their business.

We need to estimate not only the likelihood that a customer will remain active, but also their likelihood of purchasing each product category in the future. Even if a customer is not currently purchasing products from a category in the assortment the company is offering, there is a chance that they may start. There will, for example, be a probability that a bank customer who currently is engaged in the mortgage and payment service categories will extend their relationship into other product categories such as insurance, pension and investment products. This probability and the expected cash flow from such extensions should be included in the estimation of future cash flow from the customer. In fact, companies develop customer programmes aimed at customers who are not currently active in a category. The more effective these programmes are, the higher the probability that a non-user of a category will become a user. Companies capable of developing effective customer programmes will have more valuable existing customers because they can leverage their relationships with customers.

In addition to forecasting the customer's activity in various product categories, we must also predict the revenue and costs associated with each customer across these categories for each period. As mentioned earlier, some customers may be more costly to retain, and thus they should have a higher portion of the retention costs allocated to them compared with other customers. Retention costs may, for example, be additional service costs, additional discounts, additional loyalty programme reward points, additional customization of products, and so forth. It's worth noting that acquisition costs are not considered for customers who are already part of the company's portfolio.

The value of customers increases when their relationship with the company (brand) strengthens (Johnson & Selnes, 2004; Reinartz et al., 2005; Kumar, 2018; Selnes & Johnson, 2022). Stronger relationships lead to a lower probability of customer defection or churn, and an increased likelihood of increases in their purchases and reduced transaction costs. Weaker relationships increase the likelihood of customers switching to competitors, while stronger relationships reduce this probability. Customers can increase their purchasing by either increasing their share in one category (i.e. share-of-wallet) or by expanding their purchases to new categories. For example, a grocery customer can start buying meat and vegetables in addition to milk and bread. Additionally, customers with stronger relationships are more likely to become brand ambassadors and recommend the company to others.

The value of a customer portfolio not only includes current customers, but also potential customers who are not yet in the portfolio. These new customers must be assigned predicted active status across product categories and future periods, while also factoring in acquisition costs. The future value of a customer portfolio is therefore dependent on the cost of acquiring new customers. This means that companies with a strong and appealing brand, positive word of mouth, convenient locations for customers, attractive products and services, and other factors that reduce acquisition costs will have a more valuable customer portfolio.

SEGMENTATION OF CUSTOMERS

Customer heterogeneity is a fundamental characteristic of markets, meaning that customers differ in terms of what they need and how they respond to marketing activities. To address this, marketers often group similar customers into *segments* and differentiate their offerings accordingly.

We distinguish between macro- and micro-segmentation. Macro-segments are strategic and guide how companies invest in and specialize their organization-wide resources and activities. Therefore, the selection of macro- or strategic segments has a long-term perspective. Companies specialize in differentiated positions of their offering through investments and continuous product innovation (Dickson & Ginter, 1987; Dickson, 1992). Micro-segments are tactical and are used to differentiate market-related activities that do not require long-term investments and specialization of resources and activities. For instance, a company may differentiate its emails to younger and older customers because these two groups have different interests. While the macro-segments are few and strategic in nature, the micro-segments are many and vary across different types of tactical market activities. Thus, there may be one micro-segmentation variable used to differentiate price promotions, but another micro-segmentation variable used to differentiate email communication. Micro-segmentation is continuously updated, altered and adapted to changes in customer heterogeneity and competitive dynamics, and as companies learn how to make their market activities more effective.

Macro-segments refer to customer needs that remain stable over a longer period of time. This means that if a customer has a certain need today, they are likely to have the same need tomorrow and for some time after that. However, the same customer may have different stable needs for different situations. For instance, they may be a business customer of an airline in one situation, and a private customer in another. Also, notice that customer needs may change over time. The need for mortgages, for example, differs as customers move through the family cycle from single, to twosome, to family with children living at home, family without children living at home, and retirement. In the following we will discuss two different types of customer needs: those related to product qualities and those related to relationship qualities. Although presented as distinct types, they may also be combined, as we will see later.

Macro-Segments Based on Differences in Product Needs

Customers select the product that they believe will best satisfy their needs. A product can be considered a collection of product attributes, where each attribute has a different weight that reflects its importance to the customer's needs. The total utility of a product is the weighted sum of its attributes (Lancaster, 1966). Segments of customers can then be identified based on how they weigh these attributes. The basic notion is that if a company specializes in catering to a specific customer segment, customers will perceive the company as providing more valuable products and services, resulting in higher utility compared to other suppliers. This enhanced value proposition will create a preference and a willingness among customers to go the extra mile to purchase from the specialized company, such as paying a higher price or travelling a greater distance to reach the company's outlets. It also means that companies will be more effective in their investments.

It is the customers' perceptions of a product's superiority that influence their purchasing behaviour, rather than the company's own beliefs about what is more useful. If customers are already satisfied with a product, they may not see the value in switching to a new, supposedly better product. It is important to remember that a product is only as good as the problem it solves. Therefore, the economic effect of specialization is not just due to the fact that a company specializes in a particular product or service, but rather how relevant and useful that specialization is perceived to be by customers. When customers also experience the promised superiority after they have bought it, they become more satisfied, more likely to strengthen their relationship with the company (brand), and more likely to spread positive word-of-mouth about the company.

Now consider Case Study 5.1 below.

Case Study 5.1

Flytoget and Vy

In Oslo, travellers have a choice between two brands, Flytoget and Vy, for transportation between the city and the airport. Flytoget is positioned for customers who prioritize convenience and place greater importance on this attribute. These customers are willing to pay a premium, even up to twice the price of Vy. The frequency of departures and comfort on board are the two main factors that contribute to convenience, where Flytoget is perceived to be superior. The convenience segment in the airport transportation market has remained quite stable, although the expectations for convenience have evolved over the years. Flytoget has, for example, responded to this development by introducing on-board check-in for luggage, eliminating the need for customers to spend time on this when they arrive at the airport.

Image 5.1 Airport train transport

The introduction of new products can lead to the emergence or expansion of certain market segments. For instance, when Tesla entered the automobile industry, the electric car segment became significantly larger. Although established car manufacturers like BMW, Renault, Jaguar, Volvo, etc., had already developed a few models for the emerging electric segment, their investment in developing new models has accelerated due to the growing size of the electric segment.

The identification of product need segments can be achieved through two main principles: a priori and post-hoc segmentation methods.

A Priori Method

The a priori method involves defining segments based on observable characteristics such as age and gender in consumer markets, and industries, revenues, number of employees and other relevant factors in business-to-business markets. In the charter tour example discussed in Chapter 1, the Young Single, Families and 55-Plus segments were identified based on age and number of children, and these are a priori segments. The next step involves estimating the differences in product needs, i.e. the weighting of product attributes, for each segment. As shown in Table 5.1, the Young Single segment places little to no weight on hotel resort attributes except for price, while the Family segment prioritizes facilities for children and prefers to travel during school holidays. The 55-Plus segment values quality of rooms, hotel restaurants and prefers to travel during off-peak times when there are fewer children around.

Table 5.1 The a priori segmentation method illustrating differences in weights (i.e. need) for charter tour product features or attributes

	Young Single	Family	55-Plus
Room quality	Small	Medium	High
Hotel restaurants	Small	Medium	High
Children's facilities	None	High	Negative
Season preference	None	School holidays	Outside school holidays
Price	High	Medium	Small

Post-Hoc Segmentation Method

The post-hoc segmentation method involves conducting interviews with a sample of individuals to gather information on how they weigh different product attributes and what needs they want the product to fulfil. This data is then analysed using various statistical techniques to group respondents based on similarities in attribute weights. These groups are then described post-hoc in terms of observable characteristics.

A frozen-fish producer in Norway sought to identify product need segments that would appreciate a high-end brand of frozen fish. To accomplish this, a representative national sample of customers were interviewed and asked to rate the importance of a set of attributes. Using a statistical clustering method, the respondents were grouped into segments based on similarity in how they weighted the attributes. Table 5.2 reports the results, revealing the discovery of three distinct segments that were labelled according to their weight profiles. The Healthy Lifestyle segment placed emphasis not only on important nutrition but also on simplicity in cooking. The Food Lovers segment placed weight on all attributes, but relatively more on the fish's suitability for making new and exciting dishes, as well as traditional ones. The Convenience segment was clear that they did not want to buy anything that takes much time to cook. Interestingly, the three segments had similar demographic profiles, including age, gender, income and education, and other almost identical variables. Therefore, an a priori method would not have discovered the three distinct product need segments.

Table 5.2 The post-hoc segmentation method illustrating differences in weights (i.e. need) for frozen-fish product features or attributes

	Segment 1 Healthy Lifestyle	Segment 2 Food Lovers	Segment 3 Convenience
Suitable for new and exciting dishes	5.07	7.78	5.38
Suitable for traditional meals	4.74	7.68	5.49
Contains important nutrition	8.06	8.36	5.01
Simple to cook	7.28	7.02	6.28

How important are the following criteria when you are buying fish for dinner on a scale from 1 to 10 where 1 is Not Very Important and 10 is Very Important?

Macro-Segments Based on Differences in Relationship Needs

Although the basic function of an exchange relationship is fulfilled once customers receive the products and pay for them, most customers continue their relationships with suppliers (brand) once they are established (Dwyer et al., 1987). In common language we immediately think of interpersonal relationships when we talk about relationships. However, in the marketing literature we refer to relationships as exchange relationships with a set of connectors where interpersonal tie is only one. Other connectors may be brand perceptions, subscription contracts, loyalty programmes, apps, and so forth. At one end of a relationship spectrum there are few connectors and arm's length distance, whereas at the other end we observe relationships with many connectors and close collaboration with information sharing, socialization, integration, joint commitment of resources, and so forth (Heide, 1994).

Companies tend to have a mix of customers with different types of problems they need to solve (Tuli et al., 2007). PanFish was a fish-farming company that is now part of Mowi ASA, a Norwegian seafood company with over 5 billion dollars in sales and more than a 25% share of the global salmon and trout markets. To gain more control over their value chain they started to allocate all the medium-sized range of the catch to 'partners' whose machinery required minimum variation in size and weight (i.e. industrial manufacturers of smoked salmon). They developed a joint quality control and logistic solution for these customers, which brought higher margins. The bulk of smaller and larger fish were sold to regular customers (i.e. grocery store chains and other large retailers), and the remainder of the catch was sold in an opportunistic manner to customer who bought primarily on price (i.e. opportunistic buyers representing hotels and restaurants). The result was both a higher average profit per customer, lower operating costs and greater overall profits.

Customers' needs for developing relationships and connecting with suppliers differ and can be categorized into three types of relationships: acquaintances, friends and partners, based on how relationship value is created (Johnson & Selnes, 2004). Table 5.3 outlines these three types of relationship needs, factors that enhance supplier or brand attractiveness, and the fundamental qualities of suppliers and brands that are necessary in any relationship. Trust is an essential component of all relationships and is based on reliability and benevolence. Reliability is the trust that there is nothing wrong with the products, and the suppliers are honest in their communication. Benevolence is the trust that the supplier is acting in the customer's best interest and will take responsibility if something goes wrong. Trust is critical to well-functioning relationships, and the more customers trust the brand or supplier, the less effort is required in information search and contractual arrangements (Heide, 1994; Morgan & Hunt, 1994).

Table 5.3　Three different types of relationship need used for segmentation of customers

	Acquaintance	Friend	Partner
Perception of suppliers and brands	Customers perceive few or no differences between suppliers or brands	Customers perceive some suppliers or brands to have better products and services	Customers perceive themselves to be embedded in a supplier's or brand's network and ecosystem of products, services, technology or people
Attractive supplier and brand factors	Price and convenience	Product and service qualities	Customization through idiosyncratic investments in ecosystem
Fundamental supplier qualities	Reliability and benevolence	Reliability and benevolence	Reliability and benevolence

Acquaintances

The category of customer needs characterized by acquaintance is commonly observed in markets where products are largely similar. Take banks, for instance, where many individuals perceive the offered products as interchangeable. Whether it's a mortgage, a savings account or a credit card, the offerings are often identical across different banks. In such cases, what sets one bank apart from others is often a lower price. Similarly, in the realm of grocery stores, where many people see products as largely uniform, the appeal of one store over another lies in factors like lower prices or more convenient locations. Crucially, customers tend to stick with their chosen bank or grocery store as long as they don't find a superior offer (such as lower prices or increased convenience) elsewhere, and as long as they can trust their provider in terms of reliability and benevolence.

Friends

Customers of the friend type distinguish between suppliers and brands based on the perceived qualities of their products and services, leaning towards those considered superior.

Even in cases where products or services from various suppliers appear identical, customers may still gravitate towards a specific supplier due to the trust and rapport established with their customer service representative or advisor. These personal connections contribute additional value and foster a sense of loyalty that acts as a barrier against competitors.

Noteworthy distinctions may also be linked to variations in product quality, as exemplified by customers who favour brands like Nike due to the perceived excellence of their products. It's crucial to recognize that the friend type of relationship can manifest for various reasons within a company's customer base. Different customers may consider themselves friends of Nike for distinct reasons, such as the cushion construction in running shoes or the brand's design aesthetic. Moreover, the same customer can perceive a supplier as superior to others in different purchasing scenarios. For instance, an airline customer may regard the airline as superior for both business and private travel.

Partners

The partner type of customer views themselves as an essential component within the network and ecosystem of a supplier or brand, encompassing products, services, technology or people. This interconnected system generates additional value beyond the inherent worth of the products and services alone (Katz & Shapiro, 1985a; Uzzi 1996). Consider an Apple partner customer, who likely sees the integrated digital connections between various Apple products as an added advantage, amplifying the overall value of their Apple product suite. This network may extend to social systems, where aligning with a supplier or brand grants membership to a community of fellow brand users (Schau et al., 2009). For instance, LEGO fostered a community of dedicated individuals, including children of all ages, who shared their coding and play experiences across social media platforms and other settings using the Mindstorms robotic kit. As customers strengthen and enrich their ties to the supplier's or brand's network and ecosystem of products, they extract more value and perceive alternative suppliers and brands as significantly less appealing.

Notice that a supplier or brand can have customers in all three types of relationships. PanFish have acquaintances (hotels and restaurants), friends (grocery retailers) and partners (smoked salmon manufacturers). But also, companies or brands like Nike have customers in all three types of relationship segments. Some Nike customers perceive no major differences between running shoes and will choose brands based on convenience or price (i.e. acquaintances). At the other end of the relationship spectrum, Nike has customers who have adapted to the brand's ecosystem of product and services through Nike's customer club, and 'customized' their buying of a whole range of products and services. The proportion of each type of relationship segment may differ based on market dynamics and the company's strategies to transform relationships from acquaintances to friends and from friends to partners. As customers become more embedded and connected to the supplier's network and ecosystem of products and services, their value to the company increases, which motivates companies to build stronger and more collaborative relationships with them (Selnes & Johnson, 2022).

Heterogeneity in product and relationship needs can both be utilized to define strategic macro-segments. There is no single correct method of defining strategic macro-segments, and two companies can achieve success in the same market by using different segmentation models. What is important is that companies thoroughly investigate their opportunities with a long-term perspective and choose a strategic segmentation model where investments and organization-wide specialization of resources and activities will give a sustainable market position. When the strategic macro-segmentation is defined, companies will start developing the tactical micro-segmentation, which is employed to maximize the return on short-term market-related activities.

Micro-Segmentation for Tactical Purposes

Despite having similar product or relationship needs, customers can still differ in terms of economic value and their response to various market activities. For instance, a family with many children is likely to purchase more grocery products than a family with fewer children, and individuals who are active in sports tend to spend more money on sports equipment and fashion than those who are less active.

Companies aim to attract and retain their most economically valuable customers by providing differentiated value propositions and dedicating more resources to satisfying these customers. Economic value-based customer (i.e., CLV) differentiation has become a common practice in the hotel and airline industry, where top-tier loyalty programme members receive exclusive benefits. For instance, Diamond members in the Hilton Honor loyalty programme receive access to executive lounges and are guaranteed a room, even if the hotel is full. Similarly, British Airways rewards its top-tier customers with lifetime membership benefits if they remain members for ten consecutive years. Numerous fast-food restaurants, coffee shops and retailers offer loyalty programmes that reward customers with more benefits and rewards as they make more purchases, seeking to increase their share of customer spending in their respective categories.

Image 5.2   Hilton Honor loyalty programme with multiple layers of benefits for different value segments

Economic value segments can be identified through either direct spending data collected from loyalty programmes or transactions recorded in the accounting system.

In cases where direct economic value data is not available, other indicators can be used to estimate the economic value of customers. For instance, the number of children living in a household can be used to estimate the household's total spending on groceries, and the number of employees in a company can be used to estimate their total spending on office equipment and consumables.

The practice of micro-segmentation involves using variables to differentiate market-related activities. For instance, new customers of a fitness club may have different information needs concerning operating hours, equipment and personal trainers, and therefore respond differently to email promotions compared to established customers. The age of the relationship is thus a variable used to differentiate customer communication. Older customers may prefer personal service at a bank, while younger ones may prefer digital self-service, and this difference in preference will lead to different responses to service encounters. Thus, in this case age of the customer is used as a variable to differentiate customer communication. The objective of micro-segmentation is to identify segments that will enable companies to differentiate and direct their marketing activities more efficiently.

Retailers use distance from a customer's home to the retail location to determine which households to target with their mail promotions. The typical response pattern is shown in Figure 5.2, where we can observe that the response rate is about 20% when the distance is close to zero (i.e. the retailer is located next door). At 10 minutes' travel distance, the response rate decreases to half at 10%, and at 10 minutes, it further declines to 5%. Using the value of response in relation to the cost of distribution, the optimal distance (i.e. micro-segment variable) for distribution of mail promotions can be determined.

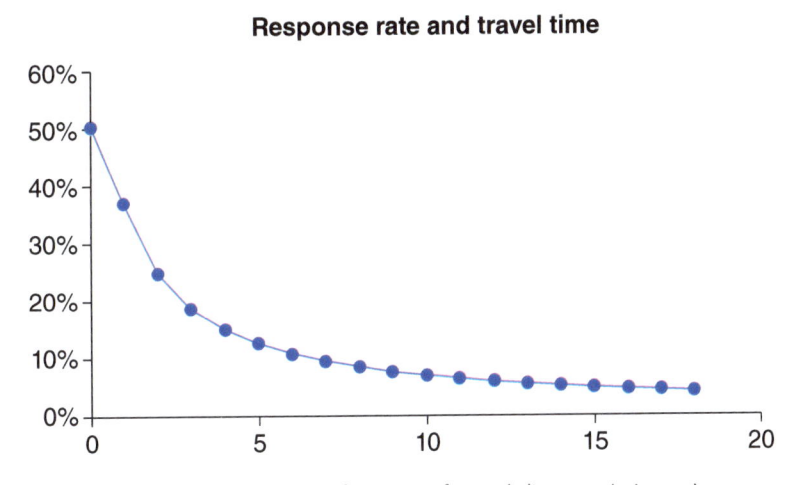

Figure 5.2 Response to promotion as a function of travel distance (minutes)

To gain a deeper understanding of micro-segmentation, companies are building customer databases with a vast array of customer characteristics, alongside developing customer and marketing analytics capabilities. This enables them to explore various factors that could potentially impact on marketing activities and determine differences in customer responses.

As the list of possible variables is extensive, companies are continuously searching for new variables that can be incorporated into their databases.

CUSTOMER DATABASE AND CUSTOMER ANALYTICS

The customer database serves as a repository for storing information about each customer in the company's portfolio. Each customer has a set of variables associated with them. For instance, one variable could be the customer's total spending or sales revenues over the past year, which is gathered from the transaction register, such as the accounting or ERP system. Another variable could be the customer's satisfaction level with the brand, which is obtained from a survey where customers rate their overall satisfaction with the supplier. Additionally, the customer's distance to the nearest store can be a variable, and this data can be gathered by combining the customer's address with publicly available geographic data. As a result, companies can get a more comprehensive view of each customer in their portfolio by integrating data from different sources.

Customers can be either individuals or groups of individuals, such as households. In the case of groceries, the consumption is done by members of a household, making the household the customer. However, one or more individuals from the household may conduct the actual shopping, and it is these individuals that are registered in the transaction records and loyalty programmes. When defining the household as the customer, individual members become representatives of the household. It's important to note that various representatives of a household may not have the same needs or responsiveness to market activities. For instance, one representative may respond positively to price promotions on coffee, while another representative may not be responsive to coffee promotions but may be responsive to promotions on fruits and vegetables. By having this information, grocery retailers can target representatives of the household with different promotion programmes.

The definition of a customer in business markets is more complex because individuals within an organization have varying roles in the buying process (Johnston & Bonoma, 1981). Additionally, organizations often have hierarchical structures with each unit being part of a larger formal structure. Consequently, purchasing decisions may be centralized in a procurement department or decentralized to individual units within the organization. In a customer database, companies need to track representatives at both the organizational unit level and the centralized organizational level. Therefore, keeping track of business customers necessitates a profound understanding of how purchasing decisions are made in different types of companies.

Customer information is often found in multiple data sources and integrated into a customer database, also known as a customer data platform, as shown in Figure 5.3. Algorithms are applied to process the data and transform it into variables that describe the customer. For example, a rule can classify customers as 'New' based on the number of days since their first transaction. The computer compares the date of the first transaction with today's date and calculates the number of days between them. If the number of days is less than a defined number, such as 40 days, a variable labelled 'New' in the customer database is set to 1.

This procedure is repeated daily, and after a defined number of days, such as 40, the 'New' variable is set to 0, indicating that the customer is no longer new. The 'New' variable can then be used to select customers for various customer programmes targeted towards new customers.

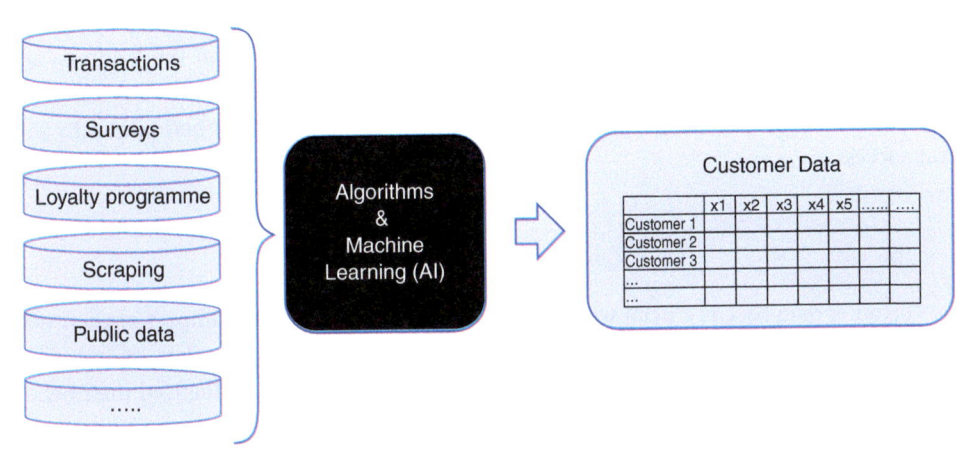

Figure 5.3 Dynamic integrating data from multiple sources and transforming data to variables through algorithms and machine learning stored in a customer data base

Companies use machine learning to improve algorithms and to enhance the intelligence of data, hence the term artificial intelligence (AI). The primary benefit of machine learning is its ability to predict future customer behaviour and thus also the expected cash flow from the customer portfolio. The first prediction is the probability of customers continuing their relationship with the company (brand). The second is prediction of future purchases and transaction costs; that is, whether customers are likely to increase their purchases within the product categories they are active. The third prediction is the probability of customers increasing their connections with the company's network and ecosystem of products and services and the expected value of their purchases in the future. This can be starting purchasing in new product categories, converting to self-service systems, becoming a member of a loyalty programme, and so forth. By updating these predictions dynamically, typically daily, companies can monitor the growth of the customer portfolio in real time.

Companies aim to predict the macro- and micro-segments to which individual customers belong. This classification of customers can be done using data from different sources, and for example combine psychological data with behavioural data. Most companies today have direct email contact with their customers and can send surveys to ask how satisfied they are, attitude towards the brand, and beliefs about competitors. These data can be combined with behavioural data like membership and usage of loyalty programmes, app usage, email campaign responsiveness, number of product categories purchased, personal relationships with sales representatives, contracts, technological systems, and more. By combining these data sources companies can predict to which segment a customer belongs; for example, whether the customer is likely to be an acquaintance, a friend or a partner.

Companies often use prediction models to identify potential new customers who are likely to respond positively to customer acquisition programmes. These models use data from existing customers to identify characteristics that can be used to identify potential customers. For example, a media company might develop a prediction model for prospective advertisers that could be targeted by their sales force. The model could use variables such as industry (e.g. retail, restaurant), number of employees, location (i.e. address) and other factors to predict the likelihood that a prospect would be interested in advertising in their media channel. By using this model, the company could schedule their sales calls with great success.

Causal Inferences (Why)

The customer data base is crucial when companies need to analyse the impact of their marketing investments on revenues and profits. By analysing the time-series data on individual customers, companies can investigate how marketing activities have influenced their behaviours. For instance, a company may discover that a particular type of email promotion boosts cash flow from customers in one segment but not in another. Armed with this knowledge, the company can redesign and tailor its email promotions for better results. As illustrated in Case Study 5.2, the higher the discounted offer, the shorter the customers lasted.

Case Study 5.2

Subscription Discount for Acquiring New Readers to a Newspaper

A newspaper company conducted a study to evaluate the effectiveness of their promotion programme, specifically the impact of different price discounts on subscription duration. As expected, larger discounts resulted in more new subscribers. Using their customer database, the newspaper was able to track the duration of these new customers and group them by the level of discount they received. Interestingly, they found that customers who received higher discounts had shorter subscription durations. The newspaper continued their investigation and conducted qualitative interviews, revealing that customers' mindsets were different depending on the level of discount. When the discount was low, customers thought about the quality of the newspaper, but when the discount was high, they focused on the discount itself rather than the quality of the newspaper. Therefore, to retain customers who were recruited with high discounts, the company needed to shift their focus from the discount to the quality of the newspaper.

Causal inference can also help to understand why certain customer behaviours occur, such as why customers leave a brand or defect. An example of this is a university college that wanted to understand why so many students left after their first year in their bachelor programmes. Based on scientific research on the topic they conducted data to test some hypotheses (Tinto, 2001). Using data from their customer database, the college analysed variables such as student activity on the learning platform, the number of study points achieved each semester (study points were awarded when exams were passed), and whether the student continued to the second year or not. To capture more psychological variables such as motivation and satisfaction, a survey was developed and sent to all students after their first year, including those who continued and those who left. A statistical model of the variables was created to understand the connections between them, as shown in Figure 5.4. The results showed that one reason students left was a lack of confidence in their choice of bachelor programme, which led to less effort in learning, lower academic integration and less social integration with other students. The second type of motivation was related to academic interest and mastery, while the third was related to social integration. Together, these three motivational factors explained 78% of the variance in learning effort and 41% in the variance of defection, which are high numbers in the social sciences. Unmotivated students put less effort into their learning, resulting in fewer study points, less satisfaction and, ultimately, defection.

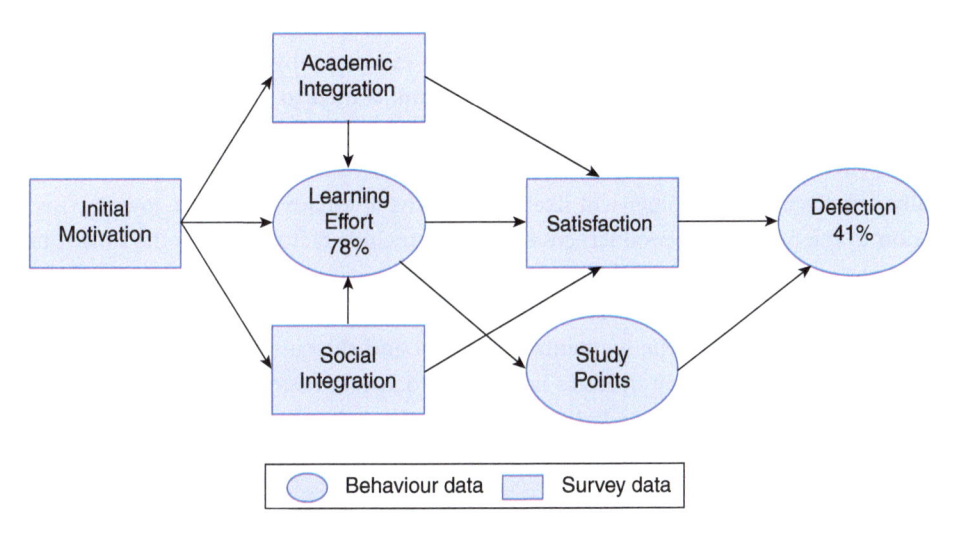

Figure 5.4 A causal model for how motivation affects defection in a university programme

Customer Privacy

The personalization privacy paradox refers to the tension between customers' desire for more relevant products and services and their concern for privacy protection (Awad & Krishnan, 2006). While customers may benefit from sharing personal information with suppliers, such as receiving better offers or personalized recommendations, there is a risk that the collected information may not always be used in their best interest. Also, customers may react negatively when information becomes too personal with a negative effect on brand attitudes (Simonson, 2005; White et al., 2006).

Companies must develop their customer databases in compliance with strict laws and regulations that protect customer privacy rights (Goddard, 2017; Wolters, 2018). The GDPR's aim is to protect all EU citizens from privacy and data breaches in an increasingly data-driven world. The regulation applies to all personal data of data subjects residing in the Union, regardless of the company's location. A breach of GDPR can result in a fine of up to 4% of annual global turnover or 20 million euros (whichever is greater). The main principle is that individuals must give their consent before companies can store their personal data. The request for consent must be given in an intelligible and easily accessible form, with the purpose for data processing attached to that consent, and it must be as easy to withdraw consent as it is to give it. People have the right to obtain confirmation from the data controller if personal data concerning them is being processed, where it is being processed, and for what purpose. This change represents a dramatic shift towards data transparency and empowering data subjects. Non-member countries in Europe like Norway and the UK have adapted to the EU regulation, and countries in other parts of the world like, for example, the USA, have implemented similar regulation that protects the privacy interests of their citizens.

CUSTOMER VALUE PROPOSITIONS

The customer value proposition is a statement that explains why customers should choose to connect with and purchase from the company, and is used to shape perceptions of their offerings. Customers tend to choose the alternative that they perceive to be best value which is most beneficial in relation to its costs. Therefore, if two alternatives are perceived to be equally beneficial, the customer will likely choose the alternative with the lowest costs. In addition to the price of the product, costs may also include factors such as the time it takes to make the purchase, the perceived risk of purchasing the product and other issues that may affect the effort required to make the purchase.

The alignment between the segmentation model and the customer value proposition is crucial. The value proposition needs to be tailored to attract customers with different needs and preferences for products or relationships. This means that the value proposition will be differentiated to fit the specific segments defined in the segmentation model.

Value Propositions for Product Needs

Companies aim to attract customers by targeting product need segments with relevant and compelling value propositions. For instance, IKEA's value proposition is focused on providing a broad selection of well-designed and functional home furnishing products at affordable prices. This value proposition is tailored to customers who seek products with decent quality and good design at reasonable prices. In order to align with their value proposition, IKEA has specialized their business activities, including streamlined and highly integrated production and logistics, which help to ensure quality and lower costs. As a result, IKEA's value proposition has successfully attracted thousands of customers worldwide and is an excellent example of strategic marketing.

Other companies may choose to specialize in multiple product need segments, such as British Airways which has different value propositions for its business and private travellers. This is explored further in Case Study 5.3 below.

Image 5.3 An IKEA store

Case Study 5.3

British Airways

For private customers, British Airways offers a premium service that comes with added value for those willing to pay a price premium. On the other hand, for the business segment, British Airways focuses on the customers' leisure time and offers a high level of comfort and service in their Club World cabin. Their value proposition for this segment is, 'Our Club World cabin offers premium levels of comfort and service with the freedom and flexibility to make every journey unique and unforgettable. Whether you're travelling for business or leisure, there's a Club World seat with your name on it' (https://www.britishairways.com/en-gb/information/travel-classes/business/club-world). This allows British Airways to offer differentiated value propositions to each segment based on their unique needs and preferences.

When companies like British Airways operate in multiple need segments under the same brand name, they often add a more general value proposition that appeals across all segments. For example, British Airways associates its brand with environmental sustainability and corporate responsibility with the following statement: 'Connecting Britain with the world and the world with Britain. British Airways is a global airline, bringing people, places and diverse cultures closer together for more than 100 years. Serving our community and planet is at the heart of everything we do, and we look forward to sharing our exciting sustainability initiatives with you' (https://www.britishairways.com/content/information/about-ba).

(Continued)

Image 5.4   A British Airways jet

Value Propositions for Relationship Needs

As previously mentioned, customers have different levels of need when it comes to connecting with suppliers. Customers tend to choose suppliers they trust and those who can assist them in fulfilling their purchasing task more efficiently. Acquaintances, friends and partners reflect the three types of needs that have been identified (see Table 5.3; p. 158).

Customers who fall under the acquaintance type of relationship need are attracted to a value proposition that offers parity value, meaning that the products offered are reliable and comparable in quality to alternative brands in the market. To make the brand more appealing to these customers, companies offer lower costs in the form of lower prices, a streamlined purchasing process, or a lower perceived risk. Ryanair provides an example of this type of value proposition (as illustrated in Image 5.5). Acquaintance-type customers also tend to choose brand names with which they are familiar, as familiarity reduces risk. Building brand awareness and familiarity through advertising can be an effective strategy for reaching these customers. However, they are unlikely to respond positively to value propositions that suggest superior products or solutions at higher prices because they believe that all products and services are more or less the same, or that better products and services do not provide them with more benefits and value.

The value proposition for the friend segment is based on offering superior value. This means that the brand's attractiveness is not only limited to the product benefits but also includes service and the customer's interaction with the brand. For instance, Nordstrom, a successful fashion retailer in America, has positioned itself as a brand with superior customer service. They are renowned for their service quality based on the slogan 'Our one rule. Use good

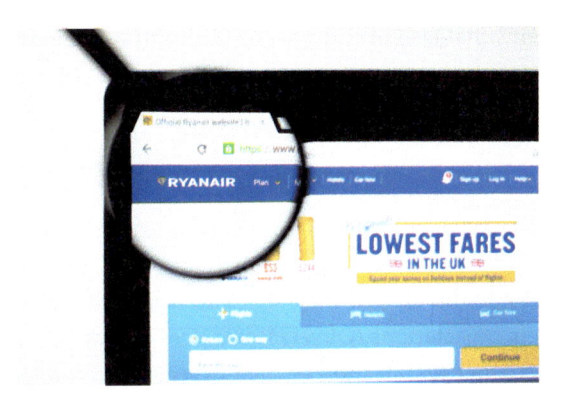

Image 5.5 Ryanair website

judgment in all situations'. Friend customers are more likely to respond positively to value propositions that suggest additional benefits and higher quality, and they are willing to pay a premium price or other costs. However, there may be differences within the friend segment regarding the type of additional benefits that they find attractive. For example, families on a resort vacation may find children's facilities appealing, while older customers may prefer spa facilities. Therefore, customers in both segments may find the brand attractive, but for different reasons, and the attraction may also depend on the situation. When a couple is travelling with their children, children's facilities are attractive, but when the couple is travelling without their children, it is likely that the spa facilities make the resort appealing.

To cater to partner customers, companies offer a superior customized value proposition, where customers are invited to invest time and effort to obtain added value. For instance, to access Starbucks' pre-order and prepayment service, customers have to be members of their loyalty programme, download the app and allow the company to withdraw payment from their bank account or credit card. With this customized set-up, customers could get their favourite coffee with less hassle. While partnering has been a common practice in business-to-business markets, the digitalization of customer interactions has accelerated customization and partnering where customers also invest in the relationship, in consumer markets as well. Partner customers are therefore likely to respond positively to value propositions that offer more benefits and lower costs.

MANAGING CUSTOMER EXPERIENCE

Companies strive to create compelling value propositions to attract customers and drive sales. However, a strong value proposition also raises customers' expectations and increases the demand for quality products and services. Meeting these expectations usually leads to customer satisfaction and retention, while failing to do so usually results in dissatisfaction and a desire to end the relationship. Effective customer experience management involves ensuring customer satisfaction as they engage with the company, including the quality of the product and the customer service they receive. A critical aspect of customer experience management is removing any incidents that lead to customer dissatisfaction, while also seeking to improve the efficiency and design of the customer's interaction with the company.

Customer Satisfaction

Customer satisfaction can be described as the feeling of pleasure derived from the fulfilment of a need, desire or goal through consumption. It is based on the customer's perception of how consumption measures up against their standard of pleasure versus displeasure, which is often shaped by their expectations (Oliver, 1980, 1997). Negative disconfirmation occurs when the customer's experiences fall short of their expectations, while positive disconfirmation occurs when their experiences exceed their expectations.

The literature has extensively documented the positive impact of customer satisfaction on financial performance, making it one of the most commonly used metrics to assess a company's market performance (Fornell et al., 2006). This effect is driven by a causal mechanism where positive experiences reinforce customers' beliefs that the brand is a good choice, generating positive feelings towards the brand that result in a favourable attitude and a willingness to continue the relationship. However, it is important to recognize that loyalty is merely an intention, and as with intentions in general, they are often not followed through.

Customer loyalty is influenced not only by satisfaction, but also by various other factors such as the nature of the relationship and the broader network in which it is embedded (Watson et al., 2015; Khamitov et al., 2019). Customers may also feel an obligation to maintain the relationship because they wish to reciprocate the efforts made by the supplier on their behalf (Bagozzi, 1995). In addition, switching costs can affect customer loyalty (Klemperer, 1987; Pick & Eisend, 2014). For instance, if a customer has already chosen a particular bank, there is a cost associated with switching to a different bank in terms of the time required to set up a new account. The decision to stay or switch to another supplier or brand also involves the comparison of alternatives (Kelley & Thibaut, 1978; Anderson & Narus, 1984). Even the most devoted customers of brands like BMW, Audi and Mercedes have switched to Tesla because the latter provided a more appealing value proposition.

Customer satisfaction is widely recognized as an important factor influencing customer loyalty (Fornell et al., 1996). However, it is not a guarantee that customers will remain loyal. Southwest Airlines is an example of a company that has consistently scored high in customer satisfaction and has outperformed its competitors for many years. Southwest's focus on reliability and customer service has helped it maintain scores around 80 on the American Customer Satisfaction Index (ACSI) since 2008. However, as shown in Figure 5.5, competitors are catching up, which means that Southwest's competitive advantage is declining (Statistica, 2023c). When customers are equally satisfied with all brands in a market, companies must innovate their products and services to find new ways to gain a competitive advantage.

To address quality failures in products or services, customer experience managers need to determine the root cause of customer dissatisfaction. There are two common measurement systems used to collect feedback: episodic and relationship monitoring.

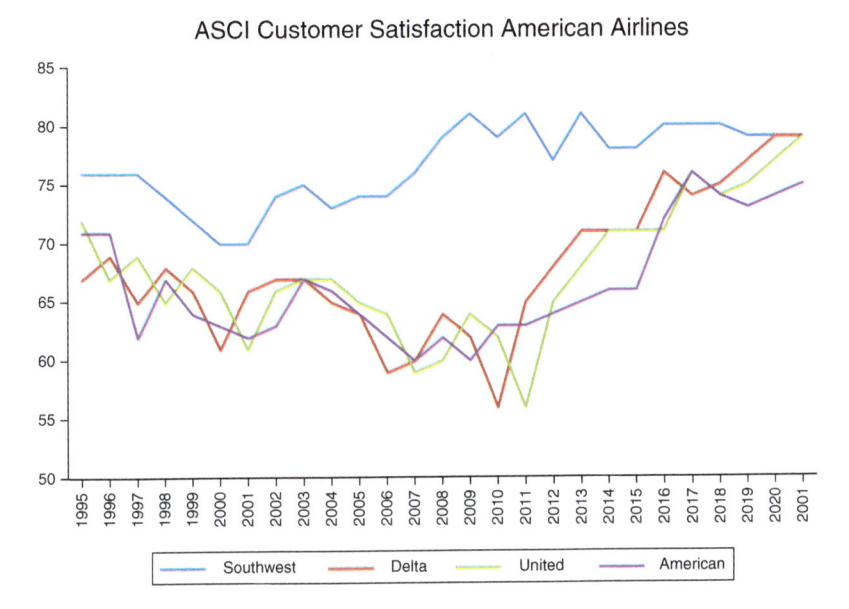

Figure 5.5 Satisfaction scores for the main airlines in USA

Episodic systems involve obtaining customer feedback on each occasion that they interact with the company or brand. For instance, if a customer has contacted a bank's service centre, they may receive a text message or email afterwards, asking whether they were satisfied with the service and, if not, the reason for their dissatisfaction. The rationale behind episodic measurement is that every interaction with the company builds overall satisfaction and loyalty. As such, it is crucial to ensure that each interaction fulfils customer expectations. For many companies, episodic measurement of customer satisfaction is a valuable tool.

A variant of the episodic measure of satisfaction is the Net Promoter Score (NPS) where customers are asked how likely it is that they will recommend the supplier or brand to others (Reichheld, 2003). Although the literature has concluded that NPS is less informative as measures of satisfaction (Keiningham et al., 2007), many companies use this method to track customer experiences.

The relationship method involves measuring the overall satisfaction that customers have with a supplier or brand. This approach assumes that the overall satisfaction is a function of many factors of more or less importance. For instance, a customer may have high satisfaction for a single interaction with a bank's service centre (i.e. high episodic satisfaction), but overall dissatisfaction due to the bank's high mortgage loan interest rates. The typical approach for the relationship method involves conducting annual interviews with customers to assess their overall satisfaction and satisfaction with quality aspects of products and services.

Product expectations are dynamic and are influenced by innovations and competitive advancements that change the relative appeal of a brand. We will explore this further in Case Study 5.4 in the example of Tesla.

Case Study 5.4

Tesla

Tesla gained a competitive edge over established car manufacturers such as Mercedes, Audi and BMW by offering superior electric cars. However, these competitors have been catching up by improving their line of electric cars, eroding Tesla's relative advantage. As a result, many of Tesla's customers may become less satisfied with the brand as it becomes less attractive in comparison to competing brands. This trend is reflected in the Norwegian Customer Satisfaction Barometer (Figure 5.6), where Tesla's customer satisfaction score peaked at 82.2 out of 100 in 2018 and has since been lower.[1] It is noteworthy that BMW and Volvo also experienced declining scores until 2020, but this trend has reversed because both manufacturers have introduced many electric models that are perceived as equal to or better than Tesla, reducing Tesla's relative attractiveness.

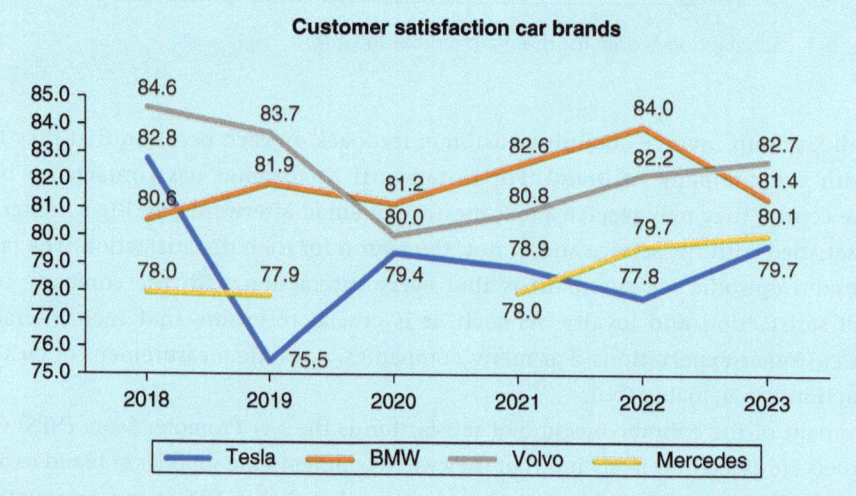

Figure 5.6   Results from the annual customer satisfaction barometer in Norway illustrating how satisfaction with Tesla has changed from 2018 to 2023

To improve customer satisfaction and loyalty, customer experience managers need to understand the different types of customer expectations (Harmeling et al., 2015). Product expectations are related to the quality of the product or service that the customer has purchased, while relational expectations refer to the quality of the customer's interactions with the supplier or brand, often referred to as service quality. A service can also be sold as a product, as,

[1] https://www.bi.no/forskning/norsk-kundebarometer/bransjeresultater-2023

for example, public transportation, hotels, airlines, and so forth. In the marketing literature there are numerous discussions on the difference between physical products and intangible (service) products (Bitner & Booms, 1981; Levitt, 1981). In this context we address service as the process of interacting with the supplier to solve a problem. Thus, an airline (which is a service product) is also contacted by customers to make a reservation, change a ticket, complain about bad experiences, and so forth. The impact of service quality on customer satisfaction and loyalty has been well-documented in the literature (Carrillat et al., 2009). The five key dimensions of service quality are reliability (dependable and accurate service delivery), responsiveness (promptness in helping customers), empathy (caring attention to individual customers), assurance (knowledge and courtesy of service providers) and tangibles (appearance of people and physical materials; Parasuraman et al., 1988). By focusing on improving these dimensions, customer experience managers can improve overall service quality and drive greater customer satisfaction and loyalty.

The foundation of a satisfactory customer experience is reliability. Customers expect suppliers to fulfil their promises, such as delivering a product on a specified date. However, simply meeting this expectation may not lead to delighted customers. The second dimension, responsiveness, is crucial as well. Customers expect suppliers to be quick to help them when needed. When combined with empathy, responsiveness creates a sense of perceived benevolence that strongly influences the fulfilment of relational expectations (Selnes & Grønhaug, 2000).

Multichannel Service Interaction

Customers engage with companies or brands to gather information, place orders, receive physical delivery of products, make payments and receive post-sale support, if necessary. Customers interact with companies through mainly one or more of the following channels:

- physical stores;
- online websites;
- catalogues;
- customer service centres;
- salespeople.

The coordination of the multichannel system is crucial, as depicted in Figure 5.7. Channels must be synchronized so that customer interactions are recorded and updated consistently across all channels. For instance, if a customer seeks information online and then visits the physical store to purchase the product, the information available online, such as product details, prices and availability, must match what the customer sees in the store. Similarly, if a customer places an order online for in-store pickup but later contacts customer service to modify the order, the customer service team must be aligned with the rest of the channels and able to fulfil the customer's request.

Some companies may include search engines, social media and digital marketplaces as a customer interaction channels, at least for information search purposes. Many customers start their search on Google and other search engines, and companies need to work on how the search engines use information on their company and brands. If the company is selling electric cars, their company name or brands should come high up in the search result field by either organic or paid presence. Many customers use Facebook and other social media to find good suppliers and brands. Also, digital marketplaces like Amazon, Alibaba and TripAdvisor, are important and frequently information sources in many markets. Companies need to align their own customer interaction channels, where they have full control, with other channels' customers use, in order to collect and disseminate information about their products and services (Lovett & Staelin, 2016).

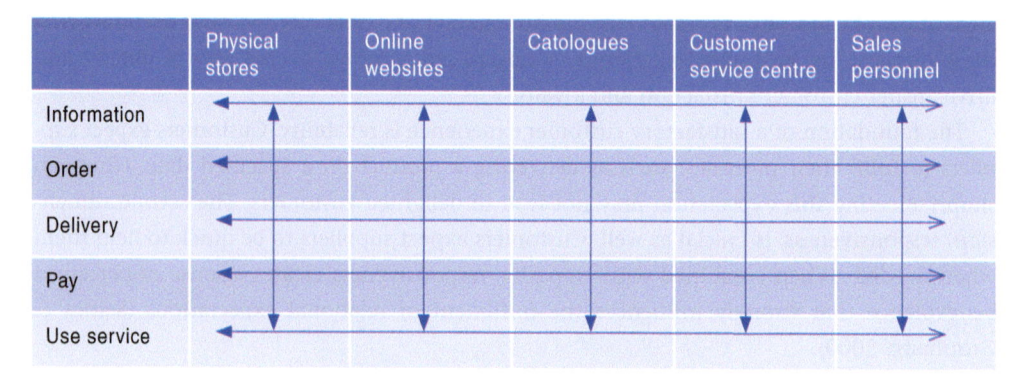

	Physical stores	Online websites	Catologues	Customer service centre	Sales personnel
Information					
Order					
Delivery					
Pay					
Use service					

Figure 5.7 Multichannel functions for customer service interaction

Service Level

Service level in multichannel interaction systems increases with one or more of the following qualities:

- speed and convenience;
- friendliness and empathy;
- assistance and competence;
- personal adjustments and customization.

The concepts of speed and convenience refer to the ease and speed with which customers can access the supplier. These factors can be improved by various means, such as having a physical location, extended opening hours and sufficient staffing. Providing a high level of service means that customers can interact with the supplier at any time and place, without having to wait. In today's market, customers expect online services to be available 24/7. For many retailers and fast-food restaurants, having a physical presence close to where people live and work is important. Being located in shopping centres can also provide faster and more straightforward access to customers, who can bundle their purchases with other items, thereby saving time.

The social dimension of customer contact is related to friendliness and empathy. Customers appreciate service employees who display sociable and friendly behaviour, maintain eye contact, offer polite phrases like 'Thank you' and 'I'm sorry' without over-doing it, and smile. Companies can enhance this dimension by cultivating a service-oriented culture, recruiting employees with strong social skills and providing service quality training to their staff.

Assistance and competence are crucial for customers when they require help to identify their product requirements and assess different options, as well as after the purchase when they begin to use the products. For instance, electronic retailers have witnessed a rise in the demand for usage support. In the past, most electronic devices only needed to be plugged into a power outlet to function. However, nowadays, such products must be configured to meet the customer's needs and other appliances in a technological network. As a result, companies operating in such situations need to enhance their post-purchase services by making them not only competent but also readily available and friendly.

By providing personalization and customization options in customer interactions, com-panies can offer better service and provide more value to their customers. Starbucks, for example, offers a pre-order service through its loyalty programme, allowing customers to order their coffee in advance and avoid waiting in line.

Managers must understand that various service-level elements will have distinct levels of usefulness for different customer segments. It is crucial to identify how customers perceive and value these different elements. For example, certain customer segments may prioritize speed and convenience while others may prioritize assistance and competence. Furthermore, elements within each contact channel may vary across segments. One customer segment may place high importance on the physical appearance of a store interior, while another segment may prioritize space and checkout facilities (Gustafsson & Johnson, 2003). For the online channels, companies use digital applications to adjust their websites dynamically for different customer segments (Hauser et al., 2009).

The significance of different contact channels varies depending on the product category. Buying airline tickets online is highly practical because the service is entirely based on digital information. However, buying a dress online may be less useful because a lot of information such as body-fit, fabrics and colours cannot be fully digitized and must be assessed physically. Nevertheless, many customers still prefer to buy their clothes online, but in that case, the physical information is less important either because they have already examined the phys-ical product or because the advantages of the digital channel outweigh the importance of the physical information (Kuan et al., 2008).

Service Interaction Design

To effectively manage customer experience, companies must also focus on designing efficient and effective service interaction processes on their customers' journeys (Edelman & Singer, 2015). Service interaction is, for example, when a customer enters a store and starts searching for information and products. Another example is when customers contact their insurance company to alter their contract. Thus, there are many encounters where customers meet or

MARKETING MANAGEMENT

interact with a company. A service interaction design process starts with defining the service concept, as illustrated in Figure 5.8, with the aim of creating positive customer experiences. Through gap analysis, which monitors deviations from defined standards, companies can systematically improve their service concept. The service concept is defined by the organization of the service production (structure), the infrastructure supporting the service production and how different service production activities are integrated. For example, if an airline wants to differentiate its service for economy class and business class passengers, it can structure the process differently, such as by implementing different check-in procedures, seating arrangements and on-board services for each segment. Coordination among different contact channels is also important to ensure that customer information is available and updated across all channels, allowing for seamless booking changes, for example.

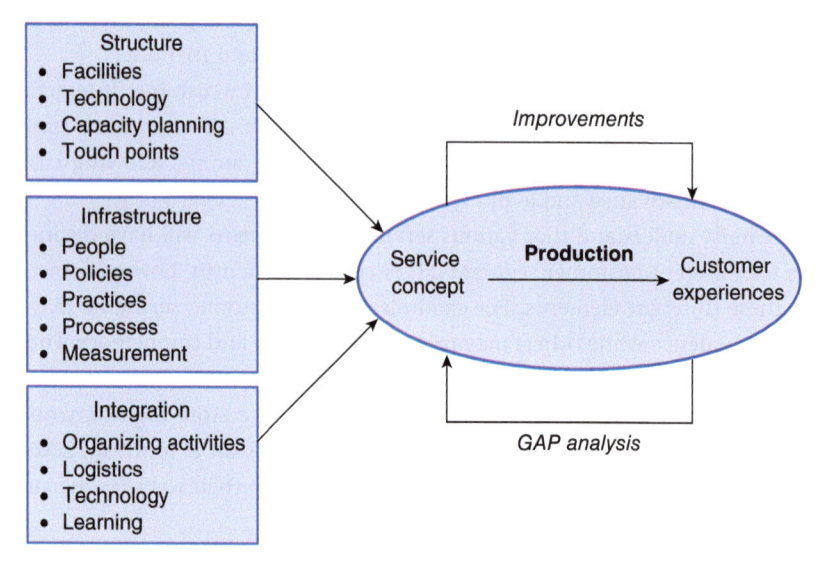

Figure 5.8 A framework for designing more effective and efficient service interaction design (Roth & Menor, 2003)

The continuous digitalization of customer service and the emergence of self-service options offer numerous opportunities for managing customer experience. In terms of financial benefits, the digitization of customer interactions can replace costly service employees with computers, thereby reducing service costs (Surprenant & Solomon, 1987; Meuter et al., 2000; Selnes & Hansen, 2001). Additionally, well-designed digital encounters can improve service quality in various ways (Parasuraman & Grewal, 2000). Firstly, computers eliminate waiting time and make services available at any time and place. Secondly, computers provide accurate information, enabling customers to change and modify their orders and contracts without the risk of human error that may occur in face-to-face interactions. Furthermore, customer relationship management (CRM) systems offer service employees access to customer data and a record of their interaction history for every service request. Each request is assigned a case number, which ensures that all personnel involved in solving the service request have access to the same data, and management can monitor how requests are resolved, including response time, quality issues, and other metrics.

Companies are increasingly turning to artificial intelligence and robots to provide customer service. Some hotels have already replaced personal room service with computer-based systems, while in the nursing home industry, robots are being deployed to perform a variety of service operations.

Image 5.6   A robot providing hotel room service

While self-service options can handle many service requests, personal assistance is still necessary for certain situations. Self-service requires customers to have a clear understanding of their request and be comfortable with technology. However, personal assistance is needed when customers have more complex service needs or lack the technical expertise to operate digital services. To accommodate different customer needs, most companies offer a combination of self-service and personal service. As technology takes care of routine service requests, service employees can focus on more complex requests that require advanced skills and personal interaction abilities, as highlighted in the service profit chain (Heskett et al., 1994; Hogreve et al., 2017).

CUSTOMER PROGRAMMES

Customer portfolio management aims to achieve several goals, such as acquiring new customers, reducing churn, positive word of mouth and increasing the degree of connectedness with existing customers, leading to higher revenue and profits. To attain these goals, companies develop customer programmes that are targeted activities to achieve these goals. It's important to note that customer programmes are different from campaigns because programmes are repeated activities while campaigns are one-time activities, such as an advertising campaign. Customer programmes are tailored to customers based on macro- and micro-segments. Customer programmes can also be referred to as relationship marketing (Palmatier et al., 2006).

Customer programmes typically begin with a message delivered through one or more communication channels. These channels may include media advertising (such as print or digital media, social media and similar platforms), direct personal channels (such as email, SMS, call centres or sales personnel), or indirectly through partners (such as retailers, financial services and similar entities). The primary goal of the initial message is to generate a response from the customer, which may occur through the same channel or a different one. For example, a company may send an email to members of its customer club, informing them of a promotion and providing a link to a website where the promotion is presented. The desired response in this case would be for the customers to click on the link, which is commonly referred to as the click-through rate (CTR).

Customer programmes are subject to continuous improvement and development, based on systematic evaluation and analytics. For example, a programme may prove to be more effective for younger customers than older ones, and a new version of the programme may then be developed to target the latter. As time passes, customer programmes become increasingly fine-grained to better accommodate the individual differences found in the customer database (i.e. micro-segments).

Below we describe a selection of customer programmes and comment on their advantages and some challenges. Companies typically have various programmes designed for acquiring new customers, retaining existing ones, creating positive word of mouth, maximizing customer value and upgrading relationships. Some programmes can serve more than one purpose. For instance, a loyalty programme may attract new customers, retain existing ones, maximize their value and enhance their relationship with the company (brand).

Customer Loyalty Programmes

A loyalty programme aims to retain customers and create brand preference by offering rewards. It consists of two main components: an earning model and a redemption model. The earning model provides customers with reward points for each purchase, with the size of the reward increasing with the amount spent. Rewards can take various forms, such as monetary rewards like a free product or discount, or benefits like fast-track, VIP lounge access and upgrades. The earning model is often linked with partners to enable customers to accumulate reward points more quickly by purchasing from programme partners (Dorotic et al., 2021). For example, Scandinavian Airlines' EuroBonus programme has partnered with 25 airlines in Star Alliance, including Lufthansa and United,[2] as well as many hotels, car rentals and other loyalty programmes such as Trumf in Norway. Hilton Honor is recognized as having one of the most successful loyalty programmes in the world, as presented in Case Study 5.5.

---

[2] See https://www.staralliance.com/en/home

Case Study 5.5

Hilton Honor Loyalty Programme

Hilton's Honor loyalty programme is widely considered one of the most successful loyalty programmes globally, with over 120 million members accounting for 50–60% of their total bookings. More than 70% of the company's sales are registered in their loyalty programmes (Digital Marketing News, 2023). In addition to providing financial incentives, the programme has also introduced other benefits catering to the specific preferences of their most valuable customers. According to a senior manager at Hilton, some customers value tangible benefits such as free Wi-Fi or breakfast, while others prefer high-touch experiences such as the ability to call the concierge or pre-order meals to their room.

The principle of rewarding customers in loyalty programmes differs greatly from ordinary discounts. With discounts, the customer receives a reduced price at the point of purchase, whereas with rewards in loyalty programmes, the customer earns points for their purchases and can redeem them for rewards at a later point in time. The reward serves as an incentive for customers to return and continue their relationship with the company (brand), and comes into play when the customer is faced with a choice between alternative suppliers or brands in the future. Due to the rewards earned in a loyalty programme, the customer perceives a potential loss by choosing another supplier or brand. According to prospect theory, people have a strong aversion to loss and are likely to choose the alternative with the least perceived loss, even if the other alternative is better (Kahneman & Tversky, 1979; Camerer, 2005). The more rewards a customer has earned, the stronger this perceived loss effect on their behaviour will be. This is known as the goal-gradient hypothesis (Kivetz et al., 2006).

Academic literature frequently debates the extent to which loyalty programmes can create a more positive and favourable attitude towards a brand, known as brand attitudinal loyalty (Dorotic et al., 2012). Critics argue that customers only take advantage of the economic rewards offered by loyalty programmes, and that their attitude towards the brand is unaffected. They suggest that as soon as the reward is redeemed, there is no further effect on behaviour. Additionally, critics argue that customers collect rewards from all the brands they use without any impact on behaviour. For instance, a customer may join all of the grocery store loyalty programmes in the neighbourhood simply to collect rewards, without any effect on their behaviour (Nunes & Drèze, 2006).

However, loyalty programmes will normally create a favourable attitude towards a brand if the benefits offered in addition to economic rewards have immense value. For example, the pre-order service offered to members of the Starbucks loyalty programme increases the attractiveness of Starbucks vis-à-vis the other coffee shops. Thus, customers expect more value from the brand after having adapted to the programme. The effort required to get access to the service is a type of investment (sunk cost) that has value only within the relationship with the supplier (brand), and thus will create a type of switching cost in favour of the loyalty programme brand.

Loyalty programmes offer a significant benefit by establishing a communication channel between the brand and the individual customer. Members provide their email address, phone number and other relevant contact information. This benefit has become even more important as traditional mass communication channels are no longer as effective due to changes in media consumption habits. For example, fewer people are watching broadcast TV or reading newspapers and magazines. As a result, email marketing has become one of the most essential communication tools in marketing. Additionally, loyalty programmes provide companies with valuable data about their customers that can be used to generate general insights about customers and competitors, as well as specific knowledge about individual customers and the effectiveness of their marketing activities.

Many companies have introduced customer membership clubs to create connections and a communication channel with their customers (Andjelic, 2022). Members of, for example, Nike's customer club receive information about new products, promotions, product and service updates, and other company-related news. Unlike loyalty programmes, customer clubs do not have an earning model, which means that rewards cannot be differentiated based on purchase history. As a result, customer clubs are less complex to manage, as companies do not have to keep track of all transactions and points earned and used in a programme. While the individual customer data collected in customer clubs may not be as extensive as those in loyalty programmes, they are still valuable. Companies can, for example, use the location data provided by customers (i.e. customers provide name and mail address in addition to email address and phone number) to analyse the potential market around their operative units, such as retailers, restaurants or other types of businesses. This information can be used to tailor digital advertising to areas with different market shares and demographic profiles.

Loyalty programmes and customer clubs are powerful marketing tools that can help to protect, expand and convert customer relationships. These programmes can even convert previous customers into loyal customers, ultimately contributing to the acquisition of new customers. Therefore, the strategic significance of loyalty programmes and customer clubs is significant, as they provide the necessary means to build a sustainable and profitable customer base.

Customer Acquisition Programmes

Companies must strike a balance between investing in existing customer relationships and creating new relationships through customer acquisition programmes (Reinartz et al., 2005). A new customer doesn't just mean someone who has never had a relationship with the company (brand) before, but can also refer to a previous customer who is no longer active. While recruiting new customers is essential for customer portfolio growth, companies should focus on attracting customers who are more likely to continue purchasing and have a higher purchase volume. Expanding the customer base is also vital for achieving economies of scale and reducing unit costs.

In general, customer acquisition involves attracting customers from competitors, with the exception being during the early stages of a product life cycle when new customers enter a category. For instance, when parents have their first child, they enter product categories related to baby-care. Given that most customer acquisition involves stealing customers from competitors, companies need to offer incentives to entice new customers to switch.

Offering price discounts is a commonly used tactic to attract new customers (Lewis, 2006). For instance, subscription-based services such as Spotify and Netflix, newspapers like *The Times* and *Bild*, magazines like *Sports Illustrated* and *Burda*, and health clubs like Bannatyne in the UK and McFit in Germany often provide discounted or even free trial subscriptions. Retailers and fast-food chains advertise price promotions in direct mail sent to non-customers and in digital campaigns. Many media channels have access to the names and addresses of their regular customers, so advertisers can match this information and send digital ads to those who are not in the customer database. Once new customers sign up, companies launch onboarding programmes that focus on communicating the value and relevance of their products and services to encourage customers to continue using them.

Image 5.7 A Netflix subscription promotion

Managing word of mouth (WOM) is crucial in influencing customers' purchasing decisions as they rely heavily on the experiences shared by other customers (de Matos & Rossi, 2008). The original definition of WOM referred to non-commercial, person-to-person communication between a communicator and a receiver about a product, brand or service. However, with the advent of social media and digital networks, electronic word of mouth (eWOM) has become an even more influential source of information for customers. TripAdvisor, which was launched in 2001, was a pioneer in eWOM. It was founded on the premise of addressing the lack of diagnostic information on hotels' websites and brochures. TripAdvisor's popularity has made it essential for hotels and restaurants to maintain a positive presence on the platform and strive for positive reviews from their customers.

Image 5.8   Tripadvisor logo

Currently, product reviews are widely available in almost every market and have become a vital source of information. Research indicates that people place their trust in digital reviews, and eWOM has a powerful influence on sales. The positivity of the reviews is crucial, and the greater the positivity, the stronger the impact on sales. However, the volume of reviews is equally important, and research has found that it has a significant impact on sales (Floyd et al., 2014; You et al., 2015). On average, a 10% increase in positivity (for example, from 6.0 to 6.6 on a 10-point scale) leads to a 5% increase in sales. Similarly, a 10% increase in the number of reviews (from 50 to 55 reviews) results in a 3% increase in sales. It should be noted that these are average effects, and there can be significant variations across markets and product categories.

Influencers with large followings are another form of important eWOM (Wies et al., 2023). They provide recommendations to their followers regarding products they like or dislike, and their followers often take note of these recommendations. These influencers are compensated by companies that want their products promoted. Surprisingly, even if followers are aware that the influencers are paid to post positive reviews, they still trust them to be impartial. This is because they believe that influencers will only take on promotion jobs if they genuinely believe in and value the product they are promoting (Hughes et al., 2019).

Price Promotion Programmes

Companies use price promotion programmes to generate more sales from their existing customer base, such as increasing the frequency of their visits and the size of their baskets. However, a price reduction comes at a cost, which is the lost profit margin, and the increase in sales volume must be greater than the cost to be effective (Gupta, 1988). While most products tend to sell more when offered at a discounted price, this does not always guarantee an increase in sales for retailers. In fact, research shows that in retailing, typically, one-third of the price-promoted product results in customer switching, meaning that customers switch from one brand to another to take advantage of the promotion. Another third of the price-promoted products leads to stockpiling, where customers purchase more during the promotion and less in the following weeks because they have stocked up. Finally, for some products, price discounts increase the overall consumption of the product, such as when people eat more chocolate and ice cream because they purchased it at a discount. Notably, price discounts are found to have a greater effect on perceived high-quality brands than ordinary brands. Therefore, a 20% discount on a high-quality brand like Heinz generates more sales than a 20% discount on a private store brand like First Price.

A price promotion can be seen as an experiment where price reduction can increase the sales of the product as well as increase the sales of other products (Russell & Petersen, 2000). By utilizing the vast amount of customer information available, companies can customize price-promotion programmes to target products and customers with the highest potential for increased sales. For example, if a grocery retailer can identify a customer in their database who has a baby but is not buying diapers or baby food from them, they can create a special price promotion on these products and target it directly to this customer. This level of personalization can increase the effectiveness of price-promotion programmes and lead to higher sales and customer satisfaction.

Personal Customer Visit Programmes

A personal customer visit is a face-to-face meeting between a sales representative and a potential or current customer. The primary goal of such visits may vary, either to convert a prospect into a customer or to strengthen existing relationships. In the latter case, the visit typically starts with the sales representative soliciting feedback from the customer about their experiences and satisfaction levels (Mohr et al., 2010). Then, the representative listens to the customer's needs and challenges. Based on this information, the representative may suggest products and services that can help the customer overcome their challenges and achieve their goals (Zoltners et al., 2009).

When the goal is to convert prospects into customers, the sales representative presents products and services and highlights the reasons why the customer should consider them. Personal presentations have an advantage over website or brochure presentations in that the representative can tailor the message to the customer's interests and expertise, making the communication more persuasive. Moreover, the representative can respond to objections and provide new perspectives on the customer's needs and product options. The more prepared the representative is about the prospective customer and their situation, the more persuasive they can be in the conversation.

Successful sales representatives are characterized by their proactive, systematic and frequent interactions with their customers, helping them solve business-related problems of various sizes. This approach is key to maintaining and developing customer relationships (Biong & Selnes, 1996) In contrast to other sales representatives, these successful individuals invest more time in such activities.

In the B2B market, the sales representative is often referred to as a key account manager (KAM). B2B relationships often involve large companies with multiple people, products and logistics processes. These complex relationships require the KAM to organize and define the roles and activities of all involved members of the customer team. One of the KAM's key responsibilities is to gather and distribute information about all relevant aspects of the relationship. For instance, if a car manufacturer is working on new electric car models, the Bosch KAM needs to be aware of this and inform the right people and divisions in order to stay relevant in their relationship with the customer (Ryals & Rogers, 2007).

One of the main objectives of personal customer visit programmes is to ensure that customers derive maximum value from the products and services they purchase from a supplier. Often, after purchasing a new car, computer or CRM system, customers may not know how to use the product to its full potential and may not have the necessary skills to acquire this knowledge. Therefore, educating customers on how to obtain more value from the product can be an essential factor in strengthening the customer–supplier relationship. A product or service can only deliver its full potential value if it is put into use and utilized effectively (Tuli et al., 2007).

SUMMARY

Customer portfolio management aims to increase the value of a company's customer portfolio by focusing on three key factors: acquiring new customers, retaining existing customers and increasing the level of engagement with each customer. As a result, the expected cash flow from the portfolio increases over time. The process of customer portfolio management involves creating a strategy for growth, implementing the plan and capturing the value that is generated.

The aim of segmentation is to identify important differences among customers to achieve greater returns on investments in marketing activities through customization and specialization. There are two types of segmentation: strategic and tactical. Strategic segmentation (macro) involves identifying large customer groups that will guide a company's investment decisions and resource allocation over the long term. In contrast, tactical (micro) segmentation focuses on tailoring marketing activities to smaller customer groups that do not require significant investments or resource specialization.

The customer database is a repository of information pertaining to each customer in the company's portfolio. Customer-related information is often stored in different databases and integrating data from different sources allows companies to gain a more comprehensive understanding of customers in their portfolio. Machine-learning algorithms are used to improve the accuracy and efficiency of data analysis, which is often referred to as artificial intelligence (AI).

Companies aim to provide compelling value propositions to attract more customers and increase their purchases of the company's products and services. However, strong value propositions raise customer expectations, which in turn increases the demand for quality in products and services. Customer experience management focuses on ensuring customer satisfaction as they begin to use the product and seek services from the company. Customers interact with companies through various channels such as physical stores, online websites, catalogues, customer service centres and sales representatives. It is important for these channels to be coordinated so that when customers interact with one channel, the interaction is registered and updated across all channels. Customer interaction channels owned by the company need to be aligned with other media channels that customers use to collect and to disseminate company and brand information.

Companies create customer programmes to attain their objectives in customer portfolio management. These programmes are specific activities aimed at acquiring new customers, maintaining customer relationships, leveraging positive word of mouth, exploiting current customer connections and upgrading customers to stronger relationships.

END-OF-CHAPTER QUESTIONS

1   Customer lifetime value is the discounted expected cash flow a customer will provide to a company. The following table shows the expected revenues, costs and cash flow for one customer in the portfolio from a grocery store. The expected cash flow is the surplus multiplied by the retention probability. Notice that the retention probability in the second year is the retention rate for the first year multiplied by the retention rate (95%). Thus, the probability is 59.9% that this customer will still be a customer in year 10. The discount rate is set to 10% which means that the value of the customer in year 1 is 4.32. CLV is the sum of the discounted cash flows.

Period	1	2	3	4	5	6	7	8	9	10
Revenues	25	25	25	25	25	25	25	25	25	25
Costs	20	20	20	20	20	20	20	20	20	20
Cash flow	5	5	5	5	5	5	5	5	5	5
Retention probability	95.0%	90.3%	85.7%	81.5%	77.4%	73.5%	69.8%	66.3%	63.0%	59.9%
Expected cash flow	4.75	4.51	4.29	4.07	3.87	3.68	3.49	3.32	3.15	2.99
Discounted cash flow	4.32	3.73	3.22	2.78	2.40	2.07	1.79	1.55	1.34	1.15
CLV	24.36									

- Set up the table in an Excel sheet and simulate what will happen to the value of this customer if the retention rate changes from 95% to 98%, and from 95% to 92%. What can the company do to increase their retention rate for their customers?
- What will happen if annual revenues increase from 25 to 30 (and the costs remain unchanged)? What can the company do to increase revenues from this customer without increasing costs? What can the company do to reduce costs for this customer?
- How and why will these changes for increasing revenues and reducing costs affect retention probability?

- How can the grocery store get the data they need in order to estimate the CLV for their customers?
- Read Berger and Nasr (1998) to get a deeper understanding of CLV.

2   Macro-segmentation is central in marketing. Think about all the different types of customers that visit a grocery store. How do you think these customers can be grouped into macro-segments that reflect the differences and principles outlined in this chapter? What will be the difference between the ad hoc and a priori methods if you were to investigate this more formally with analytics?

3   Customer satisfaction is key in predicting future customer behaviour. Imagine a scale from 1 to 10 and give a score to a selection of companies or brands you use (or have used). Make sure you have a few with high scores (8–10) and a few with low scores (1–5). List the reasons for giving low scores and discuss what the low-score companies could or should have done to prevent your low score. List the reasons for giving high scores and discuss what these companies most likely have done to deserve this evaluation. What are the consequences of low and high scores on satisfaction for how you will deal with these companies in the future?

4   Self-service is attractive for companies as this will reduce manual labour costs in handling customer requests. Chatbots are used by many service companies, but with mixed results. What are the strengths and weaknesses with chatbots in terms of creating good customer experiences? Do a database search and find a few scientific articles that have investigated how chatbots affect satisfaction and loyalty. What are the main findings from these investigations?

5   Loyalty programmes are used to motivate customers to make more purchases with the brand. A central mechanism is referred to as the goal gradient mechanism. What is this mechanism? What can companies do to take advantage of this mechanism? Read Kivetz et al. (2006).

FURTHER READING

Oliver, R.L. (1980). A cognitive model of the antecedents and consequences of satisfaction decisions. *Journal of Marketing Research*, 17(4), 460–469.

Reinartz, W. & Kumar, V. (2002). The mismanagement of customer loyalty. *Harvard Business Review*, 80(7), 86–94.

Schau, H.J., Muñiz Jr, A.M., Arnould, E. & Arnould, J. (2009). How brand community practices create value. *Journal of Marketing*, 73(5), 30–51.

Villanueva, J., Shijin, Y. & Hanssens, D.M. (2008). The impact of marketing-induced versus word-of-mouth customer acquisition on customer equity growth. *Journal of Marketing Research*, 45(1), 48–59.

Watson, J., Ghosh, A.P. & Trusov, M. (2018). Swayed by the numbers: The consequences of displaying product review attributes. *Journal of Marketing*, 82(6), 109–131.

Zhou, T., Lu, Y. & Wang, B. (2009). The relative importance of website design quality and service quality in determining consumers' online repurchase behavior. *Information Systems Management*, 26(4), 327–337.

6

PRODUCT CATEGORY MANAGEMENT

This chapter

- explores product portfolio value growth;
- presents the key principles of product categorization;
- introduces key principles in product positioning and pricing;
- introduces the management of product value delivery;
- examines the role of market and distribution network.

INTRODUCTION

To manage a company's products effectively, product category management aims to create both financial value for the company and product value for its customers. Financial value is concerned with future growth and sustainable profits, achieved by positioning the products optimally. Product value for customers involves meeting their needs better than the competition. The management of product portfolios is closely linked to customer portfolio management. Companies can benefit from economies of scale and lower costs when they have more customers who frequently purchase from multiple product categories, leading to an increase in the financial value of the product portfolio.

Product profitability is determined by historical data in the accounting system, while financial value is based on future cash-flow projections. To ensure the profitability and attractiveness of products in the future, product category management focuses on strategic positioning. This requires a thorough understanding not only of current customer needs but also of how these needs will evolve over time. Additionally, it is crucial to understand not just the current actions of competitors but also how both existing and emerging competitors will attract the same customer base the company is pursuing.

Figure 6.1 illustrates the various elements involved in product category management, with the ultimate goal of maximizing the financial value of the product portfolio. The first step is to define the categories in which the company competes, which helps to understand customer needs and competition and, in turn, inform product value positioning to ensure current and future attractiveness and profitability. Product value positioning involves setting the strategic direction for product design, delivery, and communication to the market to enhance product appeal. As customers' perceived value is a function of perceived quality relative to costs of buying the product, pricing plays a significant role. That is, if a product has a certain level of quality, it will be perceived as more valuable with a lower price. However, price has also an important effect on profitability. Although reducing prices can boost sales, it simultaneously erodes profit margins. Therefore, a critical aspect of product management involves identifying the ideal price point that maximizes profitability.

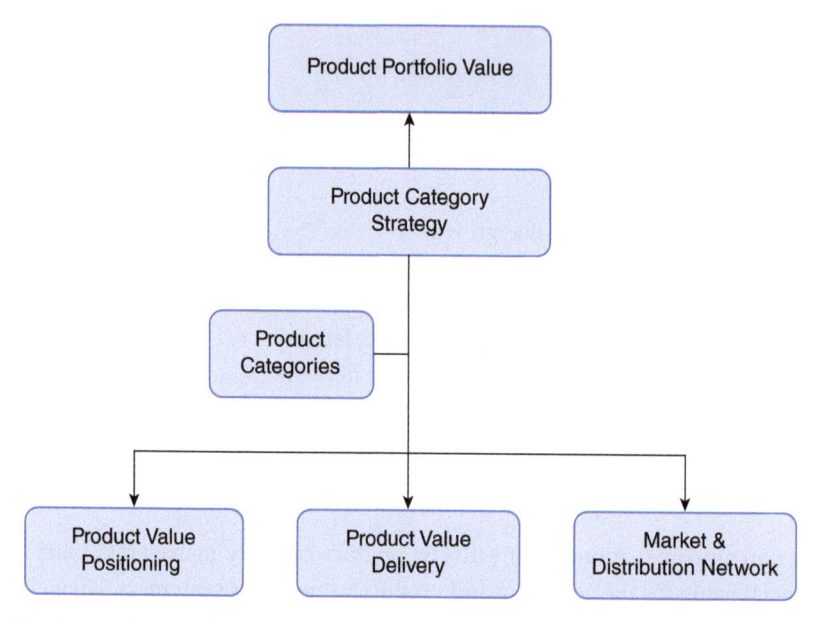

Figure 6.1 Layout for product category strategy

This chapter will explore the key principles in defining product categories from a marketing perspective. This is followed by a section where we discuss how companies can translate customer and market insight into attractive value propositions. Next, product value delivery involves ensuring customer satisfaction by meeting their expectations and managing costs associated with product delivery to maintain product profitability. Such costs can be both direct and indirect, with companies investing in advertising and sales to increase revenue and requiring analytics to determine the optimal investment level. Finally, product category management involves designing the market and distribution network to improve customer access to products, which can be achieved by expanding the company's network of locations and partners.

DEFINING PRODUCT CATEGORIES

It is crucial that companies identify the appropriate definition of product categories. While there is no right or wrong way to define them, different definitions can lead to varying strategies. For instance, as presented in Chapter 1, Tine, a Scandinavian dairy company, defined its primary category as milk instead of breakfast and lunch drinks, failing to recognize that juice and other beverages were close substitutes and stealing their market share. When defining product categories, it is important to estimate their size and growth accurately. Poor decisions on product category definitions may lead companies to overestimate or underestimate market potential, resulting in either underinvestment in categories that require more investment or overinvestment in categories that are not worth investing in. Defining the appropriate product categories is thus crucial as it sets the stage for how the company will compete and guides investment decisions in the market.

Companies must determine the appropriate level of analysis when conceptualizing their products in product category management. For example, an insurance company offers various types of insurance products, such as damage and personal health insurance, each with their own subcategories and variants. The question is: at what level should the company define their strategic categories as the unit of analysis in their product management system? The key factor in making this decision is how customers make purchasing decisions. If customers first choose between different insurance companies at the top level (damage and health insurance), then these should be treated as the two product categories. If a customer chooses damage insurance first, then that becomes the strategic category, and so on. The company must define their competitive arenas accordingly, as illustrated by Product Category A and Product Category B in Figure 6.2. In each category, there are subcategories A1, A2 and A3 for category A and B1, B2 and B3 for category B. And further, within each under-category there may be several product variants. Including more categories, sub categories and product variants (product lines) increases the overall attractiveness of the product portfolio. Thus, a grocery store with a wider assortment is normally more attractive than a grocery store with a smaller assortment. Companies can also increase the attractiveness of their product portfolio by offering higher quality products. Thus, a grocery store with fresh fruits and vegetables will be more attractive than stores with old and damaged products. Companies need to balance the costs of a broader and high-quality assortment with the overall customer appeal and revenues generated. It is important to note that not all customers follow the same decision rules, and decision rules may change over time. Therefore, companies may need to redefine their definitions of product categories as markets evolve.

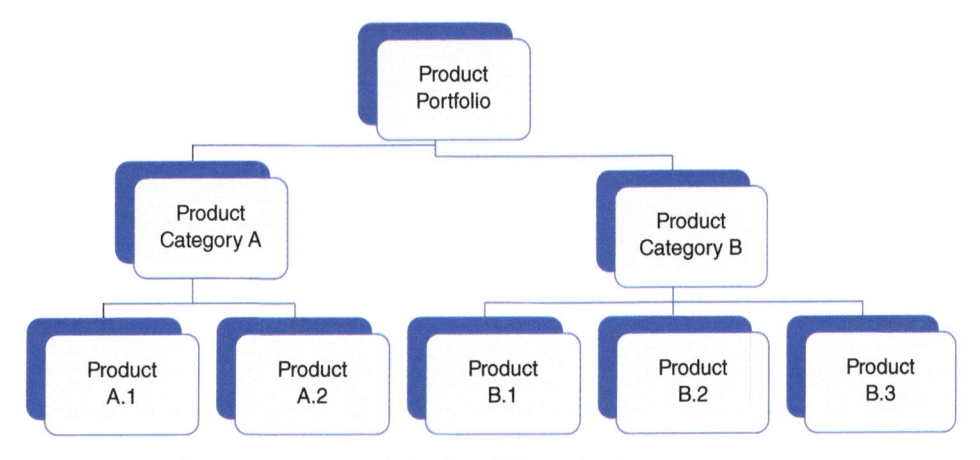

Figure 6.2 Product categories are defined at different levels

The appeal of a product category often relies on the attractiveness of other product categories as well. Therefore, the attractiveness of the fruit and vegetable section in a grocery store can be influenced by the attractiveness of other categories in the store. For instance, if a customer is already in the store because of the appeal of the meat and fish category, there will be a cost to them of going to another store to purchase fruit and vegetables. A similar example can be seen in an insurance company where the attractiveness of the health insurance product is increased if a customer has already established damage insurance with the company (e.g. for cars, houses, boats). This cost advantage may be enough to attract more customers, but it ultimately depends on the value differences between the alternatives and the size of the cost advantage. The key point is that product categories are interdependent, and therefore it is important to optimize the synergies between them. Category managers should therefore cooperate and share resources to make the whole greater than the sum of its parts.

Category management involves identifying and investing in product categories that have higher growth potential and profitability compared to others. One factor that influences growth potential is the level of competition in a category. Some categories may have weaker competition, making them more attractive for investment. For example, IKEA identified a weakness in the kitchen appliances market and successfully expanded their product category to include a range of kitchen-related products such as furniture, kitchenware, décor, electric appliances, and more. By identifying categories with higher growth potential, companies can allocate their investments more strategically and optimize their profitability as illustrated with COOP in Case Study 6.1

Case Study 6.1

COOP and Änglamark

An important factor that impacts on growth is the ability to early on identify product categories with high growth potential. For instance, the demand for ecological food products is growing faster than other grocery categories due to changing consumer preferences. Ecological food, also known as organic food, is produced without the use of synthetic pesticides, fertilizers or genetically modified organisms (GMOs). It contributes to growth by promoting sustainable farming practices that prioritize soil health, biodiversity and animal welfare. Ecological food share of groceries is estimated to be about 10% and expected to grow.[1] COOP understood this very early and invested heavily in developing a branded collection of ecological products called Änglamark. This has proven to be highly successful, resulting in both increased sales and a stronger preference for the COOP brand.[2]

---

[1]https://www.grandviewresearch.com/industry-analysis/organic-foods-beverages-market.

[2]See https://pressrum.coop.se/anglamark-ar-sveriges-gronaste-varumarke-for-nionde-gangen/.

Image 6.1 COOP's Änglamark product range

An essential part of category management is to discover and exploit new categories and new markets in which a company can utilize their existing resources (Cardozo & Smith, 1983; Devinney & Stewart, 1988). This implies that by entering a new product category or a new segment, companies can take advantage of their brand name, customer relationships, distribution network, expertise and other resources to boost sales of products in a new category. Many companies have achieved success through brand extensions, such as Apple entering the mobile-phone market, Colgate entering the mouthwash market, Caterpillar entering the boots market, and so on (Völckner & Sattler, 2006).

A classification of growth strategies was developed by Ansoff (1957). The idea is that companies should first explore growth opportunities for existing products in existing markets (or segments), referred to as market penetration, as this strategy has the lowest risk. Next, companies should explore growth opportunities with new products to existing markets or segments (referred to as product development), and growth opportunities with existing products to new markets or segments (referred to as market development). New products to new markets (or segments), referred to as diversification, is the growth strategy with the highest risk and companies need to be far more careful in pursuing this strategy than the other three. A good example of diversification is the Finnish company Nokia, which started as a paper-mill company in 1865 and diversified into rubber manufacturing in the early 20th century and into wireless communication in the late 1960s (https://www.nokia.com).

PRODUCT-VALUE POSITIONING

Positioning a product based on its value begins with formulating a product concept, which encompasses a collection of product attributes and their associated levels. These attributes are based on the customers' needs and understanding of the product. For instance, car speed is an attribute that customers can easily comprehend and utilize to determine a car's appeal. Companies then convert these customer-defined attributes into product design variables, which form the basis of product development (Hauser & Clausing, 1988). To construct speed for a car, for example, a company might consider engine size, weight of the car and type of combustion, among other factors. In general, customers perceive and comprehend a product as a collection of product attributes, and the value of each attribute determines its overall quality or utility. The overall utility of the product is the weighted sum of each attribute's utility, with different attributes having varying importance in the overall evaluation (Lancaster, 1966).

Customers make choices based on the alternative with the highest utility, assuming all other factors are equal. A product can become more attractive by increasing the value on an attribute, changing the importance of an attribute in favour of the company's product, or introducing a new and relevant attribute. This principle can be illustrated with a coffee-shop example, as seen in Case Study 6.2 and Figure 6.3.

Case Study 6.2

Coffee Shop

Imagine first a coffee shop. In this example, the company has two competitors, A and B, and the attributes used are taste, atmosphere and waiting time, weighted at 40%, 30% and 30%, respectively. The perceived level on each attribute is listed in the table, with the company scoring 7.0 on taste, 6.0 on atmosphere and 8.0 on waiting time. The total utility for the company's product is 7.0, which is equally attractive as Competitor A (7.0) and more attractive than Competitor B (6.8). Initially, we can assume that each of the three competitors gets a share of the market equivalent to their relative utility (Guadagni & Little, 1983). Our company will get 34% of the choices ((7.0:(7.0 + 7.0 + 6.8)) = 0.34), as will Competitor A, and the remaining 32% will go to Competitor B. To estimate the predicted share of choices, the initial share of 34% can be adjusted for factors such as the location of outlets relative to where people live and work (i.e. distance to competing alternatives).

Attribute	Weight	Company	Competitor A	Competitor B
Taste	40%	7.0	7.0	8.0
Atmosphere	30%	6.0	8.0	6.0
Waiting time	30%	8.0	6.0	6.0
Sum utility	100	7.0	7.0	6.8

Figure 6.3 Product concept for a coffee shop

The attractiveness of the coffee shop can be enhanced by improving one or more of its product attributes, which can increase its share of choices. For example, if the taste score of the coffee shop is increased from 7.0 to 9.0, the total utility will increase to 7.8, and the share of choices will increase from 34% to 36%. However, the company needs to carefully evaluate the effect on profitability of improving the taste attribute, as it will result in higher costs for better raw materials and processing. Another strategy to increase share of choices is to change the relative importance of the attributes, which can be achieved through advertising (Mackenzie, 1986; Chakravarti & Janiszewski, 2004). For instance, if the coffee shop were to advertise its strength of short waiting time and with this change the weights of the attributes to 40% for waiting time, 35% for taste and 25% for atmosphere, the utility score for the coffee shop would be 7.15 and its share of choices would increase to nearly 35%. The cost of changing the weights, such as advertising costs, must also be considered to ensure that the overall profitability of the strategy is positive.

To increase its share of choices, the coffee shop has a third option, which is to introduce a new attribute, such as a loyalty programme (Jaworski et al., 2000). Assume that the relative importance of this attribute is 20% and the other three attributes are reduced accordingly (as shown in Figure 6.4), and that the company scores 7 on the loyalty programme attribute, while its competitors score zero as they have not yet introduced a loyalty programme. This new attribute would increase the overall utility, resulting in a 39% share of choices for the company. Thus, introducing a loyalty programme can have a significant impact on sales. However, the costs of the programme must be estimated, and the overall profitability of the strategy must be assessed.

Thus far, we have made the assumption that competitors will not change. However, competitors don't sit still, and it is important to investigate what plans competitors have in terms of improving their products and what their likely responses will be when a company succeeds in making their product offer more attractive. For instance, one competitor may respond and introduce a similar loyalty programme as our company, thereby nullifying our competitive advantage. In such a scenario, the loyalty programme would provide no additional revenues but only costs. Once introduced, the programme cannot be stopped because that would give competitors a relative advantage. Consequently, in defining the product positioning, companies must consider not only how customers will respond but also the costs and the competitive reactions.

Attribute	Weight	Company	Competitor A	Competitor B
Taste	35%	7.0	7.0	8.0
Atmosphere	20%	6.0	8.0	6.0
Waiting time	25%	8.0	6.0	6.0
Loyalty programme	20%	7.0	0.0	0.0
Sum utility		7.0	5.6	5.6

Figure 6.4   Introducing a new product attribute to make a product concept more attractive

Product Differentiation

If all options are perceived as equal in quality, customers tend to choose the option with the lowest cost, which includes factors such as price, time and uncertainty. For instance, in the case where all grocery stores are deemed equal, customers will opt for the one that has the lowest prices, is closest to their home or work, or the one they are most familiar with (i.e. low uncertainty). To increase their market share, grocery retailers can make their stores more appealing by offering lower prices, having locations close to their target customers and employing advertising to raise brand familiarity. This low-price strategy is exemplified as A_1 in Figure 6.5. Thus, A_1 provides more value (i.e. more attractive) than competitor B. Alternatively, another strategy is to differentiate based on superior perceived quality, represented as A_2 in Figure 6.5. A grocery store could achieve this by providing a wider and/or deeper selection of products than competitors. Notice that A_2 provides more value (i.e. more attractive) than competitor B because customers get more quality for what they pay. This strategy is designed to create a willingness to pay a price premium or to travel further (i.e. an additional cost). A third strategy is to offer higher quality at the same price, demonstrated as A_3 in Figure 6.5. Thus, A_3 also provides more value (i.e. more attractive) than competitor B because customers get more quality for the same price. Indeed, in today's value-conscious consumer market, there are many examples of strong, value-priced brands (e.g. Southwest Airlines, Zara, Starbucks).

The impact of quality and cost differentiation on customer behaviour varies across different segments. One group of customers may prefer the lower-cost option, while another group may prefer higher-quality products. Furthermore, the attractiveness of different alternatives can depend on the situation. For instance, a customer may find a low-cost store more appealing in one situation buying clothes for the children, but a high-quality store more attractive when buying for oneself. Therefore, it is crucial to use analytics to gain a comprehensive understanding of customer needs.

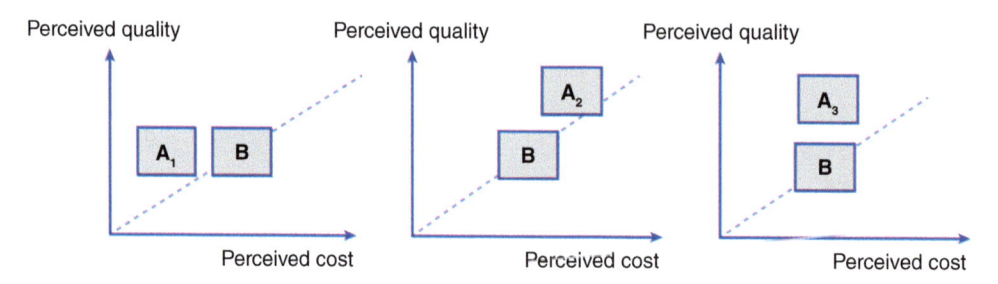

Figure 6.5 Principal strategies for product differentiation of brand A

The attributes that set a product apart from its competitors can be categorized into three groups, as illustrated in Figure 6.6:

- the core product offering;
- the exchange relationship;
- the technological and social network of products and services that surround the product.

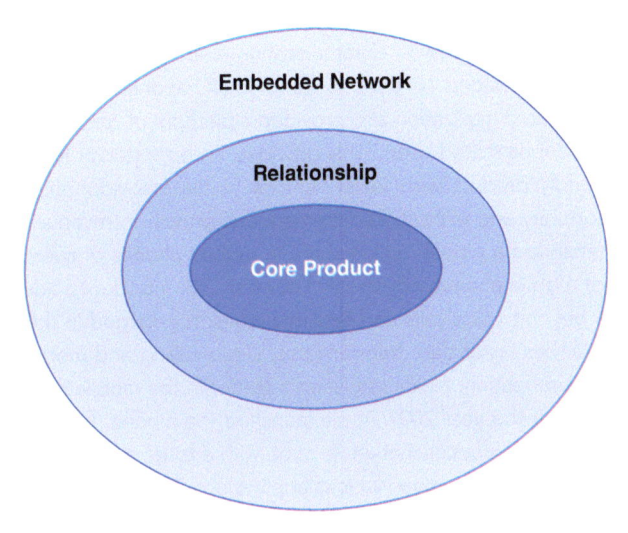

Figure 6.6 Three levels of product differentiation

Core Product Offering

The core or generic product is the tangible and material product that customers pay for, such as the coffee and physical aspects of the coffee shop, including its location, interior and employees (Levitt, 1980). Companies can differentiate their generic core product by improving the quality of raw materials, selecting a better location, enhancing the interior design, and hiring more friendly and competent staff. However, for a differentiated product to be appealing, customers must perceive it to offer better quality, such as a better-tasting coffee in the case of a coffee shop. If customers do not perceive the coffee to be better, any extra effort put into the product will be in vain. Several reasons may contribute to a lack of perception, such as unfriendly and incompetent staff, that distracts customers from the taste of the coffee.

The characteristics that can lead to successful product differentiation are not static but rather dynamic and disruptive. This is illustrated with Nokia in the mobile-phone market from 1982 and until recently in Case Study 6.3.

Case Study 6.3

Nokia in the Mobile-Phone Market

In 1982, Nokia introduced its first car phone, the Mobira Senator, which was marketed as a phone for in-car use. Sure, you could carry it around, although its weight of 9.8 kg (22 lb) made that a challenging task. The second generation of mobile phones, commonly referred to as 2G, emerged in the mid-1990s. It marked a significant advancement over the first generation by introducing digital voice communication and SMS (Short Message Service). Telephones moved from historic 1G telephones to small handheld items, which were much more portable. However, digitalization also provided a plethora of opportunities for increased functionality for the sophisticated users. This provided an opportunity for offering a simpler and more user-friendly product with fewer options to the less sophisticated users. Nokia grabbed the opportunity and experienced tremendous growth in revenue and profit. At its height Nokia commanded a global market share in mobile phones of over 50 per cent. The third generation of mobile phones, commonly known as 3G, introduced advanced communication capabilities beyond voice calls and text messages. It emerged in the early 2000s and brought features such as faster data transfer rates, video calling and mobile internet access. Despite facing stiff competition, Nokia remained a leader in the mobile-phone market during this period. However, in the year 2007 Apple launched the iPhone, which was a completely new addition to the mobile devices market. It came with a touch screen, a simple and unique design, and a great ability to download various applications. The same year, Google launched the Android operating system available for all mobile devices, which contributed to its rapid spread. By the beginning of 2010, the competing operating systems (IOS and Android) had made great progress in the market. Nokia had missed the shift towards apps pioneered by Apple (Doz, 2017). In 2011 the market value of Nokia fell from 110 billion euros to 15 billion euros. In 2023 their global market share of mobile smartphones is close to 3%, with Samsung and Apple as the market leaders.

Image 6.2 Mobira Senator, the first mobile phone by Nokia, launched in 1982

Product differentiation can be based on various production technologies. For instance, IKEA has an integrated value chain comprising product development, procurement, manufacturing, logistics and stores, where each activity is standardized to minimize costs while maintaining reasonable quality. Although IKEA's competitors can offer a broader and deeper range of furniture, their costs and therefore prices are much higher compared to IKEA.

Customer–Supplier Relationship

In Figure 6.6, the second level of product differentiation involves the relationship between customers and a supplier (or brand). The 'relationship connectors' differ from the core product in that they facilitate the buying process and can be established in various ways. The value of these connectors increases with repeated interactions, meaning that the more a customer engages with loyalty programmes, sales representatives, customer service, mobile apps, and so on, the more valuable the relationship becomes. Customers can benefit from investing and adapting to a supplier's system of customer interaction connectors, such as by disclosing personal information. This allows the supplier to send more relevant emails about new products and special promotions. For further discussion on relationship differentiation, please refer to Chapter 5, 'Customer Portfolio Management'.

Technological and Social Network of Products and Services

The third level of product differentiation, as shown in Figure 6.6, concerns the network in which the product or relationship is embedded. The network can be social, technological, or a combination of both. In a social network, people are connected through various ties, and products can serve as a means of obtaining membership in different groups or networks (Granovetter, 1973). For example, being a member of a student union can facilitate connections with other students, and the larger the network (i.e. number of other members), the more attractive it is to be a member. Similarly, online dating services like Tinder position themselves as more appealing than other dating sites by offering a vast network of members. Network effect, also known as the network externality, refers to the phenomenon where the value or utility of a product or service increases as more people use it. In other words, the more individuals or entities that join a network or adopt a particular technology, the more valuable that network or technology becomes to all participants (Uzzi, 1996).

Technological networks can take the form of an industry standard, which is an agreement among actors in a market regarding certain basic physical elements. Technological networks are physical networks that form the backbone of modern technological societies. The internet is the worldwide network of physical data connections between computers and related devices. It is a packet-switched data network, meaning that messages sent over it are broken up into packets, small chunks of data, that are sent separately over the network and reassembled into a complete message again at the other end. One example of technology standard is the Microsoft Windows operating system for computers, while another is the CCS (Combo Charging System) for electric cars. Alternatively, a technological network can be created by a single company through the development of an ecosystem of products and services that are well-integrated with each other. In such cases, the value of a new product is increased because it can be easily connected to other products and services. A well-known example of this is Apple's ecosystem for sharing data across mobile phones, personal computers, tablets and watches.

A common source of differentiation in business markets is technological networks that combine products and services into valuable solutions. Cisco is a large international company that provides enterprises with connectivity, device monitoring, security, automation and data-management services. A key element of their strategy is a customer-centric approach that involves all partners in the network to ensure that customers are utilizing the technological solutions to their fullest potential, resulting in satisfied customers.

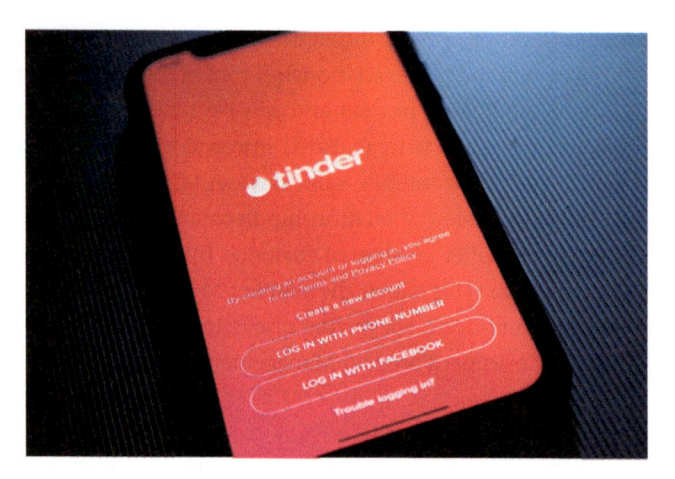

Image 6.3 A mobile phone offering to link a Tinder login to the phone number or Facebook

Relationship connectors and embedded networks are highly sustainable sources of differentiation because they are difficult, if not impossible, for competitors to replicate (von Hippel, 2005). While core features such as memory and camera specification can be easily copied by other mobile-phone brands, the relationships and ecosystem of products and services offered by Apple are unique and cannot be replicated. The costs of switching to another brand are very high due to these relationships and networks (Bell et al., 2005; Polites & Karahanna, 2012). As products and services continue to become more digitized, new opportunities for strategic differentiation through relationships and networks arise. For instance, leading companies such as Starbucks have used mobile apps to accelerate differentiation, as seen in their mobile pre-order service. Additionally, digitalization through sensors has allowed companies like Abena in the adult nappy industry to differentiate themselves by building relationships and networks with partners in hospitals and homes for the elderly.[3]

Product-Line Extensions

A product line is a collection of products within a particular category that share similar functions and features, while also catering to varying degrees of customer needs. A broader product line provides customers with a wider range of choices and improves the overall attractiveness of the category (Lancaster, 1990; Menon & Kahn, 1995; Bordley, 2003).

---

[3]See http://athenaft.com/about.php.

Coffee shops, for instance, offer various coffee flavours, ingredients and sizes to meet different customer preferences. Similarly, iPad customers can select from a variety of sizes, colours and features. Generally, a larger product line tends to attract more customers since it addresses a wider range of heterogeneous customer needs.

However, a larger product line can also result in increased costs. If every customer at a coffee shop ordered the same product, the production and delivery processes would be highly standardized, resulting in faster and cheaper operations. However, when the production and delivery processes are disrupted by product variations, it takes longer and costs more. Similarly, by focusing procurement efforts on a smaller range of products, bargaining power increases and direct product costs decrease. As a result, product category managers must find the right balance between a larger product line and product profitability. Sometimes, product lines can also become too extensive, causing increased search costs for customers. In fact, a reduction in product variety and a smaller product line can lead to increased sales and profits (Boatwright & Nunes, 2001).

Extensions into New Product Categories

Companies often expand their offerings by entering new product categories, such as banks that add insurance and pension products to their traditional offerings of payment, savings and loans. Such expansions can have significant positive effects on a company's revenue streams (Völckner & Sattler, 2006). For instance, only three years after Apple entered the music player market in 2001 with the iPod, it accounted for almost 30% of the company's revenues. Similarly, in 2009, just two years after Apple entered the mobile-phone category, the iPhone accounted for 20% of Apple's revenues, while iPod sales still contributed to more than 50% of their total revenues. Entering new product categories has been a critical strategy for Apple's growth, as its revenues increased from 5 billion dollars in 2002 to 50 billion dollars in 2009.[4]

The leverage or economies of scope mechanism, occurs in category extension, where unit production costs are lower if a company operates in two or more categories together than if they operated in separate companies. This results in synergies when resources can be shared between categories, including procurement, production, product development, distribution and communication. Apple, for example, could share resources in product technology, market communication and distribution between categories. Their brand name also creates trust and interest when they launch new categories.

Product Innovation

In order to keep up with the ever-evolving markets, companies must continuously improve and innovate their product offerings. Innovation involves developing new and more effective products. Apple's innovations, such as the iPod, iPhone, iPad and AppleTV, have helped

[4]http://www.appleinsider.com/articles/07/01/29/apple_revenues_could_catch_microsoft_by_2010.html and http://www.apple.com/pr/library/2009/04/22results.html.

the company achieve a superior market position with sustained growth and profits. Apple has not only innovated product technologies, but has also developed new pricing models, distribution networks and retail stores such as the Apple store.

Product innovations can be classified as incremental or breakthrough (Sorescu & Spanjol, 2008). Breakthrough innovations refer to new products that offer significant new benefits to the market; for example, a new packaging design like vacuum-sealed packaging for fresh salmon (such as SALMA®), or a new coffee-making concept like Nespresso coffee pods.

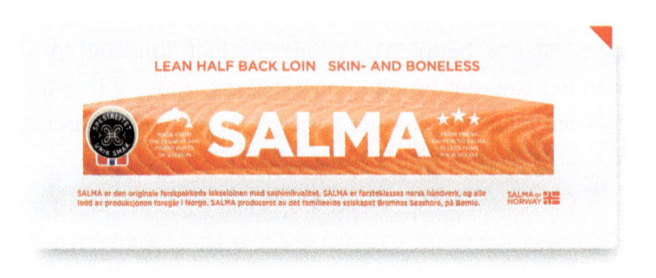

Image 6.4   An example of SALMA® vacuum-sealed salmon packaging

Smaller improvements in products are known as incremental product innovations. According to a study conducted on consumer-packaged goods, these incremental product innovations make up 86% of all new product launches. While they are the most common type of innovation, it is the breakthrough innovations that have the greatest impact on increased revenues and profits. Although breakthrough innovations are rare, they can have significant implications for growth and profitability in industries such as pharmaceuticals and technology.

Many truly new product innovations fail to gain traction because customers do not comprehend their benefits and usefulness. This is because customers often lack the knowledge needed to understand the products and their applications. Effective market communication can therefore have a significant impact on the success of these innovations (Moreau et al., 2001; Lakshmanan & Krishnan, 2011).

To achieve successful innovation, it is essential to have a comprehensive understanding of customer needs and market trends. The ultimate challenge is to anticipate future and not just current needs and to do so before customers can even express them. The emergence of electric cars, for example, took years before it became a mainstream preference, and Tesla's entry transformed the automotive industry. It takes years and large investments to develop the production rig with a supply chain, and leading car manufacturers need to make innovation decisions today on, for example, self-driving technologies that will be launched in the market two to five years from now. Their understanding and prediction of future needs is therefore critical for making the correct investments. An innovative organizational culture that fosters creativity and risk-taking, combined with a solid grasp of customer needs and market dynamics, is therefore essential for successful innovation (Urban & Hauser, 1993; Christensen, 1997).

PRICING

As explained earlier and depicted in Figure 6.6, an increase in perceived product quality should lead to a higher willingness to pay more. When a product offers more utility due to its superior quality, customers expect to pay a higher price for it. For instance, a coffee shop that serves high-quality coffee requires expensive raw materials, production equipment and skilled baristas. To make a profit, the coffee shop needs its customers to pay a premium price. The fundamental principle is that customers are willing to pay more for an improvement in quality only if the improvement also enhances their perceived utility.

It's important to note that customers are not inherently willing to pay more for a product, but they are willing to pay more for a product they perceive as having higher utility. Analysing how much more they are willing to pay can be done through various methods (Schmidt & Tammo, 2020). One way is by simply asking customers how much they are willing to pay for a high-quality product, but this can be unreliable due to the complexity of the question. A better approach is to conduct an experiment where respondents are presented with different scenarios of price differences between high-quality and ordinary products. The willingness to pay can then be inferred from the share of choices made at various price levels. Companies can also conduct real field experiments by testing out different price premiums at different locations. It is then important that the different locations are comparable (Abadie, 2021). While this method is expensive, time-consuming and informs competitors of their pricing strategy, it is probably the most valid method for detecting the optimum price premium.

Determining the best price for a product is one of the most crucial and challenging tasks for management. It's challenging because a change in price can impact on both revenue and profitability simultaneously, and it's difficult to predict the effect of price changes on sales and revenue with complete accuracy. This effect of price changes on sales is called price elasticity, and several factors can increase or decrease this response function. It is also challenging because different customer segments respond differently to price changes. Moreover, the impact of a product's price is also influenced by how competitors price their products. Economic price theory provides an analytical framework that is very useful in handling this complexity and identifying the optimal price.

Price Theory

To determine the optimal price, we must first perform some algebraic and calculus computations. The initial step towards finding the price that maximizes profits is to define the demand function, which indicates the demand (i.e. quantity of products sold) at various prices. We must rearrange the market mechanism formula, as explained in Chapter 2, to express Q (representing quantity sold) as a function of P (representing price):

$$P = a - b \cdot Q \rightarrow Q = (a - P)/b$$

Revenue (R) is the number of units sold multiplied by price and is defined by the following function:

$$R = P \cdot Q = (a - b \cdot Q) \cdot Q = a \cdot Q - b \cdot Q^2$$

Cost (C) is defined as the sum of fixed cost (F) plus the variable unit cost (c) times quantum sold:

$$C = F + c \cdot Q$$

Profit (S for surplus) is revenues (R) minus costs (C):

$$S = R - C = (a \cdot Q - b \cdot Q^2) - (F + c \cdot Q)$$

The optimal price that maximizes profit or surplus is achieved when the marginal revenue is equal to the marginal cost. The derivatives of the marginal revenue and marginal cost functions are used to determine this price. By setting these derivatives equal and substituting the respective formulas, we can calculate the optimal price (P), which is:

$$R' = a - 2 \cdot b \cdot Q$$

$$C' = c$$

$$R' = C' \rightarrow a - 2 \cdot b \cdot Q = c \rightarrow Q = (a - c)/2b \rightarrow (a - P)/b = (a - c)/2b \rightarrow$$
$$P = a - b \cdot [(a - c)/2b] \rightarrow P = (a + c)/2$$

See Case Study 6.4 for an example of how this might look in practice.

Case Study 6.4

Fitness Club Membership

An example that can be used to illustrate the process is pricing for a fitness club membership. Figure 6.7 presents the demand function, showing the number of memberships that will be sold at various prices. Assume that the fitness club has a fixed cost of 50 million euros and a variable unit cost of 500 euros. The optimal price for the fitness club membership can now be determined by substituting the numbers into the formula:

$$P = (a + c)/2 = (1667 + 500)/2 = 1083$$

Therefore, the optimal price to maximize profit (surplus) for a membership in the fitness club is 1,083 euros, resulting in approximately 175,000 members, total revenues of almost 190 million euros, and a profit of nearly 52 million euros. As can be seen in Table 6.1, both lower and higher prices will lead to lower profit (surplus). Additionally, we can observe that the price that maximizes revenue (i.e. where marginal revenue is 0) is different from the price that maximizes profit. The difference in the curve's shape for the relationship between price and revenue and the relationship between price and profit is demonstrated in Figure 6.8.

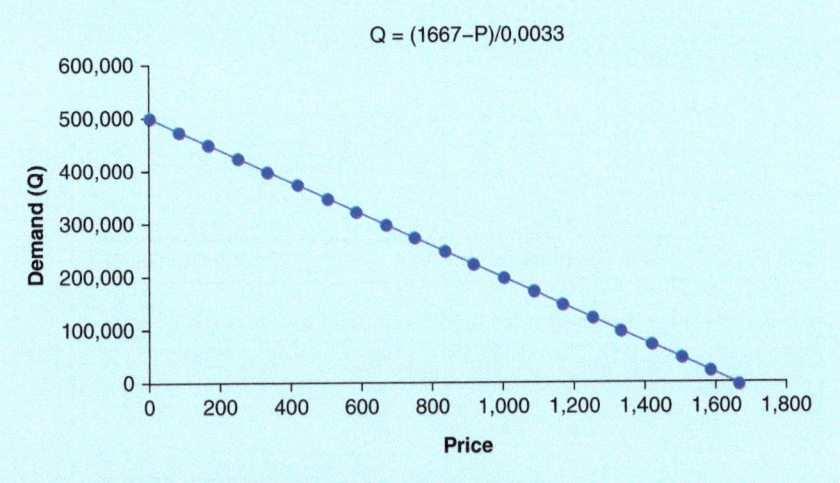

$$Q = (1667-P)/0{,}0033$$

Figure 6.7 The demand function for a fitness club

Table 6.1 Profit at different price levels

Members	Price	Revenues (million euros)	Marginal Revenue	Cost (million euros)	Marginal Cost	Profit (million euros)
350,000	500	175	−667	225	500	−50
325,000	583	190	−500	213	500	−23
300,000	667	200	−333	200	500	0
275,000	750	206	−167	188	500	19
250,000	833	208	0	175	500	33
225 000	917	206	167	163	500	44
200 000	1,000	200	333	150	500	50
175,000	1,083	190	500	138	500	52
150,000	1,167	175	667	125	500	50
125,000	1,250	156	833	113	500	44
100,000	1,333	133	1,000	100	500	33
75,000	1,417	106	1,167	88	500	19
50,000	1,500	75	1,333	75	500	0

(Continued)

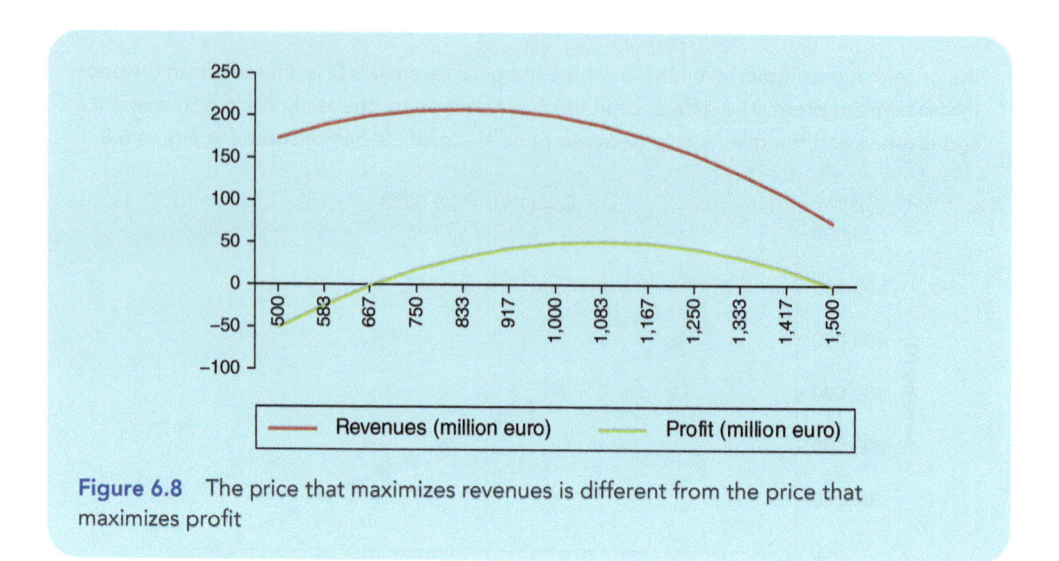

Figure 6.8 The price that maximizes revenues is different from the price that maximizes profit

Price Elasticity

Understanding the price elasticity of demand is central. When demand is not very elastic, a company can increase its price without much reduction in sales, resulting in a higher profit. However, reducing prices will not significantly increase sales, making price an ineffective competitive tool. On the other hand, when demand is highly elastic, even a small increase in price will lead to a large reduction in sales and profit. But a small reduction in price will also have a significant effect on capturing more sales, making price a highly effective competitive tool.

The relationship between price elasticity and sales volume can be illustrated by a demand curve, as shown in Figure 6.9. The price elasticity coefficient is calculated by dividing the percentage change in sales volume (i.e. number of units sold) by the percentage change in price. It's worth noting that the price elasticity coefficient is not constant across different price levels, as the relative percentage change in price and sales volume varies at different price points. For instance, a 10% increase in price will result in a different percentage change in sales volume compared to a 10% decrease in price.

Several factors have been identified in the literature that influence the degree of price sensitivity in demand, such as:

- the presence of relevant substitutes;
- the proportion of the consumer's budget allocated to the product category;
- the extent to which the product is deemed a necessity or a luxury;
- the time horizon considered (short-term vs long-term effects);
- the duration of the price change (temporary or permanent);
- the consumer's reference price and zone of tolerance;
- the difficulty of assessing true product quality;
- the number of customers using the product (network effect).

Price	Sales	Percentage Change in Price	Percentage Change in Sales	Price Elasticity
10	48			
20	46	100.0%	−4.2%	−0.042
30	44	50.0%	−4.3%	−0.087
40	41	33.3%	−6.8%	−0.205
50	38	25.0%	−7.3%	−0.293
60	34	20.0%	−10.5%	−0.526
70	30	16.7%	−11.8%	−0.706
80	24	14.3%	−20.0%	−1.400
90	18	12.5%	−25.0%	−2.000
100	11	11.1%	−38.9%	−3.500

Figure 6.9 Price elasticity is different at different price levels

The availability of **relevant substitutes** is an important factor in determining how sensitive the demand for a product is to a price change. If there are many equally attractive alternatives available, customers will be more likely to avoid products with higher prices. In this case, the price elasticity is high, which means that even a small price reduction will have a significant impact on demand. On the other hand, if a product is perceived as superior to its alternatives, the demand will be less sensitive to a price change. For instance, a coffee shop that is known for its exceptional coffee can increase its prices without losing many customers to its competitors. In contrast, the petrol station market is characterized by products that are perceived as equal, and if one gas station increases its prices, customers will quickly switch to other competitors.

Customers are less likely to be sensitive to a price change if the **percentage of their budget** spent on a product category is low, as they tend to not pay much attention to infrequent purchases. Conversely, if a larger portion of their budget is spent in a category, customers are more likely to be sensitive to price changes. The relationship between price levels and the percentage of households changing suppliers in the Norwegian electricity market is illustrated in Figure 6.10. The figure shows that as the price levels increase (i.e. more of the household's budget is spent in the category), the switching percentage also tends to increase. Interestingly this pattern was disrupted in 2020 under the COVID-19 pandemic, perhaps because consumers reduced spending in other product categories and therefore not so focused on savings.

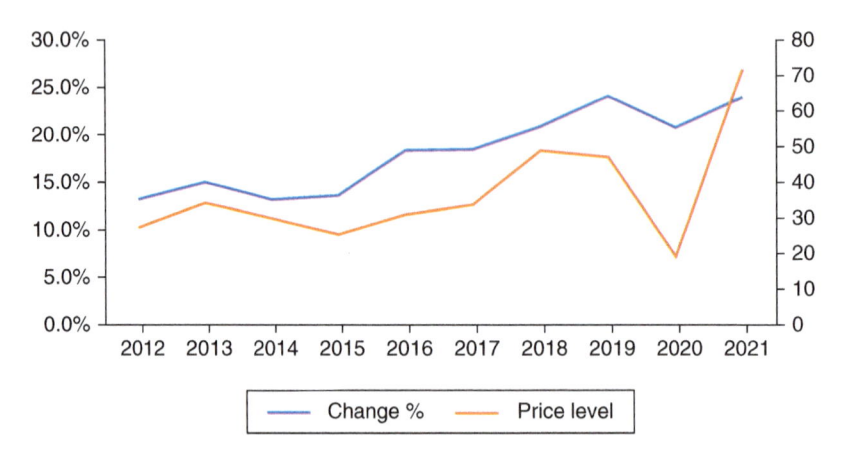

Figure 6.10 Price level and percentage of households switching supplier in the Norwegian electricity market[5]

If a product is deemed highly **necessary**, its price elasticity will be low, in contrast to 'luxury' items which tend to have high price elasticities. The overall sales of petrol for cars will likely remain the same even if prices fluctuate, as people tend to drive the same amount regardless of price. Some companies attempt to position their products as necessary, which reduces the impact of price increases. Streaming services like Netflix and Spotify have become such necessary products, and customers are not very sensitive to incremental increases in prices. For example, the premium monthly subscription price for Netflix has risen from 8 dollars in 2015 to 20 dollars in 2022, an increase of 67% over seven years, but this has not led to a significant decrease in the number of subscribers.[6]

The perspective of **long-term** versus short-term can influence how people perceive a price change. Products with longer-term perspectives, such as home insurance, are more sensitive to price increases compared to short-term products, such as travel insurance. To counteract this, companies position their products as short-term rather than long-term. For example, household insurance companies offer monthly prices instead of annual prices,

[5]Collected from https://www.ssb.no/statbank/table/09387/tableViewLayout1/ and https://www.nve.no/reguleringsmyndigheten/publikasjoner-og-data/rapporter-og-analyser/leverandorskifteundersokelsen/.

and subscription services like streaming services use monthly pricing to make their products appear more short-term. Car dealers have also been successful in selling cars with monthly lease financing, where customers focus on the short-term benefits rather than long-term costs.

The impact of a price change on sales is influenced by whether the change is **permanent** or temporary. In recent years, petrol prices have steadily risen to levels much higher than a decade or two ago. This prolonged high pricing has altered how customers purchase cars, with greater sensitivity to petrol efficiency, and electric and hybrid car technologies. Although customers are not immediately responsive to price increases in petrol, over the long term, they become more so. Consequently, the demand for petrol decreases with rising prices as customers switch to lower consumption cars or those with different technologies such as electric and hydrogen engines.

Consumers develop a mental framework known as the '**zone of tolerable prices**' around a reference price, recognizing that prices for many products fluctuate. When the price falls within this zone, the price elasticity is low, meaning that customers are less sensitive to price changes. However, if the price falls outside the zone, customers will take notice and modify their behaviour accordingly. For example, customers may have established an expectation that the price for a latte should range from 2 to 3 euros. Consequently, within this range, price sensitivity is low. However, if the price rises to 4 euros, customers are more likely to leave the coffee shop. As a result, the coffee shop should aim to price their latte close to 3 euros in order to capture as much of the customer's willingness to pay as possible.

The zone of tolerance can be influenced by communication. For instance, reducing the price of a product from 10 to 9.90 euros is more likely to impact customer behaviour than reducing it from 9.5 to 9.4 euros (Bizer & Schindler, 2005). Companies can also use a strategy of offering multiple product variants at different price points, where the most expensive option is perceived as a reference point and the other options appear to be better deals. This can influence customer behaviour and increase sales.

In product categories where it is challenging to **evaluate objective quality**, price can serve as an indicator of quality (Olson, 1977). For instance, many people assume that an expensive wine is of higher quality than a cheaper wine. The same applies to professional services such as doctors, lawyers and consultants where individuals tend to believe that an expensive professional is more competent than a cheap one. As a result, a professional with lower prices is often perceived as less competent. Therefore, when selling products and services where quality is difficult to assess objectively, it is generally not advisable to promote oneself as having the lowest prices in the market.

The **network effect** on price elasticity refers to the phenomenon where the demand for a product or service increases as more people use it (Katz & Shapiro, 1985b). This is because the value of a network increases as more people join it, which in turn makes it more difficult for users to switch to a different network. As a result, the demand for the product or service

---

See https://www.theverge.com/2022/3/24/22993562/netflix-price-increase-us-plans-2022.

becomes less elastic, meaning that the price can be increased without significantly reducing the number of users. The network effect can be seen in the case of operating systems such as Windows and macOS. The more people who use these operating systems, the more software developers will create applications for them, which in turn makes them more valuable to users. This makes it difficult for users to switch to a different operating system, even if the price were to increase. The network effect is also observed in social media where the most popular influencers pay lower prices (or get the product for free) if they promote the product to their followers (Fainmesser & Galeotti, 2020).

After analysing numerous scientific publications on price elasticity, researchers have discovered that the average price elasticity is –2.6, with most elasticities falling between –1 and –3 (Bijmolt et al., 2005). This implies that a 1% price decrease will, on average, lead to a 2.6% increase in sales. Additionally, the researchers found that the price elasticity of a product increases when it is frequently sold on price promotions. Therefore, products that are frequently promoted on price are more responsive to changes in price.

Differentiated Pricing

The optimal price determined following price theory where marginal revenue equals marginal costs, assumes that there is only one fixed price for the product. However, there are many instances where customers possess different levels of willingness to pay for a product, presenting an opportunity to capture the maximum value from each customer. Customers who are willing to pay a higher price for the product are of course pleased when offered a lower, fixed price. This is viewed as a surplus for the customers, as they obtain the product at a price lower than what they believe it's worth. At the same time, this as a loss for the company since they could have earned more from these customers by charging a higher price. The solution, if feasible, is to charge customers varying prices that align with their willingness to pay.

One type of differentiated prices is dynamic pricing, which is also referred to as yield pricing. Companies use complex computer algorithms that take multiple variables into account to set prices dynamically, including time and online search history. Airlines have been utilizing dynamic pricing since the late 1970s. If they, for example, have a goal (yield) to fill 80% of their seats for a coming flight, the machine will suggest lowering the price until the forecast has reached the yield. If the forecast is above the yield, the machine will suggest increasing the price (to achieve a higher profit). As a consequence of this pricing strategy two passengers in the same row may pay different prices for the same product. The success of dynamic pricing in the airline industry has led to its adoption by many other companies, such as hotels and car rentals.

Dynamic pricing can also be seen in the retail industry for selling fashion and perishable goods. In the textile industry, for instance, companies renew their collections at least once a year to follow the latest fashion trends. Some customers are eager to wear the latest fashion and are willing to pay more to get it early, while others are less eager and not willing to pay such a premium. They wait a few weeks until the prices drop. Similar patterns can be observed in furniture, sports equipment, electronics, cars, and more. With this type of dynamic pricing, companies can capture more of the willingness to pay by setting a high price early in the cycle and then gradually reducing it through price discounts from the initial price.

Figure 6.11 illustrates the mechanism. The demand curve represents varying levels of willingness to pay, so when the price is low, many customers are willing to pay, and demand is high. In the left graph, the price is fixed at 'p', and demand is at level 'd'. The square is a measure of revenues (p*d). With a fixed price, there are customers who won't buy (lost volume) and customers who would pay more (lost price premium). The mechanism with differentiated prices is shown in the right graph, where we have three price levels (p_1, p_2 and p_3), and we see the increased revenues as the added red boxes. For example, let's say Armani has launched a new dress and has 100 potential customers. With a fixed price of 3,000 euros only 75 would buy the product, and they would gain 225,000 euros in revenues. However, with differentiated and dynamic pricing, they can capture more of the value in the market. Suppose 25% of the customers are willing to pay 8,000 euros for the product, generating 200,000 euros in revenue. Additionally, let's assume that the next segment is 50% of the customers and they are willing to pay 3,000 euros, which gives 150,000 euros in revenue. Lastly, the final segment pays only 1,500 euros, and the revenue from this segment is 37,500 euros. The total revenue with differentiated dynamic pricing has increased from 225,000 euros to 387,500 euros without any further action than differentiating the prices.

Figure 6.11 The difference between fixed price (to the left) and differentiated prices (to the right)

The two-component model is a type of differentiated pricing where customers pay a fixed price to gain access to a product or service and then pay a variable price based on their usage. An example of this is a fitness club that charges a fixed membership fee for access to their facilities and then charges a variable price based on the number of times the customer uses the gym. The variable price can be made dynamic so that during periods of low demand the price is lower and during high demand periods the price is higher. By doing this, the fitness club can manage overcrowding during peak hours and increase customer satisfaction while also increasing their total revenues.

Price discrimination can sometimes be based on objective customer characteristics, such as age or product preferences. For example, public transportation often offers child and senior prices, while airlines can charge more for seats in the front of the aircraft by labelling them as business class tickets. By adding a free meal or other minor product variations, airlines can further increase prices and signal quality differences that attract certain customers. These small alterations in product characteristics allow companies to capture more of the willingness to pay from different customer segments.

Digital interaction with customers is expected to lead to a rise in differentiated pricing since differentiation can be executed more easily in the digital realm where individuals cannot observe the prices other customers receive. For example, loyalty programme members and other customer clubs often enjoy discounted prices, providing companies with another way to reward their most valued customers. In addition, retailers and restaurants can charge higher prices during peak hours without informing everyone about these differences. Although customers may initially react negatively to dynamic pricing, they are likely to become accustomed to it over time, as was observed with airlines and hotels (Weisstein et al., 2013).

Premium Brand Pricing

Premium brands like Häagen-Dazs (ice cream), Redken (shampoo), BMW (automobiles), Gucci (fashion), Apple (electronics), Hoka (running shoes), Ritz-Carlton (hospitality) and Equinox (fitness club) charge relatively high prices to leverage their strong brand image (Aaker, 1991; Keller, 1993). The success of premium price brands lies in their ability to create a sense of aspiration and desirability among consumers. By associating themselves with exceptional quality, luxury and prestige, these brands tap into the human desire for quality, social status and self-expression. One important underlying mechanism lies in how consumers use extrinsic cues, such as price or brand name, when inferring true (i.e. intrinsic) product quality that is difficult or impossible to infer (Olson, 1977). Companies invest in product development, advertising, and packaging to develop the desired brand associations (Kirmani & Wright, 1989). On average, consumers seems to be willing to pay a price premium of about 10% for national advertised grocery brands over retailer private label brands (Steenkamp et al., 2010).

Pricing in Online Auctions

Prices can also be set through auctions where customers bid on what a seller offers. During in-person auctions, a seller will typically announce an asking price and the customer with the highest bid (i.e. price) wins the auction. An online auction is a type of auction that's held over the internet, unlike in-person auctions. The best part of holding an online auction is the freedom of bidding from any location with bidders connected through the internet. Online auctions can be business-to-business (B2B), business-to-consumer (B2C) and consumer-to-consumer (C2C).

Pricing strategy depends on type of auction. *English auctions* are one of the most popular formats where one item is auctioned at a time. The auctioneer announces the starting bid, and individual bidders will increase the price with every bid until no one can outbid the last bidder. Sellers prefer auctions with many bidders (participants) and will typically set their starting price low to engage many bidders in the bidding process. The *Dutch auction* is like an English auction, except that prices start high and are successively dropped until a bidder accepts the going price, at which point the auction ends. *First-price sealed-bid auctions* is like an English auction, but the bidding process is different. In these auctions, every bidder provides a single bid, and at the end of the bidding process, all the bids are compared for the highest one to win the auction. Again, sellers prefer auctions with many bidders or participants. Unlike English auctions, the bid price in *Reverse auctions* has a lower ceiling. In reverse auctions, there are multiple sellers who sell their items to a single buyer. So, instead of outmatching other bidders for a higher price, sellers try to give the lowest possible price until it matches the expectation of a bidder. The pricing strategy will here be a mix of economic factors and the potential for developing a long-term relationship with the buyer.

In business-to-business, online procurement reverse auctions have become common practice in many industries. The buyer invites a set of prequalified suppliers and issues a request for purchase that details the nature of the contract as well as product, delivery and handling specifications and expectations. The suppliers are not told who their competitors are or how many suppliers are bidding against them. However, after the auction begins, suppliers can view each of their competitors' bids and respond in real time. The buyer may then take four to six weeks to evaluate the individual bids and select a winner. The pricing strategy in these procurement online auctions is a trade-off between long-term relational factors and short-term economic factors. Suppliers with long-term relational strategies will therefore submit fewer bids, bid less often and make fewer price concessions as a result (Jap & Haruvy, 2008).

Auction houses can use automation and create a virtual bidder (i.e. computer) that bids on behalf of the bidders on-site. Each time an online bid is placed, the system records it. Further, based on this record, a virtual clerk places the bid, and an operator updates the web interface for all the bidders to view in real time. Programmatic advertising is a method of buying and optimizing digital advertising in real time through automated systems. It involves the use of software to purchase and manage ad placements in real time, based on specific criteria such as audience demographics, interests and behaviours. This allows advertisers to target their ads more effectively and efficiently, and to optimize their campaigns in real time. Programmatic advertising commonly involves real-time bidding (RTB) on ad inventory, where advertisers bid on impressions and the winning bid's ad is instantly displayed to the targeted audience (Malthouse et al., 2018).

Competitive Pricing

In Chapter 2, we discussed how markets differ in terms of pricing strategies and how competitors respond to price changes. In oligopoly markets, where there are few suppliers and products are relatively similar, competitors tend to follow immediately when one of the players lowers their prices. This is commonly observed in the petrol industry, where customers will switch to a cheaper supplier unless competitors follow suit. However, the response of competitors is different when prices are increased. In this case, competitors are less likely to follow unless prices are increased incrementally, so customers don't notice the changes.

In markets with many competitors, price discrimination is less visible, and customers and competitors are slower to respond. This may change for products where customers do their research online, as competitors respond more quickly to price changes in this scenario. With the help of modern analytics, companies can monitor each other's websites and track how prices change. It's crucial to note that pricing is not just about customers and their willingness to pay, but also about how competitors price their products and services. Therefore, companies need to consider both customers and competitors when analysing and making pricing decisions.

PRODUCT VALUE DELIVERY

The management of product value delivery involves both meeting customer expectations and ensuring product profitability. Meeting customer expectations leads to satisfaction and increased likelihood of repeat business and positive word-of-mouth recommendations. Conversely, customers become dissatisfied when the quality of products and services fall short of their expectations. While increasing investment in product quality and customer service may improve customer satisfaction, it also increases costs and may hurt short-term profitability. As a result, product managers must find a balance between investing in quality to meet customer expectations and achieving long-term profitability.

Product Quality and Customer Satisfaction

To effectively manage product delivery, companies must implement a system to measure customer satisfaction. As previously discussed in Chapter 5, 'Customer Portfolio Management', customer satisfaction is defined as the pleasurable fulfilment of a need, desire or goal. This means that customers must feel that they have achieved outcomes that meet or exceed their expectations. Expectations serve as the standard for comparison, and when experiences fall short of expectations, this is known as negative disconfirmation. Conversely, when experiences exceed expectations, this is known as positive disconfirmation. Customer satisfaction is therefore a reflection of the perceived quality of the experience relative to the expected quality, which is based on the quality proposed and the value proposition that convinced customers to choose the product.

On the one hand, a strong value proposition can attract more customers because they expect more, but it also raises the bar for the level of quality that must be delivered. For example, if a fitness centre promises a superior quality personal trainer, this may attract more customers to the centre. However, the centre must then demonstrate to their customers that they truly have high-quality personal trainers. If the centre merely makes promises without increasing the quality, customers will not only be dissatisfied, but they may be even more dissatisfied and less likely to continue their relationship with the centre. Notice, however, that higher expectations lead to higher satisfaction, given that the expected quality and benefits are delivered and expectations are fulfilled. Thus, if the training centre delivers higher quality on personal trainers this will lead to more satisfied customers and a higher probability of continuity and positive word of mouth.

We explore quality and satisfaction further in Case Study 6.5.

Case Study 6.5

Scandinavian Fitness Chain

A survey was sent by a Scandinavian fitness chain to its customers, enquiring about their satisfaction levels with key quality factors as shown in Figure 6.12. The survey also included questions related to overall satisfaction, loyalty and brand attitude. Individual usage data was obtained from a production system database and linked to each respondent in the survey. The red colour in Figure 6.12 represents low satisfaction (1–5 on the 10-point scale), yellow represents moderate satisfaction (6–7 on the 10-point scale) and green represents high satisfaction (8–10 on the 10-point scale). The blue box, Usage, is the average number of visits per month collected from the check-in system where members used their card when entering the training centre. A statistical analysis was conducted to estimate the partial effect of each quality factor on overall satisfaction. Usage and brand attitude were entered as control variables. The results showed that low satisfaction with personal trainers and the pricing model caused overall dissatisfaction (i.e. low scores). An increase of one point in the satisfaction score with personal trainers led to an estimated increase of 0.35 points in overall satisfaction. Similarly, an increase of one point in the satisfaction score with the pricing model led to an estimated increase of 0.25 points in overall satisfaction. Customers were only moderately satisfied with equipment, and an increase of one point on this factor would increase overall satisfaction by 0.45 points. The model also estimated the effect of an increase in overall satisfaction on loyalty. Thus, improving satisfaction with personal trainers, the pricing model and equipment would lead to reduced churn rates. With these findings, the product manager could estimate the economic effect of investing in better quality in these three factors on increased revenues due to more customers continuing their relationship with the training centre.

(Continued)

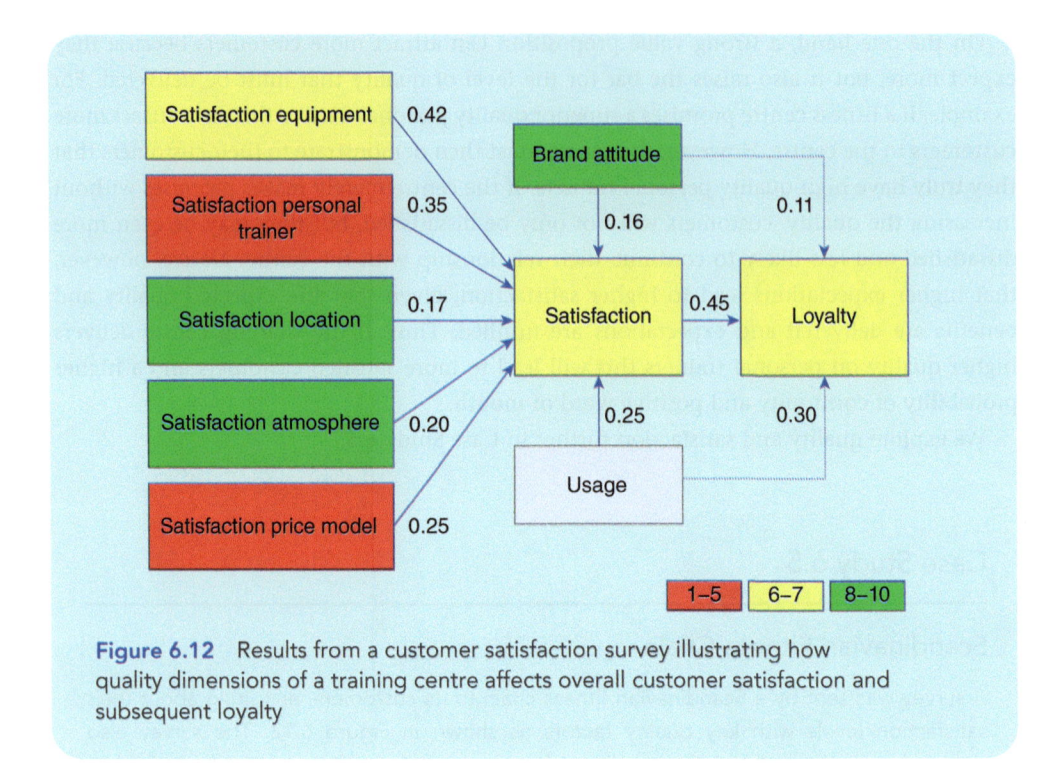

Figure 6.12   Results from a customer satisfaction survey illustrating how quality dimensions of a training centre affects overall customer satisfaction and subsequent loyalty

Delivering Product Profitability

The process of determining product category profitability involves several steps, as shown in Table 6.2. The first step is to analyse the number of customers, their average purchase frequency and the price paid of the product. This information is closely related to customer portfolio management, which focuses on acquiring new customers, retaining existing ones and expanding relationships across different product categories. For example, if there are 1.2 million customers buying Product Category A with an average of 12 purchases per year at a price of 68 euros, the total revenue generated from this product category would be 979 million euros.

To determine the profitability of a product category, it is necessary to subtract the costs associated with producing and selling the product from the revenues generated. These costs can be either directly related to the number of products sold (known as direct variable product unit costs), or indirectly related to other activities involved in producing and selling the product (known as indirect product costs). Direct variable costs can include input materials and labour costs in manufacturing, as well as procurement costs paid by retailers to manufacturers. Additionally, variable selling costs like commissions paid to distributors or sales representatives for each product they sell can also be considered direct variable costs.

In the example presented in Table 6.2, the direct cost for one unit sold in Product Category A is 20 euros, resulting in total direct costs of 288 million euros. After subtracting these costs from the revenues generated by the sale of the product, the gross margin for Product Category A is calculated to be 691 million euros.

In order to determine the net profit, indirect product costs must be subtracted from the gross margin. Indirect costs are costs that are related to the product but do not change with the number of units produced or sold. These costs must be allocated to the appropriate products. They include costs for activities such as advertising, sales force, product development and management. Activity-based allocation is the most used method to allocate these costs, which involves assigning costs based on how much of an activity related to a specific cost is devoted to the various products (Cooper & Kaplan, 1991). For example, if 20% of the sales force's time is dedicated to a particular product category, 20% of the sales force's costs are allocated to that category. In the given example, the indirect cost for Product Category A is 489 million euros. This amount is then subtracted from the gross margin, resulting in a net profit of 201 million euros. Notice that while all three product categories have positive gross margins, only Category A and Category B have positive net profit. Thus, the investments in indirect costs for Product Category C (i.e. advertising, sales, and so forth) have a too weak effect on sales to create a positive net profit. The response function for how investments in advertising, sales and other indirect costs have on sales is therefore important to understand and estimate.

Table 6.2 Estimating product category profitability

	Product Category A	Product Category B	Product Category C
Number of customers	1,200,000	800,000	400,000
Number of purchases (year)	12	8	2
Price paid	EUR 68	EUR 98	EUR 154
Revenues	MEUR 979.0	MEUR 627.2	MEUR 123.2
Direct costs	MEUR 288.0	MEUR 192.2	MEUR 68.0
Gross margin	MEUR 691.0	MEUR 435.0	MEUR 55.2
Indirect costs	MEUR 489.0	MEUR 313.6	MEUR 79.0
Net profit	MEUR 201.0	MEUR 121.4	– MEUR 23.8

Advertising and Sales Response Functions

To determine the optimal investment in advertising and sales, we must estimate their response functions. Typically, these response functions are assumed to follow an S-shaped curve, as shown in Figure 6.13, where advertising costs are plotted on the X-axis and the number of new customers is plotted on the Y-axis. In this case we focus on the effect on attracting new customers, but the principle would have been the same if we had sales as the dependent variable. There are multiple ways to specify a response function mathematically, and the formula for the function depicted in the figure is:

$$Y = a_0 + (a_1 - a_0) \cdot (X a_2 / (a_3 + X a_2))$$

In the formula, Y is number of new customers and X is advertising costs, a_0 is the number of new customers without advertising, a_1 is the maximum number of new customers, and a_2 and a_3 are coefficients that determines the shape of the function.

In the numerical illustration in Figure 6.13, a_0 is 15, a_1 is 150, a_2 is 5 and a_3 is 35. If, for example, Product Category A managers are increasing their investments in advertising from 250,000 to 350,000 euros, the number of new customers will increase from 1,144 to 1,416. Assuming these new customers continue and are purchasing the same number of times per year as other customers and pay the same, revenues will increase by 221,823 euros ((1,416 – 1,144)*12*68 euros). The gross margin will increase by 156,580 euros (272*12*(6,820) euros). Thus, by increasing advertising by 100,000 euros the net profit of the category will increase by 56,580 euros (increased gross margin is 156,580 euros minus the additional 100,000 euros in indirect advertising costs). In this case, increasing advertising spending for Product Category A with 100,000 euros is very profitable. Notice that if the new customers do not continue as customers, the profitability of advertising will drop dramatically.

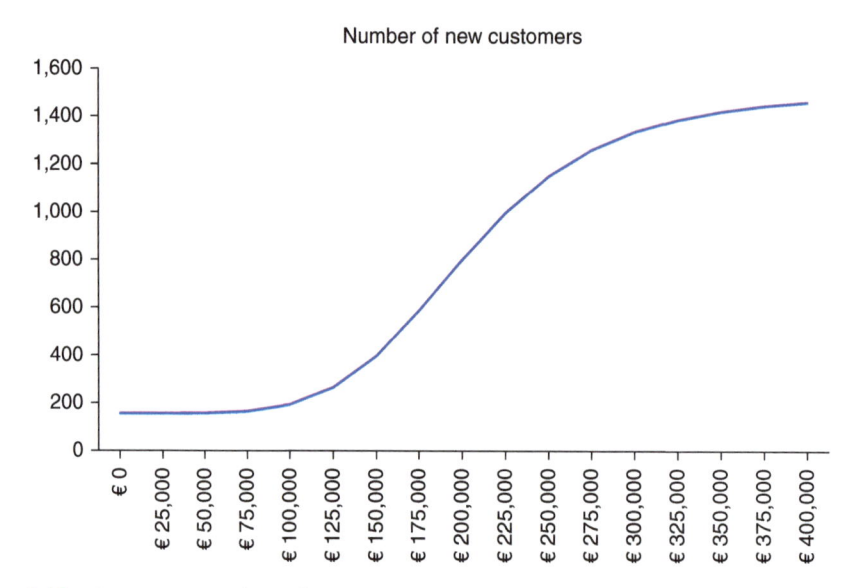

Figure 6.13   Response (number of new customers) to advertising investments

Understanding the response function for advertising and sales is a critical factor in decision-making for these types of investments. Studies have shown that, on average, a 10% increase in advertising increases revenues by around 1% (Tellis, 2009; Sethuraman et al., 2011). However, it is essential to note that this is an average estimate, and numerous factors can affect the size of the response. For instance, the position of the company's current spending on the S-curve plays a crucial role, as demonstrated in the numerical example above. When a company increases advertising at the beginning of the steep curve, the effect is larger than when it increases from a level at the top. Additionally, the response to advertising depends on whether the product is new or well-known. Generally, advertising has a stronger impact on newer products than established ones. Advertising is also more effective in high-frequency categories where customers do not have strong brand preferences, and they choose brands that are most familiar or/and the brand that comes to mind most easily in a choice purchase situation (i.e. forefront-of-mind).

Companies have multiple ways to estimate their response function for advertising. One way is through statistical analysis of time-series data on advertising spending, sales and relevant control variables, known as marketing-mix modelling. This method uses the natural variation in past advertising spending to analyse the effect (Powell, 2008). Another way is to conduct field experiments where various levels of advertising are tested against control groups to estimate the response function. Field experiments have become more accessible and important in digital advertising due to the ability to develop sophisticated treatment and control groups (Sahni, 2016). Therefore, it is recommended that companies invest in this type of analytics to estimate their response function accurately if advertising plays a significant role in stimulating sales (Lilien et al., 2007).

Other Mechanisms for Increasing Sales

Referring to the example above, notice that new customers in Product Category A can in principle be achieved by encouraging customers that the company already has a relationship within Product Category B and/or Product Category C. To do this, managers must collaborate to identify effective ways of motivating customers to expand their purchases across categories. A natural first step in this process is to investigate why 'internal' customers are not buying from other categories, and use this understanding to develop strategies and tactics.

Category managers can also enhance revenues and profits by increasing the frequency of customer purchases. For instance, if the number of purchases per customer in Product Category A is increased from 12 to 13, revenues will increase by over 8%. To stimulate frequency, companies can use loyalty programmes and price promotions, as discussed in Chapter 5 on customer management.

Expanding the distribution network and market presence is another way to increase the number of customers and revenues. Branded chains such as retailers, fitness centres, hotels and restaurants constantly search for new locations to open new outlets. Before investing in new locations, companies estimate the expected number of new customers across categories and their expected purchases and evaluate the potential profitability. The key to expanding a distribution network is to identify locations with many potential customers and low competition (Kalnins, 2004).

Price promotions and various pricing formats in loyalty programmes can motivate customers to increase their total spending in a category or increase the share of purchases directed to the company. The response to discounts and promotions is different from the response to different levels of the 'normal' price (Nijs et al., 2001). Price promotions don't necessarily increase the number of purchases or the number of customers. Instead, they may simply alter the timing of the purchase, as customers who make a promotion-based purchase will wait longer until they buy again since they don't consume more. For example, if a customer purchases toothpaste on promotion, they will wait longer until the next purchase because they don't consume more toothpaste. The risk, therefore, is that price promotions don't generate more sales and therefore the effect on profitability is negative because discounted products have lower margins.

Indirect Costs and Economies of Scale

Product profitability improves with larger volume because of the economies of scale effect. Indirect costs related to the product, such as machinery in a factory or distribution locations in a retailer outlet, can be divided among more units when volume increases. As a result, the cost per unit decreases with the increase in volume. For example, if a manufacturer sells 100 units of a product, the cost of machinery or distribution outlet will be divided by 100. However, if the manufacturer sells 200 units, the cost will be divided by 200, which means the cost per unit will be halved. A company with higher volume than its competitors will have a cost advantage on activities such as product development, administration, sales force, advertising campaigns and distribution network, which are all indirect costs. Notice that companies invest in indirect costs like product development, advertising and distribution to increase sales. In other words, companies spend money to earn money! These investments are successful if the overall effects on sales volume are large enough to cover more than the costs and thus reduce unit costs. Therefore product category managers have growth in volume as one of the important objectives for their market activities. A notable example that highlights the significance of economies of scale is the introduction of the Model T Ford, as presented in Case Study 6.6.

Case Study 6.6

Model T Ford and Economies of Scale

While other car manufacturers were catering to the wealthy with their highly personalized cars, Henry Ford aimed to target the middle class with a standardized product that offered low price due to economies of scale from making one standardized product rather

Image 6.5 A Model T Ford car

than making numerous variants with lower volumes. Henry Ford was renowned for the slogan 'You can have any color you want, as long as it's black'. Instead of providing customers with a range of extravagant features to choose from, Ford offered an affordable car that was made in large quantities. The price on Model T was reduced from $850 in 1908 to $300 in 1924, making the car affordable to many new customers. The Model T Ford was launched on 1 October 1908. During the next 18 years the Model T dominated the sales of cars. In this period Henry Ford earned more money than all other car manufacturers together. However, in 1926 other competitors surpassed Ford with more successful car models based on many of the principles of standardization and economies of scale.

MARKET AND DISTRIBUTION NETWORK

Product managers must ensure that their products are available in locations where customers are willing to purchase them. Customers engage with companies or brands to gather information, place orders, receive physical delivery of products, make payments and receive post-sale support, if necessary. While some companies such as IKEA own all of their contact channels, others like Nike and McDonald's use a combination of their own channels and intermediaries. Nike, for example, have their own Nike concept stores with only Nike products in combination with retail chains that also sell competing brands. McDonald's have a franchise system with a combination of outlets (restaurants) they own themselves and outlets owned by others (franchisees) (Kashyap et al., 2012). Regardless, customers expect coordination and consistency across channels, and lack of coordination can lead to dissatisfaction and affect their preferences for suppliers, as discussed in Chapter 5.

When intermediaries are involved, coordination is crucial and needs to be integrated into distribution and market network contracts (Kumar & Venkatesan, 2005; Simons & Bouwman, 2006). As actors in the distribution network become more integrated, they also become more interdependent with potential risks for opportunistic behaviour. So, companies must carefully weigh the benefits of closer collaboration and integration against the risks of negative consequences (Heide & John, 1988; Heide, 1994).

When designing a multichannel system for customer interaction, companies need to find a balance between generating revenues and managing costs. As the level of service provided in distribution channels increases, so do the potential revenues. However, this also leads to higher costs for the company.

Distribution Intensity and Market Share

Product category managers increase their revenues by investing in a number of locations where customers can purchase their products or services. The relationship between distribution intensity (i.e. distribution coverage) and sales or market share is, however, not linear and the shape of the curve depends on type of product category. For convenience products where customers purchase a product or service frequently, the shape of the curve is normally convex (Reibstein & Farris, 1995). Convexity arises from the choices made by small stores to

MARKETING MANAGEMENT

carry predominantly popular brands and the willingness of certain consumers to 'settle' for less favoured brands for these types of products. The curve is convex because when many stores start providing the product its popularity will increase, motivating even more stores to carry the product. Another effect for service brands like petrol stations, grocery stores and fast food is that their brands become more visible with higher distribution density. And as we know from branding theory, increased familiarity results in more sales, all others equal. As illustrated in the first chart in Figure 6.14, the effect of increasing distribution will be even higher for the companies that already have high distribution.

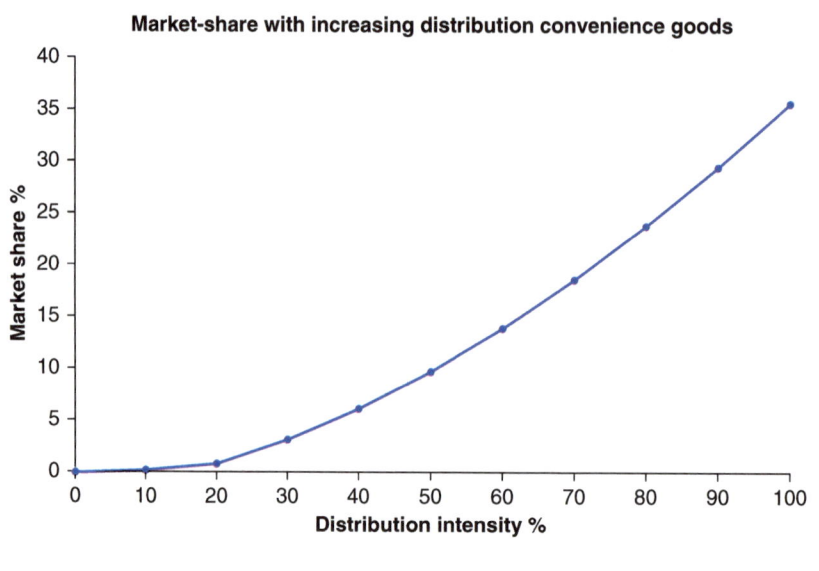

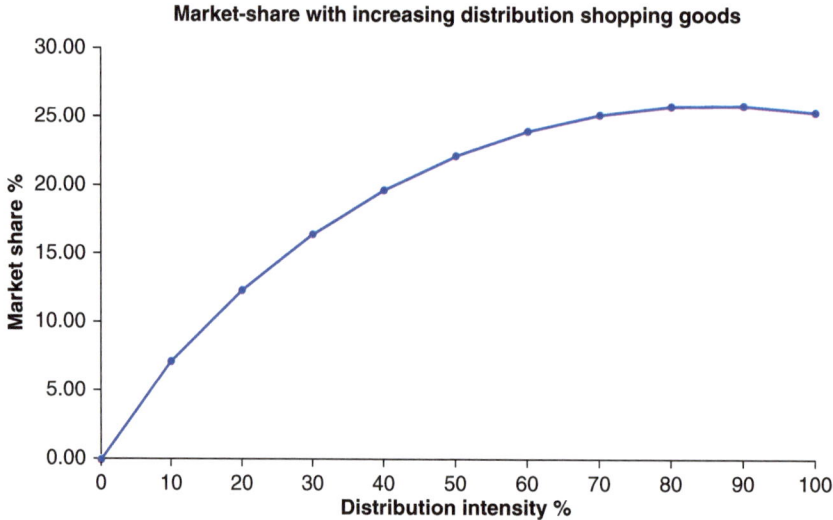

Figure 6.14   The expected relationship between increases in distribution intensity on market share for convenience (convex) and shopping (concave) goods

When it comes to shopping goods, consumers often desire ample information about products prior to making a purchase. The responsibilities of a reseller extend beyond offering spatial convenience and a diverse product range; they also involve providing additional marketing support, such as sales assistance and product demonstrations. To offset these expenses, resellers require protection from excessive price competition from other resellers. That is, retailers avoid carrying brands where customers collect information and get recommendations in their store and then go to a nearby store or an ecommerce retailer who offers the same product at a lower price (but without their service level). Through the implementation of a selective distribution strategy, suppliers can mitigate unwanted price competition by limiting the number of outlets within a specific trading area. The trade-off between coverage and reseller support implies that the link between distribution intensity and market share is likely to follow a concave pattern (Bucklin et al., 2008). This is illustrated in the second graph in Figure 6.14 where we observe a diminishing effect of distribution coverage on market-share increase.

Costs in Distribution Channels

The cost structure, with regard to fixed and variable costs, is influenced by the design of the market and distribution system, whether intermediaries are involved or not. When intermediaries are used, the company typically pays for distribution services based on the number of units sold, resulting in mainly variable costs. However, in the absence of intermediaries, the company establishes and maintains its own distribution operations, resulting in fixed costs that are not dependent on the number of units sold.

A significant and noteworthy feature of distribution networks that involve intermediaries is that the overall costs in the system are lower compared to a fully integrated distribution system. This effect is demonstrated in Figure 6.15, where M represents the manufacturers, C represents the customers, W represents the wholesaler and D represents the distributors (retailers). The left graph shows a direct distribution system with a link from each of the three

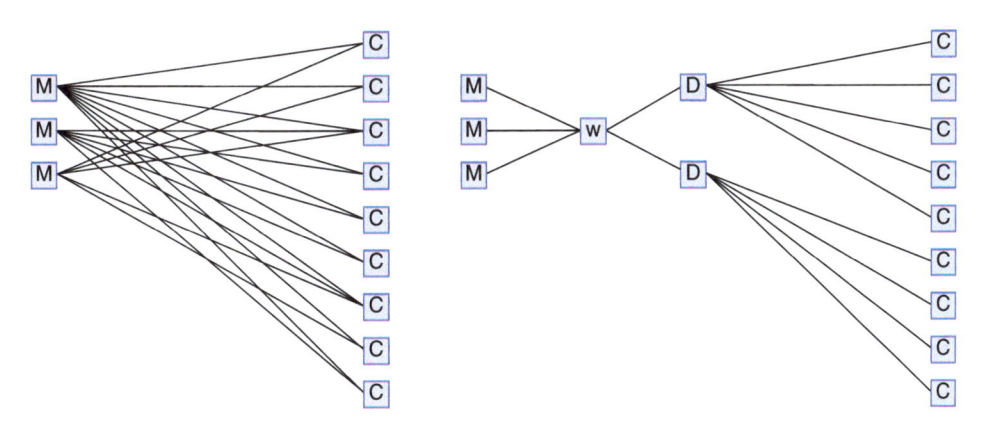

Figure 6.15 Number of activities is reduced with intermediaries in distribution systems (supply chain)

manufacturers to each of the nine customers (a total of 27 connections). In contrast, the right graph shows that the three manufacturers send their products to the wholesaler, who collects and distributes the products to the two distributors (retailers) who connect with two segments with five and four customers. The number of connections with intermediaries is reduced from 27 to 14, which significantly decreases the total amount of distribution activities. Consequently, arranging a distribution system with intermediaries has the potential to lower total distribution costs in a supply chain.

Flows in Distribution Systems

In distribution systems that involve intermediaries, the involved parties work together to organize the necessary tasks. These tasks are often referred to as flows (Coughlan et al., 2006):

- physical flow;
- flow of ownership;
- flow of payment;
- flow of information;
- flow of promotion.

Physical Flow

The physical flow in distribution systems involves logistics, which encompasses the transportation and storage of products from manufacturing through to delivery to the end user. The degree to which each participant in the distribution system performs logistics tasks may vary, and the logistics may also involve third-party suppliers, such as specialized transportation for perishable goods. Advanced tracking systems are often used to digitalize the physical logistic system, allowing all parties, including end users, to trace products through the system and supply chain. For instance, a consumer purchasing fresh salmon can trace its physical flow back to the salmon farm and even trace the suppliers of fodder and medicine used in the salmon farms. This technological development has contributed substantially to developing more sustainable business models. Sustainability and the idea of circular economy is becoming an important element in distribution system design (Kazancoglu et al., 2020). Developments in block-chain technology can contribute significantly to more sustainable distribution systems (Sternberg et al., 2021). An increasing number of companies are designing products that can be fully decomposed back to raw materials, such as Polestar, which designs products that can be recycled throughout the entire value chain.[7]

Flow of Ownership

The flow of ownership refers to the transfer of ownership from the manufacturer to the end customer, which is typically handled by the distributors in distribution systems. By taking

---

[7]https://www.polestar.com/us/news/striving-for-zero-the-2030-climate-neutral-car-plan/.

ownership of the products, distributors also take the risks associated with selling them, such as the possibility of products perishing or going out of fashion, or of there being quality defects. The distribution contract specifies the responsibilities and risks of each party, and the level of risk assumed by the distributors influences the fees they can charge the suppliers for distributing their products.

Flow of Payment

The flow of payment refers to the transfer of funds between manufacturers and end customers, which is closely tied to the transfer of ownership. In many consumer markets, customers pay for products upon delivery, while products with longer lead times, such as cars, often require a deposit (or advance payment) at the time of order and payment in full upon delivery. Wholesalers and retailers who stock the product typically receive a credit period of one to two months before payment is due. Some distributors manage to sell products and receive payment before they pay their suppliers, reducing their need for working capital but increasing the suppliers' need for working capital.

Flow of Information

The flow of information in distribution systems involves sharing information about local markets, competitors and customers. To stay market-oriented, suppliers need information about end customers' buying behaviour, preferences and satisfaction. Intermediaries also want information about how the market is developing on customer needs, competition, regulation, economics and technology. Sharing information benefits both parties, but it requires trust that the other party will not exploit the information (Selnes & Sallis, 2003). However, information sharing also poses a potential conflict of who owns the customer, i.e. whether it is the manufacturer or the retailer. Therefore, it is crucial to address and resolve such questions through good working relationships in the distribution systems.

Flow of Promotion

Although distribution systems with intermediaries can reduce distribution costs, dividing the cost savings among the parties involved is not a straightforward process. In these systems, distribution power is a critical factor, and the party with the most power typically claims a larger share of the profit generated in the system. By creating popular branded products that customers demand, manufacturers can increase their power and leverage over retailers, who want to stock these products to attract customers. The more appealing a brand is to consumers, the more likely they are to prefer retailers that carry that brand – a strategy known as a pull-strategy. Brands such as Nike have significant influence, allowing them to more or less dictate the terms of distribution services and pay less for distribution than less popular brands. Retailers can on their side increase bargaining power by having more stores in areas where people shop, giving them leverage to negotiate better terms with manufacturers. However, excessive market power concentrations can lead to monopolies, which is why regulatory authorities, such as the European Competition Network (EU) and the Federal Trade Commission (USA), have established regulations to promote competition and prevent monopolies. Collaboration benefits all parties in the distribution system in the long run, and they must be forward-thinking and anticipate market turbulence, technological shifts and changes in customer preferences in order to stay ahead of the curve (Heide & John, 1988; Heide, 1994).

Franchise Systems

A franchise model is a business arrangement in which one party, known as the franchisor, grants another party, known as the franchisee, the right to operate a business using the franchisor's established brand, business model and support systems. The franchisee, in return, pays fees or royalties to the franchisor and agrees to operate the business according to the franchisor's standards and guidelines. When a company has developed a successful concept and wants to grow, it can do so by either establishing its own local operations in other locations or by using a franchising model where independent companies own the local operations. The big advantage with the franchising alternative is that the company can grow with less capital and with less risk. One of the most well-known and successful franchise systems is McDonald's. The history starts with a very popular and successful fast-food restaurant in California. In 1954 they opened their first franchise restaurant in Chicago, which was an immediate hit. By 1963, McDonald's had 500 restaurants in America. Today there are around 36,000 McDonald's eateries around the world, 80% of which are franchises.

The franchisor is the party that owns or controls the business concept, brand and intellectual property rights. The franchisor provides the franchisee with the necessary tools, training and ongoing support to replicate the business successfully. The franchisee is the entity that invests in and operates the franchise unit. The franchisee benefits from using the established brand, business model and support services provided by the franchisor. Franchisees typically pay initial fees, such as franchise fees or licence fees, to obtain the right to operate a franchise unit. Additionally, franchisees pay ongoing royalties, which are a percentage of their revenue or profits, to the franchisor.

There are many factors that will influence the success of franchising models (Nijmeijer et al., 2014). Research indicates that franchisors should assist in site selection and provide exclusive territories to franchisees. Although the franchisors needs to provide high-quality systems and support on local operations, some decision-making needs to be decentralized, allowing the franchisee to use local knowledge and find good solutions to secure ownership and dedication.

The franchise model allows businesses to expand rapidly and leverage the entrepreneurial spirit and local market knowledge of franchisees. The Body Shop depicted in Case Study 6.7 illustrates how successful the model can be.

Case Study 6.7

The Body Shop

In 1976, Dame Anita Roddick established The Body Shop in Brighton, England. It originated as a small store offering high-quality skincare products in eco-friendly refillable containers, founded on the belief that business could serve as a positive force for both people and the planet – the wellspring of true beauty.

The company operates a worldwide network of retail outlets, providing customers with an immersive experience in its offerings. These stores are renowned for their organic aesthetics and unwavering commitment to ethical brand messaging.

Since its inception, The Body Shop has evolved into a global retail powerhouse, catering to the needs of over 30 million customers across the globe. The company employs 10,000 individuals, complemented by an additional 12,000 team members in its franchise operations, spanning approximately 3,000 stores situated in over 70 countries.

The Body Shop is steadfast in its dedication to responsible sourcing of natural and sustainable ingredients. It actively champions fair-trade principles and embraces community-centric suppliers. The company's unwavering commitment to ethically sourced, top-quality ingredients distinguish it from its peers. The company was a pioneer in reporting sustainability goals (Livesey & Kearins, 2002).

Moreover, The Body Shop has long been at the forefront of the cosmetics industry's battle against animal testing. Its product range includes a wide array of cruelty-free, vegetarian and vegan options, aligning seamlessly with its core principles of animal welfare.

The brand places a pronounced emphasis on curbing its ecological footprint. It takes proactive measures to diminish packaging waste, employs environmentally friendly materials

Image 6.6 A Body Shop store

(Continued)

and actively participates in reforestation endeavours. Notably, initiatives like the 'Refill and Reuse' programme have been instrumental in reducing plastic waste.

The Body Shop goes beyond being just a cosmetics company; it serves as a powerful catalyst for positive change. The company wholeheartedly commits to social and environmental advocacy, actively supporting causes like ending animal testing, fostering self-esteem and advocating for human rights. These initiatives have not only resonated with customers but have also cultivated profound loyalty among its advocates.

In February 2024, the UK branch of Body Shops, along with several other branches in Europe, came under administration to address the company's financial difficulties. This unfortunate event occurred after a period of declining revenue and profitability, possibly due to changes in the business model under different ownerships, heightened competition from companies offering ethical and sustainable products, and increased production costs resulting from widespread price inflation. Even strong brands with wide distribution networks are not immune to competition and changes in customer needs and preferences, and must continuously improve the value they create for owners, customers, and other stakeholders.[8]

SUMMARY

Product category management involves managing a company's products to achieve both financial value for the company and product value for its customers. Financial value is focused on future growth and sustainable profits, while product value for customers is centred on meeting their needs better than the competition and keeping their customers satisfied.

Product category management involves determining the appropriate level at which a product should be conceptualized for effective strategic management. This guiding principle is based on the level at which customers make their buying decisions. Defining product categories is a crucial strategic decision as it guides a company's investments and competition. Companies should invest in categories that have the potential for growth and profitability and reduce investments in categories that are declining in volume and profitability.

When defining and positioning a product, we rely on a product concept to assess its attractiveness. These concepts are constructed based on a set of product attributes and their respective levels, which are connected to customers' needs and their perceptions of the product. Customers will choose the alternative that provides the highest utility, assuming all other factors are equal. If all alternatives are perceived as equal in quality, customers will

[8]For information on the financial difficulties in 2024, see https://www.standard.co.uk/business/business-news/the-body-shop-what-went-wrong-and-what-happens-next-b1138941.html; https://www.retaildetail.eu/news/beauty-care/concerns-for-the-body-shop-extend-to-germany-france-benelux/.

choose the option with the lowest cost, which can include factors such as price, time and uncertainty.

When a product offers higher quality, it is expected that customers will be willing to pay more for it. This is because they perceive a greater utility from the product. It's not that customers necessarily want to pay more, but they are willing to pay extra for the added utility. Companies often try to differentiate their prices to capture the maximum value from each customer by reflecting their varying willingness to pay. One popular strategy for implementing differentiated pricing is dynamic pricing, which has become prevalent in many industries where customers interact online.

The management of product value delivery involves fulfilling customer expectations and ensuring product profitability. Customer satisfaction increases when their expectations are met, leading to repeat purchases and positive word-of-mouth recommendations. On the other hand, customers become dissatisfied when the product's quality falls short of their expectations. Product managers must determine the appropriate level of investment in quality to maintain customer satisfaction, retain customers, and balance long-term revenues and costs.

To calculate the profitability of a product category, several factors must be considered. The first step is to assess the number of customers, their average number of purchases and the price paid. After assessing these factors, the product category profitability can be calculated by subtracting the product-related costs from the revenues. The costs can be either directly related to the number of products sold, such as direct variable product unit costs, or indirectly related to other activities involved in producing and selling the product. It is important to understand the response function for advertising and sales to make informed decisions regarding investments in these areas. Product profitability can benefit from economies of scale as indirect product-related costs can be spread over more units when volume increases.

Product managers increase revenues and market share through investment in distribution networks. For convenience goods, increased distribution intensity has an increasing positive effect on sales and market share (convex), whereas the shape for shopping (i.e. search goods) is concave. The quality of service in distribution channels can be improved by offering fast and convenient service, demonstrating friendliness and empathy, providing competent assistance, and making personalized adjustments and customizations as needed.

The cost structure of a distribution system depends on whether intermediaries are involved or not. When intermediaries are present, the cost structure is primarily made up of variable costs. Conversely, in fully integrated distribution systems that operate without intermediaries, the costs are fixed and do not depend on the number of units sold. It is worth noting that distribution networks with intermediaries often have lower total costs than those without intermediaries. Distribution power plays a crucial role in such systems, as the party with the most power tends to claim a greater share of the benefits.

END-OF-CHAPTER QUESTIONS

1   Compare an iPhone and a Samsung mobile phone. What are the differences in the core product between these two brands? Discuss why customers have different

preferences for the two brands, and how these differences are related to relational and network factors.

2   What is your acceptable price range for a takeaway pizza (or sushi if you prefer)? How can a takeaway restaurant motivate you to select from the upper part of this price range? Interview a few friends and ask them to specify their acceptable price range and what they think companies can do to motivate them to select in the upper part. Do you all have the same price range? How can a takeaway restaurant motivate customers to increase the upper limit in their acceptable price range?

3   How can a car dealership motivate households with two cars to buy both cars from the dealership, and to not only have both cars, but also buy additional services like maintenance, insurance and finance? Investigate a few car dealerships' websites and try to find out what they offer households with two cars. Discuss why car dealerships have different value propositions to households with two cars.

4   Identify a radically new product. What is or can be the value proposition, and how will you communicate it to create an interest and a desire to try the new product? Test out your communication concept on a few friends and investigate their thinking about and interest in the new product. What does this tell you about the challenges for market success for radically new products?

5   Many companies invest heavily in social media advertising. How can a company find out the effects of these investments, that is if there is a positive return on the investments? Read Gordon et al. (2019) and Frick et al. (2022).

FURTHER READING

Cillo, V., Petruzzelli, A.M., Ardito, L. & Del Giudice, M. (2019). Understanding sustainable innovation: A systematic literature review. *Corporate Social Responsibility and Environmental Management*, 26, 1012–1025. https://doi.org/10.1002/csr.1783.

Levitt, T. (1980). Marketing success through differentiation of anything. *Harvard Business Review*, 58(1), 83–91.

Leiblein, M.J., Chen, J.S. & Posen, H.E. (2023). Uncertain learning curves: Implications for first-mover advantage and knowledge spillovers. *Academy of Management Review*, 48(1), 123–148.

7

BRAND MANAGEMENT

This chapter

- defines brand and its strategic role;
- introduces the key levels in brand strength hierarchy;
- presents the road-map in brand strategy;
- identifies the key measures in brand management;
- discusses branding in business markets.

INTRODUCTION

Throughout this chapter, you will learn the essence of what a brand is, including understanding how it extends far beyond just a name or logo, and discover the profound impact it can have on customer perceptions. You will learn the crucial roles a brand plays, for both the customer and the company. You will learn the key elements that make up a strong and valuable brand. From brand awareness to brand loyalty, we will dissect the components that contribute to a brand's success. Further, you will gain knowledge of how to position the company's brand strategically in relation to competitors and within the company's own brand portfolio, including how to communicate the brand. You will also discover the dynamics of managing and measuring established brands. Finally, you will get some insights on branding in business markets.

WHAT IS A BRAND AND ITS STRATEGIC ROLES?

A brand refers to a distinctive name, term, design, symbol or other identifiable element that distinguishes the goods or services of one seller from those of others.[1] It serves two fundamental purposes: to identify the seller and to communicate its unique qualities. These two functions form the foundation of brand management, which we will explore in more detail below. A brand resides in the customer's memory and its value is determined by the level of

---

[1] Definition of 'brand' from the American Marketing Association.

awareness, preference, loyalty and usage it enjoys among people. The objective is to translate these factors into financial value by generating a steady stream of revenue and cash flow from customers who choose the brand. This cash flow increases when more people adopt the brand, use it frequently, are willing to pay a premium for it and exhibit loyalty towards it, desiring to continue using it in the future. The brand plays a crucial role in the consumer's decision-making process. When a need arises, the consideration of various brands within the relevant product category comes into play. For example, when thinking about ice cream, brands like Magnum and Ben & Jerry's come to mind. The greater the positive experiences and knowledge a customer possesses about a brand, the higher the likelihood that they will select that brand. Consequently, brand management entails shaping customer perceptions and knowledge about the brand in a manner that creates a positive and appealing image within their consciousness.

Brand knowledge can be visualized as a network of connections centred around the brand name, which acts as a focal point within this network. Case Study 7.1 and Figure 7.1 provide an example of how this might work in practice.

Case Study 7.1

Samsung

Figure 7.1 depicts knowledge as an interconnected network associated with Samsung.

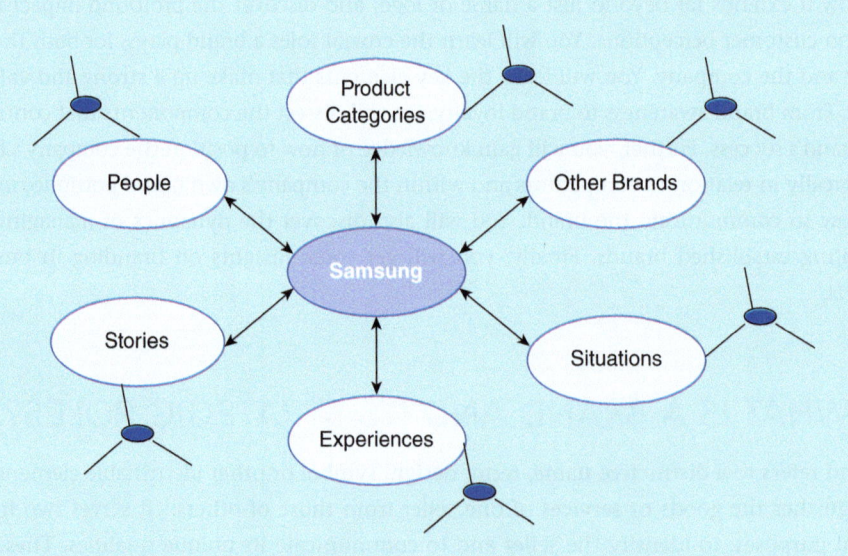

Figure 7.1 Brand knowledge represented as an associative network in memory, with the brand name as the node in the network of associations

This network represents the information and associations customers have about the brand. When a customer thinks of Samsung, they associate it with specific product categories, such as mobile phones. Additionally, the customer may link Samsung with other brands in the mobile-phone category, such as Apple, Sony and HTC. When the customer's knowledge of mobile phones is activated during a purchasing process, Samsung and other brands appear in their consciousness. This is referred to as unaided brand recall since the brand comes to mind without any explicit exposure to Samsung's name, logo or other branding elements. Conversely, if exposure to a brand element is necessary for the brand to come to mind, it is termed aided recall. As mentioned earlier, a crucial role of a brand is to *identify* the brand with a specific product category in the customer's mind. If Samsung and the associated knowledge are not activated when the mobile-phone category is considered, it indicates poor brand positioning. In such cases, Samsung is less likely to be included in the customer's consideration set. Brands that reside in the customer's memory and are spontaneously activated when considering a product (unaided familiarity) are more likely to be chosen. If a customer already has a positive relationship with certain brands in mind, they are unlikely to search for additional brands. Therefore, a significant task for brand management is to cultivate strong associations between the brand and its product category, enabling the brand name to naturally come to mind, or being identified during relevant purchase situations.

The *unique* aspects of a brand are also stored in memory, like how we store information about other individuals, such as our friends. Each friend possesses specific characteristics, like being a skilled chef, which we remember and utilize when describing them to others. Likewise, we store information about a brand's unique properties that set it apart from other brands. For instance, we might say, 'Samsung excels in terms of functionality'. This allows us to categorize and compare brands to determine our preferences. Knowledge of a particular brand comprises various elements that describe its attributes. As depicted in Figure 7.1, Samsung may be associated with other people, such as celebrities or friends.

Additionally, some individuals may have associations related to the company's history, technology, employees and country of origin. Those who have prior experience with a Samsung product would have stored positive or negative experiences as well. These associations play a vital role as they influence customer perceptions and emotions towards the brand and contribute to its distinctiveness in comparison to other brands. Thus, a crucial aspect of brand management is to ensure that the brand stands out and possesses unique qualities.

Brand knowledge serves as a framework for processing new information. When encountering new information about a brand, such as through advertisements, existing knowledge networks play a crucial role in interpreting and evaluating the new information. If the new information aligns with the existing knowledge, including one's current perception of the brand, customers typically incorporate the information to update their knowledge. However, if the new information is unexpected and contradicts the existing knowledge, it requires more cognitive capacity to process it. Also, as discussed in Chapter 4, 'Marketing Communication', attitudes people hold about brands are hard to change. Customers need to be motivated to allocate this cognitive capacity, which is more likely to occur if the information is relevant and interesting. If individuals lack motivation, the new information will be rejected outright. This means that the information is perceived as irrelevant or untrustworthy, and the brand knowledge remains unchanged. See Case Study 7.2 for an example of how McDonald's attempted to change perception of their food.

Case Study 7.2

McDonald's

To address negative perceptions surrounding their brand, McDonald's implemented the 'Our Food, Your Questions' advertising campaign. Through this campaign, McDonald's aimed to enhance transparency and debunk misconceptions about the quality, sourcing and nutritional value of their food. This initiative was in response to the growing consumer preference for healthier and more transparent food options, as well as the increasing scrutiny faced by McDonald's regarding health and transparency concerns.

The campaign was initially launched in Canada in 2012 and achieved recognition as the marketer of the year. It was later extended to the United States, Australia and Finland, and proved to be highly effective in terms of communication. Notably, in Finland, the perception of McDonald's food quality increased by 29%, the company's trust score rose by 35% and overall sales grew by 14% during the campaign period.

Despite its success, however, the campaign may not have achieved a lasting transformation in people's attitudes towards fast food. McDonald's global sales revenues have exhibited a steady decline since 2013, except for the years 2021–2022.[2]

This contradiction between the campaign's message and the established perceptions of fast food requires considerable cognitive effort to process the information. Should the advertising fail to capture interest, the message is likely to be disregarded without further consideration.

What can McDonald's do to change people's attitudes towards its food?

In such cases, the veracity of the message becomes less significant. Holding onto established attitudes and perceptions about brands simplifies decision-making processes, allowing for practical choices without the need for constant deliberation. This is the primary reason why changing attitudes towards a brand becomes challenging once people have formed an opinion. The reluctance to invest cognitive effort creates difficulty in transforming a negative perception of a brand into a positive one.[3]

There are two key insights to learn from this. The pre-existing brand knowledge shapes how customers understand and absorb new information, and customers are hesitant to alter their existing perceptions of a brand.

---

[2]Statista https://www.statista.com/statistics/208917/revenue-of-the-mcdonalds-corporation-since-2005/; https://time.com/3501921/mcdonalds-transparency-campaign; http://marketingmag.ca/advertising/marketer-of-the-year-2012-mcdonalds-canada-70067/; https://nordddb.com/case/our-food-your-questions

[3]These arguments stem from social judgement theory and assimilation and contrast effects (Sherif & Hovland, 1961).

Individuals gather information about brands and enhance their brand knowledge from diverse information sources. Advertising from the company and its competitors serves as a significant source. Additionally, customers' personal experiences with owning and using a brand are an important factor. These experiences are often shared through word of mouth, which becomes another influential source of brand information. Some of these sources lie outside the company's direct control. For example, a company cannot direct control or restrict what someone writes about their brand on social media, nor prevent journalists from writing unfavourably about the brand.

While many of these sources lie outside the company's direct control, the company still possesses opportunities to shape and influence how people perceive its brands. For instance, they can actively participate in discussions on social media platforms, address inaccuracies, provide supplementary information, correct factual errors and guide individuals in rectifying misconceptions.

Before a company can initiate marketing initiatives to strengthen its brand, it is crucial to understand the perceptions and sentiments of customers towards the brand. By conducting comprehensive analyses, the brand manager can assess potential issues and uncover opportunities. The objective is to shape customers' understanding in a manner that fosters positive views of the brand and cultivates high expectations regarding its offerings.

The Role of the Brand for Customers

The brand provides three benefits to customers (Aaker, 1991):

- it simplifies the interpretation and processing of information for customers;
- it establishes a sense of assurance when making purchase decisions;
- it delivers a feeling of gratification during usage.

The brand creates a cognitive structure in customers' minds that provides coherence to product and market information. With the constant exposure to advertising and other information, the brand's knowledge framework aids individuals in distinguishing relevant information worth retaining for future use from irrelevant details that can be disregarded. Essentially, the brand knowledge functions as a mechanism for selectively storing vital information to remember that simplifies interpretation and processing.

Consider the contrasting reception of an advertising message from Samsung versus a brand unfamiliar to customers. Information about Samsung is likely to be processed, retained and recalled due to its relevance. On the other hand, storing information about an unfamiliar brand is more challenging. There is no pre-existing mental space to store details about the unknown brand, necessitating the creation of a new node to expand memory capacity. However, people tend to resist creating new nodes as it requires mental effort. As mentioned earlier, humans naturally conserve mental resources to avoid unnecessary strain. Processing and remembering all the information one encounters would be chaotic and practically impossible.

Brands also instil confidence in decision-making. When an individual has previously gathered information and developed an impression regarding the quality of specific brands, they experience reduced risk and heightened assurance when selecting those brands. Consequently, well-known brands embody a sense of confidence and trust.

When customers are unfamiliar with brands within a specific product category, they face uncertainty in deciding which supplier to choose. They perceive a possibility of selecting a supplier offering low-quality or unsuitable products. To alleviate this uncertainty, they actively seek additional information about different brands until their uncertainty reaches a minimum level. However, in the case of well-known brands, relevant information is already stored and can be readily accessed, reducing the customer's motivation to gather information about other brands in the market. Thus, brand knowledge aids in swiftly identifying reputable products and mitigating the risk of making a poor choice.

A significant implication arises from the fact that brands alleviate uncertainty, leading to an increased willingness to pay for reduced risk. Consequently, customers are more inclined to pay a premium for products bearing a well-known brand compared to those associated with an unknown brand. The extent of this willingness to pay varies based on multiple factors. It is essential to highlight that the fundamental principle is that brand familiarity presents an opportunity to command a higher price.

A brand serves as a symbol that can enhance the value of a product beyond its functional aspects. Merely owning an Apple product, for instance, can generate feelings of gratification. The symbolic value associated with different brands may vary significantly. For instance, the symbolic value attributed to LG is likely lower compared to the symbolic value of Apple. People enjoy showcasing their new iPhone, and it is reasonable to assume that this behaviour is motivated by the desire to signal ownership of an iconic symbol.

Symbolic value can manifest in two ways: inward-directed and outward-directed. Inward-directed symbolic value refers to the personal pleasure derived from owning a specific brand. For instance, a professional photographer may experience immense satisfaction and fulfilment from owning a Hasselblad camera, fulfilling a long-held dream. Similarly, art collectors may find joy in owning a painting by a renowned artist. On the other hand, a brand can also serve as an icon or symbol that positions individuals within their social circles.[4] This outward-directed symbolic value often revolves around notions of prestige, signifying

---

[4]Certain branding experts will probably consider symbolic value as an aspect of brand personality. The logic behind brand personality is that customers relate to brands in the same way as they relate to other people, where others' personality is very important for whether you want to relate to them. Symbolism is a broad concept that captures the meaning of the brand. This meaning can be linked to the fact that the brand is a symbol of a certain type of personality. However, the brand can also have a meaning that does not have to do with personification. Hasselblad, in the example above, has a meaning for professional photographers who can be linked to a dream that has come true.

belonging or hierarchical status. A brand can symbolize traits such as youthfulness, intellectualism, friendliness, masculinity, femininity, and more. Consequently, some individuals may purchase paintings not solely for personal enjoyment but also to impress others. Likewise, it is reasonable to assume that the symbolic value associated with a brand like iPhone influences some consumers' purchasing decisions. Brands with high symbolic value effectively fulfil customers' needs for self-assurance, role alignment, group affiliation and identification (Park et al., 1986).

The symbolic value associated with a brand not only shapes customer preferences but also drives a willingness to pay a premium. However, the extent to which customers are willing to pay more varies based on multiple factors. In the case of perfume and fashion brands, customers might be willing to pay a price that is twice as high as that of an unknown product offering the same technical quality. The underlying principle is that a brand name with a strong symbolic value can inspire customers to pay a higher price. Nevertheless, it is a challenging task to cultivate a brand with a substantial symbolic value.

Image 7.1 The act of possessing a Hasselblad camera can in itself provide a sense of pleasure due to its symbolic value

The Role of the Brand for Companies

Brands represent highly valuable assets for companies and possess substantial financial worth. The magnitude of this financial value is contingent upon various factors. A brand's significance lies in its ability to enhance the effectiveness and impact of marketing efforts, resulting in several key advantages (Aaker, 1991):

- increases willingness among customers to pay a premium;
- strengthens customer loyalty;
- increases efficiency of marketing activities;
- provides a robust foundation for introducing new products under the same brand name;
- enhances bargaining power when dealing with distributors and suppliers;
- contributes to greater employee motivation and the cultivation of an organizational culture.

A strong brand generates a willingness among customers to pay a premium, allowing for higher pricing of products. When faced with a choice between a well-established brand and an unknown one, customers tend to opt for the former, even if it comes with a higher price tag. Blind tests conducted with recognized and unfamiliar beer brands have shown that individuals often cannot discern their preferred brands based on taste alone. In fact, many participants perceive the unknown brands as tasting better. However, when asked if they would switch from the well-known brands to the unknown ones, most respond that they will continue purchasing the familiar brands, despite the taste difference. Similar patterns have emerged across various product categories, not limited to beer. Consequently, investments in branding can prove highly profitable as customers are willing to pay a premium for brands due to the reduced uncertainty and the additional meaning and symbolic value they provide beyond the inherent product value.

The extent to which customers are willing to pay more varies depending on the circumstances. In the fast-moving consumer goods sector, strong brands often command prices that are 10–30% higher than non-branded products of the same quality, such as private label brands (Sethuraman, 2000; Apelbaum et al., 2003). Consequently, many manufacturers in this market invest in branding to achieve higher price points. Manufacturers with established strong brands typically allocate around 10% of the brand's revenue to brand-building advertising, aimed at reinforcing positive brand associations (Kerin & O'Regan, 2008).

However, for new or low market-share brands, this percentage is likely to be higher. This is because advertising costs remain constant regardless of brand size, and brands with a larger market share can distribute these costs across a greater number of products, resulting in lower unit costs. Strong brands foster customer loyalty.[5] Customers have higher expectations from well-established brands, and they derive greater benefits from them. As long as these expectations are met, customers will continue using the brand. When customers are satisfied, they have no reason to switch to a competitor's brand.

Brand loyalty plays a pivotal role in amplifying the impact of marketing activities. When customers are loyal to a brand, the need for extensive advertising and promotional campaigns diminishes as they are already convinced to purchase products from that particular

---

[5]Oliver (1999) argues that we can distinguish between different types of loyalty based on the role the brand has for the person. At the lowest level are only those who are loyal simply because they are satisfied. At a higher level, the brand becomes a symbol that reinforces self-esteem and identity (for example Rolex), and the ultimate is a loyalty where the brand acts as a symbol of group belonging (for example, Harley-Davidson in the motorcycle community).

company. For instance, if Samsung, a well-established brand, invests 10,000 euros in an advertising campaign to drive customers to its website, it is likely to attract more visitors compared to an unknown or weaker brand running a similar campaign. In other words, Samsung can allocate fewer resources to attract website visitors because its strong brand recognition already exists among customers.

Strong brands also enhance the effectiveness of personal selling. For example, a salesperson representing Volkswagen will likely find it easier to sell cars in a European country compared to a salesperson from Tata (http://www.tatamotors.com). While Tata is a prominent car manufacturer in India, it lacks widespread brand recognition outside of India. Therefore, a Tata salesperson must first establish trust and credibility in the brand before making their case for choosing their cars. On the other hand, a Volkswagen salesperson can bypass this initial step since people are already familiar with the brand. Selling a well-known brand thus requires less time per sale, resulting in reduced sales costs.

Image 7.2 Tata is a leading car manufacturer brand in India, but a relative unknown brand in many other countries

Furthermore, strong brands facilitate more efficient customer service processes by instilling trust. Customers generally have confidence in service representatives of recognized brands and believe that they can effectively resolve any issues. For instance, in the event of a manufacturing defect, a Tata customer may attribute it to the brand's unfamiliar quality. Conversely, a Volkswagen customer, aware of the brand's reputation for high quality, is likely to perceive the defect as an isolated incident rather than a reflection of overall low quality. As a result, the service process is streamlined for strong brands, consuming less time and operating more efficiently.

A strong brand also fosters positive WOM, which acts as a magnet for attracting new customers. In essence, the brand enhances the effectiveness of various marketing activities, resulting in reduced marketing costs and increased profitability.

Established brands frequently serve as a launching pad for introducing new products and expanding a company's presence into new product categories (Aaker & Keller, 1990). As discussed in Chapter 6, the Apple brand is an example of this role. Initially known as a personal computer brand, Apple has achieved remarkable success in leveraging its brand to establish a strong foothold in various product categories. The Apple brand has served as a powerful platform for positioning the company as a key player in the MP3 player segment with the iPod, the mobile-phone industry with the iPhone, the tablet market with the iPad, and even in the realm of streaming services with Apple TV.

Introducing a new product under an established brand name offers advantages in terms of leveraging the brand's value, image and associations, while simultaneously reducing customer uncertainty. This strategic approach is known as brand extension (Völckner & Sattler, 2006). However, it is important to note that using brand extensions to launch new products is not without risks. Introducing an established brand into a different product category can potentially confuse and frustrate customers, face resistance from retailers, dilute the brand's meaning or even harm the parent brand. For instance, some argue that Calvin Klein may have confused customers and diluted the brand's integrity by expanding into numerous categories such as underwear, swimwear and baby clothes.

Strong brands empower companies with stronger bargaining power when dealing with retailers and distributors. Retail chains are typically drawn to popular consumer brands because they attract customers and influence consumer perceptions associated with the store's own brand name. For example, consumer electronics retailers such as Power (Scandinavia), Dixons (Europe) and Best Buy (US) aim to include the Samsung brand in their product offerings as it enhances their profile. The more appealing the brand is to consumers, the more enticing it becomes for retailers. Brand owners like Samsung utilize this brand-based influence to negotiate favourable terms, including better pricing and lower distribution costs.

Strong brands also have a favourable impact on employee motivation and organizational culture (Morgan, 2004; Maxwell & Knox, 2009). Companies with positive brand values, for example linked to competence, ethical leadership or sustainability programmes, are often appealing to employees for various reasons. It is widely believed that organizations with strong brands possess competent and driven employees. As a result, many individuals aspire to work in such companies, anticipating challenging and rewarding experiences. Moreover, being employed by a well-known brand can enhance one's social status. Individuals may regard someone working for Apple, for instance, as both intriguing and competent. The positive associations tied to the brand extend to the people associated with the company. Working for companies with strong brands can also positively influence one's career prospects, as prospective employers typically view candidates with prior experience in renowned brand companies as more competent and sociable. Therefore, companies with strong brands tend to attract skilled and motivated employees. When employees have a positive perception of the brand, they become effective brand ambassadors, contributing to the brand's reinforcement (Morhart et al., 2009).

The brand represents one of the company's most significant assets, known as brand equity (Aaker, 1991; Keller, 1998; Keller & Lehman, 2006). Strong brands possess considerable value as they positively impact both revenue and profitability. Unlike tangible assets, the brand is classified as an intangible asset due to its abstract nature, making it non-transferable like other company assets. Its true value becomes evident during acquisitions and sales of companies. This can be observed through the market value of publicly traded companies. For instance, a substantial portion of the Coca-Cola Company's market value is attributed to its robust portfolio of brands. The financial value of a brand relies on its level of recognition and awareness. The greater the number of individuals who are aware of, prefer, use and remain loyal to the brand, the higher its financial worth. Conversely, if a brand is relatively unknown, lacks preference, has limited usage and lacks loyalty, its financial value will be correspondingly low. Consequently, brand building involves influencing the thoughts and emotions of customers in the market towards the brand.

BRAND-STRENGTH HIERARCHY

The concept of brand building, or branding, can be viewed as a hierarchical structure in which a higher level within the hierarchy indicates a stronger brand, as depicted in Figure 7.2.[6] The hierarchy consists of four levels that measure brand strength: brand awareness, brand expectations, brand usage and brand loyalty. Typically, customers progress through a learning

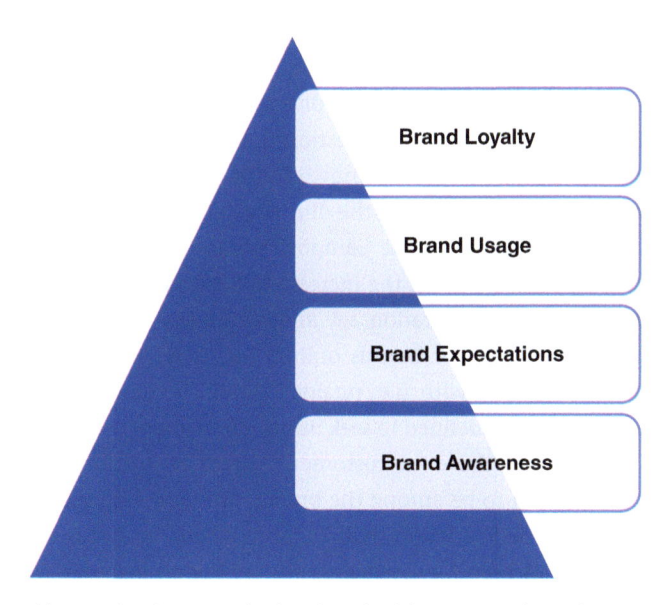

Figure 7.2 Brand hierarchy showing the levels in building strong brands

---

[6]In the marketing literature, there are several models that define different levels of brand strength. One recognized model is Keller (2001). This and other models are derived from attitude theory, which claims that an attitude's strength is a combination of cognitions, emotions and action intentions.

process starting from the lowest level (awareness) and ascending to the highest level (loyalty). Consequently, the number of individuals at each level varies, meaning that not everyone who is aware of the brand has developed expectations, and so on. Branding involves the implementation of diverse marketing activities targeted at one or more of the four levels in the hierarchy. The overall strength of a brand increases with the extent of brand awareness and the position individuals hold within the brand hierarchy. A stronger brand yields a greater influence on customer behaviour and ultimately enhances the brand's financial value.

Brand Awareness

Brand awareness refers to the state where the brand is stored in memory and connected with one or more product categories. In order for someone to possess brand awareness, the brand needs to be associated with the relevant product category and easily come to mind. When customers are asked about their knowledge of mobile-phone brands, their response indicates not only their awareness of the specific brand in question but also their knowledge of other brands. Therefore, brand awareness serves as a metric to gauge how many individuals within a market associate a brand with its respective product category. Brand awareness is considered low if only a small number of people link the brand to the product category, while it is deemed high if a significant number do so. It is important to note that the question does not enquire whether the customer recognizes a brand upon hearing its name, such as asking 'Have you heard about HTC?' (aided recall). Many people might have heard of HTC, but fewer individuals will mention HTC when asked 'Which mobile-phone brands do you know?' (unaided recall). Significantly fewer individuals will include HTC in their response during unaided recall, and it is this latter question that reveals the strength of the brand. A relevant example is the brand Campbell's, known for its quality soups. Their challenge arose when people contemplated brands within the dinner category but failed to activate the association with soups, and consequently the Campbell's brand did not come to mind either.

The value of brand awareness lies in the increased likelihood of brands known to customers being included in their consideration set and ultimately chosen. For instance, when individuals search for mobile-phone brands online, they tend to first visit the websites of brands they are already familiar with (i.e. unaided recall). If they find the desired product from these brands, they are less inclined to seek information about other brands. On the other hand, if a brand is not among those the customer is aware of, it is unlikely to be considered or selected. Thus, it is crucial to be among the brands that potential customers immediately think of, preferably being the first brand that comes to mind, known as *top of mind*.

Another consequence of brand awareness is the ability to generate a preference solely through awareness. When customers are aware of a brand's existence, even without extensive knowledge about it, certain circumstances can lead to a preference for that brand. For instance, when a customer is browsing a shelf of numerous beer brands at a grocery store, they are more likely to select a brand they recognize rather than one they have never encountered before. This phenomenon arises due to the reduction of perceived risk through recognition, making a familiar brand more appealing compared to an unfamiliar one, assuming all other factors are equal.

Image 7.3 Cambell's famous condensed tomato soup

Advertising plays a pivotal role in establishing brand awareness as the primary method. Its initial objective is to generate interest in processing brand-related information that can be stored in memory within the product category. While occasional curiosity exists in learning about new brands, the majority of individuals lack interest primarily due to their absence of desire to acquire further knowledge. Typically, people already purchase and utilize brands that satisfy them, leaving little room for the need for novelty. Hence, the challenge lies in crafting a message that captures attention and creates a lasting recollection of the brand.

In addition to advertising, positive WOM serves as a significant avenue for brand recognition. When individuals consider purchasing something unfamiliar, seeking advice from others is a common practice. With readily available online reviews, the significance of WOM has significantly amplified. Some categories even have specialized websites dedicated to reviews, such as TripAdvisor in the tourism industry.

Although brand awareness represents just the starting point of brand strength, its importance cannot be understated in competitive situations. Brands that are not automatically associated with a specific product category are at a disadvantage when it comes to being chosen, as demonstrated by the case of Campbell's. Similarly, unfamiliar brands are perceived as more uncertain and are thus less likely to be selected. Consequently, companies have the opportunity to achieve significant market gains by enhancing their familiarity. This involves seamlessly integrating the brand as a familiar and recognized choice within the product category, thereby strengthening its association with customers.

Brand Expectations

One of the fundamental aspects of branding involves the cultivation of associations that raise expectations surrounding the brand. This process of association development is a cognitive one, wherein beliefs and emotions become linked to the brand name. For these associations to be valuable, they must result in customers having higher expectations for the brand compared to its competitors. When faced with multiple brand options, customers tend to select the brand that aligns with their highest expectations, assuming the price difference is negligible. Consequently, customers are often willing to pay a premium for a brand that promises greater fulfilment of their expectations.

Brand preference is rooted in the expectation that a particular brand will deliver greater value compared to its alternatives. In this context, value refers to the customer's evaluation of the benefits received in relation to the price paid. Consequently, a preference for one brand, such as Toyota, may outweigh the preference for another brand, such as BMW, based on the perception that the more affordable option provides better value, even if it may not necessarily be superior in quality or performance.

Perceptions of a brand, which form expectations and preferences, are influenced by a variety of factors. Some of these factors pertain to the quality of the products (transactional properties), while others are related to the customer's relationship with the brand (relational characteristics). Transactional properties encompass aspects such as the physical quality of the products, their functional capabilities, the brand's symbolic value, the time and effort required to obtain them, their cost and other attributes typically associated with what customers pay for. Many companies initially focus on developing the product's properties in terms of quality and functionality. An example of this is Tesla, which has achieved remarkable success by advancing battery technology to enable longer ranges, thereby contributing to the creation of a strong preference for the Tesla brand among numerous customers.

The relational properties of a brand are closely tied to the customer's relationship with the brand supplier. These properties encompass factors such as the customer's confidence in receiving the expected value for their purchase, the assurance of assistance in unforeseen and negative situations, recognition and appreciation as a customer, and the perception that the supplier understands and prioritizes their best interests. Relational properties hold particular significance in the formation of preferences for service-oriented companies, where customer–brand interactions and relationships play a crucial role. In industries like banking and insurance, preference formation largely occurs through customers' experiences at the various touchpoints with the brand. Exceptional experiences with a bank consultant, for instance, can be influential in generating high expectations for brands such as BNB Parisbas and Rabobank.

The specific properties that create preference vary depending on the customers' unique needs and requirements. For instance, a business traveller may prioritize an airline's convenient flight schedule, while someone on a leisurely vacation may value other aspects more. Similarly, an active athlete would place greater emphasis on the quality and functionality of products compared to someone who engages in sports merely for exercise. Thus, comprehensively understanding the customers' needs is crucial for successfully identifying the properties that the brand should be associated with, both overall and across different customer segments.

Marketing communication plays a significant role in the process of learning and establishing brand associations. Within this context, companies can utilize advertising to shape desired associations. Advertisements have the power to inform consumers about the advantages of a brand's characteristics, both transactional and relational in nature. They can highlight the specific attributes and benefits that set the brand apart from competitors. Additionally, advertising can be employed to enhance the perceived importance of certain properties. For instance, an airline that is already renowned for its high service quality, such as Qatar Airways, can utilize advertisements to emphasize the significance of service quality, thereby making their brand more appealing to consumers. In contrast, Ryanair, a low-cost carrier, can underscore budget-friendly prices and offers various deals and promotions to remind customers about these features.

Through strategic communication efforts, brands can effectively shape consumer perceptions and strengthen their position in the market.

Marketing communication can also serve as a tool to amplify the symbolic value of a brand (Levy, 1959). Apple, for example, is not only recognized for its quality products but is also associated with a range of values such as imagination, freedom, innovation, enthusiasm, youthfulness and simplicity. The brand has transcended beyond being just a provider of functional goods and has become a symbol representing a desirable way of life. Creating symbolic value involves expanding the brand's meaning beyond its utilitarian dimensions to encompass a more abstract significance that enhances the individual's life.

Identifying and defining this symbolic meaning poses a significant challenge, as does persuading customers to alter their perceptions of a brand. Should the brand be associated with symbolic individuals, such as Louis Vuitton with Steffi Graf and Angelina Jolie? Should it be tied to specific usage situations, such as Quality Street chocolates being linked to Christmas? Alternatively, should the brand limit its distribution in order to maintain an exclusive image, as exemplified by Armani? These are all strategic considerations that brands face when seeking to establish and enhance their symbolic value. See Case Study 7.3 for an example of the use of symbolic brand properties.

Case Study 7.3

Volvo

The value of brand symbols lies in their alignment with the underlying values of customers. The importance of these values evolves alongside societal developments. For instance, frugality held significant importance in Western countries in the years following the Second World War. During this period, Volvo symbolized frugal luxury and gained considerable popularity. However, as societal values shifted over time, frugality gradually gave way to other values such as equality, health and individualism.

Recognizing this shift in values, Volvo embarked on a quest to identify emerging values that could replace frugality as the key value associated with their brand.[7] They identified personal security as a potential candidate. Through creative communication and targeted product development, Volvo successfully transformed the symbolic value of their brand. They transitioned from being primarily associated with frugality to becoming synonymous with security. Moreover, Volvo further adjusted their brand associations to incorporate a rugged and sporty lifestyle, emphasizing the brand's commitment to safety.

Image 7.4 Sporty lifestyle with Volvo. Copyright © Volvo Car Corporation

This example illustrates Volvo's impressive ability to adapt and evolve its brand's symbolic value in response to changing societal values. By staying attuned to emerging values and strategically managing their brand associations, Volvo effectively repositioned themselves to resonate with their target audience.

---

[7]Volvo wanted to expand its US market, where established brands like Ford and some of the GM brands already held this position. They needed a unique symbolic value which could make the Volvo brand more interesting.

Media coverage serves as a significant communication tool for establishing brand associations. Unlike advertising, which often takes a back seat in media channels, media coverage garners distinct attention and engagement. A notable example is Apple's launch of the iPad on 27 January 2010, which generated extensive worldwide media coverage and publicity. This media event played a crucial role in bolstering Apple's image as an innovative, cool and consumer-friendly company, as we will now explore further in Case Study 7.4.

Case Study 7.4

Apple's iPad Launch

The iPad launch was meticulously planned, part of a well-executed product launch strategy. Months in advance, Apple announced the upcoming launch, strategically leaking small titbits of information to the press to build anticipation and curiosity. Journalists began discussing comparisons between Apple's new iPad and Amazon's Kindle, as well as exploring how publishers could safeguard their books from piracy. It's important to note that the January 27 event was not the actual product launch but rather an announcement about the forthcoming iPad and a glimpse of its prototype.

Image 7.5 An Apple iPad

Following the announcement, Apple commenced advertising the product and began accepting pre-orders. Apple enthusiasts had to wait until 10 April 2010 to finally obtain the highly anticipated iPad. The media coverage leading up to the launch played a pivotal role in creating buzz, raising expectations and generating excitement among consumers. This example underscores the power of media coverage as an effective tool for brand communication and association building.

Packaging serves as an essential communication channel for establishing brand associations, particularly in the realm of consumer goods. Through the shape, size, colour and logos on product packaging, brands effectively convey their desired associations. Iconic examples, such as the distinctive shape of the classic Coca-Cola bottle and the unique Absolut Vodka bottles, showcase how brands can create distinct visual signals that foster immediate recognition and identification.

The form of packaging plays a crucial role in conveying specific meanings and generating brand associations. Different shapes evoke different perceptions and associations, contributing to the overall brand image. Similarly, colours play a significant role in triggering associations. For instance, the colour red is often associated with attributes like aggressiveness, passion, strength and vitality. It's no coincidence that Ferrari utilizes red in their marketing, as it aligns with the brand's characteristics. On the other hand, blue evokes associations with authority, dignity, safety and trustworthiness, effectively signalling a sense of responsibility.

By strategically utilizing packaging design elements such as shape, size, colour and logos, brands can communicate their desired associations and create a distinctive visual identity that resonates with consumers. This allows them to establish a unique presence in the market and reinforce their brand image.

Employees play a crucial role in communicating brand associations, as they serve as important channels for shaping customer perceptions. This holds especially true in service industries, encompassing both consumer and business markets. Within sectors like management consultancy, law firms and advertising agencies, employees' behaviour and appearance significantly influence how customers perceive the respective brands. It goes beyond vocational qualifications, as employees' attire and communication style also contribute to the brand's image.

In professional service industries, such as advertising agencies, it is essential for employees to align with the brand's desired attributes. For instance, if an agency aims to establish itself as the epitome of creativity, employees should dress and behave in a manner that reflects their creative flair. This sets them apart from employees in, say, an audit firm, where a more formal and conservative approach may be expected.

By embodying the brand's values and characteristics through their appearance and conduct, employees become ambassadors who shape customer perceptions. Their interactions with customers directly influence how the brand is experienced and remembered. Therefore, businesses in service industries must recognize the pivotal role of employees in conveying brand associations and ensure they are aligned with the brand's desired image.

For retailers, restaurants, hotels and other service-oriented companies, brand development often centres around cultivating a perception of outstanding service. When a retail chain aims to establish a friendly brand image, it becomes crucial to train their staff to genuinely embody friendliness towards customers. This ensures that customers can authentically experience the brand's value first-hand.

Focusing on service-oriented branding, these companies prioritize creating positive interactions and memorable experiences for their customers. Through comprehensive training programmes, staff members are equipped with the necessary skills and knowledge to embody the brand's friendly image. This includes fostering a warm and welcoming demeanour, actively engaging with customers, and consistently going above and beyond to fulfil their needs.

The ultimate objective is for customers to perceive and appreciate the brand's unwavering commitment to exceptional service through their direct interactions with well-trained and friendly staff. By consistently delivering on the promise of friendliness, trading companies can solidify their brand's reputation and cultivate long-lasting customer loyalty. A notable example of effective employee utilization in brand building is Geek Squad.

Case Study 7.5

Geek Squad

The communication strategy of Geek Squad, a subsidiary of Best Buy Company, showcases a team of passionate and knowledgeable individuals, often referred to as computer geeks, who possess a profound dedication to computer technology. They approach the task of resolving computer problems with utmost seriousness and demonstrate a genuine desire to assist customers. This consistent portrayal has significantly contributed to Geek Squad's positive reputation in the US market, primarily because their employees align their interactions with customers to reflect the brand's promised attributes.

Geek Squad ensures that customers can engage with their employees through various channels, including Best Buy stores, online platforms, customer centres and even within customers' homes. This extensive accessibility further reinforces the brand's commitment to delivering reliable and expert technology assistance.

Image 7.6 Geek Squad is a brand that communicates that the employees have both expertise in computers and a high service mindset

(Continued)

By consistently providing customers with the exceptional experience they expect from the brand, Geek Squad's employees play a pivotal role in establishing and maintaining the brand's reputation. Customers' interactions with these knowledgeable and dedicated team members reaffirm the brand's promises and solidify its position in the market.

Creating new and improved products is undoubtedly a significant strategy to generate higher expectations for a brand. Volvo's introduction of Polestar, for instance, forged fresh associations with the Volvo brand as a prominent electric car manufacturer. However, it's essential to recognize that the company's perception of a product's superiority may not necessarily align with how it is perceived by customers. Merely claiming a product is better does not make it so – its actual value lies in its ability to effectively address a specific problem. Customers often discern that a product is supposedly superior, but if it fails to demonstrate relevance and credibility, it fails to provide a valid reason for heightened expectations.

Image 7.7 The launch of the Volvo Polestar has created high expectations for the Volvo brand as a leading car manufacturer of electric cars

Individuals exhibit variances in their associations with the same brand. For instance, while some may associate McDonald's with positive attributes such as good food, others may associate it with negative connotations like unhealthy food. This diversity in brand associations is evident across most brands. The range of associations directly influences the expectations people hold for a particular brand.

An integral aspect of brand management involves understanding and mapping the spectrum of associations and their impact on expectations. It is crucial to gather factual information regarding these variations and gain insights into which marketing initiatives will influence different groups with distinct associations. By doing so, brand managers can tailor their strategies to cater to diverse audience segments and shape their expectations of the brand accordingly.

Brand Usage

The financial value of a brand largely depends on the extent to which customers engage with it, indicating their increased purchasing of various products offered by the brand. Essentially, the more customers use the brand and the more frequently they use it across different situations, the greater the cash flow generated. Let's consider the example of Costa, a coffee retailer brand in the UK, and how customers interact with their products and services. If more people choose to visit Costa instead of competing cafés or restaurants, the cash flow will increase. By persuading more individuals to choose Costa, the company's revenue and cash flow will grow. Since a significant portion of their costs remains consistent irrespective of the number of visiting customers, the additional income from new users positively impacts profitability. In addition, Costa offers a line of home products, and if they succeed in convincing customers to purchase their coffee capsules or instant coffee for home use, this will further contribute to an enhanced cash flow.

After a customer acquires and begins using a brand, a new stage of the customer journey starts at which the customer gains experience and acquires new knowledge about the brand. Figure 7.3 illustrates that this experience plays a role in shaping the associations the customer develops with the brand. Through experience, brand associations created through marketing communication can be either reinforced, extended or diminished and thus lead to updating of brand expectations. As long as the brand consistently meets or exceeds the customer's high expectations, a positive sentiment towards the brand develops, leading to what we commonly refer to as brand loyalty.

Enhancing the appeal of a brand, or increasing its attractiveness, is a crucial objective in branding. However, this process also leads to higher expectations from customers. As expectations rise, the brand must strive harder to meet or exceed those expectations. This implies that attractive brands require more efforts to generate excitement and carry a higher risk of encountering dissatisfied customers. Consequently, it becomes essential to acknowledge that customers may hold varying expectations, and the company should prioritize providing exceptional care to those with the highest expectations.

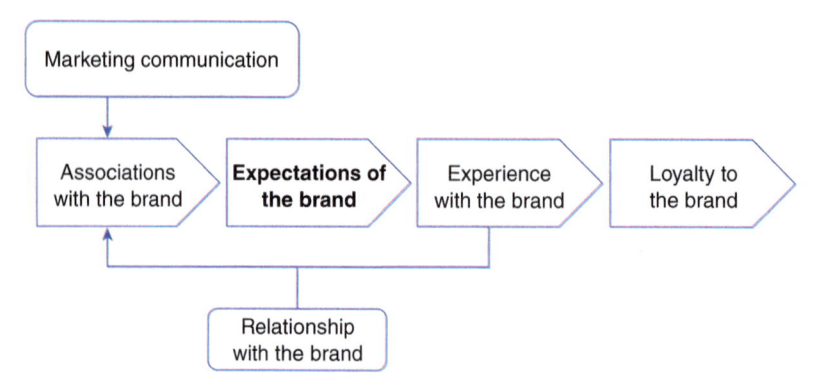

Figure 7.3 Branding is about developing associations (knowledge) linked to the brand so that these create higher expectations. Associations are created partly through brand communication and partly through experiences with using the brand and the relationship that develops between the person and the brand. Experiences play a central role in the learning process

In certain product categories, elevated expectations can influence the subjective perception of quality, resembling a placebo effect. This phenomenon is particularly relevant in categories where evaluating quality objectively is challenging or impossible. Take, for instance, the evaluation of wine, which poses difficulties for most individuals to assess using objective criteria. Consequently, many people rely on external cues such as the brand name, price and bottle design as indicators of the wine's inherent quality. In such cases, these external factors play a significant role in shaping the perception of quality.

Consequently, a well-established wine brand is likely to be perceived by many as having a superior taste. This demonstrates that in various scenarios, elevated expectations result in more positive evaluations and increased satisfaction. However, it is crucial for the brand to consistently meet and exceed these expectations over time in order to maintain a competitive edge. Despite the inherent difficulty for customers to objectively evaluate quality, the brand should continuously strive to deliver high-quality products and services.

The organization's ability to deliver quality across all customer touchpoints is a crucial factor in ensuring customer satisfaction. Primarily, the quality of the products provided must meet or exceed customer expectations. For instance, customers anticipate that GoAhead's train and bus services will be punctual. The company may have valid reasons such as signal failure, heavy traffic or adverse weather conditions for any delays, but customers are not interested in hearing excuses. Instead, they will attribute the failure to deliver on time to the GoAhead brand, resulting in reduced satisfaction and a more negative attitude towards the brand. This principle applies to all interactions between the customer and the brand, including communication from the company and how customers are handled when filing complaints. At each touchpoint, the brand must deliver at the very least what is expected, and ideally surpass those expectations whenever possible.

Put simply, branding encompasses the entire organization across all levels. It is crucial to acknowledge that as customer expectations rise, the brand becomes stronger. Therefore, a significant undertaking is to systematically elevate customers' expectations in alignment with their experiences of the brand. This implies that during customer interactions, the company can leverage the opportunity to introduce new and improved ways of utilizing the brand. For instance, establishing a customer club that sends newsletters and exclusive offers to members can be a valuable strategy. When customers join the customer club, it creates an expectation that adds to the existing ones they already have, further reinforcing the brand's influence.

Promotional campaigns serve as a highly effective tool to stimulate brand usage. In the fast-moving consumer goods (FMCG) industry, it is commonplace for leading brands to employ promotional campaigns as a means to boost sales. For instance, the UK snack brand Walkers utilizes sales promotions to maintain a strong market share and attract customers from competing brands[8] Typically, promotional campaigns in FMCG categories result in a significant surge in sales during the campaign period, followed by a subsequent decline, resulting in overall unchanged total units sold (Van Heerde et al., 2003; Dekimpe et al., 2005). Therefore, the immediate impact of promotional campaigns is not primarily increased short-term revenue, but rather a long-term effect achieved by fostering greater brand usage that disrupts competitors' attempts to fit into customers' consumption patterns.

Promotions are also actively employed by retail and restaurant chains to enhance the frequency of brand usage among customers. By encouraging customers to visit their establishments more frequently, these brands increase their visibility in people's consciousness, thereby boosting the likelihood of customers returning on subsequent occasions.

Many leading brands are now developing integrated solutions that combine products and services, aiming to provide customers with a more convenient and efficient brand experience. The advancement of digitalization has significantly expanded the possibilities for creating such solutions. The automotive industry serves as a notable example of this evolving trend. In the past, customers would purchase cars from dealerships, where the car manufacturer's brand (such as Volvo) and the dealership's brand (such as Endeavour) were distinct entities. The dealership would handle all practical aspects of car maintenance, while the manufacturer focused solely on producing the vehicles.

However, today we witness a shift towards manufacturer brands that encompass all aspects of car ownership. Brands like Toyota and Tesla exemplify this approach by offering both the products (the cars themselves) and a comprehensive range of services. When customers purchase a car from Tesla, for instance, it becomes a bundled package, streamlining the customer experience under a single brand. Once customers establish this package deal with Tesla, it becomes easier for them to extend the package to include multiple cars, provides options for renting vehicles during holidays, financing, insurance, tire changes, car washing, and more.

---

[8]https://www.smylies.com/latest-news/crisp-snack-market-review-2019/; https://www.campaignlive.co.uk/article/promotion-works-walkers/798496.

In fact, one can even envision scenarios where Tesla provides entertainment tailored to passengers during car journeys, facilitates pre-ordering of groceries from the supermarket on the way to a holiday home and offers various other conveniences. The aim is to create an integrated ecosystem where the brand seamlessly integrates with various aspects of the customers' lives, enhancing their overall experience.

Expanding the range of product categories under a brand, known as brand extension, is a significant growth strategy for many brands (Völckner & Sattler, 2006). The financial market provides a good example of this trend. In the past, customers would have separate accounts and loans at a bank, insurance policies at an insurance company and pension plans at a pension insurance provider. However, nowadays, it is possible to access all these product categories under a single brand. Instead of dealing with multiple branded entities, customers can receive a wide range of financial products and services from a single supplier. This consolidation offers customers a simpler and more streamlined solution, while the brand benefits from increased income derived from the customer portfolio across various product categories.

It is important to recognize that the value of a brand is realized when customers not only purchase its products but also actively use them. A crucial aspect of brand product development is to ensure that customers make regular and comprehensive use of the brand's offerings. The goal is for customers to incorporate the brand into their daily lives, rather than simply making occasional purchases. The more people who actively use the brand, the higher the cash flow generated by the brand. Therefore, encouraging widespread usage of the brand becomes a key driver of success.

Brand Loyalty

Brand loyalty refers to customers having a favourable disposition towards purchasing, recommending and exploring new products and services from a particular brand. It entails developing a strong relationship with the brand embedded in a network of products and services, fostering a sense of community, and having confidence that the brand values and cherishes this connection. Within this relationship, a set of norms and expectations emerge, and it is crucial for the brand to uphold them.

As customers adapt to the relationship through repeated purchases and product/service usage, their expectations for the brand's recognition of this commitment intensify (Morgan & Hunt, 1994; Brakus et al., 2009). This behaviour aligns with basic relational expectations (i.e. social norms). To illustrate, imagine regularly buying groceries from a local store where you frequently visit. Over time, you become acquainted with the employees, and you expect them to recognize you in return. It becomes natural to exchange greetings and smiles when encountering each other at the checkout counter. If, however, the person operating the cash register fails to reciprocate your smiles, you perceive it as a violation of the social norm within this particular relationship.

In certain cases, the strength of a relational norm can create a sense of discomfort when considering switching to a different brand. Harley-Davidson has successfully built a powerful brand that symbolizes membership in the Harley-Davidson community. Owners of Harley motorcycles feel a strong sense of camaraderie and connection with one another, with the brand serving as the unifying factor. Some Harley owners even display their deep affinity by getting tattoos of the brand's logo. Through effective brand building, Harley-Davidson has been able to sell their motorcycles at a significantly higher price compared to other brands in the same category. In addition to motorcycles, the company also boasts a substantial merchandise business, with around 20% of their total sales revenue derived from motorcycle-related products (http://investor.harley-davidson.com). Leveraging the community aspect, Harley-Davidson can cost-effectively disseminate information about new products and models. This allows them to achieve better sales revenue compared to many of their competitors, considering the advertising expenditure involved.

While Harley-Davidson stands as a prominent example, other brands have also cultivated similar communities, including Apple and certain car brands such as Alfa Romeo, Jaguar and Land Rover. This phenomenon is also prevalent among fan clubs, such as those associated with Manchester United, Real Madrid and PSG. Brand communities are not limited to technology brands and sports clubs. The athletic apparel brand Lululemon has an online community platform called 'The Sweat Life'. This platform allows customers to connect virtually, share workout routines and wellness tips, and inspire each other through photos and stories. It also includes features like a blog with articles on fitness, nutrition and mental well-being.

Lululemon has built a strong brand community by creating a sense of belonging and shared values among its customers. They have retail stores where they host community events, such as yoga or fitness classes, in-store workshops and wellness seminars. These events provide a platform for individuals to connect with each other, share their experiences and learn from experts in the field.

Through these initiatives, Lululemon has successfully created a brand community that not only centres around their products but also fosters a supportive environment for customers to connect, engage and celebrate their active lifestyles.

It is essential to recognize that brand loyalty is a psychological phenomenon rooted in the customer's perception. The community and relationship associated with a brand do not have tangible, formal rules for membership, official agendas or organized meetings. Rather, individuals simply perceive themselves as belonging to the brand. By owning certain brands, they experience a sense of exclusivity and affiliation with a specific group. It is worth noting that this sense of brand engagement can coexist with more formal communities. For instance, many football teams have organized supporter clubs with official memberships. The club members naturally demonstrate a strong brand commitment, specifically to the club. However, there may also be supporters who exhibit an equally strong brand commitment (commitment to the club) despite not being formal members of the supporter club. Therefore, formal membership in organized brand communities cannot be reliably used as a measure of brand engagement.

In essence, brand loyalty entails fostering a favourable disposition towards purchasing, recommending and exploring new products and services from a specific brand. This strong positive attitude acts as a protective barrier against competitors' efforts to lure away the brand's customers. Consider a customer who is a member of Starbucks' loyalty programme and has also downloaded a service enabling them to pre-order their coffee. This enhanced experience increases the brand's appeal and raises customer expectations, resulting in a further positive attitude and loyalty towards the brand. In the short term, this may not directly translate into increased profits through higher sales since the customer already purchases their morning and afternoon coffee at Starbucks. However, the real value emerges when a competitor opens a coffee shop nearby or when the customer relocates to a new area. In such scenarios, the brand loyalty pays off as the customer remains devoted to the brand despite external factors or temptations.

Case Study 7.6

Four Brands, Four Strengths

The Swedish music streaming service Spotify enjoys remarkable brand awareness in the market.[9] In the UK, aided brand recognition, which involves both the brand name and logo, stands at a remarkable 95%. Meanwhile, in Germany and the USA, it maintains a solid 91% – a notable lead over its competitors, including industry pioneer Napster, as well as later entrants like Amazon Music, Apple Music and Tidal.

In the realm of online dating, the American app Tinder is the most preferred option worldwide, measured in terms of a 16% market share. This is nearly double the market share of its closest competitor, Bumble, at 9%, with Badoo and Hinge each accounting for 5% of the global online dating market.[10]

The German online fashion retailer Zalando has a commendable usage rate of 30%. Notably, in Germany, where Zalando's brand awareness among online fashion shoppers reaches 92%, the usage rate among those aware of the brand is 33%. In the UK, among the 43% of online fashion shoppers who are aware of Zalando, 12% use the platform.[11]

---

[9] https://www.statista.com/forecasts/1328344/spotify-digital-music-brand-profile-in-the-united-states; https://www.statista.com/forecasts/1328625/spotify-digital-music-services-brand-profile-in-the-uk; https://www.statista.com/forecasts/1334571/spotify-digital-music-services-brand-profile-in-germany

[10] https://www.statista.com/statistics/1200234/most-popular-dating-apps-worldwide-by-number-of-downloads/

[11] https://www.statista.com/forecasts/1288480/zalando-second-hand-apparel-online-shops-brand-profile-in-germany

Spanish competitor Zara's usage rates in these two markets are fairly consistent. Among the 81% of German online fashion shoppers aware of Zara, 20% opt to use it. Similarly, in the UK, among the 86% of brand-aware online shoppers, 21% engage with Zara.

In the smartphone arena, American tech giant Apple has garnered exceptionally high loyalty scores among US customers. A staggering 90% of iPhone users express their intent to stick with the brand for their next smartphone purchase.[12] For South Korean powerhouse Samsung, the loyalty score remains robust at 86 in the same market, reflecting the steadfast loyalty of Apple and Samsung customers in comparison to competitors like LG and Motorola.[13] In contrast, just over 61% of Motorola and LG phone users express the same commitment to their respective brands.

BRAND STRATEGY

Brand strategy is a comprehensive plan that outlines the growth and value preservation of a business's brands. The collective strength of a brand grows as more people become familiar with the brand and ascend in its brand hierarchy (see Figure 7.2). The brand's strength is evident in its performance across different brand levels: awareness, expectations, usage and loyalty. A stronger brand has a greater impact on customer behaviour, leading to increased revenue and profitability (i.e. brand equity). As depicted in Figure 7.4, brand strategy encompasses positioning, brand architecture and brand communication. To establish a robust brand, a company must first define a clear positioning strategy, determining the desired customer associations with the brand. Additionally, a strategy for how the brand interacts with other brands within the company's brand portfolio, known as brand architecture (branded house, sub-brands, endorsed brands and house of brands), is crucial. Lastly, the brand strategy encompasses various elements of brand communication, including the name, logo, slogan, creative aspects of communication and how brand messages are conveyed through branded contact points.

---

[12]https://www.statista.com/forecasts/1335456/apple-wearables-brand-profile-in-the-united-states

[13]https://www.statista.com/forecasts/1335552/samsung-smart-home-brand-profile-in-the-united-states

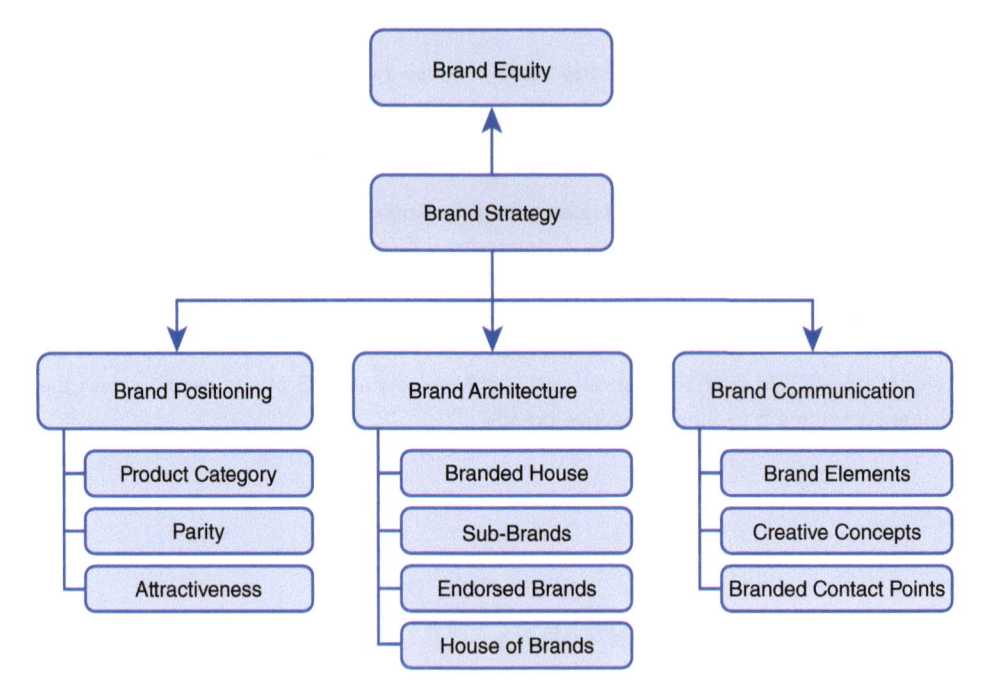

Figure 7.4 A framework for developing a brand strategy

We will now explore each of the three main areas (brand positioning, brand architecture and brand communication) in more detail.

Brand Positioning

The brand's positioning establishes the associations that should be connected with it.[14] This primarily revolves around the following three enquiries (Keller et al., 2002):

- Does the brand have a connection to the product category?
- Is the brand relevant?
- Is the brand attractive relative to its competitors?

First and foremost, the brand strategy needs to address the following aspect: What is the brand's competitive product category? Although this may seem like a simple question, answering it can be challenging due to various reasons. It is crucial to consider the customers'

---

[14]David Aaker uses the term brand identity to define how the company wants their brand to be perceived (Aaker, 1996).

perspective when defining the product category, taking into account how customers perceive the category in relation to their needs, and which products and brands they consider relevant and potential substitutes. The company must conduct a thorough analysis and gain a comprehensive understanding of the customers' actual purchasing behaviour.

As previously mentioned, it is essential for the brand to be closely associated with the product category so that it swiftly becomes part of the customer's consideration set. Defining the product category determines how the company chooses to compete in the market, and success often hinges on establishing this definition carefully. For example, a fish meal manufacturer defined its product category as 'ready-meal dinner products' instead of just 'fish products'. This decision was based on the understanding that customers' primary motivation is to purchase dinner ingredients, and their dinner category encompasses not only fish but also meat and chicken. The manufacturer's strategy aimed to ensure that their brand of fish products became part of consumers' consideration set when contemplating their dinner purchases.

Effective positioning begins with brand awareness. If the fish meal brand or the previously mentioned Campbell's soup do not come to mind when consumers make decisions about tonight's dinner, neither is likely to be chosen. An indication that the brand is well-positioned is if customers mention the brand when asked which dinner brands they know (i.e. unaided recall). If the brand does come to mind, there is a significant probability that it will be selected. Therefore, a well-positioned brand plays a vital role in driving increased sales.

The second query revolves around the brand's relevance to customers and its association with the qualities that make it a member of the product category. What does it take for a brand to be valued by customers as a viable option during purchasing decisions? The criteria that determine this are known as points of parity. Even if a brand is connected to a product category and is within customers' brand awareness, it is not guaranteed that it will be considered a relevant choice or be included in the customers' consideration sets.

The elements that constitute points of parity, transitioning the brand from the awareness set to the consideration set, vary across product categories, customer segments and over time. In some cases, new parity factors can become so significant that they actually exclude category members who fail to meet certain standards. A notable example is McDonald's in the fast-food industry and the film *Super Size Me*, which we will now explore in Case Study 7.7.

Case Study 7.7

Super Size Me

The 2004 documentary film *Super Size Me* featured filmmaker Morgan Spurlock consuming only McDonald's food and beverages for 30 days, resulting in an 11-kilo weight gain. This film altered public perception of fast food to such an extent that nutrition

(Continued)

became a parity element within the fast-food category. Healthy meals became a pre-requisite for fast food, and brands associated with unhealthy food were excluded from consideration. Although many had long considered McDonald's food as unhealthy, it did not strongly impact on the brand until the film sparked a media debate about the dangers of fats and sugars. With the emergence of healthy meals as a requirement, the points of parity in the fast-food category changed almost overnight. McDonald's lost its position because it did not meet the new demands. The perception that McDonald's food was high in fat and sugar disqualified the brand from many customers' considera-tion sets. Since then, McDonald's has worked diligently to make a comeback by revamping their menus, introducing healthier options and communicating these quali-ties effectively.

Image 7.8   Healthy meals bring McDonald's back into the fast-food category

The third enquiry pertains to what sets the brand apart from its competitors and makes it more appealing – known as the brand's points of difference. These points of difference ele-vate the brand from being merely considered by customers to becoming an attractive and preferred choice within their choice set.

Selecting an overall positioning strategy involves deciding which of the customer needs the company should specialize in satisfying. This decision is based on evaluating current and future customer requirements, as well as the positioning strategies employed by competitors. Additionally, the chosen positioning strategy must consider what the company is genuinely capable of excelling at, taking into account its resources, capabilities and objectives. IKEA exemplifies strategic positioning with its clear mission to meet people's needs for affordable furniture of high-quality and modern design.

Case Study 7.8

IKEA

The IKEA brand strategically focuses on fulfilling the desires of customers, particularly those who are young and furnishing their first home. These customers seek furniture that is affordable and lasts for a few years, rather than a lifetime or across generations.

To capture this market segment, IKEA positions itself as providing 'high quality' rather than emphasizing durability. Additionally, the brand recognizes that young customers also prioritize modern aesthetics, which is reflected in its overall positioning strategy. IKEA has consistently adhered to this strategic positioning since its establishment, with only minor adjustments. All key functions and activities within the company are dedicated to achieving this goal, which has become ingrained in its core values.

In terms of brand positioning, IKEA strategically differentiates itself through associations with low prices, high quality and modern design. This unique combination of attributes makes IKEA more appealing than its competitors. The brand effectively communicates these differentiating associations through its websites, advertising and other marketing communications.

Image 7.9 The now retired IKEA catalogue shows the differentiating elements: low price and modern design

In the case of IKEA, the distinguishing associations are primarily linked to product attributes, such as affordability, quality and design. However, many brands also emphasize supplier attributes as the basis for differentiation. These attributes reflect the quality of the relationship between the customer and the company. Examples include fast and accessible service, friendly assistance, expertise-based support, personalized interactions and cooperative engagement. Service attributes can complement differentiation based on product characteristics or serve as independent points of distinction. Several successful companies have creatively combined product and service attributes to their advantage. Southwest Airlines is an example of a successful business that combines low ticket prices with friendly and helpful customer service. Southwest Airlines prioritizes providing the highest-quality customer service, which embodies warmth, friendliness and pride in both the industry and the company. This approach has led to strong customer preferences for the Southwest brand.

Image 7.10 Southwest in the air

Symbolic associations can also contribute to brand differentiation (Park et al., 1986). Brands that are associated with attractive symbols tend to achieve stronger levels of differentiation. A compelling and appealing symbolic association allows the brand to occupy a more prominent position in the choice set and sometimes even become the sole brand in consideration. However, for a brand to attain symbolic status or become an icon, the company must possess a deep understanding of how customers think and feel (Bhat & Reddy, 1998; Aaker et al., 2001; Azoulay & Kapferer, 2003). When seeking to build symbolic associations, it is crucial to grasp the values that guide customers, which may be expressed more or less explicitly. Nevertheless, convincing customers that a brand genuinely deserves to be a symbol is no easy task. Companies that successfully maintain their symbolic brand value over time are often recognized as innovators and leaders in the market. For instance, Disney, an established company, has solidified its position as an icon of quality in the family entertainment category through continuous innovation and the introduction of new forms of entertainment.

Some companies invent new concepts or ideas that capture the public's attention and become icons themselves. A notable example is Absolut Vodka, which strategically worked to position its brand as a symbol of sophistication. This was accomplished through the development of a creative concept and modern design. The brand gained significant publicity and enhanced its credibility as a symbol of sophistication when the renowned pop artist Andy Warhol featured Absolut Vodka in one of his artworks.

Overall, leveraging symbolic associations requires a deep understanding of customer values, continuous innovation and strategic positioning to establish and maintain the brand's symbolic status.

Hence, brand positioning involves formulating a comprehensive strategy for how the brand should be portrayed in the customers' minds and how this portrayal can lead to acceptance and recognition within the product category by meeting the criteria for points of parity. The subsequent phase in the positioning strategy is to determine the factors driving the brand's appeal, specifically what sets the brand apart and makes it attractive.

Brand Architecture

Numerous companies possess multiple brand names, necessitating the establishment of a defined relationship between these brands. Brand architecture serves as an organizational structure for the brand portfolio, outlining the roles of each brand and guiding their interrelationships. Figure 7.5 illustrates the four primary types of brand architecture (Aaker & Joachimsthaler, 2000).

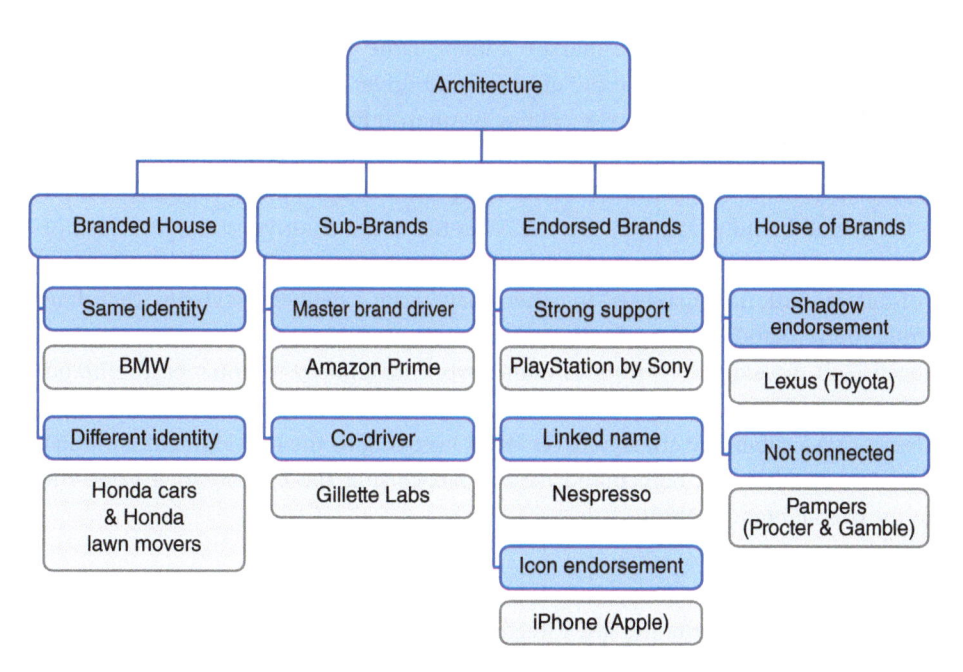

Figure 7.5 The brand relationship spectrum, illustrating different strategies for brand architecture (adapted from Aaker & Joachimsthaler, 2000)

House of Brands

The 'House of Brands' represents an extreme scenario in which the brands within a company's portfolio are independent entities, and the intention is for customers to remain unaware (or at least not actively consider) that these brands are provided by the same company. General Motors exemplifies this strategy with its diverse range of brands, including Buick, Cadillac, Chevrolet and GMC. The rationale behind this approach is that it allows the company to position each brand more precisely within various segments and price categories. When a company desires to offer both low-cost and exclusive products, a 'House of Brands' strategy proves suitable. Some companies may employ a shadow support approach as part of this strategy to bolster the focal brand. For instance, Lexus is presented as a brand within the Toyota family (with Toyota acting as the shadow supporter). However, the connection between the two is deliberately kept weak, and the Lexus brand is often communicated without explicit linkage to Toyota.

Branded House

On the opposite side of the spectrum lies the 'Branded House' architecture. In this type of brand architecture, the company primarily associates simple descriptive elements with its main brand to distinguish between different products or models. A prime illustration of this approach is BMW, which employs descriptive elements such as I, X, M, 7, 5, 3 or Z4 for its various models within the product line. The main BMW brand encompasses all brand associations and values.

Sub-Brands

The sub-brand represents a third category of brand architecture, wherein the company introduces two brand names to the market: a main name and a sub-name. This strategy manifests in two primary variations: the master brand-driver and the co-driver approaches. An example of the master brand-driver strategy is Amazon Prime. It comprises the Amazon brand as the main driver of the combined brand. The Amazon brand serves to differentiate Amazon Prime from its competitors, emphasizing the strength of the Amazon name in driving the overall brand perception. On the other hand, the co-driver strategy is exemplified by Gillette Labs. Both Gillette and Labs are brands that possess distinct meanings and points of differentiation. When used together, they create a deliberate synergy that draws value from both brand names. A similar instance of this strategy is observed with Volkswagen Golf, where the two brand names work in tandem to enhance the brand's positioning and recognition.

Implementing a sub-brand strategy necessitates investing in the development and establishment of associations for both brand names, recognizing the collaborative value they bring to the overall brand identity.

Endorsed Brands

The endorsed brand represents the last category of brand architecture, wherein a primary brand receives support or endorsement from another well-established brand. The distinctive brand qualities reside within the main brand, while the supporting brand's role is primarily to enhance trust in the main brand. An endorser strategy is commonly employed during the introduction of new brands, where the supporting brand's role is most significant in the initial stages. A notable example is the endorsement of the iPhone by Apple during the first few months after its introduction as a new brand. As the iPhone gained a firm foothold in the market, Apple's role as an endorser became relatively minor, as the iPhone brand had become well-established in its own right.

When formulating brand architecture, one crucial aspect to consider is effectively differentiating the company's offerings from competitors across various markets.[15] However, developing multiple brands can be financially demanding, prompting the need to design an architecture that balances differentiation with synergy effects. In recent times, numerous companies have significantly reduced the number of brands in their portfolios due to the high costs associated with maintaining them. Managing multiple brands requires extensive efforts and resources, such as internal coordination and governance. We are witnessing an ongoing shift where brands are expanding their appeal across multiple product categories and targeting diverse customer segments (Kumar, 2003). Apple serves as a prime example of this trend. Initially, Apple was primarily associated with the personal computer category and catered to a customer segment focused on creativity and design. Throughout the years, Apple has successfully broadened its product offerings to encompass a wide range of electronic devices, expanding beyond the initial focus on personal computers. Moreover, the customer segments targeted by Apple have significantly expanded to encompass a diverse array of consumer types. This impressive expansion has contributed to Apple's position as one of the most powerful and influential brands globally.

Brand Communication

Brand communication aims to influence customers' perceptions and emotions towards a brand, fostering strong brand awareness, expectations, usage and loyalty. To ensure effectiveness, companies must establish clear communication goals and possess a profound understanding of their target customers. Crafting impactful brand communication necessitates creative concepts and their skilful execution. While mass media advertising typically yields the best results, various direct channels are also employed to communicate and disseminate the brand's unique qualities.

Brand Elements

Brand communication comprises essential components such as the brand name, brand logo and slogan. Companies invest considerable effort in selecting the brand name since it is challenging to alter later (Bao et al., 2008). Ideally, the brand name should be straightforward, easily pronounceable, memorable, distinctive and should evoke solely positive associations. A brand name should convey associations that align with the company's desired image and identity. On 1 January 2001, Andersen Consulting rebranded as Accenture, recognizing that the former name no longer resonated with their identity. The name Accenture, a combination of 'accent' and 'future', aptly signifies the company's focus on accentuating the future for their customers. The new name has proven to be immensely successful as a brand identity.

---

[15]In the branding literature the hybrid architecture is frequently referred to reflecting that companies end up with many architectural designs.

Logos possess significant potential to create appealing brand associations and enhance the effectiveness of communication. The renowned Apple logo serves as an illustration of this evolution over the years. Initially, the logo depicted Isaac Newton sitting under a tree, accompanied by the text 'Newton ... A mind forever voyaging through strange seas of thought ... Alone'. Subsequently, the rainbow apple replaced this logo. The bite taken out of the apple cleverly played on the words 'bite' and 'byte'. The fundamental structure of the rainbow apple then became the foundation for Apple's present-day logos. Nike's Swoosh logo and McDonald's golden arches also stand as highly successful logos globally. These instances suggest that a good logo is characterized by its ease of remembrance, while repetition generates interest rather than monotony (Janiszewski, 2001).

Apple's First Logo (1976)   1976-1998   Current logo

Image 7.11 Progress of the Apple logo

Slogans serve as a means to highlight the primary advantages of a branded product. Similar to other elements of a brand, a slogan should be easily memorable. It should also stimulate contemplation and evoke related associations. For several decades, the insurance company Allstate has utilized the slogan 'You're in Good Hands', emphasizing the functional benefits of their insurance products. The slogan 'Diamonds are Forever', employed by the world's leading diamond company DeBeers, conveys the practical value of diamonds, implying their worth as both an investment (with enduring value) and an expression of love. Other widely recognized slogans that are evocative and symbolic include BMW's 'The Ultimate Driving Machine' and Nike's 'Just Do It'.

Creative Branding Concept

The reception of a brand and the expenses involved in its establishment are influenced by the quality of the creative brand concept. When aiming for high-quality creative concepts, it is common to seek assistance from professional advertising agencies. The Swedish brand Absolut Vodka, in its efforts to establish its brand name in the US market, collaborated closely with an agency to develop a creative concept rooted in modern art. Creative communication concepts can revolve around ideas, situations, themes or concepts that effectively illustrate and convey the essence of a brand. In 1973, Duracell introduced the concept of the Duracell bunny in an advertising campaign, highlighting the superior longevity of their alkaline batteries compared to regular batteries. The advertisement showcased a small, fluffy pink bunny powered by Duracell batteries, capable of leaping for an extended period beyond its competitors. Over the years, Duracell has maintained a consistent advertising strategy, continuously evolving the bunny character in tandem with advancements in quality and technology.

Image 7.12 The Duracell bunny is an example of a successful communication concept used to create brand associations

Case Study 7.9

Scottish Widows

Scottish Widows, an insurance company, devised another impactful creative concept for brand communication. This concept centred around a young woman donning an elegant, vintage black suit, symbolizing the Scottish widow. By embracing this concept, Scottish

(Continued)

Widows aimed to rejuvenate their brand values of quality and care. Typically, life insurance companies are perceived as impersonal entities, but the introduction of the widow concept allowed customers to establish a personal connection with a brand they trusted. The widow concept was launched in a campaign in 1986 and achieved immediate success. Surveys indicated a remarkable increase in unaided recall of the company's name, soaring from 30 to over 80% in the weeks following the campaign. Subsequent advertisements leveraging this concept propelled Scottish Widows to become the most popular icon in the insurance, pensions and investments markets. The brand's resilience has shielded Scottish Widows during economic downturns, and it consistently ranks among the strongest brands in the financial services industry.

Image 7.13   Scottish Widows uses this creative concept – based on a young widow

Branded Contact Points

Exposure to the brand name or logo alone, without any accompanying message, plays a vital role in brand visibility and serves as a significant branding tool. These instances where the brand name is presented are known as branded contact points. Owned channels encompass various branded contact points, including employee uniforms, building and premises signage, transportation, email communications and company websites. Additionally, companies can invest in brand exposure through sponsorships of sports and cultural events. The underlying theory (ELM) suggests that such exposure, with minimal cognitive processing, fosters a positive attitude towards the brand by associating it with positive emotions (Petty & Cacioppo, 1981). For example, seeing Formula 1 driver Lewis Hamilton on the podium with the Puma logo on his race boots may enhance one's perception of the Puma brand due to the transfer of positive feelings associated with

Hamilton. The concept of mere exposure influencing brand attitudes has been extensively documented, although the magnitude of the effect may vary based on several factors. The effect is stronger when the recipient is in a positive mood during exposure because it is the positive emotions that are transferred and linked to the brand. Furthermore, the effect increases with repeated exposures over time, as the positive association's duration is relatively short-lived. While cognitively processed advertising messages tend to be remembered for an extended period, positive associations formed through exposure (often occurring unconsciously) fade more quickly from consciousness.

Sports and cultural events have emerged as highly sought-after platforms for brand building. Volvo, for instance, was a trailblazer in sponsoring golf tournaments, even being the first sponsor of the PGA tournament. This sponsorship had a significant impact on the strength of the Volvo brand, particularly in the United States. Volvo benefitted from its association with a sport that embodies values such as quality, integrity and longevity. Many companies now vie for sponsorship opportunities at major sporting events, including the FIFA World Cup, PGA tournaments and the Olympic Games. However, there is a potential risk of negative associations being transferred to a brand through events or individual athletes. A notable example is golfer Tiger Woods, who faced extensive negative media coverage due to his extramarital affairs. Sponsors such as Accenture, AT&T and Gillette withdrew their support to mitigate the damage caused by the negative press and preserve their own brand reputation.

BRAND MANAGEMENT

To effectively manage a brand, a company requires comprehensive information about how consumers perceive and engage with the brand. This includes aspects such as brand awareness, brand expectations, brand usage and brand loyalty, which are all part of the brand hierarchy. However, there is ongoing debate and no consensus in both academic literature and industry practices regarding the measurement of these brand dimensions (e.g. Farris et al., 2009). The following examples illustrate some ways brands can be measured, but it's important to note that these methods are not necessarily the only or best approaches. The appropriate measurement techniques will vary depending on factors such as company characteristics, market dynamics, customer preferences and competitive landscape. What is important is that the brand management uses a set of indicators, that these indicators or measures are repeated over time, and that the measures provide valid and reliable indications of what customers think and feel about the brand.

Descriptive statistics regarding brand performance serve the purpose of monitoring performance, identifying trends and identifying any unexpected market developments. This information enables companies to take corrective actions if necessary. Descriptive statistics related to brand development are also utilized to evaluate marketing activities aimed at enhancing brand performance. By analysing these statistics, companies can gain a deeper understanding of the underlying mechanisms involved in building stronger brands. This, in turn, enables them to quantify the financial impact of brand-building investments and make more effective decisions regarding resource allocation, directing investments towards activities that yield the greatest impact on the brand.

Managing Brand Awareness

The initial aspect we aim to assess is the level of brand awareness, which provides us with a percentage metric indicating the number of individuals in the market who are familiar with the brand. To obtain this information, we must survey a representative sample of individuals within the market. Marketing research companies offer this service and employ statistical sampling techniques to ensure accuracy within the defined population. The survey typically includes two measures of brand awareness: unaided and aided. The unaided measure involves an open-ended question where respondents are asked to list the brands they associate with a specific product category, and their answers are recorded. The aided recall measure asks respondents if they have heard of specific brands from a provided list. For the brands they are aware of, a follow-up question gauges their familiarity with the brand on a scale ranging from very low to very high.

Using these statistics, companies can track the progress of brand awareness, such as the changes in the percentage of unaided brand recall over time and across different market segments. It is important to note that brand awareness is measured in relation to competitors, since companies are in competition for customers and need to understand their competitors' strategies and success in capturing the market.

To enhance brand awareness, companies invest in marketing communication activities. They must identify the most effective types of marketing communication and determine the optimal level of investment required to build brand awareness. Consequently, companies need a comprehensive understanding of how increases in brand awareness translate into future revenue and cash flow.

Managing Brand Expectations

The management of brand expectations involves cultivating a strong brand attitude that leads to brand preference. The underlying concept is that customers will favour and choose brands that they anticipate will provide the greatest value in relation to the effort required, whether in terms of price or the effort involved in obtaining the brand. These measures are typically obtained through surveys using representative sampling and direct questions about attitudes or preferences. To gauge brand attitude, companies often enquire about the level of liking for the brand, using a seven-point scale ranging from negative to positive, non-desirable to desirable, or bad to good (Park et al., 2010). Brand preference can also be assessed by simply asking respondents about their likelihood of choosing the focal brand in a typical decision-making situation. For example, they may be asked 'What is the likelihood you will choose [target brand] the next time you go shopping for groceries?', with response options ranging from 'definitely not' to 'certainly'.

Companies adopt various strategies for positioning their brand, highlighting different strengths where expectations will be high. For instance, one grocery chain may position their brand based on price, another on convenience and a third on product assortment. To determine the success of their positioning efforts, companies aim to measure their brand's relative position on a set of dimensions. In the context of grocery brands, they want to assess whether their brand is perceived as superior or more attractive in the targeted position. A typical survey question in this regard would be: 'How do you perceive [brand name] relative to alternative brands regarding "product assortment"?', with response options ranging from 'much worse' (–2) to 'much better' (+2). In terms of marketing communication, they need to identify the most effective types of communication and determine the optimal level of investment required to build brand preference and raise expectations in the chosen position. Regarding product development, they must understand which product and service elements contribute to a superior position on the selected dimension. For a grocery store, certain items may hold more importance than others in establishing a superior position, such as a diverse range of fresh food items like meat, fish, vegetables and fruit. Consequently, companies require a comprehensive understanding of how increases in brand expectations translate into future revenue and cash flow.

Managing Brand Usage

Effectively managing brand usage is closely intertwined with managing the customer portfolio, as explained in Chapter 5. The more frequently customers utilize a brand and the greater number of product categories they engage with the brand, the higher the revenues and cash flow generated from that brand.[16] In addition to survey-based measurements of brand usage, companies augment their data with information from accounting and loyalty programmes, where customers register their purchases to earn rewards.

The frequency of brand usage can increase in two ways: either customers allocate a larger share of their usage to the brand compared to competitors (known as share-of-wallet), or customers increase their overall usage within the product category, progressing from being light users to heavy users. A survey question that captures relative usage involves asking respondents to indicate the percentage of their purchases attributed to the focal brand versus other brands. To assess category usage, a survey question may enquire about how often respondents make purchases within a specific category. For example, they might be asked 'How often do you visit a coffee shop?', with response options ranging from 'every day' to '2–3 times per month'.

When metrics are collected from transaction data or loyalty programme data, precise measures of usage frequency can be derived directly. For instance, for each customer, the

---

[16]The transformation of brand value into financial results is discussed in Srivastava et al. (1998).

average number of brand usages per week over the past month can be calculated. These numbers can be aggregated across all customers to obtain the exact average and variance in brand usage among the entire customer base.

To enhance brand usage, companies invest in both marketing communication and product development activities. While marketing communication aimed at building brand awareness and brand expectations primarily relies on advertising in purchased channels, marketing communication aimed at increasing brand usage heavily relies on owned channels. Examples of customer programmes that promote brand usage can be found in Chapter 5, 'Customer Portfolio Management'.

Managing Brand Loyalty

Brand loyalty, as conceptualized in the marketing literature, refers to a positive and enduring inclination towards purchasing, recommending and exploring new products and services from a specific brand (Dick & Basu, 1994; Oliver, 1999). It signifies that customers consistently choose to buy the brand despite situational influences and marketing efforts that could potentially lead to switching behaviour. Additionally, brand loyalty involves the development of a strong relationship and emotional connection with the brand.

Measuring brand loyalty encompasses both psychological (related to thoughts and feelings) and behavioural aspects. Psychological measures are obtained through surveys that enquire about the likelihood of customers continuing their relationship with the brand, recommending it to others and considering it as their preferred choice (Chaudhuri and Holbrook, 2001; Brakus et al., 2009).

Various scales have been proposed to assess the strength of the relationship customers have with brands (Khamitov et al., 2019). One such scale is the Brand Attachment scale (Thomson et al., 2005), which includes questions about whether individuals perceive the brand to be affectionate, friendly, loved and peaceful. Another commonly used measure is the Self-Brand Connection scale (Escalas & Bettman, 2003), which includes statements such as '[target brand] reflects who I am', 'I can identify with [target brand]' and 'I feel a personal connection to [target brand]'. A third popular scale is Brand Identification (Bhattacharya et al., 1995), which includes statements like 'When someone criticizes [target brand], it feels like a personal insult', 'When I talk about [target brand], I usually say we rather than they' and '[target brand]'s successes are my successes'.

To enhance brand loyalty, companies invest in various marketing activities, including marketing communication, product development, customer programmes, and more. Managing customer brand loyalty requires close coordination with the management of both the company's customer segment portfolio and the product category portfolio. This approach represents the essence of customer-centric marketing management, as discussed throughout this book.

A summary of often-used brand measures is depicted in Table 7.1. Notice that there may be other measures that are more adequate given product categories and markets, and that the measures in the table are simply meant to be examples.

Table 7.1 Brand strength – examples of measures and metrics

Brand Level	Measure	Metric
Awareness	Which brands come to mind when you think about … [**product category**]?	Percentage of customers who mention brand *Alpha*.
Expectations	Do you consider the brand Alpha as worse (−3, −2, −1), about the same as (0), or better than (+1, +2, +3) other brands in … [this product category] on the following dimensions? • [Dimension 1] …… • [Dimension 2] …… • [Dimension 3] …… • [Dimension 4] …… • Dimension n] …… Scale −3 −2 −1 0 +1 +2 +2	Percentage who consider Alpha to be better than other brands in the category among those who are aware (unaided recall) of brand Alpha. (**Better** is calculated as those assigning the brand +1 or higher on an average of the dimensions 1 through n.)
Usage	How often do you buy products in …… [this category]? Which percentage of your purchases are brand *Alpha?* (If the brand is present in multiple categories, questions are repeated for each category.)	Mean **percentage** among those who consider Alpha to be better than other brands. (Can be compared to percentage among all users. We want to capture conversion from higher expectation to usage.)
Loyalty	How likely is it that you would: • Continue to use the Alpha brand? • Have the Alpha brand as your first choice? • Recommend the Alpha brand to others? • Try out new products and services from the Alpha brand? Scale: 1 (very unlikely) to 10 (very likely) • [**Target brand**] reflects who I am* • I can identify with [**Target brand**]* • I feel a personal connection to [**Target brand**]* • I would use [**Target brand**] to communicate who I am to other people* • I think [**Target brand**] could help me become the type of person I want to be* • I consider [**Target brand**] to be me** • [**Target brand**] suits me well* Scale*: 0 (Not at all) to 100 (Extremely well) Scale**: 0 (Not me) to 10 (Me)	Percentage of use that has a **loyalty score of [target metric]** or higher. (The loyalty score is calculated as the average of the answers to the four questions about loyalty. What we want to measure is the conversion from use to loyalty.) (The Self Brand Connection score is calculated as the average of the answers to the seven questions about connection to the brand.) What we want to measure is the extent to which our brand is part of the consumers' self-identities.

Case Study 7.10

Brand Management at Tony's Chocolonely[17]

Tony's Chocolonely, a Dutch chocolate manufacturing company founded in 2005, has a profound mission to eradicate child labour in the cocoa production industry. The company's brand management revolves around a strong commitment to promoting ethical and sustainable chocolate production and consumption.

In terms of brand awareness, Tony's Chocolonely has crafted distinctive and vibrant packaging that stands out on store shelves and in marketing communication materials. The company actively engages with farmers in Africa, collaborates with stakeholders such as NGOs and governments and publishes an annual 'Fair' report to transparently document their progress, challenges and endeavours in fulfilling their mission. They maintain an active presence on social media platforms, engage with consumers, partner with schools and educational institutions to develop informative material, and organize advocacy workshops to raise awareness about the issues within the chocolate industry. Their global expansion efforts further contribute to creating earned media coverage in both social and traditional media outlets.

The brand's awareness in the UK stands at 47%, while in Germany and the USA it reaches 26% and 24%, respectively.

When it comes to brand expectations and preferences, Tony's Chocolonely employs both product and relationship properties. One distinctive feature is the unevenly sized chocolate bar pieces, symbolizing the inequality in the chocolate industry. This creative concept effectively conveys their message. Another significant brand element is the slogan 'Crazy about chocolate, serious about people', which further reinforces their mission.

Remarkably, Tony's Chocolonely is the leading purchase brand in its home country, the Netherlands. In 2015, 8.8% of the chocolate bars sold in Dutch supermarkets were Tony's Chocolonely bars, and by 2020, this figure had risen to just under 17%.

The company is known for its high-quality chocolate, which comes with a relatively premium price tag, reflecting both its quality and the fact that Tony's Chocolonely pays cocoa farmers a higher price, enabling them to earn a living income. The company maintains consistent messaging around its mission and values to ensure that customers can trust the brand's commitment to its principles over time. Collaborations with NGOs and

---

[17]https://www.creativereview.co.uk/tonys-chocolonely-branding-chocolate; https://www.forbes.com/sites/afdhelaziz/2020/10/30/how-the-netherlandsno-1-chocolate-brand-tonys-chocolonely-is-winning-fans-in-the-usand-helpingpeople-vote; https://www.schoolofmarketing.co/the-marketing-education-guy/tonys-chocolonely-10x-growth; https://www.statista.com/forecasts/1352675/tonys-chocolonely-chocolate-brand-profile-in-the-uk; https://www.statista.com/forecasts/1352744/tony-s-chocolonely-chocolate-brand-profile-in-germany; https://www.statista.com/forecasts/1352571/tony-s-chocolonely-chocolate-brand-profilein-the-united-states; https://www.statista.com/statistics/942628/revenue-marketshare-of-tony-s-chocolonely-in-the-netherlands

co-branding with ethical standards-associated brands like Ben and Jerry's ice cream further connect Tony's Chocolonely with symbolic properties. Hence, when consumers purchase a chocolate bar from Tony's Chocolonely, they have the opportunity to align themselves with a desirable image.

The usage experience is strengthened by the wrapping paper of their chocolate bars, within which customers can read about the brand's mission, the chocolate-making process and the challenges in the cocoa industry.

Visitors to their superstore in Amsterdam will, in addition to gaining insight into the same topics, have the chance to immerse themselves in a multisensory experience. Of the 47% who are aware of the brand in the UK, 19% consume it, making a total of 9% usage rate. Corresponding usage figures for Germany and the USA stand at 5% and 4%, respectively.

To cultivate brand loyalty, the company organizes online and offline events to engage with their community. These events often feature elements tied into their mission, providing consumers with opportunities to deepen their understanding of the cause. Additionally, the continuous addition of new partners gives consumers more reasons to support the brand and, in turn, remain loyal. Notably, 78% of 9% who use their products express loyalty to the brand. Corresponding loyalty figures for Germany and the USA are 60% and 75%, respectively.

BRANDING IN BUSINESS MARKETS

Brand building in business markets is not as common as in consumer markets, as evidenced by the dominance of consumer brands on Interbrand's list of most valuable brands globally (https://interbrand.com/best-global-brands/). While there have been a few notable B2B brands featured on the list, such as IBM, Cisco, SAP, Microsoft, Intel, Oracle, Accenture and J.P. Morgan, the overall emphasis on branding is lower in business markets.

One reason why branding has been less emphasized is the rational decision-making characteristic of business markets, where emotional aspects typically associated with consumer market brands have limited relevance (Leek & Christodoulides, 2011). B2B purchases involve complex decision-making processes, with businesses considering factors like cost-effectiveness, return on investment, compatibility with existing systems and long-term benefits. The information necessary to evaluate these factors may not be encapsulated in a brand name. Moreover, businesses in these markets are well-equipped to handle complex purchases and may not rely on the simplification mechanism provided by well-known brands. However, research has shown that brands can still offer benefits in business markets, both for seller and for buyers.

Benefits

Benefits for sellers are similar to those in consumer markets. These benefits include the following:

- increases willingness among business customers to pay a premium;
- strengthens business customers' loyalty;

- increases efficiency of marketing activities;
- provides a robust foundation for introducing new products under the same brand name;
- enhances bargaining power in the distribution network.

(Leek & Christodoulides, 2011)

Regarding buyers in business markets, research has found brands to convey several intangible benefits (Leek & Christodoulides, 2011), including:

- it reduces business customers' level of perceived risk;
- it establishes a sense of confidence when making a purchase;
- it delivers a higher degree of satisfaction with a purchase.

Brand Equity

A brand's equity in a business market is derived from the totality brand associations perceived by customers (Michell et al., 2001). In the business market, brand equity consists of two sub-dimensions: brand associations and awareness. High equity provides competitive advantages, such as the ability for the brand to command a price premium.

Buyers in business markets prioritize overall brand identity, while consumer markets focus on products (Hague & Jackson, 1994; Leek & Christodoulides, 2011). Furthermore, research has emphasized that B2B brands function not only as entities but also as processes (Stern, 2006; Ballantyne & Aitken, 2007). Therefore, branding in business markets is most effective at the corporate level (Bendixen et al., 2004), where a brand summarizes information regarding the company's assets, people and organization's capacity to create value. At the corporate level, there are three main sources of brand association: innovativeness, customer orientation and social responsibility (Keller, 1998).

Innovativeness refers to the company's capabilities relevant to product production, such as technological innovation and manufacturing expertise (Brown & Dacin, 1997). For example, demonstrating expertise and thought leadership in a specific industry or domain can significantly impact brand equity in a business market. Essentially, this dimension reflects the qualities of the company and how they create benefits for the consumer. An innovative corporate image, for example, is based on consumers' perceptions of a company developing new and unique marketing programmes and emphasizing new product introductions or improvements. Brands that are seen as experts and leaders in their field gain trust, credibility and a competitive edge.

Customer orientation involves the company's people and relationships, and it refers to the company's ability to provide the consumer with the right solutions, including incorporating the voice of the consumer into product development. A customer-oriented company is seen as one that listens to consumers, has their best interests in mind and avoids exploiting them. Moreover, brands that go beyond transactions and focus on fostering partnerships, collaboration and personalized service are more likely to generate brand equity (Keller, 1998).

The third dimension involves values and programmes and reflects the company's philosophy and actions regarding organizational, social, political or economic issues. A socially responsible company is seen as contributing to community programmes, supporting artistic and social activities, and generally striving to improve the welfare of society. Similarly, an environmentally oriented company is believed to conduct its business in a manner that protects or improves the environment and makes efficient use of scarce natural resources (Keller, 1998).

It is important to note that brands in the consumer market can also leverage associations from the corporate level, in addition to product-level associations.

Brand awareness plays a significant role in driving brand equity in business markets (Davis et al., 2008). One obvious reason is that in order for the corporate-level association sources to be effectively utilized, business customers must have an awareness of the company. In the business market, brand awareness is defined as the ability of the decision-makers in organizational buying centres to recognize or recall a brand (Homburg et al., 2010, 202).

Brand awareness also conveys information about product quality and supplier commitment. High levels of brand awareness signal high-quality products and a firm's investment in building awareness. Only high-quality firms can afford significant investments in brand awareness. Brand awareness also signifies the presence, distribution and popularity of a brand, reducing the buyer's incentive to gather information on low-awareness brands.

Additionally, brand awareness reduces personal and organizational risk for decision-makers and buying firms. Decision-makers prefer brands with high-awareness levels to minimize personal risk in decision-making and avoid blame for potential mistakes. Organizations perceive high-awareness brands as likely to be purchased by other firms, reducing organizational risk (Homburg et al., 2010).

SUMMARY

A brand is a unique name, term, design, symbol or element that sets apart the products or services of one seller from others. It serves two main purposes: identifying the seller and communicating its distinct qualities. A brand resides in the customer's memory and its value is determined by the level of awareness, preference, loyalty and usage it enjoys. The goal is to convert these factors into financial value by generating a consistent stream of revenue from brand-loyal customers.

Brands offer several benefits to customers. They simplify the understanding of information, establish trust and security in purchasing decisions, and provide a sense of satisfaction during usage.

For companies, brands are highly valuable assets with substantial financial worth. They enhance the effectiveness and impact of marketing efforts, increase customer willingness to pay a premium, strengthen loyalty, improve marketing efficiency, facilitate new product introductions, enhance bargaining power, motivate employees and cultivate a strong organizational culture.

Brand knowledge can be visualized as a network of connections centred around the brand name. This network represents the information and associations customers have regarding the brand.

Brand building follows a hierarchical structure, with higher levels indicating a stronger brand. The hierarchy consists of four levels: brand awareness, brand expectations, brand usage and brand loyalty. Customers progress through these levels, starting from awareness and ascending to loyalty. Brand awareness refers to the brand being stored in memory and associated with specific product categories. Brand expectations are built through cultivating positive associations. Brand preference is based on the belief that the brand delivers superior value. The financial value of a brand depends on customer engagement and usage, resulting in cash flow. Brand loyalty involves favourable dispositions towards purchasing, recommending and exploring new products and services from the brand.

Brand strategy is a comprehensive plan for growing and preserving a business's brands. It includes positioning, brand architecture and brand communication. A clear positioning strategy defines desired customer associations. Brand architecture determines how the brand interacts with others in the brand portfolio. Brand communication covers elements such as the name, logo, slogan, creative aspects and messaging through various contact points.

Effective brand management requires factual knowledge and understanding consumer perceptions and engagement. This includes aspects of brand awareness, expectations, usage and loyalty, all part of the brand hierarchy. Managing brand loyalty involves coordinating with customer segment and product category portfolios. This customer-centric approach is central to successful marketing management.

Branding in business markets is less common than in consumer markets, although many of the benefits of branding identified in consumer markets also can be found in business markets. Typically, a business market company will build brand equity from corporate-level associations.

END-OF-CHAPTER QUESTIONS

1   Interview two individuals – one an owner of an iPhone and one an owner of a Samsung. Ask them what they know about both brands and how they feel about them. Use Figure 7.1 (association network; p. 232) to organize your findings. Do they feel happy, excited or joyful when thinking about iPhone or Samsung? Ask them how they became familiar with the brands (e.g. through advertisements, newspapers, internet, friends, personal experiences, or contact with the manufacturer). Use Figure 7.2 (brand hierarchy; p. 241) to analyse the brand strength of these two brands.

2   Read Keller et al. (2002), 'Three Questions You Need to Ask About Your Brand'. Choose a brand from the grocery store (Uncle Ben's, Pampers or Bonaqua). Imagine yourself as the brand manager and try to answer the three questions in the article.

3   Compare the brand architecture of two companies competing in the same market (such as Toyota and GM, Procter & Gamble and Unilever, or Hewlett-Packard and Dell)

(see Figure 7.5, brand architecture; p. 262). What are the differences? What are the advantages of the different strategies?

4   Identify three creative concepts for brand communication that correspond to the Duracell bunny and the Scottish Widows 'widow'. Investigate the history behind the communication concepts. When were they first launched? What are the key changes in advertising themes? What are the likely effects on sales and revenue?

5   Ask two individuals to guess the prices of a well-known brand and a store brand within a range of product categories (such as beer, frozen fish, pasta sauce and toilet paper). Use an open-ended question, tell them that the products have the same quality (made by the same manufacturer) and ask them to guess the price. The price they guess is their price expectation. Ask them which brand they prefer or would choose, and why. Finally, conduct a blind test and ask the two individuals to identify the brand they prefer. What have you learned about the effect of brands?

FURTHER READING

Brakus, J.J., Schmitt, B.H. & Zarantonello, L. (2009). Brand experience: What is it? How is it measured? Does it affect loyalty? *Journal of Marketing*, 73(3), 52–68.

Chaudhuri, A. & Holbrook, M.B. (2001). The chain of effects from brand trust and brand affect to brand performance: The role of brand loyalty. *Journal of Marketing*, 65(2), 81–93.

Dick, A.S. & Basu, K. (1994). Customer loyalty: Toward an integrated conceptual framework. *Journal of the Academy of Marketing Science*, 22(2), 99–113.

Oliver, R.L. (1999). Whence consumer loyalty? *Journal of Marketing*, 63, 33–44.

Park, C.W., MacInnis, D.J., Priester, J., Eisingerich, A.B. & Iacabucci, D. (2010). Brand attachment and brand attitude strength: Conceptual and empirical differentiation of two critical brand equity drivers. *Journal of Marketing*, 74(6), 1–17.

8

DEVELOPING THE STRATEGIC MARKETING PLAN

This chapter

- introduces the strategic marketing plan;
- describes the stages in the planning process;
- introduces the structure and content of the strategic marketing plan (document);
- examines the key critical success factors for implementing the strategic marketing plan.

INTRODUCTION

The strategic marketing plan outlines the steps a company intends to take to achieve its revenue and profit objectives within a two- to three-year timeframe. The structure for the plan is based on the market-matrix we introduced in Chapter 1 where companies identify revenues and profit across product categories and customer segments. Developing a strategic marketing plan is both a working process and writing of a document. We will in this chapter illustrate in detail how the market-matrix is used to structure the working process for a chocolate company. We will also use this company to illustrate analysis of profitability, market and competitive dynamics, customer behaviour and marketing audit. Writing the strategic marketing plan document should also follow a few important principles we will illustrate with a fitness centre. Both the quality of the process and the document are important in developing a successful strategic marketing plan.

As illustrated in Figure 8.1, marketing management is conceptualized as a collection of activities and resources aimed at generating value for various customer segments and product categories in the market-matrix. The marketing strategy's aim is to identify how this system of linked market activities and resources can be optimized to seize opportunities and mitigate risks. Through a methodical analysis of profitability, market and competition, customer needs and behaviour, and marketing effectiveness, companies will develop a comprehensive plan involving all departments and functions. The strategic marketing plan explains how the system of market activities and resources will be improved to attract more customers, retain existing ones, and cultivate stronger and more profitable customer relationships. The plan is supported by a budget that details the amount of funds and other resources the company will commit to the proposed initiatives and how these investments will impact revenues and profits in the coming two to three years. The plan also specifies implementation and how key performance indicators will be tracked to ensure that the strategy is executed as intended. The quality of the planning process and the creation of a strategic marketing plan showcases a company's market-oriented approach (Pulendran & Speed, 1996; Pulendran et al., 2002).

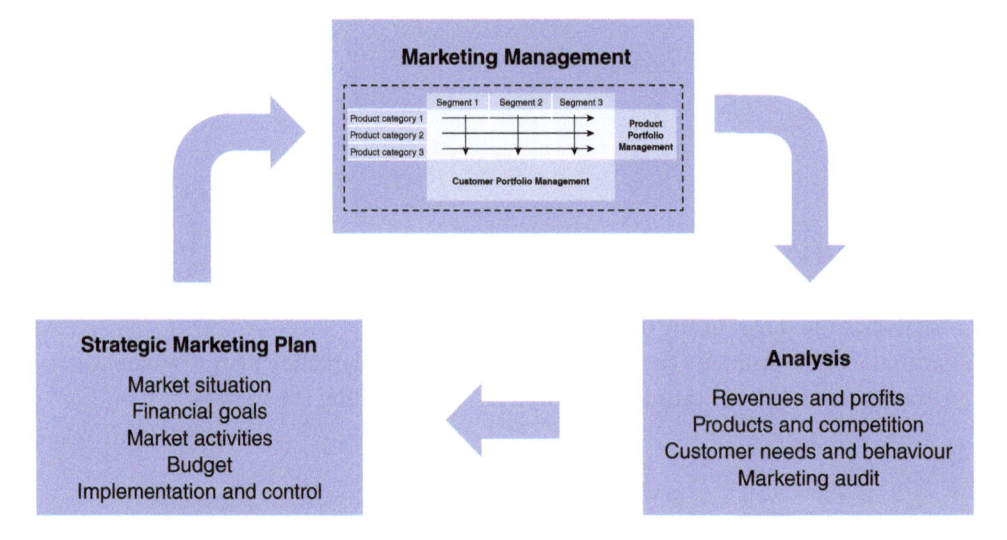

Figure 8.1   Strategic marketing planning

Strategic marketing planning is a systematic process for analysing the market situation and for developing a strategic marketing plan as illustrated in Figure 8.1. The process is also iterative, as illustrated in Figure 8.2[1] and starts with a comprehensive analysis where the purpose is to pinpoint the primary strategic obstacles hindering the company from achieving its financial objectives and other goals. During the crafting of strategic actions and goal setting, the need for additional information and analysis may arise, prompting a review and refinement of the analysis. This can also happen later in the process, such as during resource allocation or while developing metrics for measuring progress in implementation. The output of the planning process is a plan document that communicates the new strategy.

---

[1]The conceptual model for developing a strategic marketing plan as described here is inspired by McDonald (2009) and Kotler & Keller (2015).

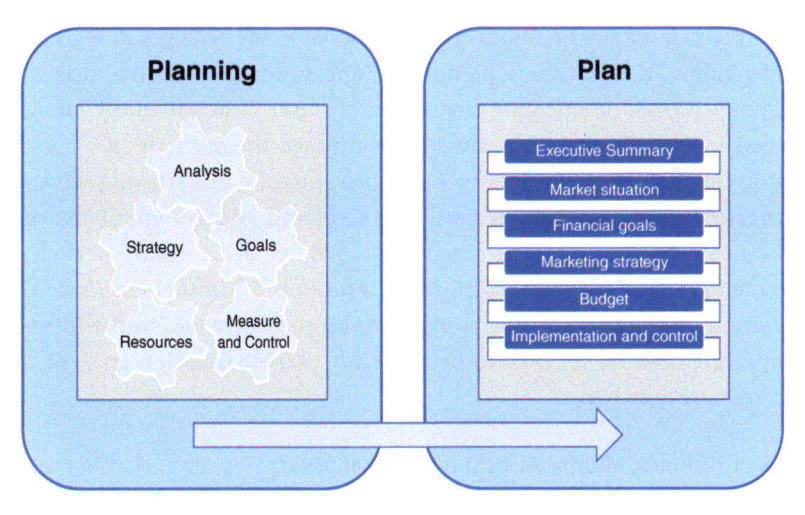

Figure 8.2 Strategic marketing planning process and writing the plan document go together

ANALYSING THE MARKET SITUATION

The primary aim of market situation analysis is to enhance the efficiency and effectiveness of the system of market-related activities and resources. We can think of the market-related activities and resources of a company as a micro-system of economic activities and decisions interlinked within a complex system of macro- and meso-economic factors (Dopfer et al., 2004). Macro level includes institutions and policy-makers, and economic factors of interest are phenomena like economic growth, inflation, unemployment, sustainability, and so forth. Meso level includes social groups, regions and industries, and economic factors of interest are consumer trends, innovation, competitions, and so forth.

In the analysis of the market situation, we attempt to identify significant changes at the meso and macro levels of the economic system that are likely to provide opportunities for growth or threats to revenues and profit. Companies aim to understand and predict future customer needs and behaviour by analysing emerging trends at the meso level. Currently it is, for example, crucial to keep an eye on changes in customer needs and behaviour related to global sustainability where the goals set by the UN play a significant role. The growing need for being sustainable is leading customers to demand more sustainable products and services. In a study of consumer-packaged goods in the US it was found that products promoted as environmental or sustainable experienced higher sales growth than comparable products without such claims (McKinsey & NielsenIQ, 2023). As such, sustainability is driving several trends that are changing customer attitudes, and while these trends have yet to translate into changes in behaviour, it is likely that they will have a significant impact on all markets in the future. These trends at the meso level are also affecting factors at the macro level, and in the case of sustainability we can observe many changes in legislation, taxes, government funding of new energy production, and so forth. Therefore, it is essential for companies to keep track of emerging trends and scenarios that will affect future customer needs and behaviour both directly and indirectly through the macro level.

Examining the market scenario proves to be an intricate undertaking, given the company's intricate integration into a complex economic system involving meso- and macro-level elements. The analysis should not merely tackle issues at each level (i.e. macro, meso and micro) but strive to cultivate a profound comprehension of their interconnections and their impact on the company both presently and in the future. There is no right or wrong method for how to organize the market situation analysis, but it will typically consist of four parts:

- analysis of revenues and profit in the market-matrix;
- analysis of products and competitive dynamics;
- analysis of customer needs and behaviour;
- marketing audit.

Analysis of Profitability in the Market-Matrix

The strategic marketing plan revolves around the understanding of how revenues and profits are generated in the market-matrix. Profit, in our use of the term, is simply revenues minus costs and is more formally referred to as earnings before interest, taxes, depreciation and amortization (EBITDA). We will now explore how this might look in practice in Case Study 8.1, returning to the example of the Scandinavian tourism company first introduced in Chapter 1.

Case Study 8.1

Scandinavian Tourism Company

In Chapter 1, it was revealed that the Scandinavian tourism company earned most of its revenues in the Sun & Beach product category within the Family segment. To estimate the profit generated across products and customers, costs are subtracted from revenues. Costs are incurred due to activities undertaken by companies to produce and sell products to different customers. Direct costs, such as material and labour used in production, can be allocated directly. However, indirect costs, such as administration, technology, advertising, sales, and so forth, pose a challenge in terms of allocation. To address this issue, companies use various techniques, with activity-based costing being the most prevalent (Cooper & Kaplan, 1991). The principle behind activity-based costing for our purpose is to allocate indirect costs based on the amount of activity connected to a product category and a customer segment.

Table 8.1 illustrates that by deducting costs from the revenues in each respective cell, we can determine the profit generated by different product categories and customer segments. The table shows that the Family segment contributes to 64% of the company's total profit, while the Sun & Beach product category accounts for 62% of the profit. It is interesting to note that the Sun & Beach product category in the Family segment alone contributes to over 55% of the total profit. On the other hand, although the Young & Single segment generates 19% of the revenues, it does not generate any profit for the company.

Table 8.1 Revenues and profit for a Scandinavian tourism company

Revenues	Young & Single	Family	55-Plus	
Sun and Beach	20	290	60	67%
Winter	80	20	20	22%
City Weekend	5	15	40	11%
	19%	59%	22%	100%

Profit (EBITDA)	Young & Single	Family	55-Plus	
Sun and Beach	−3	26	6	62%
Winter	2	2	5	19%
City Weekend	1	2	6	19%
	0%	64%	36%	100%

It is crucial not to jump to conclusions early in the planning process. For instance, a decision to drop the Young & Single customer segment might be premature without further investigation. Therefore, it is essential to dig deeper into the underlying causes. In this case, the company investigated the prices paid in each segment, which revealed a significant difference. The Family segment had the highest prices, followed by the 55-Plus segment, and the Young & Single segment had the lowest prices. And although the profit in the Young & Single segment was close to zero, the marginal profit could have been positive if the customers in this segment had filled up capacity that would otherwise not have been sold (i.e. last-minute prices).

MARKETING MANAGEMENT

An important principle in analysing is to examine patterns in the data. For instance, a chocolate company noticed an increase in revenue from 26.5 million euros to 30 million euros over the past three years. Table 8.2 shows that the growth in different product categories varied greatly. Notably, there was remarkable growth in the Pick & Mix category, with revenue increasing from 3.5 million euros to 15 million euros. However, revenue for Bags & Boxes and Chocolate Bars declined. Notice also that the overall gross margin and profitability improved over the last three years as well.

Table 8.2 Financial development in a chocolate company

	Year −2	Year −1	This Year
Pick & Mix	3.50	7.50	15.00
Children	2.00	5.00	10.00
Young Adults	1.00	2.00	4.00
Adults	0.50	0.50	1.00
Bags & Boxes	16.00	14.00	10.00
Children	1.00	1.00	1.00
Young Adults	8.00	7.00	6.00
Adults	7.00	6.00	3.00
Chocolate Bars	7.00	6.00	5.00
Children	0.00	0.00	0.00
Young Adults	1.00	1.00	1.00
Adults	6.00	5.00	4.00
Revenues	26.50	27.50	30.00
Direct costs	15.90	15.03	15.05
Gross margin	10.60	12.47	14.95
	40.00%	45.35%	49.83%
Indirect production and logistics costs	2.65	2.85	2.95
Indirect sales and marketing costs	6.00	7.00	9.50
Profit (EBITDA)	1.95	2.62	2.50
	7.36%	9.53 %	8.33 %

The objective of analysing revenues and profits is to comprehend and depict how they are created across different product categories and customer segments. Several methods can be employed for this analysis, but obtaining all the desired data can sometimes be challenging or costly. It is not necessary to have a flawless and complete description of every aspect of the analysis, but rather a rough approximation, so that the company can identify the most suitable strategic challenges to move forward.

Analysis of Product Markets and Competition

In Chapter 6, we learned that the financial value of a product category increases with the number of customers, their purchase frequency and their willingness to pay the price. As shown in Table 8.3, the Pick & Mix category has experienced tremendous growth of over 100% in recent years. It has 4.8 million customers, half of whom are young adults (50%) and almost half are children (47%). The number of customers is closely linked to distribution coverage, as the products need to be available where people shop, especially for fast-moving consumer goods. The distribution coverage for Pick & Mix is 65%, which is much higher than the other two categories. A review of consumer statistics shows that brand awareness is low for all product categories. When asked 'Which brands do you remember?' in the Pick & Mix category, only 25% of consumers mentioned the brand name. The numbers are even worse for the other product categories. Brand preference is also low in all categories, with only 17% of consumers believing that the brand is better than other competitors in the Pick & Mix category. The trial statistic is high for Pick & Mix products, but low for the other two categories. Upon closer examination of the product portfolio, the Pick & Mix category was found to be growing rapidly compared to the other two categories. This category is also well-distributed. Another important observation is that the brand statistics indicate a weak brand presence in the minds of consumers.

Table 8.3 Analysis of the product portfolio for a chocolate company

	Product Portfolio		
	Pick & Mix	**Bags & Boxes**	**Chocolate Bars**
Revenues	EUR 15,000,000	EUR 10,000,000	EUR 5,000,000
Annual growth	107%	–21%	–16%
Number of customers	4,800,000	3,960,000	780,000
Children	47%	7%	12%
Young Adults	50%	59%	32%
Adults	3%	34%	56%
Distribution coverage (% of shops)	65%	28%	18%
Other statistics (all market)			
Brand cognition (% brand to category)	25%	15%	2%
Trial (% tried product from this brand)	65%	18%	10%
Brand preference (% +1 and +2)	17%	3%	4%

There are multiple factors that may be significant in analysing competitive dynamics, and firms seek to estimate market growth and the intensity of price competition.

To evaluate the level of price competition in the market, it is recommended to analyse the five competitive forces in Porter's 5C model, as explained in Chapter 4 (Porter, 2008). An increase in price competition intensity can be expected if competitors intensify their efforts to gain market share, if customers or suppliers have more bargaining power, if new players enter the market with low entry barriers, or if new products are likely to replace traditional ones. Changes in one or more of these factors indicate changes in the price competition intensity in the market. For the chocolate company, the biggest concerns are the possibility of strong chocolate brands in the Chocolate Bars and Bags & Boxes categories extend their brands into the Pick & Mix category, and the possibility that major grocery retailer brands develop their private labels in this category. In the absence of a strong brand presence in the minds of consumers, the chocolate company is therefore likely to face intense price competition in the Pick & Mix category.

In analysing competitive dynamics, companies attempt to predict the actions of competitors in the coming years. The first step is to identify who these competitors are. In markets with only a few global or national players, identifying competitors is easy as the players have extensive knowledge about each other. However, in markets with many small or medium-sized competitors, and where the product category (market) definition is not well-defined, identifying competitors can be challenging. For instance, the competitors in the health-related services sector are diverse and include public and private hospitals, specialists such as gynaecologists and eye specialists, physiotherapists, chiropractors, etc. Some of these are small companies that operate locally, making it challenging to obtain information about them. But with recent advances in machine learning, analysts have developed tools that systematically analyse several sources of data to interpret information about competitors. Through triangulation of information, companies acquire more accurate information about their competitors and a better understanding of their potential behaviour, thereby enabling them to make more informed decisions.

Analysis of Customer Needs and Behaviour

Chapter 5 taught us that expanding the customer base, reducing customer churn and increasing customer spending are key factors in growing the value of a customer portfolio. This is achieved by increasing the frequency of customer purchases, fulfilling customers' expectations so that they are satisfied and continue to buy products from the company, encouraging customers to buy from multiple product categories, reducing transaction costs through, for example, self-service options, and developing brand familiarity and preference to recruit new customers. By focusing on these growth drivers, companies can enhance the value of their customer portfolio and achieve sustained success.

Table 8.4 demonstrates that the chocolate company has 7.5 million unique customers, including 2.3 million children, 3.45 million young adults and 1.75 million adults. It is important to note that the number of unique customers is less than the sum of customers for the three product categories in Figure 8.6 because one customer can purchase products from more than one category. The Children segment shows a high growth rate, with 600,000 new customers last year (850,000 – 250,000), while the middle segment also experienced growth of 200,000 customers (850,000 – 650,000). However, the Adult segment saw a decline of 300,000 customers (150,000 – 450,000).

The number of purchases also provides valuable information. We see that the 2,300,000 customers in the Children segment have 6,850,000 purchases of Pick & Mix, which means an average of almost three purchases per customer from this product category. The number of purchases per customer varies across segments, with the Children segment having the highest number of purchases per customer for the Pick & Mix category. The young adults tend to purchase from the Pick & Mix and Bags & Boxes categories, while adults tend to purchase Chocolate Bars. The frequency of purchases is low, with 94% of young adults and 90% of adults reporting less than five purchases per year. This is far below the average purchase frequency of chocolate products in the population. The company's brand has the strongest position in the Children segment, with a satisfaction score of 8.3 and more customers who believe the brand is better or much better than alternatives. Although the company is strongest in the Children segment for the Pick & Mix category, their position is still weak when compared to the established chocolate brands.

Table 8.4 Analysis of the customer portfolio in the chocolate company

	Customer Portfolio		
	Children	Young Adults	Adults
Revenues	EUR 11,000,000	EUR 11,000,000	EUR 8,000,000
Number of customers	2,300,000	3,450,000	1,750,000
New customers last year	850,000	850,000	150,000
Lost customers last year	250,000	650,000	450,000
Average revenue per customer	EUR 4.78	EUR 3.19	EUR 4.57
Number of purchases	7,200,000	6,950,000	3,650,000
Pick & Mix	6,250,000	2,000,000	400,000
Bags & Boxes	500,000	2,000,000	1,000,000
Chocolate Bars	0	1,000,000	4,000,000
Number of purchases per customer			
10 or more	9%	1%	1%
5–10	25%	5%	9%
1–5	66%	94%	90%
Other statistics			
Customer satisfaction (1–10)	8.3	6.1	6.7
Brand attractiveness (% +1 or +2)	25%	5%	6%
Brand's share of customer's purchases	18%	4%	3%

Companies want to understand their customers and how customers can be grouped into segments with different needs for products and how these differences will materialize in their evaluation and choice of alternative products and brands. The chocolate company conducted a survey where consumers were asked to rate the importance of a set of product attributes related to what type of chocolate they preferred. The results are reported in Table 8.5, and we observe that the most important attributes in the Children segment is that the chocolate should be fun and sweet. This is very different from in the Adult segment, where consumers prefer bitter taste, exclusive packaging and chocolates suited for relaxation and enjoyment. The Young Adult segment has most focus on product characteristics related to energy. This is important information guiding both product development and brand communication, and thus the strategic direction for positioning of the company. If the company chooses to have a strong position in the Children segment their brand should be associated with sweet and fun to become more attractive. This may, however, push younger adults and adults away from the brand, assuming they use the same brand across segments. Building different brand positions across segments is an opportunity but it means spreading scarce resources across more activities, which may result in week positions in all three segments.

Table 8.5 Product attributes' relative importance by segments

Product Attributes	Segments		
	Children	Young Adults	Adults
Sweet	40	20	0
Bitter	0	10	30
Fruit and nuts ingredients	0	20	0
Exclusive design	0	0	30
Fun	60	0	0
Energy	0	40	10
Relaxation and enjoyment	0	10	30
Sum	100	100	100

Companies like the chocolate company should attempt to identify important trends at the meso level and interpret these to their own business. Related to sustainability, is it so that people are eating less chocolate to be better aligned with these values? Companies rely on various data sources to collect data at macro and meso levels. National statistical bureaus such as the Office for National Statistics in the UK and Das Statistische Bundesamt in Germany are a good starting point. Industry associations, which collect data from most participants in the market, also provide statistics on growth and other relevant trends. Additionally, national directorates for health provide data on the consumption of certain products, such as chocolate, which can be useful for companies to understand the impact of health-related concerns. These statistics show that despite health concerns related to sugar, people continue to consume chocolate, which is important information for companies such as the chocolate company. Thus, so far, the emerging trend on sustainability does not seem to have had any major impact on the chocolate market.

Marketing Audit

Businesses allocate resources towards marketing activities with the goals of acquiring new customers, retaining current customers and increasing relationship engagement. Evaluating the effectiveness of these activities and their costs is crucial to determine whether they are meeting the intended objectives. There is no one-size-fits-all approach for conducting such an analysis, as it must be tailored to the individual company and their specific marketing initiatives.

To attract new customers, companies have activities (and costs) in advertising, pricing strategies, salesforce deployment, distribution network expansion and new product development. To evaluate the effectiveness of these costs, companies can for example use sales modelling or marketing-mix modelling (Powell, 2008; Dawes et al., 2018). These are statistical methods that compare sales and advertising over a longer period of time to investigate their relationship. By controlling for other factors that may influence sales, such as seasonality and competitor spending, these methods estimate the impact of advertising on sales by calculating the increase in sales at various levels of advertising expenditure. This is well illustrated in Case Study 8.2 and the effect of Google search advertising on sales.

Case Study 8.2

CV Services and Google Search Advertising

A company that provides a digital service for publishing job applicants' CVs invested heavily in Google search advertising to attract new customers to their subscription service. Weekly data on spending and customer acquisition were collected and analysed to estimate the effectiveness of this spending. A simple regression model was used to show the relationship between Google search advertising and the number of new customers, as illustrated in the first tableau of Figure 8.3. The dots in the figure represent weekly observations of advertising spending on the X-axis and number of new customers on the Y-axis. The line in the figure represent the estimated regression line and illustrates the effect of increased advertising on the number of new customers. The effect (regression coefficient) was found to be strong and significant. However, when control variables for seasonality

(Continued)

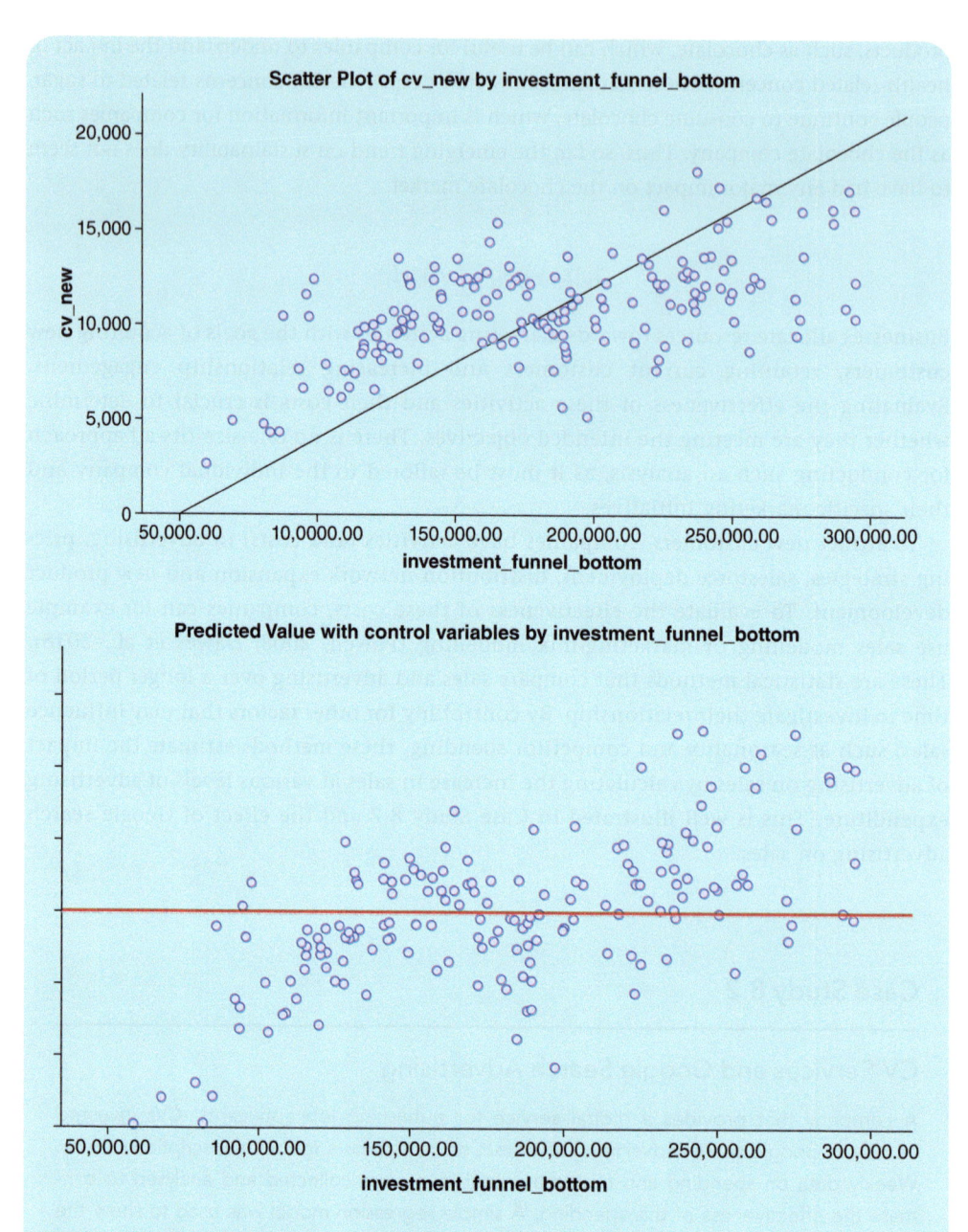

Figure 8.3 Sales modelling for estimating the effect of advertising without (first graph) and with and control of seasonality (second graph red line)

were added to the model, the significant relationship disappeared, as illustrated by the red line in the second tableau.

This can be partly explained by the pricing model for Google search advertising, where companies only pay for ads that people click on. Therefore, during seasons when people are searching more for a product, there will be more clicks simply because there are more potential customers in the 'store'. The other part of the explanation is when people were searching, they simply clicked on the company's brand name in the search field. Thus, Google made it easier and more convenient to get in contact with the brand. In other words, it was the familiar brand name and not Google advertising that brought new customers to the company. The company could therefore reduce their Google search advertising without losing sales. The main takeaway is that assessing the causal effect of advertising and other market activities is usually complex and requires good data and sound methodological skills.

Businesses allocate resources to activities aimed at developing stronger relationships with their customers, resulting in higher cash flow from them. These activities may include, but are not limited to, designing loyalty programmes with flexible earning and redemption options, offering cross-product solutions, expanding the brand into new product categories, adopting self-service formats, and more. It is worth repeating that such market activities aimed at increasing customers' cash flow are typically not confined to the marketing department, but rather require collaboration across various functions and departments within the organization.

To evaluate the effectiveness of differentiated pricing, the Scandinavian tourism company mentioned previously investigated why the 55-Plus segment had low profitability. It was discovered that the company sold its Beach & Sun products at a much lower price outside of the school holiday season, considering it as off-season and using lower prices to stimulate demand. However, a closer examination of the 55-Plus customers revealed that they preferred travelling outside of the school holiday season, not due to lower prices, but because they found the resorts more appealing when there were fewer children around. The presence of children was deemed noisy and disruptive to the relaxing holiday experience that customers in this segment desired. Upon realizing these differences in customer preferences, the company increased prices for the periods outside of school holidays and adjusted its marketing communication (websites, emails, catalogues, etc.) to differentiate communication across the two segments.

The task of analysing the market situation is a complex one that requires various investigations. These analyses encompass a broad range of investigations, utilizing both quantitative and qualitative methods. With the advent of big data and statistical tools such as machine learning, there are ample opportunities for evaluating the effectiveness of market-related activities (Wedel & Kannan, 2016). However, there is no set formula for what the analysis should cover. Rather, it is crucial to involve the right analysis team who can offer a comprehensive perspective and collaborate with others to generate innovative analytics that address the organization's strategic challenges.

SWOT and Identification of Key Strategic Challenges

The analysis stage of the planning process can be viewed as a funnel, where multiple analyses are conducted to gain a comprehensive understanding of the market situation (see Figure 8.4). To synthesize the diverse observations from the analysis process, many companies employ the SWOT technique. With SWOT, all the findings are sorted and prioritized according to their categorization into Strengths, Weaknesses, Opportunities and Threats. Through a systematic thought process based on the content of the four SWOT categories, one identifies the top three to five strategic challenges that need to be addressed in the strategic marketing planning process. At this stage it is no longer about collecting more data but about distilling what is already collected (Hart, 1992; Baer et al., 2014).

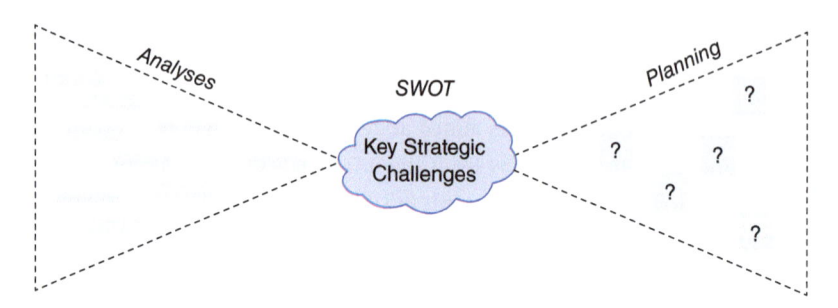

Figure 8.4   The funnel in the strategic marketing planning processes

The chocolate company's findings suggest the SWOT analysis presented in Figure 8.5. They believe that the 'Pick & Mix' and 'Small and flexible organization' are the most significant strengths of the company. It is important to note that this is a strategic judgement based on a subset of the collected facts. Therefore, others can have a different opinion regarding the strengths of the company. For instance, another group might consider efficient machinery and logistics to be the primary strengths, leading the company to identify different strategic challenges and make different strategic decisions. The same is true for the weaknesses, opportunities and threats categories as well. As people perceive and interpret information differently based on their experience and expertise, companies should ensure that their strategic teams comprise members with diverse experience and strategic expertise.

Figure 8.5   SWOT for the chocolate company

Reducing the number of elements in each of the four boxes is an important aspect of the SWOT process. The team usually begins with a long list in each category, but it's important to shorten the list to get to the essence of the strategic challenges. The reason for this is to make the strategic problem clearer and more concise. In addition, an element may be classified in two boxes. For example, a weak brand may also be seen as an opportunity to build a stronger brand. To resolve such issues, it's important to remember that strengths and weaknesses are related to the company, while opportunities and threats are related to external circumstances.

The chocolate company formulated these two strategic challenges:

- How to achieve a stronger brand positioned as the most attractive alternative in the Pick & Mix product category?
- How to develop a stronger partner relationship with retailer chains including all product categories?

After the SWOT process has reduced the number of elements in each category, the team should identify the key strategic challenges. These challenges can be thought of as specific strategic problems that need to be solved. It is essential to formulate these problems accurately, as the formulation of a problem is often more critical than the solution itself (Baer et al., 2014). To do this, we need to classify the findings into 'causes' and 'symptoms'. For example, is a weak brand a cause or a symptom for the chocolate company? If it is a symptom, we must determine why the brand is weak and identify the cause. The output of this process is a set of questions or challenges that specify the strategic problems to be solved. Ideally, there should be no more than three problems to ensure a focused and powerful strategy. The set of questions or challenges becomes the input for the strategy development process, which is essentially about finding the solutions to the strategic problems.

SETTING GOALS

The following step in the planning process (see Figure 8.2; p. 281) is establishing goals for the new strategy. Goals play a crucial role as they determine both the direction and distance required to bridge a gap. Starting with financial objectives such as revenues and profits, the strategic team must determine how the strategic challenges, or problems, will be addressed to attain these goals. For instance, if the chocolate company aims to increase revenues from 30 to 40 million euros and profits from 2.5 to 5.0 million euros within two years, how should they tackle the strategic challenges of strengthening their brand (in the Pick & Mix category) and forging a stronger partnership with retailers? It's important to remember that the strategy development process is iterative, which means that these initial goals and strategic challenges may be revised as the process evolves.

Research from motivation psychology suggests that ambitious and specific goals create higher motivation because they are more challenging and tap into people's need for achievement (Locke, 2000). When goals are set, attention and effort can be directed towards desired activities while minimizing the focus on less relevant tasks. The process of setting challenging goals can also encourage creative thinking, leading to innovation. Additionally, involving the company's management team, representing various functions and departments, in the goal-setting process can further enhance motivation to achieve these goals. Participation creates a sense of ownership and accountability for the goals, increasing the likelihood of successful implementation.

CRAFTING THE STRATEGY

Formulating the new strategy involves determining how the company will change its current market-related activities and strategic resources to achieve the goals. Therefore, the emphasis is on what the company will change, rather than a complete overhaul of all market-related activities and strategic resources. Typically, this means that most market-related activities and resources will remain unchanged. Developing a strategic map that illustrates the causal chain of effects can be a useful initial step in this process. The strategic map facilitates a common thinking among the team regarding which market-related activities and resources are central to the new strategy (Kaplan & Norton, 1996 and 2004).

The chocolate company initially categorized the strategic initiatives into the three product categories, as shown in the strategic map in Figure 8.6. Their aim for the Pick & Mix category is to increase the number of customers buying the product and the frequency of their purchases. To achieve this, they believe that creating a more attractive product, such as adding fun figures to the Pick & Mix assortment, and dedicating resources to advertising to build a

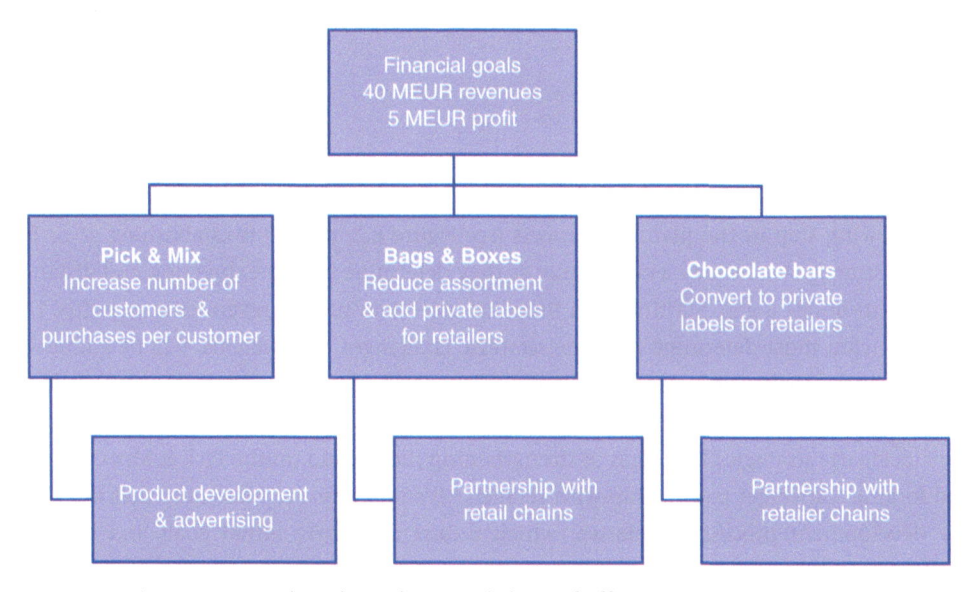

Figure 8.6 Strategic map describing the causal chain of effects

strong brand preference among children and young adults, will do the work. For the Bags & Boxes and Chocolate Bars categories, the new strategy suggests partnering and producing retailers' private label assortment. As retailer chains are expanding their private label assortments into new categories, they are searching for suppliers that can deliver reasonably good-quality products at low prices. By increasing volume on a few product variants, the chocolate company can utilize its machinery and logistics resources more efficiently, reduce unit costs through economies of scale, and provide lower prices to support the private label strategy.

RESOURCE PLANNING AND BUDGETING

The subsequent stage in the planning process is resource allocation and budgeting. The fundamental principle is that companies must spend and invest resources such as money and time to generate revenue, and the strategy is about finding a way to spend and invest more intelligently. Because market-related activities during one period can have delayed and/or lasting effects on customer behaviour, a budget for the next few periods is required. In the following sections, we will use the accompanying Excel market-plan model to demonstrate how a strategic budget can be created.

Figure 8.7 reports the allocation of revenues and costs for the chocolate company across product categories and customer segments in Year –1, that is the last year before the new strategy is implemented. The allocation provides valuable insights into the business. One observation is that the price per unit varies between segments for Pick & Mix and Bags & Boxes, as Young Adults and Adults tend to buy more items and bigger packages compared to the Children segment. Another important observation is the uneven distribution of marketing costs, with 60% (5.75 of 9.50 million euros) in the Pick & Mix category. Due to these high costs, the net profit for this category is negative. The growth in sales seems to be a result of the company's investment in advertising efforts to build consumers' familiarity and preference for the brand. The main questions are whether these investments have a long-term effect on sales and whether the level of investment in advertising is at the optimal level.

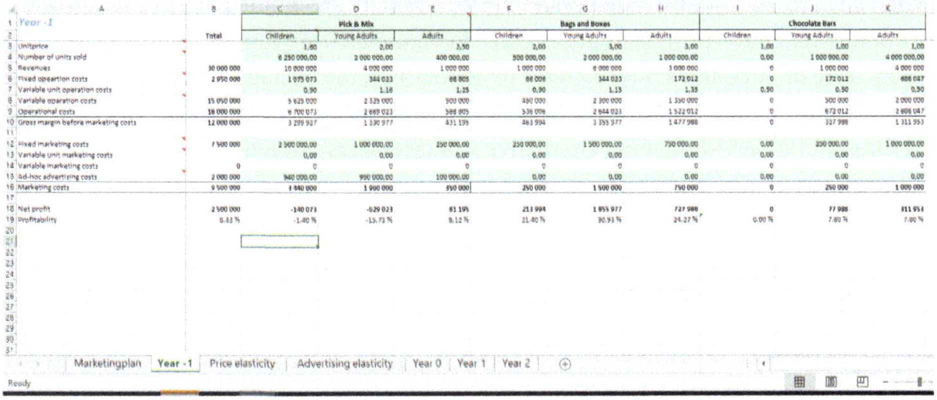

Year -1		Pick & Mix			Bags and Boxes			Chocolate Bars		
	Total	Children	Young Adults	Adults	Children	Young Adults	Adults	Children	Young Adults	Adults
Unitprice		1,60	2,00	2,50	2,00	3,00	3,00	1,00	1,00	1,00
Number of units sold		6 250 000,00	2 000 000,00	400 000,00	500 000,00	2 000 000,00	1 000 000,00	0,00	1 000 000,00	4 000 000,00
Revenues	30 000 000	10 000 000	4 000 000	1 000 000	1 000 000	6 000 000	3 000 000	0	1 000 000	4 000 000
Fixed opeartion costs	2 950 000	1 075 073	344 023	68 805	86 006	344 023	172 012	0	172 012	688 047
Variable unit operation costs		0,90	1,16	1,25	0,90	1,15	1,35	0,50	0,50	0,50
Variable operation costs	15 050 000	5 625 000	2 325 000	500 000	450 000	2 300 000	1 350 000	0	500 000	2 000 000
Operational costs	18 000 000	6 700 073	2 669 023	568 805	536 006	2 644 023	1 522 012	0	672 012	2 688 047
Gross margin before marketing costs	12 000 000	3 299 927	1 330 977	431 195	463 994	3 355 977	1 477 988	0	327 988	1 311 953
Fixed marketing costs	7 500 000	2 500 000,00	1 000 000,00	250 000,00	250 000,00	1 500 000,00	750 000,00	0,00	250 000,00	1 000 000,00
Variable unit marketing costs		0,00	0,00	0,00	0,00	0,00	0,00	0,00	0,00	0,00
Variable marketing costs	0	0	0	0	0	0	0	0	0	0
Ad-hoc advertising costs	2 000 000	940 000,00	960 000,00	100 000,00	0,00	0,00	0,00	0,00	0,00	0,00
Marketing costs	9 500 000	3 440 000	1 960 000	350 000	250 000	1 500 000	750 000	0	250 000	1 000 000
Net profit	2 500 000	-140 073	-629 023	81 195	213 994	1 855 977	727 988	0	77 988	311 953
Profitability	8,33 %	-1,40 %	-15,73 %	8,12 %	21,40 %	30,93 %	24,27 %	0,00 %	7,80 %	7,80 %

Figure 8.7 Revenues, costs and profit for the chocolate company

The subsequent stage is to define the strategic initiatives in detail by determining how they will impact the parameters in the strategic budget for the upcoming years (i.e. Year 0, Year 1 and Year 2). Regarding Pick & Mix, the proposed strategic initiatives involve investing in product development and advertising to create a more appealing brand that will attract more customers and enhance their purchasing frequency.

The strategic team has proposed product development to increase brand strength by adding more fun items to the assortment. Most of these costs will be allocated to marketing research related to concept development, which involves generating ideas through focus groups and evaluating and prioritizing them using statistical methods. After consulting with several marketing research firms, they found that they will need to invest approximately 1 million euros in this activity. The additional cost will be included in fixed marketing costs and allocated equally between the Children and Young Adult segments. The team expects that the new product assortment will lead to a 10% increase in brand strength in the respective segments, resulting in more customer acquisitions and increased purchase frequency.

To determine the appropriate level of advertising, the team must estimate the response function of advertising to sales. This is done in the Excel sheet under 'Advertising elasticity'.[2] The company assumes that this market is highly responsive to advertising, and thus adjusts the coefficients in the table from the default value of 0.8 to 0.25. A coefficient of 0.8 means that a 10% increase in advertising will result in a 1.2% increase in sales (measured in units sold). On average research has found that a 10% increase in advertising leads to 1% increase in sales (Sethuraman et al., 2011). The team expects a stronger effect than the average as this type of product is more sensitive (i.e. responsive) for advertising.

In principle a stronger brand should create a higher willingness to pay, and in the budgeting process we need to specify the size of this willingness. The price elasticity reflects the expected change in sales if there is a certain reduction in price, and research has found that on average a 10% price decrease will lead to a 26% increase in sales (Bijmolt et al., 2005). Given that the product category typically has a low sensitivity to price changes, the company assumed that a 10% reduction in price would only increase sales by 2%. Conversely, a 10% increase in price is expected to result in a 2% decrease in sales. This information is entered under 'Price elasticity' in the Excel model.

When advertising response function and price elasticity are defined, we can simulate the effects of different advertising and price levels. In Figure 8.10 we can see that in Year 0 with a 10% increase in price and a 50% increase in advertising, the overall revenues and profit for Pick & Mix in the Children segment is 13,447,216 euros and 1,085,726 euros. With the help of the Excel worksheet, simulating alternative strategies does not require much effort.

The company carried out similar analyses for the other two product categories. Here they planned for a lower price per unit sold but a substantial increase in distribution due to the private label initiative. The overall results for Year 0 are presented in Figure 8.8, where we can see that the estimated revenues are around 38 million euros, which is an increase of 8 million

---

[2]The formula used for the advertising response function is explained in the accompanying Excel market-plan model.

euros, and the net profit is expected to be around 3.6 million euros, an increase of about 1 million euros. Notably, the Children segment in Pick & Mix is expected to be highly profitable in Year 0, while the Young Adult segment is not expected to be profitable this year. Nonetheless, the company anticipates that the investments made in Year 0 will continue to have positive effects in the upcoming years.

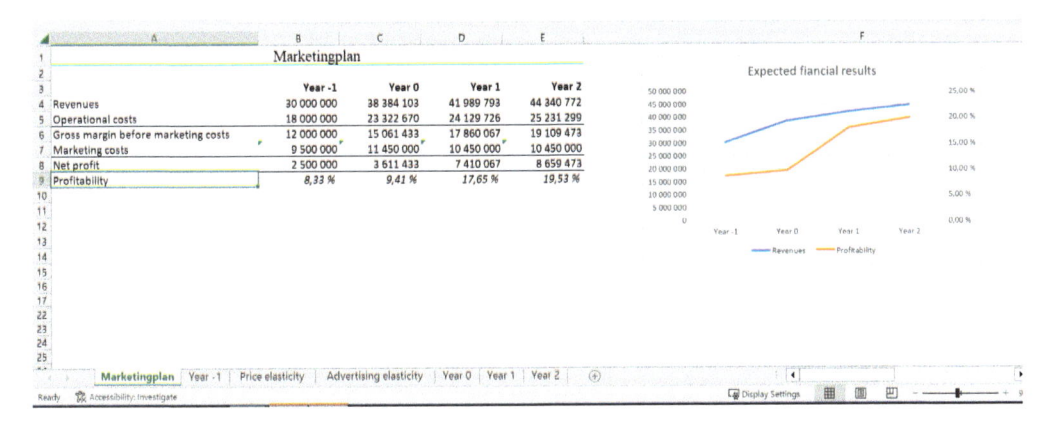

Figure 8.8 Strategic budget for Year 0 for the chocolate company

After specifying the effects for Year 1 and Year 2, we can now analyse the overall impact of the strategic initiatives by looking at the 'Marketing Plan' section. As shown in Figure 8.9, they expect the initiatives to result in an increase in both revenues and profits over the next years. Notice that the accuracy of the budget is contingent on the assumptions made regarding the required investments and expected outcomes.

Figure 8.9 Strategic budget for next three years for the chocolate company

MEASURE AND CONTROL

The impact of market-related activities on revenues and profits is mediated through other variables we refer to as causal mechanisms. For instance, one causal mechanism is that advertising will increase brand awareness, which in turn will lead to (i.e. cause) an increase in sales from new customers. In this case, brand awareness and new customers act as mediators between the advertising activity (i.e. market-related cost) and new revenues. To determine whether the strategy is working as intended, these mediators are monitored, and we can empirically verify whether the increase in advertising spending is causing a corresponding increase in brand awareness. Thus, if there is an actual increase in brand awareness after increasing the advertising, this indicates that the strategic initiative is working as intended. The strategic marketing plan must specify which variables (i.e. mediators) companies will monitor and measure to control whether the strategy is working. We refer to these measures as key performance indicators, abbreviated to KPIs. The identification of the appropriate KPIs is an essential aspect of designing a strategy performance measurement system and plays a critical role in strategic management (Pun & White, 2005). KPIs need to have a causal relationship with financial goals, be easy to understand, be sensitive to changes in the market and stimulate market-related activities.

Figure 8.10 outlines the process of developing and implementing effective KPIs. The process begins by identifying the goals that the strategic activities aim to impact. These goals may include psychological variables such as brand awareness, brand preference, customer satisfaction and customer loyalty, as well as behavioural variables such as purchase frequency, order sizes, contract renewals and loyalty programme membership.

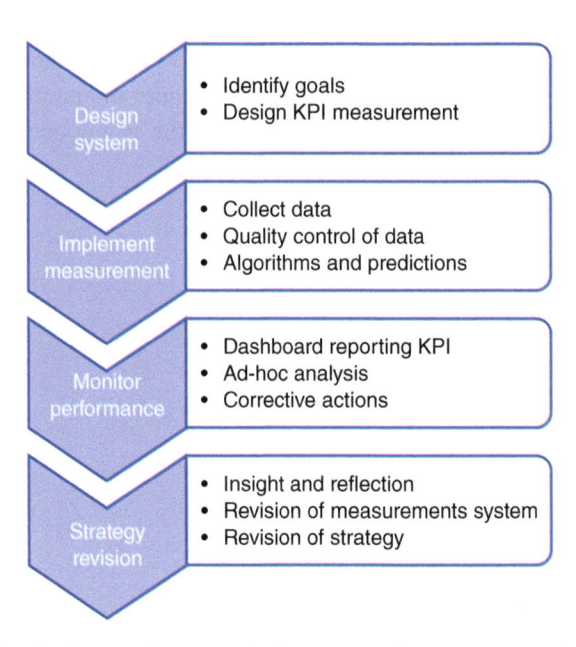

Figure 8.10   Developing key performance indicators used to monitor marketing strategy performance

In marketing, many of the mediators between market activities and financial outcomes are related to changes in how customers think and feel. In the example above, brand awareness is a psychological variable. Another example is satisfaction, which is a link between quality and loyal behaviour. The first point is that to measure psychological variables, interviews need to be conducted (i.e., survey questionnaires). The other point is that most of the psychological variables we want to measure need to be assessed through multiple indicators. Brand attitude, for example, cannot be measured directly but only through indicators for example measured with three even-point indicators anchored at Bad to Good, Negative to Positive, Non-desirable to Desirable (Gardner, 1985; Park et al., 2010). Measuring and operationalizing these indicators challenging, and companies often consult academic literature and marketing research companies to find reliable and valid measures (Bendle et al., 2021).

Behavioural data is typically gathered from multiple sources, such as transaction data, website traffic, email responses, and more. A grocery retailer, for example, can measure the number of shopping baskets containing fresh fruit and vegetables by analysing the occurrence of product numbers for fruits and vegetables (i.e. EAN, or European Article Numbers) in all transactions (i.e. all cash receipts). They can employ this indicator to monitor how well the retailers in their chain are performing and which stores are underperforming or overperforming. Companies can also use algorithms to forecast whether something is likely to happen in the coming periods. For example, many firms have developed models that predict customer churn (i.e. customer departure) and customer potential (i.e. interest in a new product). In this manner, the company gets an early warning of how performance is likely to develop and therefore the opportunity to implement corrective actions.

Companies can gain valuable insights by using descriptive statistics on KPIs to monitor whether their strategies are achieving the expected results (Berman & Israeli, 2022). Additionally, a well-designed management information system collects underlying data, enabling managers to conduct ad hoc analyses to obtain a more in-depth understanding of issues with underperformance. For example, if there is a drop in customer satisfaction, managers can investigate the cause by comparing satisfaction levels across different customer segments, product categories, locations and other factors. This approach can help identify the underlying problem and enable corrective actions to be taken.

The measurement system must undergo periodic revisions to evaluate whether they need to be changed. This becomes especially critical when the strategy itself undergoes changes.

Related to the UN sustainability initiative, companies have started to report their performance on the environmental, social and governance (ESG) goal. Environmental criteria assess how a company performs as a keeper of nature; social criteria examine how it manages relationships with employees, suppliers, customers and the communities where it operates; and governance deals with a company's leadership, executive pay, audits, internal controls and shareholder rights. It's a way for businesses to consider more than just financial factors in their decision-making processes, and research conducted by McKinsey indicates that leading companies can increase their performance on ESG together with growth in revenues and profit (McKinsey, 2023). Given the importance of sustainability, most companies are now revising their performance measurement system and integrating them into their strategic marketing plans.

The measurement and control development constitutes the end of the planning process. The next step is to put the plan in writing in the strategic marketing plan document. Such a document is needed to get the approval from the board of directors. They want to know how the management team intends to achieve sustainable growth and profitability before they approve the market activities and the related costs and investments that follow.

STRATEGIC MARKETING PLAN DOCUMENT

The strategic marketing plan is an output of the planning process, as illustrated in Figure 8.2. The plan outlines the strategic initiatives that a company intends to undertake in order to achieve its financial objectives over a period of three to five years.

The primary audience for this document is the board of directors, who represent the company's shareholders. Their primary responsibility is to ensure that the company is taking appropriate actions to secure and maximize future profitability for the benefit of all stakeholders, including employees. Therefore, the strategic marketing plan must give confidence in the top management team's ability to maintain control and execute sound and effective strategic initiatives.

The marketing strategy plan also plays a crucial role in fostering a shared understanding among leaders and employees of the challenges and opportunities in the market, as well as developing consensus around the strategic initiatives. When the document is approved by the board of directors, managers will work together to achieve the goals outlined in the plan. As we have discussed earlier, marketing success hinges on the entire organization's coordinated response and understanding of market opportunities and challenges.

In the strategic marketing plan document, the writing style is crucial. The content must be concise and accurate, with a focus on carefully crafted words and sentences. Avoiding technical terms and jargon is essential, and tables and figures should be integrated with the text and easy to read. The document should contain relevant and well-documented facts presented in context, so the reader can understand their meaning and implications. A good strategy document must also have a logical flow that connects all the pieces and is easy to follow (Johnson, 2004). The recommendation is that the plan should have the following structure:

- executive summary;
- market situation;
- financial goals;
- marketing strategy;
- budget;
- implementation and control.

We will use the Scandinavian fitness chain Vital to illustrate how the marketing strategy plan should be written. Vital is not a real company but contains elements based on facts from real companies. The primary reason we can't provide real examples is that this type of document is very sensitive information.

Executive Summary

The main aim of an executive summary is to provide readers with a brief overview of a large amount of information. It typically includes a short summary of the strategic challenges and opportunities, major findings or facts, key elements of the strategy and financial goals. Figure 18.11 provides an example of an executive summary for Vital.

Executive summary

The annual market growth in Scandinavia is expected to be 10–15 % over the next three years. The market is composed of three larger fitness chains which account for 60% of the Scandinavian market. The other 40% is composed of many small and local competitors. Vital is in a good position to increase their market share in the Scandinavian market.

Vital will increase number of customers through three strategic initiatives:

- Reduce churn by delivering a more satisfactory customer experience
- Attract more new customers by offering a more attractive product in the *55-Plus* segment
- Attract more new customers by opening 25 new locations.

The strategic financial goal is over the next three years to increase revenues from last year's 1,150 million euros to 2,175 million euros and net profit from last year's 180 million euros to 595 million euros.

Figure 8.11 Executive summary for Vital

Market Situation

The objective of this section is to provide a brief overview of customer, market, competitor and marketing performance data. These factors have led to the identification of primary strategic challenges that need to be resolved.

The market situation report for Vital is presented in Figure 8.12 (a, b, c). Notice that the document is brief and to the point. The content is also selective in terms of the elements to report in the document from the analysis. During the analysing process, several areas are analysed, such as the profitability of customer segments and product categories, competition, customer behaviour and marketing audit, but they are not necessarily reported in the final document. The report should only include the most significant findings and what they represent in terms of challenges and opportunities. Notice also that the final part of this section contains the main elements of the SWOT analysis and the strategic problems the company needs to resolve. This is the bridge to the remainder, which is about how these strategic problems is meant to be solved.

Market situation

Customers

The *55-Plus* segment provides the largest growth potential with an annual growth in number of customers of 7.9% (average is 2.4%), an average revenue per customer of 1,200 euros (average is 936 euros), a high score on customer satisfaction with 7.8 (average is 7), and an attractiveness score with 35% perceiving the brand to be more attractive than competing brands (average is 22%).

Performance in the *Adult* segment is not acceptable and must be improved. The low level of satisfaction and the low level of brand attractiveness is related to poor customer experiences, primarily with the booking system and the perceived quality of personal trainers.

Performance in the *Young Adult* segment is not acceptable and must be improved. The low level of satisfaction and the low level of brand attractiveness is primarily related to price level and the rigid nature of the membership price model.

	Customer Portfolio		
	Young Adults	Adults	55-Plus
Revenues	EUR 150,000,000	EUR 650 000 000	EUR 350,000,000
Number of customers	214,286	722,222	291,667
New customers lost year	40,520	122,607	35,500
Lost customers last year	30,470	127,605	10,489
Growth	4.5%	−0.7%	7.9%
Average revenue per customer	EUR 700,00	EUR 900,00	EUR 1 200,00
Customer satisfaction (1–10)	6.5	6.8	7.8
Brand attractiveness (% +1 or +2)	5%	25%	35%

Figure 8.12a   Market situation for Vital

Financial Goals

The primary focus of the board of directors is to ensure that the company has a solid strategy for achieving sustainable and profitable growth. Ultimately, all organizations must generate revenues that exceed their expenses, resulting in a surplus. This surplus is essential as it serves as a source of dividends for shareholders, motivating their continued investment in the company. In the case of non-profit organizations, this surplus is necessary to build a reserve that can protect against unforeseen decreases in revenue or unexpected expenditures.

In the short term, the board of directors might endorse a budget deficit when the company is investing to obtain future revenue and profit growth. For instance, a start-up company foresees incurring a deficit during its initial years as it creates and nurtures its organization, products and customer relationships. Additionally, various other organizations

Market

The adult population in Scandinavia between 18 and 80 years old constitutes about 16 million people, increasing 8% annually. The share of the population that is active and exercises every week is 80% (12.8 million) and growing 10% annually. The trend is that more people switch from outdoor training to indoor training with exercise equipment, and the trend is particularly strong in the segment 55 years and older. The total number of members in training centres is estimated to be 3.2 million, which is about 25% of the active population between 18 and 80 years old. The expected annual growth in the market for training centre membership is estimated to be 10–15% the next three years.

Competitors

Fitness Scandinavia and *MFGT* together with *Vital* are the three major competitors in Scandinavia, with a total share of the training centre market of about 60%. There are few differences in the product offerings from the three competitors and every successful innovation is quickly copied by the others. While Vital is primarily following an organic growth strategy through opening new locations and building stronger relationships with their customers, the two competitors also grow through acquisition of small and local training centres.

As there are small entry barriers in the market, many entrepreneurs see an opportunity to start fitness centres. The number of small and local training centres has therefore been steadily growing. The small competitors are not able to offer the same assortment of products and services as the three larger competitors and therefore use price as their main strategy to attract new customers. This results in lower gross margins and therefore poor financial performance.

Figure 8.12b Market situation for Vital

Marketing effectiveness

The general effect of advertising to attract new customers is on average positive and provides acceptable customer acquisition costs in the *Young Adult* and *Adult* segments. The effect of advertising targeted at the *55-Plus* segment is, however, very low, resulting in a high customer acquisition cost in this segment. A closer examination shows that Vital is perceived to be weaker than competing brands on products and services related to the specific needs in this segment (i.e., physiotherapy, massage, dietary supplements, etc.), which is believed to explain the lower effectiveness of advertising in this segment.

The guiding principle for building the distribution system has been to find locations close to where people live and work. However, the demographics of the *55-Plus* segment shows that this segment have other preferences for where they want to live than younger people. The result is that Vital is underrepresented in areas with a higher population density of people 55 years and older.

Vital is underperforming in terms of fulfilling expectations in the *Young Adult* and the *Adult* segments, resulting in low satisfaction, termination of memberships, and negative word of mouth in social media. The negative disconfirmations are primarily related to digital self-service of bookings in the mobile apps, and to negative experiences with some of the personal trainers.

Strategic marketing challenges

The major strength of Vital is their large market share in a growing market. There are weaknesses in fulfilling customer expectations in some of the market segments, leading to high customer churn. The major opportunity for Vital is to capture a larger share of the fast-growing segment of people 55 and older. This also constitutes the major threat as competitors may be more successful in capturing the new customers from this segment. Together this suggests three main strategic challenges:

- High churn caused by low satisfaction in the *Young Adult* and the *Adult* segments
- Low product attractiveness among potential customers in the *55-Plus* segment
- Low location attractiveness for customers in the *55-Plus* segment.

Figure 8.12c Market situation for Vital

need to restructure and may experience temporarily higher costs than revenues. Ideally, companies should strive to strike a balance where they not only enhance their market position but also sustain profitability simultaneously.

Financial goals for Vital are illustrated in Figure 8.13. Notice that this part of the document only specifies the overall financial numbers. More comments as to the specifics in costs are discussed in the budget part of the document.

Financial goals

The strategic financial goal is over the next three years to increase revenues from last year's 1,150 million euros to 2,175 million euros and net profit from last year's 180 million euros to 595 million euros.

The average annual growth is expected to be 20%, which is higher than the expected market growth of 10%. The growth will come from attracting more new customers in the *55-Plus* segment, a lower churn, and a higher average price paid due to more customers from the *55-Plus* segment.

Overall profitability is expected to increase from 15.65% to 27.36%.

Figure 8.13   Financial goals for Vital

Marketing Strategy

This section outlines how the company intends to solve the strategic problems, that is the specific strategic initiatives aimed at addressing the identified challenges (i.e. strategic problems to be solved) and achieving the financial goals. It is important to note that the strategy only focuses on what needs to be changed and not a comprehensive description of all market-related activities. The goal is to address the system of market-related activities that require improvement through specific strategic initiatives.

The marketing strategy reflects the market-matrix and the three management areas in marketing. That is, the strategic initiatives that will increase the value of the customer portfolio, the strategic initiatives that will increase the value of the product portfolio and the strategic initiatives that will increase the attractiveness of the company's brands. Remember also that the success of a company is closely related to how well the company coordinates and creates synergies among the three areas. For Vital, the strategic endeavours related to the market are structured into three areas of marketing management, as illustrated in Figure 8.14. It's worth noting that this document provides succinct descriptions for each strategic initiative.

Budget

The budget is a projection of the expected revenue and profit growth for the strategic period of three to five years. The strategic initiatives outlined in the plan involve investments that may result in increased costs but are also expected to yield higher revenues. The strategic budget for Vital is presented in Figure 8.15.

Marketing strategy

To solve the strategic market challenges and achieve the financial goals, a number of strategic initiatives will be taken.

Customer portfolio strategy:

- Improve customer experience with digital interaction. Current digital applications will be replaced with a new technological solution offered by a leading software supplier.

- Improve customer experience with personal trainers. Capabilities of the personal trainers will be improved with a new skill development programme and by replacement of personal trainers that underperform.

Product category strategy:

- Develop a new value proposition for the product offering targeted towards the *55-Plus* segment to attract more new customers. The new product concept will include products and services related to specific challenges in training in this age group, which include physiotherapy, massage, and dietary supplements.

- In the next 12 months establish 25 new locations targeted specifically at the *55-Plus* segment to attract more new customers. The property team has acquired a new analytical tool that can identify white spots where the size and density of *55-Plus* is high, and competition is weak.

Branding strategy:

- Improve brand familiarity and brand preference in the *55-Plus* segment to attract more new customers. The advertising team will develop a new communication concept based on the new value proposition for the product offering. Digital media advertising will be used to targeting potential customers in the right age group and in areas where Vital already have or are establishing new locations. The advertising team will also redesign the websites in accordance with the need for a more diversified communication to the different segments.

Figure 8.14 Marketing strategy for Vital

The strategic budget represents a consolidation of the forecasted changes within the market-matrix. This process is an integral part of the planning phase, as previously explained using an Excel tool in the case of the chocolate company. A similar analysis was conducted for Vital, where the strategic team assessed the potential impact of strategic initiatives on revenue and profit across customer segments and product categories. As an illustration, endeavours aimed at enhancing the customer experience through digital interactions and personal trainers were expected to boost customer satisfaction, consequently fostering greater brand loyalty.

Typically, organizations often turn to marketing and business analytics to gain valuable insights during this stage of the planning process. These insights are then employed to formulate a strategic budget, detailing when and how increased expenditures are expected to translate into higher revenues and profits.

Budget

The increase in operating costs is mainly due to the opening of 25 new locations. There is also a smaller increase in operating costs due to replacement of personal trainers with more skilled employees with higher salaries. The cost of a new technology application for digital interaction is also included in operating costs in Year 0.

The increase in marketing costs is from the new product positioning of an attractive product targeted at *55-Plus*. Advertising spending is reallocated from targeting younger potential customers to older customers.

	Year −1	Year 0	Year 1	Year 2
Revenues	1,150,000,000	1,363,150,581	1,565,933,015	2,175,109,065
Operational costs	870,000,000	1,000,500,000	1,100,550,000	1,452,726,000
Gross margin before marketing costs	280,000,000	362,650,581	465,383,015	722,383,065
Marketing costs	100,000,000	114,000,000	118,200,000	127,240,500
Net profit	180,000,000	248,650,581	347,183,015	595,142,565
Profitability	15.65%	18.24%	22.17%	27.36%

Figure 8.15 Budget for Vital

Implementation and Control

The final section of the marketing strategy plan is Implementation and Control, which outlines how the strategic initiatives will be monitored to ensure that they achieve the expected outcomes on the KPIs that are essential for increasing revenues and profits. For instance, an increase in customer satisfaction may indicate that the strategic initiatives have led to improved customer experience, which in turn may reduce customer churn and ultimately boost revenues. However, other factors may also influence customer satisfaction, making it necessary to use analytical methods to confirm the true effects of the strategic initiatives. In the Vital case illustrated in Figure 8.16, some of the KPIs will be monitored monthly while others will be tracked biannually.

Certain strategic initiatives may necessitate alterations in the structure of the organization and the responsibilities of management roles. For example, a customer-oriented company may introduce a policy where sales representatives are primarily responsible for customer satisfaction, so their bonuses become a combination of customer satisfaction and sales, not just sales as has been the case previously. Another example could be that a marketing director is given overall responsibility for ensuring that new customers return and start using a brand, not just the responsibility for recruiting new customers as it has been previously. As the renowned management professor Peter Drucker (1967) wrote: 'What you measure is what you get!' Leaders and other employees in a company will act in accordance with what they are measured on. Therefore, if different behaviour is desired, the company should change what they measure their leaders and other employees on.

> **Implementation and control**
>
> The following key performance indicators will be monitored by the top management team and reported to the board:
>
> - Number of new and lost customers (monthly)
>
> - Customer satisfaction overall and with digital interaction and personal trainer (monthly)
>
> - Brand attractiveness among existing customers (biannual)
>
> - Brand familiarity and attractiveness among potential customers (biannual)
>
> All indicators will be broken down by customer segment and by location.
>
> The strategic initiatives will be implemented within the existing organizational structure.

Figure 8.16   Implementation and control for Vital

CHARACTERISTICS OF SUCCESSFUL STRATEGIES

Not all strategies lead to success, and various explanations have been proposed. A study of British companies found that the most important success factor is trust in the process among those affected by the strategy (Piercy & Morgan, 1994). This involves trust that the process was both thorough and comprehensive. Companies should therefore allocate sufficient resources and time to work with the strategy process, formalize tasks and provide a budget for the strategy team to get assistance from consultants and analytics if specialized capabilities are needed. Other studies of successful marketing strategies also highlight the importance of analytics (Pulendran & Speed, 1996; Menon et al., 1999; Pulendran et al., 2002). Thus, companies with extensive analysis and facts about customers, markets and competitors are more likely to succeed.

The writing style in the marketing strategy document is crucial. The content must be concise and accurate, with a focus on carefully crafted words and sentences. Strategic teams invest substantial effort in crafting precise wording that captures the core of the problem and outlines the planned solutions.

The document should contain relevant and well-documented facts presented in context, so the reader can understand their meaning and implications. A recurring characteristic of poor marketing strategy plans is that they are too long! Ideally the document should be limited to 20–30 pages (Calkins, 2008). If the document becomes a report of all the analysis and evaluation done in the process it will miss the point. Expressing ideas concisely is a challenging yet vital skill. Winston Churchill, renowned for his speeches, once remarked: 'If you want me to speak for two minutes, it will take me three weeks of preparation; if you want me to speak for an hour, I am ready now.'

SUMMARY

The strategic marketing plan outlines the steps a company intends to take to achieve its revenue and profit objectives within a two- to three-year timeframe. The marketing strategy's aim is to identify how the system of market-related activities and resources can be optimized to seize opportunities and mitigate risks. Through a methodical analysis of revenue, profits, competition, customer needs and behaviour, and marketing effectiveness, companies will develop a comprehensive plan involving all departments and functions.

The initial step in the planning process involves conducting a comprehensive analysis to pinpoint the primary strategic obstacles hindering the company from achieving its financial objectives. Undertaking an in-depth analysis of the situation is critical since it enables the management team to establish a shared understanding of the challenges facing the organization. To distil the insights gained from the situation analysis into key strategic challenges, companies often use a technique known as SWOT. After the SWOT process has reduced the number of elements in each category of the SWOT, the team should identify the key strategic challenges. These challenges can be thought of as specific problems that need to be solved. It is essential to formulate these problems accurately, as a solution to the wrong problem will rarely have an effect. The formulation of a problem is therefore more critical than the solution itself.

Formulating the new strategy involves determining how the company will modify its current market-related activities to achieve their goals. Goals play a crucial role as they determine both the direction and effort required to bridge the gap. The subsequent stage in the planning process is resource allocation and budgeting. The fundamental idea is that companies must allocate costs and invest resources to generate revenue; that is, companies must spend money to earn money. The purpose of the planning process is to invest or spend money more intelligently. The identification of KPIs is an essential aspect of designing a strategy performance measurement system and plays a critical role in strategic management.

The primary audience for the marketing strategy document is the board of directors, who represent the company's shareholders. Their primary responsibility is to ensure that the company is taking appropriate actions to secure and maximize future profitability for the benefit of all stakeholders, including employees. And remember that the writing style in the marketing strategy document is crucial.

END-OF-CHAPTER QUESTIONS

1   Open the marketing planning Excel model on this book's companion website, developed for the chocolate company, to see the number behind the output in Table 8.10.

- What is the likely rationale behind the allocation of 'Ad-hoc advertising costs' and therefore the high share of costs for their 'Pick & Mix' product category? What would profitability for the product categories have looked like if they allocated the 'Ad-hoc advertising costs' simply as a percentage of revenues?
- What is the likely rationale behind the allocation of 'Fixed operation costs' and therefore the high share of costs for their Pick & Mix product category?

What would profitability for the product categories have looked like if they allocated the 'Fixed operation costs' simply as a percentage of revenues?

- The advertising coefficient was set to 0.25 for the children and young adults in the Pick & Mix category (the other columns were set to 0.5). Examine how revenues and profit for the company (in the marketing plan sheet) will change if you set these coefficients to 0.5 and 0.10 with the same amount of advertising in the strategy period (Year 0, Year 1 and Year 2).

- The price elasticity coefficient was set to 2% for the Pick & Mix category (the other categories were set to 5%). Examine how revenues and profit for the company (in the marketing plan sheet) will change if you set these coefficients to 5% and 1% with the same pricing in the strategy period (Year 0, Year 1 and Year 2).

- The increase in brand strength for the Pick & Mix category was modelled with setting the coefficient for 'Change in brand strength' larger than 1.0. That is, the 1.1 in Year 0 means an increase in brand strength of 10%. What is the mechanism between stronger brands and revenues and how is it captured in the excel model? (Hint: look at cell C12 in the Year 0 sheet.) If the strategic initiatives with product development and advertising are less successful, the brand strength will not increase as much as assumed. What happens with overall revenues and profit if the brand strength remains unchanged (the coefficient is then 1.0)?

2   The strategic importance of a strong brand is evidenced in the chocolate company. What would you recommend as a KPI to track their development in brand strength?

3   Read Kaplan and Norton (1996) on balanced scorecard and strategic maps. Use the suggested method to develop a strategic map for Vital. What do you see as the benefits and problems with using this method in a strategy planning process?

4   Why do you think many companies choose to allocate marketing costs as a percentage of revenues? Selnes (1992) can be useful in this exercise.

5   Read Risitano et al. (2022) on how sustainability goals affect marketing management and the success of marketing strategies.

FURTHER READING

Baer, M., Dirks, K.T. & Nickerson, J.A. (2014). Microfoundations of strategic problem formulation. *Strategic Management Journal*, 34(2), 197–214.

Kaplan, R.S. & Norton, D.P. (1996). Linking the balanced scorecard to strategy. *California Management Review*, 39(1), 53–79.

Piercy, N.F. & Morgan, N.A. (1994). The marketing planning process: Behavioral problems compared to analytical techniques in explaining marketing plan credibility. *Journal of Business Research*, 29(3), 167–178.

Risitano, M., Romano, R., Rusciano, V., Civero, G. & Scarpato, D. (2022). The impact of sustainability on marketing strategy and business performance: The case of Italian fisheries. *Business Strategy & the Environment*, 31(4), 1538–1551.

Selnes, F. (1992). Analyzing marketing profitability: Sales are a dangerous cost driver. *European Journal of Marketing*, 26(2), 15–26.

REFERENCES

Aaker, D.A. (1991). Firm resources and sustained competitive advantage. In *Managing Brand Equity: Capitalizing on the Value of a Brand Name*. The Free Press.

Aaker, D.A. (1996). *Building Strong Brands*. The Free Press.

Aaker, D.A. & Joachimsthaler, E. (2000). The brand relationship spectrum: The key to the brand architecture challenge. *California Management Review*, 42(4), 8–23.

Aaker, D.A. & Keller, K.L. (1990). Consumer evaluations of brand extensions. *Journal of Marketing*, 54(1), 27–41.

Aaker, D.A., Stayman, D.M. & Hagerty, M.R. (1986). Warmth in advertising: Measurement, impact, and sequence effects. *Journal of Management*, 17(1), 99–120.

Aaker, J.L., Benet-Martínez, V. & Garolera, J. (2001). Consumption symbols as carriers of culture: A study of Japanese and Spanish brand personality constructs. *Journal of Personality & Social Psychology*, 81(3), 492–508.

Abadie, A. (2021). Using synthetic controls: Feasibility, data requirements, and methodological aspects. *Journal of Economic Literature*, 59(2), 391–425.

Abernethy, A.M. & Franke, G.R. (1996). The information content of advertising: A meta-analysis. *Journal of Advertising*, 25(2), 1–17.

Abidin, C. (2015). Communicative intimacies: Influencers and perceived interconnectedness. *Ada: A Journal of Gender, New Media, & Technology*, 8, 1–16.

Adams, J.S. (1963). Toward an understanding of inequity. *Journal of Abnormal and Social Psychology*, 67(5), 422–436.

Aguilar, F. (1967). *Scanning the Business Environment*. Macmillan.

Ajzen, I. (1985). From intentions to actions: A theory of planned behavior. In J. Kuhl & J. Beckmann (eds), *Action Control: From Cognition to Behavior* (pp. 11–39). Springer.

Ajzen, I. & Fishbein, M. (1980). *Understanding Attitudes and Predicting Social Behavior*. Prentice-Hall.

Akçura, M.T. & Srinivasan, K. (2005). Customer intimacy and cross-selling strategy. *Management Science*, 51(6), 1007–1012.

Allan, D. (2008). A content analysis of music placement in prime-time television advertising. *Journal of Advertising Research*, 48(3), 404–417.

AMA. (2023). Branding. Retrieved from https://www.ama.org/topics/branding/

Ambler, T. (2000). Marketing metrics. *Business Strategy Review*, 11(2), 59–66.

Anderson, J.C. & Narus, J.A. (1984). A model of the distributor's perspective of distributor–manufacturer working relationships. *Journal of Marketing*. 48(4), 62–74.

Andjelic, A. (2022). Want more loyal customers? Offer a community, not rewards. *Harvard Business Review Digital Articles*, February 9, 1–4.

Andreassen, T.W. (1999). What drives customer loyalty with complaint resolution? *Journal of Service Research*, 1(4), 324–332.

Ansoff, I.H. (1957). Strategies for diversification. *Harvard Business Review*, 35(5), 113–124.

Apelbaum, E., Gerstner, E. & Naik, P. (2003). The effects of expert quality evaluations versus brand name on price premiums. *Journal of Product and Brand Management*, 12(3), 154–165.

Ariely, D. (2008). *Predictably Irrational: The Hidden Forces that Shape Our Decisions*. HarperCollins.

Aristotle. (2010). *Rhetoric* (W. Rhys Roberts, trans. & W.D. Ross, ed.). Cosimo.

Awad, N.F. & Krishnan, M.S. (2006). The personalization privacy paradox: An empirical evaluation of information transparency and the willingness to be profiled online for personalization. *MIS Quarterly*, 30(1), 13–28.

Azoulay, A. & Kapferer, J.-N. (2003). Do brand personality scales really measure brand personality? *Journal of Brand Management*, 11(2), 143–155.

Baer, M., Dirks, K.T. & Nickerson, J.A. (2014). Microfoundations of strategic problem formulation. *Strategic Management Journal*, 34(2), 197–214.

Bagozzi, R.P. (1995). Reflections on relationship marketing in consumer markets. *Journal of the Academy of Marketing Science*, 23(4), 272–277.

Bagozzi, R.P. & Dholakia, U. (1999). Goal setting and goal striving in consumer behavior. *Journal of Marketing*, 63(4), 19–32.

Ballantyne, D. & Aitken, R. (2007). Branding in B2B markets: Insights from the service-dominant logic of marketing. *Journal of Business & Industrial Marketing*, 22(6), 363–371.

Bao, Y., Shao, A.T. & Rivers, D. (2008). Creating new brand names: Effects of relevance, connotation, and pronunciation. *Journal of Advertising Research*, 48(1), 148–162.

Barney, J. (1991). Firm resources and sustained competitive advantage. *Journal of Management*, 17(1), 99–120.

Barry, J.M. & Gironda, J. (2018). A dyadic examination of inspirational factors driving B2B social media influence. *Journal of Marketing Theory and Practice*, 26(1–2), 117–143.

Barry, T.E. & Howard, D.J. (1990). A review and critique of the hierarchy of effects in advertising. *International Journal of Advertising*, 9(2), 121–135. https://doi.org/10.1080/0265 0487.1990.11107138

Bass, F.M. (1969). A new product growth model for consumer durables. *Management Science*, 15(5), 215–227.

Batra, R. & Ray, M.L. (1986). Situational effects of advertising repetition: The moderating influence of motivation, ability, and opportunity to respond. *Journal of Consumer Research*, 12(4), 432–445. https:/doi.org/10.1086/208528

Beard, F.K. (2005). One hundred years of humor in American advertising. *Journal of Macromarketing*, 25(1), 54–65. https://doi.org/10.1177%2F0276146705274965

Bearden, W.O. & Etzel, M.J. (1982). Reference group influence on product and brand purchase decisions. *Journal of Consumer Research*, 9(2), 183–194.

Belch, G.E., Belch, M.A. & Villarreal, A. (1987). Effects of advertising communications: Review of research. *Research in Marketing*, 9, 59–117.

Bell, S.J., Auh, S. & Smalley, K. (2005). Customer relationship dynamics: Service quality and customer loyalty in the context of varying levels of customer expertise and switching costs. *Journal of the Academy of Marketing Science*, 33(2), 169–183.

Bendixen, M., Bukasa, K.A. & Abratt, R. (2004). Brand equity in the business-to-business market. *Industrial Marketing Management*, 33(5), 371–380.

Bendle, N., Farris, P.W., Pfeifer, P. & Reibstein, D. (2021). *Marketing Metrics*, 4th edn. Pearson FT Press.

Berger, P.D. & Nasr, N.I. (1998). Customer lifetime value – marketing models and applications. *Journal of Interactive Marketing*, 12(1), 17–30.

Berman, R. & Israeli, A. (2022). The value of descriptive analytics: Evidence from online retailers. *Marketing Science*, 41(6), 1074–1096.

Bettman, J.R. (1979a). Memory factors in consumer choice: A review. *Journal of Marketing*, 43(2), 37–53.

Bettman, J.R. (1979b). *An Information Processing Theory of Consumer Choice*. Addison-Wesley.

Bhat, S. & Reddy, S. (1998). Symbolic and functional positioning of brands. *Journal of Consumer Marketing*, 15(1), 32–43.

Bhattacharya, C.B., Rao, H. & Glynn, M.A. (1995). Understanding the bond of identification: An investigation of its correlates among art museum members. *Journal of Marketing*, 59(4), 46–57.

Bijmolt, T.H.A., Heerde, H.J. & Pieters, R.G.M. (2005). New empirical generalizations on the determinants of price elasticity. *Journal of Marketing Research*, 42(2), 141–156.

Bilnytt (2023). https://www.bilnytt.no/subscriber/showArticle.aspx?articleID=11276

Biong, H. & Selnes, F. (1995). Relational selling behavior and skills in long-term industrial buyer–seller relationships. *International Business Review*, 4(4), 483–498.

Biong, H. & Selnes, F. (1996). The strategic role of the salesperson in established buyer–seller relationships. *Journal of Business-to-Business Marketing*, 3(3), 5–42.

Bitner, J. & Booms, B. (1981). Marketing strategies and organizational structures for service firms. In J. Donnelly & W. George (eds), *Marketing of Services* (pp. 47–51). American Marketing Association.

Bizer, G.Y. & Schindler, R.M. (2005). Direct evidence of ending-digit drop-off in price information processing. *Psychology & Marketing*, 22(10), 771–783.

Boatwright, P. & Nunes, J.C. (2001). Reducing assortment: An attribute-based approach. *Journal of Marketing*, 65(3), 50–63.

Bolton, R.N. & Lemon, K.N. (1999). A dynamic model of customers' usage of services: Usage as an antecedent and consequence of satisfaction. *Journal of Marketing Research*, 36(3), 171–186.

Bonoma, T. (1982). Major sales: Who really does the buying? *Harvard Business Review*, 84(7/8), 172–181.

Bordley, R. (2003). Determining the appropriate depth and breadth of a firm's product portfolio. *Journal of Marketing Research*, 40(1), 39–53.

Bower, G.H., Gilligan, S.G. & Monteiro, K.P. (1981). Selectivity of learning caused by affective states. *Journal of Experimental Psychology: General*, 110(4), 451–473.

Brakus, J.J., Schmitt, B.H. & Zarantonello, L. (2009). Brand experience: What is it? How is it measured? Does it affect loyalty? *Journal of Marketing*, 73(3), 52–68.

Brown, T.J. and Dacin, P.A. (1997). The company and the product: Corporate associations and consumer product responses. *Journal of Marketing*, 61 (January), 68–84.

Brucks, M. (1985). The effects of product class knowledge on information search behavior. *Journal of Consumer Research*, 12(1), 1–16.

Bucklin, R.E., Siddarth, S. & Silva-Risso, J.M. (2008). Distribution intensity and new car choice. *Journal of Marketing Research*, 45(4), 473–486.

Burnham, T., Frels, J.K. & Mahajan, V. (2003). Consumer switching costs: A typology, antecedents, and consequences. *Journal of the Academy of Marketing Science*, 31(2), 109–126.

Business of Apps (2023). https://www.businessofapps.com/data/amazon-statistics/

Calkins, T. (2008). *Breakthrough Marketing Plans: How to Stop Wasting Time and Start Driving Growth*. Palgrave Macmillan.

Camerer, C. (2005). Three cheers – psychological, theoretical, empirical – for loss aversion. *Journal of Marketing Research*, 42(2), 129–133.

Campbell, C. & Farrell, J.R. (2020). More than meets the eye: The functional components underlying influencer marketing. *Business Horizons*, 63(4), 469–479.

Cardozo, R.N. & Smith, D.K. (1983). Applying financial portfolio theory to product portfolio decisions: An empirical study. *Journal of Marketing*, 47(2), 110–120.

Carrillat, F.A., Jaramillo, F. & Mulki, J. (2009). Examining the impact of service quality: A meta-analysis of empirical evidence. *Journal of Marketing Theory & Practice*, 17(1), 95–110.

Chai, B. (2013, 15 November). How Volvo created the Jean-Claude Van Damme 'Epic Split' video. *Wall Street Journal*. https://www.wsj.com/articles/BL-SEB-78277

Chaiken, S. (1980). Heuristic versus systematic information processing and the use of source versus message cues in persuasion. *Journal of Personality and Social Psychology*, 39(5), 752–766. https://psycnet.apa.org/doi/10.1037/0022-3514.39.5.752

Chakravarti, A. & Janiszewski, C. (2004). The influence of generic advertising on brand preferences. *Journal of Consumer Research*, 30(4), 487–502.

Chan, K.K. & Misra, S. (1990). Characteristics of the opinion leader: A new dimension. *Journal of Advertising*, 19, 53–60. https://psycnet.apa.org/doi/10.1080/00913367.1990.10673192

Chattopadhyay, A. (1998). When does comparative advertising influence brand attitude? The role of delay and market position. *Psychology and Marketing*, 15(5), 461–475. https://doi.org/10.1002/(SICI)1520-6793(199808)15:5%3C461::AID-MAR4%3E3.0.CO;2-5

Chaudhuri, A. & Holbrook, M.B. (2001). The chain of effects from brand trust and brand affect to brand performance: The role of brand loyalty. *Journal of Marketing*, 65(2), 81–93.

Christensen, C.M. (1997). *The Innovator's Dilemma: When New Technologies Cause Great Firms to Fail*. Harvard Business School Press.

Cline, T.W. & Kellaris, J.J. (2007). The influence of humor strength and humor-message relatedness on ad memorability: A dual process model. *Journal of Advertising*, 36(1), 55–67. https://doi.org/10.2753/JOA0091-3367360104

Colley, R.H. (1961). *Defining Advertising Goals for Measured Advertising Results*. Association of National Advertisers.

Cooper, R. & Kaplan, R.S. (1991). Profit priorities from activity-based costing. *Harvard Business Review*, 69(3), 130–135.

Cornwell, T.B., Weeks, C.S. & Roy, D.P. (2005). Sponsorship-linked marketing: Opening the black box. *Journal of Advertising*, 34(2), 21–42.

Coughlan, A., Anderson, E., Stern, L.W. & El-Ansary, A. (2006). *Marketing Channels*. Prentice Hall.

Court, D., Elzinga, D., Mulder, S. & Vetvik, O.J. (2009). The consumer decision journey. *McKinsey Quarterly*, 3, 96–107.

Cova, B. & Cova, V. (2002). Tribal marketing: The tribalisation of society and its impact on the conduct of marketing. *European Journal of Marketing*, 36(5/6), 595–620.

Credit Suisse (2003). *Global Wealth Report*. https://www.ubs.com/global/en/family-office-uhnw/reports/global-wealth-report-2023.html

Cummings, W.H. & Venkatesan, M. (1976). Cognitive dissonance and consumer behavior: A review of the evidence. *Journal of Marketing Research*, 13(3), 303–308.

Davis, D.F., Golicic, S.L. & Marquardt, A.J. (2008). Branding a B2B service: Does a brand differentiate a logistics service provider? *Industrial Marketing Management*, 37(2), 218–227.

Dawes, J., Kennedy, R., Green, K. & Sharp, B. (2018). Forecasting advertising and media effects on sales: Econometrics and alternatives. *International Journal of Market Research*, 60(6), 611–620.

Day, G. (1981). The product life cycle: Analysis and application. *Journal of Marketing*, 45(4), 60–67.

de Matos, C.A. & Rossi, C.A.V. (2008). Word-of-mouth communications in marketing: A meta-analytic review of the antecedents and moderators. *Journal of the Academy of Marketing Science*, 36(4), 578–596.

de Pelsmacker, P., Geuens, M. & van den Bergh, J. (2018). *Marketing Communications: A European Perspective*. Pearson.

Dekimpe, M.D.G., Hanssens, D.M., Nijs, V.R. & Steenkamp, J.E.M. (2005). Measuring short- and long-run promotional effectiveness on scanner data using persistence modelling. *Applied Stochastic Models in Business and Industries*, 21(4–5), 409–416.

Delboeuf, F.J. (1865). Note sur certaines illusions d'optique: Essai d'une théorie psychophysique de la manière dont l'oeil apprécie les distances et les angles [Note on certain optical illusions: Essay on a psychophysical theory concerning the way in which the eye evaluates distances and angles]. *Bulletins de l'Académie Royale des Sciences, Lettres et Beaux-arts de Belgique*, 19, 2nd ser., 195–216.

Devinney, T.M. & Stewart, D.W. (1988). Rethinking the product portfolio: A generalized investment model. *Management Science*, 34(9), 1080–1095.

Devinney, T.M., Stewart, D.W. & Shocker, A.D. (1985). A note on the application of portfolio theory: A comment on Cardozo and Smith. *Journal of Marketing*, 49(4), 107–112.

Dhar, R., & Wetenbroch, K. (2000). Consumer choice between hedonic and utilitarian products. *Journal of Marketing Research*, 37, 60–71.

Dick, A.S. & Basu, K. (1994). Customer loyalty: Toward an integrated conceptual framework. *Journal of the Academy of Marketing Science*, 22(2), 99–113.

Dickson, P.R. (1992). Toward a general theory of competitive rationality. *Journal of Marketing*, 56 (January), 69–83.

Dickson, P.R. & Ginter, J.L. (1987). Market segmentation, product differentiation, and marketing strategy. *Journal of Marketing*, 51(2), 1–10.

Digital Marketing News. (2023). https://www.dmnews.com/personalization-is-the-key-to-hilton-worldwides-customer-loyalty/

Digital Synopsis. (n.d.). Jean-Claude Van Damme's epic split for Volvo goes super viral online. https://digitalsynopsis.com/advertising/volvo-van-damme-epic-split

Dopfer, K., Foster, J. & Potts, J. (2004). Micro–meso–macro. *Journal of Evolutionary Economics*, 14(3), 263–279.

Dorotic, M., Bijmolt, T.H.A. & Verhoef, P.C. (2012). Loyalty programs: Current knowledge and research directions. *International Journal of Management Reviews*, 14(3), 217–237.

Dorotic, M., Fok, D., Verhoef, P.C. & Bijmolt, T.H.A. (2021). Synergistic and cannibalization effects in a partnership loyalty program. *Journal of the Academy of Marketing Science*, 49(5), 1021–1042.

Doz, Y.L. (2017). https://knowledge.insead.edu/strategy/strategic-decisions-caused-nokias-failure

Drucker, P.F. (1967). The effective executive. HarperCollins.

Dwyer, R.F., Schurr, P.H. & Oh, S. (1987). Developing buyer–seller relationships. *Journal of Marketing*, 51 (April), 11–27.

Eat This, Not That! (2021). https://www.eatthis.com/news-dangerous-side-effects-eating-mcdonalds-every-day/

Edelman, D.C. & Singer, M. (2015). Competing on customer journeys. *Harvard Business Review*, 93 (November), 88–100.

Egan, J. (2007). *Marketing Communications*. Thomson Learning.

Elder, R.S. & Krishna, A. (2010). The effects of advertising copy on sensory thoughts and perceived taste. *Journal of Consumer Research*, 36(5), 748–756. https://doi.org/10.1086/605327

Elliott, S. (2012, 24 September). For Oreo campaign finale, a twist on collaboration. *New York Times*. https://www.nytimes.com/2012/09/25/business/media/oreos-daily-twist-campaign-finale-enlists-consumers.html

Engel, J.E., Blackwell, R.D. & Miniard, P.W. (1994). *Consumer Behavior*. Dryden.

Escalas, J.E. & Bettman, J.R. (2003). You are what they eat: The influence of reference groups on consumers' connections to brands. *Journal of Consumer Psychology*, 13(3), 339–348. https://doi.org/10.1207/S15327663JCP1303_14

Fainmesser, I.P. & Galeotti, A. (2020). Pricing network effects: Competition. *American Economic Journal: Microeconomics*, 12(3), 1–32

Farris, P.W., Bendle, N.T., Pfeifer, P.E. & Reibstein, D.J. (2009). *Key Marketing Metrics*. Pearson.

Festinger, L. (1957). *A Theory of Cognitive Dissonance*. Stanford University Press.

Fichte, J.G. & Breazeale, D. (1993). *Fichte: Early Philosophical Writings*. Cornell University Press.

Fishbein, M. & Ajzen, I. (1975). *Belief, Attitude, Intention and Behavior: An Introduction to Theory and Research*. Addison-Wesley.

Fiske, S.T. & Taylor, S.E. (1991). *Social Cognition*, 2nd edn. McGraw Hill.

Fiske, S.T., Cuddy, A.J.C., Glick, P. & Xu, J. (2002). A model of (often mixed) stereotype content: Competence and warmth respectively follow from perceived status and competition. *Journal of Personality and Social Psychology*, 82(6), 878–902.

Floyd, K., Freling, R., Alhoqail, S., Cho, H.Y. & Freling, T. (2014). How online product reviews affect retail sales: A metameta-analysis. *Journal of Retailing*, 90(2), 217–232.

Ford, D. (2002). *The Business Marketing Course: Managing in Complex Networks*. John Wiley & Sons.

Fornell, C., Johnsen, M.D., Anderson, E., Cha, J. & Bryant, B.E. (1996). The American Customer Satisfaction Index: Nature, purpose and findings. *Journal of Marketing*, 60(4), 7–18.

Fornell, C., Mithas, S., Morgeson III, F.V. & Krishnan, M.S. (2006). Customer satisfaction and stock prices: High returns, low risk. *Journal of Marketing*, 70(1), 3–14.

Fournier, S. (1998). Consumers and their brands: Developing relationship theory in consumer research. *Journal of Consumer Research*, 24(4), 343–373.

Freud, S., Strachey, J., Freud, A. & Rothgeb, C.L. (1953). *The Standard Edition of the Complete Psychological Works of Sigmund Freud*. Hogarth Press and the Institute of Psycho-Analysis.

Frick, T.W., Belo, R. & Telang, R. (2022). Incentive misalignments in programmatic advertising: Evidence from a randomized field experiment. *Management Science*, 69(3), 1665–1686.

Garber, M. (2012, 26 July). The future of advertising (will be squirted into your nostrils as you sit on a bus). *The Atlantic*. https://www.theatlantic.com/technology/archive/2012/07/the-future-of-advertising-will-be-squirted-into-your-nostrils-as-you-sit-on-a-bus/260283/

Gardner, M.P. (1985). Does attitude toward the ad affect brand attitude under a brand evaluation set? *Journal of Marketing Research*, 22(2), 192–198.

Gigerenzer, G. & Gaissmaier, W. (2011). Heuristic decision making. *Annual Review of Psychology*, 62, 451–482.

Gladwell, M. (2000). *The Tipping Point: How Little Things Can Make a Big Difference*. Little, Brown and Company.

Goddard, M. (2017). The EU General Data Protection Regulation (GDPR): European regulation that has a global impact. *International Journal of Market Research*, 59(6), 703–705.

Golder, P.N. & Tellis, G.J. (2004). Growing, growing, gone: Cascades, diffusion, and turning points in the product life cycle. *Marketing Science*, 23(2), 207–218.

Gordon, B.R., Jerath, K., Katona, Z., Narayanan, S., Shin, J. & Wilbur, K.C. (2021). Inefficiencies in digital advertising markets. *Journal of Marketing*, 85(1), 7–25.

Gordon, B.R., Zettelmeyer, F., Bhargava, N. & Chapsky, D. (2019). A comparison of approaches to advertising measurement: Evidence from big field experiments at Facebook. *Marketing Science*, 38(2), 193–225.

Gorn, G.J. (1982). The effects of music in advertising on choice behavior: A classical conditioning approach. *Journal of Marketing*, 46(1), 94–101. https://doi.org/10.2307/1251163

Granovetter, M. (1973). The strength of weak ties. *American Journal of Sociology*, 78, 1360–1380.

Grønhaug, K. (1976). Exploring environmental influences in organizational buying. *Journal of Marketing Research*, 13(3), 225–229.

Guadagni, P. & Little, J.D.C. (1983). A logit model of brand choice calibrated on scanner data. *Marketing Science*, 2(3), 203–238.

Gupta, S. (1988). Impact of sales promotions on when, what, and how much to buy. *Journal of Marketing Research*, 25(4), 342–355.

Gustafsson, A. & Johnson, M. (2003). *Competing in a Service Economy: How to Create a Competitive Advantage through Service Development and Innovation*. Stephen M. Ross Business School, University of Michigan.

Hague, P. & Jackson, P. (1994). *The Power of Industrial Brands*. McGraw Hill.

Hallén, L., Johanson, J. & Seyed-Mohamed, N. (1991). Interfirm adaptation in business relationships. *Journal of Marketing*, 55(2), 29–37.

Harmeling, C.M., Palmatier, R.W., Houston, M.B., Arnold, M.J. & Samaha, S.A. (2015). Transformational relationship events. *Journal of Marketing*, 79(5), 39–62.

Hart, S.L. (1992). An integrative framework for strategy-making processes. *Academy of Management Review*, 17(2), 327–351.

Hatton, G. (2018, 13 February). Micro influencers vs macro influencers. *Social Media Today*. https://www.socialmediatoday.com/news/micro-influencers-vs-macro-influencers/516896

Hauser, J.R. & Clausing, D. (1988). The house of quality. *Harvard Business Review*, 66(3), 63–73.

Hauser, J.R., Urban, G.L., Liberali, G. & Braun, M. (2009). Website morphing. *Marketing Science*, 28(2), 202–223.

Heide, J.B. (1994). Interorganizational governance in marketing channels. *Journal of Marketing*, 58(1), 71–85.

Heide, J.B. & John, G. (1988). The role of dependence balancing in safeguarding transaction-specific assets in conventional channels. *Journal of Marketing*, 52(1), 20–35.

Heide, J.B. & John, G. (1990). Alliances in industrial purchasing: The determinants of joint action in buyer–supplier relationships. *Journal of Marketing Research*, 27(1), 24–36.

Heide, J.B. & Weiss, A.M. (1995). Vendor consideration and switching behavior for buyers in high-technology markets. *Journal of Marketing*, 59(1), 30–43.

Helson, H. (1948). Adaptation-level as a basis for a quantitative theory of frames of reference. *Psychological Review*, 55(6), 297–313. https://psycnet.apa.org/doi/10.1037/h0056721

Herzberg, F. (1966). *Work and the Nature of Man*. World Publishing.

Heskett, J.L., Jones, T.O., Loveman, G.W., Sasser Jr., W.E. & Schlesinger, L.A. (1994). Putting the service-profit chain to work. *Harvard Business Review*, 72(2), 164–170.

Hogg, M. & Vaughan, G. (2005). *Social Psychology* (4th edn). Prentice-Hall.

Hogreve, J., Iseke, A., Derfuss, K. & Eller, T. (2017). The service–profit chain: A meta-analytic test of a comprehensive theoretical framework, *Journal of Marketing*, 81(3), 41–61.

Holbrook, M.B. (1993). Nostalgia and consumption preferences: Some emerging patterns of consumer tastes. *Journal of Consumer Research*, 20(2), 245–256. http://www.jstor.org/stable/2489272

Homburg, C., Klarmann, M. & Schmitt, J. (2010). Brand awareness in business markets: When is it related to firm performance? *International Journal of Research in Marketing*, 27(3), 201–212.

Hovland, C.I., Janis, I.L. & Kelley, H.H. (1953). *Communication and Persuasion: Psychological Studies of Opinion Change*. Yale University Press.

Howard, J.A. & Sheth, J.N. (1969). *The Theory of Buyer Behavior*. Wiley.

Hughes, C., Swaminathan, V. & Brooks, G. (2019). Driving brand engagement through online social influencers: An empirical investigation of sponsored blogging campaigns. *Journal of Marketing*, 83(5), 78–96.

Iveson, A., Hultman, M. & Davvetas, V. (2022). The product life cycle revisited: An integrative review and research agenda. *European Journal of Marketing*, 56(2), 467–499. https://doi.org/10.1108/EJM-08-2020-0594

Janiszewski, C. (2001). Effects of brand logo complexity, repetition, spacing on processing fluency and judgment. *Journal of Consumer Research*, 28(1), 18–32.

Jap, S.D. & Haruvy, E. (2008). Interorganizational relationships and bidding behavior in industrial online reverse auctions. *Journal of Marketing Research*, 45(5), 550–561.

Jaworski, B.J. & Kohli, A.K. (1993). Market orientation: Antecedents and consequences, *Journal of Marketing*, 57(3), 53–70.

Jaworski, B., Kohli, A.K. & Sahay, A. (2000). Market-driven versus driving markets. J*ournal of the Academy of Marketing*, 57(3) *Science*, 28(1), 45–54.

Jensen Schau, H., Muñiz, A.M. & Arnould, E.J. (2009). How brand community practices create value. *Journal of Marketing*, 73(5), 30–51.

Johnson, M. & Selnes, F. (2004). Customer portfolio management: Toward a dynamic theory of exchange relationships. *Journal of Marketing*, 68(2), 1–17.

Johnson, M.D., Anderson, E.W. & Fornell, C. (1995). Rational and adaptive performance expectations in a customer satisfaction framework. *Journal of Consumer Research*, 21(4), 695–707.

Johnson, W. (2004). *Powerhouse Marketing Plans*. American Marketing Organization (AMACOM).

Johnston, J.W. & Bonoma, V.T. (1981). The buying center: Structure and interaction patterns. *Journal of Marketing*, 45(3), 143–156.

Kahle, L.R. & Homer, P.M. (1985). Physical attractiveness of the celebrity endorser: A social adaptation perspective. *Journal of Consumer Research*, 11(4), 954–961. https://doi.org/10.1086/209029

Kahneman, D. (2003). Maps of bounded rationality: Psychology for behavioral economics. *American Economic Review*, 93(5), 1449–1475. https://www.jstor.org/stable/3132137

Kahneman, D. (2011). *Thinking, Fast and Slow*. New York: Farrar, Straus and Giroux.

Kahneman, D. & Tversky, A. (1979). Prospect theory: An analysis of decision under risk. *Econometrica*, 47(2), 263–291.

Kallbekken, S. & Sælen, H. (2013). 'Nudging' hotel guests to reduce food waste as a win–win environmental measure. *Economics Letters*, 119(3), 325–327.

Kalnins, A. (2004). An empirical analysis of territorial encroachment within franchised and company-owned branded chains. *Marketing Science*, 23(4), 476–489.

Kaplan, R.P. & Norton, D.P. (2004). *Strategy Maps: Converting Intangible Assets into Tangible Outcomes*. Harvard Business School Publishing.

Kaplan, R.S. & Norton, D.P. (1996). Linking the balanced scorecard to strategy. *California Management Review*, 39(1), 53–79.

Kashyap, V., Antia, K.D. & Frazier, G.L. (2012). Contracts, extracontractual incentives, and ex post behavior in franchise channel relationships. *Journal of Marketing Research*, 49(2), 260–276.

Katz, E. & Lazarsfeld, P.F. (1955). *Personal Influence: The Part Played by People in the Flow of Mass Communication*. Free Press.

Katz, M.L. & Shapiro, C. (1985a). Network externalities, competition, and compatibility. *The American Economic Review*, 75(3), 424–440.

Katz, M.L. & Shapiro, C. (1985b). Technology adoption in the presence of network externalities. *Journal of Political Economy*, 94(4), 822–841.

Kazancoglu, I., Kazancoglu, Y., Yarimoglu, E. & Kahraman, A. (2020). A conceptual framework for barriers of circular supply chains for sustainability in the textile industry. *Sustainable Development*, 28(5), 1477–1492.

Keiningham, T.L., Cooil, B., Andreassen, T.W. & Aksoy, L. (2007). A longitudinal examination of net promoter and firm revenue growth. *Journal of Marketing*, 71(3), 39–51.

Keller, K.L. (1993). Conceptualizing, measuring, and managing customer-based brand equity. *Journal of Marketing*, 57 (January), 1–22.

Keller, K.L. (1998). *Strategic Brand Management: Building, Measuring, and Managing Brand Equity*. Prentice Hall.

Keller, K.L. (2001). Building customer-based brand equity: A blueprint for creating strong brands. Marketing Science Institute Working Paper series, report no. 01–107.

Keller, K.L. & Lehman, D.R. (2006). Brands and branding: Research findings and future priorities. *Marketing Science*, 25(6), 740–759.

Keller, K.L., Sternthal, B. & Tybout, A.M. (2002). Three questions you need to ask about your brand. *Harvard Business Review*, 80(9), 80–89.

Kelley, H.H. & Thibaut, J.W. (1978). *Interpersonal Relations: A Theory of Interdependence*. Wiley.

Kerin, R.A & O'Regan, R. (2008). *Marketing Mix Decisions: New Perspectives and Practices*. American Marketing Association.

Khamitov, M., Wang, X. & Thomson, M. (2019). How well do consumer–brand relationships drive customer brand loyalty? Generalizations from a meta-analysis of brand relationship elasticities. *Journal of Consumer Research*, 46(3), 435–459.

Kivetz, R., Netzer, O. & Schrift, R. (2008). The synthesis of preference: Bridging behavioral decision research and marketing science. *Journal of Consumer Psychology*, 18(3), 179–186.

Kivetz, R., Urminsky, O. & Zheng, Y. (2006). The goal-gradient hypothesis resurrected: Purchase acceleration, illusionary progress, and customer retention. *Journal of Marketing Research*, 43 (February), 39–58.

Klemperer, P. (1987). Markets with consumer switching costs. *The Quarterly Journal of Economics*, 102(2), 375–394.

Knoeferle, K. & Spence, C. (2021). Sound in the context of (multi)sensory marketing. In J. Deaville, T. Siu-Lan & R. Rodman (eds), *The Oxford Handbook of Music and Advertising* (pp. 833–858). Oxford University Press.

Kohli, A. & Jaworski, B.J. (1990). Market orientation: The construct, research propositions, and managerial implications. *Journal of Marketing*, 54 (2), 1–18.

Kotler, P. & Keller, K.L. (2015). *Marketing management*. Pearson Prentice Hall.

Kraljic, P. (1983). Purchasing must become supply management. *Harvard Business Review*, 61(5), 109–117.

Krugman, H.E. (1965). The impact of television advertising: Learning without involvement. *Public Opinion Quarterly*, 29(3), 349–356. https://doi.org/10.1086/267335

Krugman, H.E. (1966). The measurement of advertising involvement. *Public Opinion Quarterly*, 30(4), 583–596. https://doi.org/10.1086/267457

Kuan, H.-H., Bock, G.-W. & Vathanophas, V. (2008). Comparing the effects of website quality on customer initial purchase and continued purchase at e-commerce websites. *Behaviour & Information Technology*, 27(1), 3–16.

Kumar, N. (2003). Kill a brand. *Harvard Business Review*, 81(12), 86–95.

Kumar, V. (2018). A theory of customer valuation: Concepts, metrics, strategy, and implementation. *Journal of Marketing*, 82(1), 1–19.

Kumar, V. & Venkatesan, R. (2005). Who are the multichannel shoppers and how do they perform? Correlates of multichannel shopping behavior. *Journal of Interactive Marketing*, 19(2), 44–62.

Lakshmanan, A. & Krishnan, H.S. (2011). The Aha! experience: Insight and discontinuous learning in product usage. *Journal of Marketing*, 75 (6), 105–123.

Lancaster, K. (1990). The economics of product variety: A survey. *Marketing Science*, 9(3), 189–205.

Lancaster, K.J. (1966). A new approach to consumer theory. *Journal of Political Economy*, 74(2), 132–148.

Lavidge, R.J. & Steiner, G.A. (1961). A model for predictive measurements of advertising effectiveness. *Journal of Marketing*, 25(6), 59–62.

Leek, S. & Christodoulides, G. (2011). A literature review and future agenda for B2B branding: Challenges of branding in a B2B context. *Industrial Marketing Management*, 40(6), 830–837.

LEGO. (2024a). *Revenue of the LEGO Group from 2003 to 2023 (in billion Danish kroner). Statista*. Statista Inc.. Accessed: June 22, 2024. https://www.statista.com/statistics/282870/lego-group-revenue/

LEGO. (2024b). *Net profit of the LEGO Group worldwide from 2009 to 2023 (in billion Danish kroner). Statista*. Statista Inc.. Accessed: June 22, 2024. https://www.statista.com/statistics/292305/lego-group-net-profit/

Leiblein, M.J., Chen, J.S. & Posen, H.E. (2023). Uncertain learning curves: Implications for first-mover advantage and knowledge spillovers. *Academy of Management Review*, 48(1), 123–148.

Lembke, A. (2021). *Dopamine Nation: Finding Balance in the Age of Indulgence*. New York: Penguin Audio, 2021.

Lemon, K. & Verhoef, P.C. (2016). Understanding customer experience throughout the customer journey. *Journal of Marketing*, 80(6), 69–96.

Lessin, J.E. (2013, 5 February). Apple tries (a little) harder to get its message out. *Wall Street Journal*. http://blogs.wsj.com/digits/2013/02/05/apple-tries-a-little-harder-to-get-its-message-out/

Levitt, T. (1960). Marketing myopia. *Harvard Business Review*, 38(4), 24–47.

Levitt, T. (1965). Exploit the product life cycle. *Harvard Business Review*, 43(6), 84–94.

Levitt, T. (1980). Marketing success through differentiation—of anything. *Harvard Business Review*, 58(1), 83–91.

Levitt, T. (1981). Managing intangible products and product intangibles. *Harvard Business Review*, 59(3), 94–102.

Levy, S. (1959). Symbols for sale. *Harvard Business Review*, 37(4), 117–124.

Lewis, M.M. (2006). Customer acquisition promotions and customer asset value. *Journal of Marketing Research*, 43(2), 195–203.

Lilien, G.L., Rangaswamy, A. & De Bruyn, A. (2007). *Principles of Marketing Engineering*. Trafford Publishing.

Livesey, S.M. & Kearins, K. (2002). Transparent and caring corporations? A study of sustainability reports by The Body Shop and Royal Dutch/Shell. *Organization & Environment*, 15(3), 33–258.

Locke, E.A. (2000). *Handbook of Principles of Organizational Behavior*. Blackwell.

Lovett, M.J. & Staelin, R. (2016). The role of paid, earned, and owned media in building entertainment brands: Reminding, informing, and enhancing enjoyment. *Marketing Science*, 35(1), 142–157.

Machleit, K.A., Madden, T.J. & Allen, C.T. (1990). Measuring and modeling brand interest as an alternative ad effect with familiar brands. *Advances in Consumer Research*, 17 223–230.

MacInnis, D.J. & Jaworski, B. (1989). Information processing from advertisements: Toward an integrative framework. *Journal of Marketing*, 53(4), 1–23 .

MacInnis, D.J. & Park, C.W. (1991). The differential role of characteristics of music on high- and low-involvement consumers' processing of ads. *Journal of Consumer Research*, 18(2), 161–173. https://doi.org/10.1086/209249

Mackenzie, S.B. (1986). The role of attention in mediating the effect of advertising on attribute importance. *Journal of Consumer Research*, 13(2), 174–195.

MacNeil, I. (1980). *The New Social Contract*. Yale University Press.

Malthouse, E.C., Maslowska, E. & Franks, J.U. (2018). Understanding programmatic TV advertising. *International Journal of Advertising*, 37(5), 769–784.

Marketing Accountability Standards Board. (2020). In *Common Language Marketing Dictionary*. https://(2008).Breakthrough marketing-dictionary.org/

Marshall, A. (1890). *Principles of Economics*. Macmillan.

Maslow, A.H. (1943). A theory of human motivation. *Psychological Review*, 50, 370–396.

Maxwell, R. & Knox, S. (2009). Motivating employees to 'live the brand': A comparative case study of employer brand attractiveness within the firm. *Journal of Marketing Management*, 25(9/10), 893–907.

McAlexander, J.H., Schouten, J.W. & Koenig, H.F. (2002). Building brand community. *Journal of Marketing*, 66(1), 38–54. https://doi.org/10.1509/jmkg.66.1.38.18451

McDonald, M. (2009). *Marketing Plans: How to Stop Wasting Time and Start Driving Growth*. Palgrave Macmillan. Elsevier.

McKinsey. (2023). The triple play: Growth, profit and sustainability. https://www.mckinsey.com/capabilities/strategy-and-corporate-finance/our-insights/the-triple-play-growth-profit-and-sustainability#/

McKinsey and NielsenIQ. (2023). Consumers care about sustainability – and back it up with their wallets. https://www.mckinsey.com/industries/consumer-packaged-goods/our-insights/consumers-care-about-sustainability-and-back-it-up-with-their-wallets?stcr=DCA7D436BA08453A869FE9EAF41801C4&cid=other-eml-alt-mip-mck&hlkid=363c920a27b74f5997c38bdd25127765&hctky=10204615&hdpid=48b4aabe-b8ce-4100-b260-2c12748a7464#/

Menon, A., Bharadwaj, S.G., Adiam, P.T. & Edison, S.W. (1999). Antecedents and consequences of marketing strategy making: A model and a test. *Journal of Marketing*, 63(2), 18–40.

Menon, S. & Kahn, B.E. (1995). The impact of context on variety seeking in product choices. *Journal of Consumer Research*, 22(3), 285–295.

Meuter, M.L., Ostrom, A.L., Roundtree, R.I. & Bitner, M.J. (2000). Self-service technologies: Understanding customer satisfaction with technology-based service encounters. *Journal of Marketing*, 64(3), 50–64.

Michell, P., King, J. & Reast, J. (2001). Brand values related to industrial products. *Industrial Marketing Management*, 30(5), 415–425.

Mohr, J., Sengupta, S., Slater, S.F., Iacobucci, D. & Churchill, G. (2010). *Marketing Research: Methodological Foundations*, 10th edn. South-Western/Cengage Learning.

Mohr, J.J., Sengupta, S. & Slater, S.F. (2010). *Marketing of High-Technology Products and Innovations*. Prentice Hall.

Moncrief, W.C. & Marshall, G.W. (2005). The evolution of the seven steps of selling. *Industrial Marketing Management*, 34, 13–22.

Moreau, C.P., Lehmann, D.R. & Markman, A.B. (2001). Entrenched knowledge structures and consumer response to new products. *Journal of Marketing Research*, 38(1), 14–29.

Morgan, A. (2004). *The Pirate Inside: Building a Challenger Brand Culture Within Yourself and Your Organization*. John Wiley & Sons.

Morgan, R.M. & Hunt, S.D. (1994). The commitment–trust theory of relationship marketing. *Journal of Marketing*, 58(3), 20–38.

Morhart, F.M., Herzog W. & Tomczak, T. (2009). Brand-specific leadership: Turning employees into brand champions. *Journal of Marketing*, 73(5), 122–142.

Muehling, D.D., Sprott, D.E. & Sprott, D.E. (2004). The power of reflection: An empirical examination of nostalgia advertising effects. *Journal of Advertising*, 33(3), 25–35.

Muniz, A.M. Jr. & O'Guinn, T.C. (2001). Brand community. *Journal of Consumer Research*, 27(4), 412–432. https://doi.org/10.1086/319618

Nadeau, J. & Casselman, R.M. (2008). Competitive advantage with new product development: Implications for life cycle theory. *Journal of Strategic Marketing*, 16(5), 401–411.

Neslin, S.A., Grewal, D., Leghorn, R., Shankar, V., Teerling, M.L., Thomas, J.S. & Verhoef, P.C. (2006). Challenges and opportunities in multichannel customer management. *Journal of Service Research*, 9(2), 95–112.

Neuhaus, T., Millemann, J.A. & Nijssen, E. (2022). Bridging the gap between B2B and B2C: Thought leadership in industrial marketing – a systematic literature review and propositions. *Industrial Marketing Management*, 106, 99–111.

Nijmeijer, K.J., Fabbricotti, I.N. & Huijsman, R. (2014). Making franchising work: A framework based on a systematic review. *International Journal of Management Reviews*, 16(1), 62–83.

Nijs, V.R., Dekimpe, M.G., Steenkamp, J.-B. & Hanssens, D.M. (2001). The category-demand effects of price promotions. *Marketing Science*, 20(1), 1–22.

Nunes, J.C. & Drèze, X. (2006). Your loyalty program is betraying you. *Harvard Business Review*, 84(4), 124–131.

Ohanian, R. (1990). Construction and validation of a scale to measure celebrity endorsers' perceived expertise, trustworthiness, and attractiveness. *Journal of Advertising*, 19(3), 39–52. https://doi.org/10.1080/00913367.1990.10673191

Oliver, R.L. (1980). A cognitive model of the antecedents and consequences of satisfaction decisions. *Journal of Marketing Research*, 17(4), 460–469.

Oliver, R.L. (1997). *Satisfaction: A Behavioral Perspective on the Consumer*. McGraw Hill.

Oliver, R.L. (1999). Whence consumer loyalty? *Journal of Marketing*, 63(Special Issue), 33–44.

Oliver, R.L. & Winer, R.S. (1987). A framework for the formation and structure of consumer expectations: Review and propositions. *Journal of Economic Psychology*, 8(4), 469–499.

Olson, E.L. & Thjømøe, H.M. (2009). Sponsorship effect metric: Assessing the financial value of sponsoring by comparisons to television advertising. *Journal of the Academy of Marketing Science*, 37, 504–515.

Olson, E.L. & Thjømøe, H.M. (2011). Explaining and articulating the fit construct in sponsorship. *Journal of Advertising*, 40(1), 57–70.

Olson, J.C. (1977). Price as an informational cue: Effects on product evaluations. In A.G. Woodside, J.N. Sheth and P.D. Bennett (eds), *Consumers and Industrial Buying Behavior* (pp. 267–286). Elsevier.

Otto, A.S., Szymanski, D.M. & Varadarajan, R. (2020). Customer satisfaction and firm performance: insights from over a quarter century of empirical research. *Journal of the Academy of Marketing Science*, 48(3), 543–564.

Palmatier, R.W. & Sridhar, S. (2017). *Marketing Strategy: Based on First Principles and Data Analytics*. Palgrave.

Palmatier, R.W. & Sridhar, S. (2021). *Marketing Strategy: Based on First Principles and Data Analytics*. Palgrave.

Palmatier, R.W., Dant, R.P., Grewal, D. & Evans, K.R. (2006). Factors influencing the effectiveness of relationship marketing: A meta-analysis. *Journal of Marketing*, 70(4), 136–153.

Parasuraman, A. & Grewal, D. (2000). The impact of technology on the quality–value–loyalty chain: A research agenda. *Journal of the Academy of Marketing Science*, 28(1), 168–174.

Parasuraman, A., Zeithaml, V.A. & Berry, L.L. (1988). SERVQUAL: A multiple-item scale for measuring consumer perceptions of service quality. *Journal of Retailing*, 64(1), 12–40.

Park, C.W., Jaworski, B.J. & MacInnis, D.J. (1986). Strategic brand concept-image management. *Journal of Marketing*, 50(4), 135–145.

Park, C.W., MacInnis, D.J., Priester, J., Eisengerich, A.B. & Iacabucci, D. (2010). Brand attachment and brand attitude strength: Conceptual and empirical differentiation of two critical brand equity drivers. *Journal of Marketing*, 74(6), 1–17.

Payne, J., Bettman, J. & Johnson, E. (1992). Behavioral decision research: A constructive processing perspective. *Annual Review of Psychology*, 43, 87–131.

Percy, L. & Rosenbaum-Elliott, R. (2021). *Strategic Advertising Management*, 6th edn. Oxford University Press.

Persvold, A.Z. (2018, 7 May). Nostalgi. I Store norske leksikon. https://snl.no/nostalgi

Peter, C. & Ponzi, M. (2018). The risk of omitting warmth or competence information in ads: Advertising strategies for hedonic and utilitarian brand types. *Journal of Advertising Research*, 58(4), 423–432. https://doi.org/10.2501/JAR-2018-005

Peteraf, M.A. (1993). The cornerstone of competitive advantage: A resource-backed view. *Strategic Management Journal*, 14, 171–191.

Petty, R.E. & Cacioppo, J.T. (1981). *Attitudes and Persuasion: Classic and Contemporary Approaches*, 1st edn. Routledge. https://doi.org/10.4324/9780429502156

Petty, R.E. & Cacioppo, J.T. (1986a). *Communication and Persuasion: Central and Peripheral Routes to Attitude Change*. Springer Verlag.

Petty, R.E. & Cacioppo, J.T. (1986b). The elaboration likelihood model of persuasion. *Advances in Experimental Social Psychology*, 19, 123–205. https://doi.org/10.1016/S0065-2601(08)60214-2

Petty, R.E., Cacioppo, J.T. & Goldman, R. (1981). Personal involvement as a determinant of argument-based persuasion. *Journal of Personality and Social Psychology*, 41, 847–855. https://doi.org/10.1037/0022-3514.41.5.847

Pick, D. & Eisend, M. (2014). 'Buyers' perceived switching costs and switching: A meta-analytic assessment of their antecedents. *Journal of the Academy of Marketing Science*, 42(2), 186–204.

Piercy, N.F. (1987). The marketing budgeting process: Marketing management implications. *Journal of Marketing*, 51(4), 45–59. https://doi.org/10.1177%2F002224298705100405

Piercy, N.F. & Morgan, N.A. (1994). The marketing planning process: Behavioral problems compared to analytical techniques in explaining marketing plan credibility. *Journal of Business Research*, 29(3), 167–178.

Pindyck, R.S. & Rubinfeld, D.L. (2017). *Microeconomics*. Pearson Prentice Hall.

Plott, C.R. & Zeiler, K. (2007). Exchange asymmetries incorrectly interpreted as evidence of endowment effect theory and prospect theory? *American Economic Review*, 97(4), 1449–1466.

Polites, G.L. & Karahanna, E. (2012). Shackled to the status quo: The inhibiting effects of incumbent system habit, switching costs, and inertia in new system acceptance, *MIS Quarterly*, 36 (1), 21–A13.

Porter, M. (1985). *Competitive Advantage: Creating and Sustaining Superior Performance*. The Free Press.

Porter, M.E. (1979). How competitive forces shape strategy. *Harvard Business Review*, 57(2), 137–145.

Porter, M.E. (1980). *Competitive Strategy: Techniques for Analyzing Industries and Competitors*. The Free Press.

Porter, M.E. (1996). What is strategy? *Harvard Business Review*, 74(6), 61–78.

Porter, M.E. (2008). The five competitive forces that shape strategy. *Harvard Business Review*, 86(1), 78–93.

Powell, G.R. (2008). *Marketing Calculator: Measuring and Managing Return on Marketing Investment*. John Wiley.

Price, L.L. & Arnould, E.J. (1999). Commercial friendships: Service provider–client relationships in context. *Journal of Marketing*, 63(4), 38–56.

Pulendran, S. & Speed, R. (1996). Planning and doing: The relationship between marketing planning styles and market orientation. *Journal of Marketing Management*, 12(1/3), 53–68.

Pulendran, S., Speed, R. & Widing, R. II (2002). Marketing planning, market orientation and business performance. *European Journal of Marketing*, 37(3/4), 476–497.

Pun, K.F. & White, A.S. (2005). A performance measurement paradigm for integrating strategy formulation: A review of systems and frameworks. *International Journal of Management Reviews*, 7(1), 49–71.

Punj, G.N. & Staelin, R. (1983). A model of consumer information search behavior for new automobiles. *Journal of Consumer Research*, 9(4), 366–380.

Putrevu, S. (2008). Consumer responses toward sexual and nonsexual appeals: The influence of involvement, need for cognition (NFC), and gender. *Journal of Advertising*, 37(2), 57–70. https://doi.org/10.2753/JOA0091-3367370205

PWC. (2021). Power shifts: Altering the dynamics of the E&M industry. https://www.pwc.com/gx/en/entertainment-media/outlook-2021/perspectives-2021-2025.pdf

Ratneshwar, S., Pechmann, C. & Shocker, A.D. (1996). Goal-derived categories and the antecedents of the hypothetical bias, across-category consideration. *Journal of Consumer Research*, 23(3), 240–250.

Reibstein, D.J. & Farris, P.W. (1995). Market share and distribution: A generalization, a speculation, and some implications. *Marketing Science*, 14(3), 190–203.

Reichert, T. & Ramirez, A. (2000). Defining sexually oriented appeals in advertising: A grounded theory investigation. *NA – Advances in Consumer Research*, 27, 267–273. https://www.acrwebsite.org/volumes/8402/volumes/v27/NA-27

Reichert, T., Heckler, S.E. & Jackson, S. (2001). The effects of sexual social marketing appeals on cognitive processing and persuasion. *Journal of Advertising*, 30(1), 13–27. https://doi.org/10.1080/00913367.2001.10673628

Reichheld, F.F. (2003). The one number you need to grow. *Harvard Business Review*, 81(12), 46–54.

Reinartz, W. & Kumar, V. (2002). The mismanagement of customer loyalty. *Harvard Business Review*, 80(7), 86–94.

Reinartz, W., Thomas, J.S. & Kumar, V. (2005). Balancing acquisition and retention resources to maximize customer profitability. *Journal of Marketing*, 69(1), 63–79.

REQ Marketing. (2015, 16 May). The million dollar quiz [case study]. *REQ Marketing Insights*. https://req.co/insights/article/million-dollar-quiz-case-study

Rigby, D.K., Reichheld, F.F. & Schefter, P. (2002). Avoid the four perils of CRM. *Harvard Business Review*, February, 5–12.

Risitano, M., Romano, R., Rusciano, V., Civero, G. & Scarpato, D. (2022). The impact of sustainability on marketing strategy and business performance: The case of Italian fisheries. *Business Strategy & the Environment*, 31(4), 1538–1551.

Rogers, E.M. (1962). *Diffusion of Innovations*. Free Press of Glencoe.

Rosenberg, M. & Hovland, C. (1960). Cognitive, affective and behavioral components of attitudes. In M. Rosenberg & C.I. Hovland (eds), *Attitude Organization and Change* (pp. 1–14). Yale University Press.

Roth, A.V. & Menor, L.J. (2003). Insights into service operations management: A research agenda. *Production & Operations Management*, 12(2), 145–164.

Rothschild, W. (1979). Competitor analysis: The missing link in strategy. *Management Review*, 68(7), 22–32.

Russell, C.A. (2002). Investigating the effectiveness of product placements in television shows: The role of modality and plot connection congruence on brand memory and attitude. *Journal of Consumer Research*, 29(3), 306–318. https:/doi.org/10.1086/344432

Russell, G.J. & Petersen, A. (2000). Analysis of cross category dependence in market basket selection. *Journal of Retailing*, 76(3), 367–392.

Ryals, L. & Rogers, B. (2007). Key account planning: Benefits, barriers and best practice. *Journal of Strategic Marketing*, 15(2/3), 209–222.

Saad, G. (2015). Behavioral decision theory. *Wiley Encyclopedia of Management*, 1–3. Wiley.

Sahni, N.S. (2016). Advertising spillovers: Evidence from online field experiments and implications for returns on advertising. *Journal of Marketing Research*, 53(4), 459–478.

Samuelson, W. & Zeckhauser, R. (1988). Status quo bias in decision making. *Journal of Risk and Uncertainty*, 1, 7–59. https://doi.org/10.1007/BF00055564

Schiffman, L.G. & Kanuk, L.L. (2007). *Consumer Behavior*. Pearson Prentice Hall.

Schmidt, J. & Bijmolt, T.H.A. (2020). Accurately measuring willingness to pay for consumer goods: A meta-analysis. *Journal of the Academy of Marketing Science*, 48(3), 499–518.

Selnes, F. (1992). Analyzing marketing profitability: Sales are a dangerous cost driver. *European Journal of Marketing*, 26(2), 15–26.

Selnes, F. & Grønhaug, K. (2000). Effects of supplier reliability and benevolence in business marketing. *Journal of Business Research*, 49(3), 259–271.

Selnes, F. & Hansen, H. (2001). The hazard of self service in developing customer loyalty: The mediating role of interpersonal relationships. *Journal of Service Research*, 4(2), 79–90.

Selnes, F. & Johnson, M.D. (2022). Manage your customer portfolio for maximum lifetime value. *MIT Sloan Management*, 64(1), 22–27.

Selnes, F. & Sallis, J. (2003). Promoting relationship learning. *Journal of Marketing*, 67(3), 80–95.

Selnes, F. & Troye, S.V. (1989). Buying expertise, information search and problem solving. *Journal of Economic Psychology*, 10(3), 411–429.

Senft, T.M. (2008). *Camgirls: Celebrity & Community in the Age of Social Networks*. Peter Lang.

Sethuraman, R. (2000). *What makes consumers pay more for national brands than for store brands: Image or quality?* Marketing Science Institute Report nr. 00–110.

Sethuraman, R., Tellis, G.J. & Briesch, R.A. (2011). How well does advertising work? Generalizations from meta-analysis of brand advertising elasticities. *Journal of Marketing Research*, 48(3), 457–471.

Shah, D., Rust, R.T., Parasuraman, A., Staelin, R. & Day, G.S. (2006). The path to customer centricity. *Journal of Service Research*, 9(2), 113–124.

Shankar, V., Carpenter, G.S. & Krishnamurthi, L. (1999). The advantages of entry in the growth stage of the product life cycle: An empirical analysis. *Journal of Marketing Research*, 36(2), 269–276.

Shapiro, B.P. (1988). What the hell is 'market oriented'? *Harvard Business Review*, 66(6,) 119–125.

Shapiro, B.P., Rangan, V.K., Moriarty, R.T. & Ross, E.B. (1987). Manage customers for profits (not just sales). *Harvard Business Review*, 65(5), 101–108.

Sherif, M. & Hovland, C.I. (1961). *Social Judgment: Assimilation and Contrast Effects in Communication and Attitude Change*. Yale University Press.

Shmueli, G. (2010). To explain or to predict? *Statistical Science*, 25(3), 289–310.

Shocker, A.D. (1985). A note on the application of portfolio theory: A comment on Cardozo and Smith. *Journal of Marketing*, 49(Fall), 107–112.

Shocker, A.D., Ben-Akiva, M., Boccara, B. & Nedungadi, P. (1991). Consideration set influences on consumer decision-making and choice: Issues, models, and suggestions. *Marketing Letters*, 2(3), 181–197.

Simons, L. & Bouwman, H. (2006). Extended QFD: Multi-channel service concept design. *Total Quality Management & Business Excellence*, 17(8), 1043–1062.

Simonson, I. (2005). Determinants of customers' responses to customized offers: Conceptual framework and research propositions. *Journal of Marketing*, 69(1), 32–45.

Simonson, I. (2008). Will I like a 'medium' pillow? Another look at constructed and inherent preferences. *Journal of Consumer Psychology*, 18(3), 155–169.

Simonson, I. & Drolet, A. (2004). Anchoring effects on consumers' willingness-to-pay and willingness-to-accept. *Journal of Consumer Research*, 31(3), 681–690. https://doi.org/10.1086/425103

Simonson, I. & Rosen, E. (2014). *Absolute Value: What Really Influences Customers in the Age of (Nearly) Perfect Information*. HarperCollins.

Slovic, P. (1995). The construction of preference. *American Psychologist*, 50(5), 364–371.

Slovic, P., Fischhoff, B. & Lichtenstein, S. (1977). Behavioral decision theory. *Annual Review of Psychology*, 28(1), 1–39.

Smith, A.K. & Bolton, R.N. (2002). The effect of customers' emotional responses to service failures on their recovery effort evaluations and satisfaction judgments. *Journal of the Academy of Marketing*, 30(1), 5–23.

Smith, R.E. & Yang, X. (2004). Toward a general theory of creativity in advertising: Examining the role of divergence. *Marketing Theory*, 4(1–2), 31–58. https://doi.org/10.1177/1470593104044086

Smith, R.E., Chen, J. & Yang, X. (2008). The impact of advertising creativity on the hierarchy of effects. *Journal of Advertising*, 37(4), 47–61. doi: 10.2753/JOA0091-3367370404

Smith, R.E., MacKenzie, S.B., Yang, X., Buchholz, L.M. & Darley, W.K. (2007). Modeling the determinants and effects of creativity in advertising. *Marketing Science*, 26(6), 819–833.

Sorescu, A.B. & Spanjol, J. (2008). Innovation's effect on firm value and risk: Insights from consumer-packaged goods. *Journal of Marketing*, 72(2), 114–132.

Spreng, R., Mackenzie, S. & Olshavsky, R. (1996). A reexamination of the determinants of consumer satisfaction. *Journal of Marketing*, 60(3), 15–32.

Srinivasan, N. & Ratchford, B.T. (1991). An empirical test of a model of external search for automobiles. *Journal of Consumer Research*, 18(2), 233–242.

Srivastava, R.K., Shervani, T.A. & Fahey, L. (1998). Market-based assets and shareholder value: A framework for analysis. *Journal of Marketing*, 62(1), 2–18.

Stabell, C.B. & Fjeldstad, Ø.D. (1998). Configuring value for competitive advantage: On chains, shops, and networks. *Strategic Management Journal*, 19(5), 413–443.

Stanovich, K.E. (2020). Why humans are cognitive misers and what it means for the Great Rationality Debate. In R. Viale (ed.), *Routledge Handbook of Bounded Rationality*, 1st edn (pp. 1–3). Routledge. https://doi.org/10.4324/9781315658353

Statista. (2023, 22 February). Value of the denim jeans market worldwide from 2022 to 2030 (in billion U.S. dollars) [Graph]. In Statista. https://www.statista.com/statistics/734419/global-denim-jeans-market-retail-sales-value/

Statista. (2023a). Most valuable brands worldwide in 2024. https://www.statista.com/statistics/264875/brand-value-of-the-25-most-valuable-brands/

Statista. (2023b). U.S. customer satisfaction with Amazon.com from 2000 to 2023. https://www.statista.com/statistics/185788/us-customer-satisfaction-with-amazon/

Statista. (2023c). American customer satisfaction index scores for Southwest Airlines in the United States from 1995 to 2024. https://www.statista.com/statistics/422062/american-customer-satisfaction-index-for-southwest-airlines-us/

Statista. (2024a). https://www.statista.com/statistics/286547/pepsico-advertising-spending-worldwide/

Statista (2024b). Instagram accounts with the most followers worldwide 2024. https://www.statista.com/statistics/421169/most-followers-instagram/

Steenkamp, J.B., Van Heerde, H.J. & Geyskens, I. (2010). What makes consumers willing to pay a price premium for national brands over private labels? *Journal of Marketing Research*, 47(6), 1011–1024.

Stern, B.B. (2006). What does brand mean? Historical-analysis method and construct definition. *Journal of the Academy of Marketing Science*, 34(2), 216–223.

Sternberg, H.S., Hofmann, E. & Roeck, D. (2021). The struggle is real: Insights from a supply chain blockchain case. *Journal of Business Logistics*, 42(1), 71–87.

Stigler, G.J. (1958). The economies of scale. *The Journal of Law & Economics*, 1 (October), pp. 54–71.

Stout, P.A. & Leckenby, J.D. (1988). Let the music play: Music as a nonverbal element in television commercials. In S. Hecker & D.W. Stewart (eds), *Nonverbal Communication in Advertising* (pp. 207–233). Lexington Books.

Strong, E. (1925). *The Psychology of Selling*. McGraw Hill.

Surprenant, C.F. & Solomon, M.R. (1987). Predictability and personalization in the service encounter. *Journal of Marketing*, 51(2), 86–96.

Tellis, G. (2009). Generalizations about advertising effectiveness in markets. *Journal of Advertising Research*, 49(2), 240–245.

Thaler, R.H. & Sunstein, C.R. (2008). *Nudge: Improving Decisions About Health, Wealth, and Happiness*. Yale University Press.

Thomson, M., MacInnis, D.J. & Whan Park, C. (2005). The ties that bind: Measuring the strength of consumers' emotional attachments to brands. *Journal of Consumer Psychology*, 15(1), 77–91.

Tine. (2022). Annual report. https://www.tine.no/om-tine/TINE-aarsrapport-2022.pdf

Tinto, V. (2001). *Rethinking the First Year of College*. Syracuse University Press.

Top Speed. (2023). Tesla Models Are Pocket-Burning Expensive. https://www.topspeed.com/why-people-hate-tesla-and-why-they-might-be-right/#tesla-models-are-pocket-burning-expensive

Tormala, Z.L., Brinol, P. & Petty, R.E. (2006). When credibility attacks: The reverse impact of source credibility on persuasion. *Experimental Social Psychology*, 42(5), 684–691. doi: 10.1016/j.jesp.2005.10.005

Tostivint, C., Östergren, K., Quested, T., Soethoudt, J.M., Stenmarck, A., Svanes, E. & O'Connor, C. (2016). Food waste quantification manual to monitor food waste amounts and progression, FUSIONS – European Commission (FP7), Coordination and Support Action – CSA – Contract number: 311972.

Trusov, M., Bucklin, R.E. & Pauwels, K. (2009). Effects of word-of-mouth versus traditional marketing: Findings from an internet social networking site. *Journal of Marketing*, 73(5), 90–102.

Tueanrat, Y., Papagiannidis, S. & Alamanos, E. (2021). Going on a journey: A review of the customer journey literature. *Journal of Business Research*, 125, 336–353.

Tuli, K.R., Kohli, A. & Bharadwaj, S. (2007). Rethinking customer solutions: From product bundles to relational processes. *Journal of Marketing*, 71(3), 1–17.

Turn Around H&M. (2018). Low wages in H&M supply chain lead to gender based violence. https://turnaroundhm.org/2018-06-04/

Tuten, T.L. (2020). *Social Media Marketing*. Sage.

Tuten, T.L. & Solomon, M.R. (2016). *Social Media Marketing*. Sage.

Tversky, A. & Kahneman, D. (1981). The framing of decisions and the psychology of choice. *Science*, 211(4481), 453–458.

United States Department of Justice. (2018, July 31). *Herfindahl–Hirschman Index*. justice. gov. Retrieved January 29, 2024, from https://www.justice.gov/atr/herfindahl-hirschman-index

Urban, G.L. & Hauser, J.R. (1993). *Design and Marketing of New Products*. Prentice Hall.

Uslay, C., Altintig, Z.A. & Winsor, R.D. (2010). An empirical examination of the 'Rule of Three': Strategy implications for top management, marketers, and investors. *Journal of Marketing*, 74(2), 20–39.

Uzzi, B. (1996). The sources and consequences of embeddedness for the economic performance of organizations: The network effect, *American Sociological Review*, 61(4): 674–698.

Van Heerde, H.J., Gupta, S. & Wittink, D.R. (2003). Is 75% of the sales promotion bump due to brand switching? No, only 33% is. *Journal of Marketing Research*, 40(4), 481–491.

Van Ittersum, K. & Wansink, B. (2012). Plate size and color suggestibility: The Delboeuf illusion's bias on serving and eating behavior. *Journal of Consumer Research*, 39(2), 215–228.

Venkatesh, R., Kohli, A.K. & Zaltman, G. (1995). Influence strategies in buying centers. *Journal of Marketing*, 59(4), 71–82.

Verhoef, P.C., Kooge, E., Walk, N. & Wieringa, J.E. (2021). *Creating Value with Data Analytics in Marketing: Mastering Data Science*. Routledge.

Vieira, V., Santini, F. & Araujo, C. (2018). A meta-analytic review of hedonic and utilitarian shopping values. *Journal of Consumer Marketing* 35, 426–437. doi: 10.1108/jcm-08-2016-1914

Villanueva, J., Yoo, S. & Hanssens, D.M. (2008). The impact of marketing-induced versus word-of-mouth customer acquisition on customer equity growth. *Journal of Marketing Research*, 45(1), 48–59.

Völckner, F. & Sattler, H. (2006). Drivers of brand extension success. *Journal of Marketing*, 70(2), 18–34.

Voldsgaard, A. & Rüdiger, M. (2022). Innovative enterprise, industrial ecosystems, and sustainable transition: The case of transforming DONG Energy to Ørsted. In M. Lackner, B. Sajjadi & W.Y. Chen (eds), *Handbook of Climate Change Mitigation and Adaptation* (pp. 3,633–3,684). Springer. https://doi.org/10.1007/978-3-030-72579-2_160

von Hippel, E. (2005). *Democratizing Innovation*. Cambridge, MA: MIT Press.

Wanamaker, J. (2020, December 8). In *Britannica*. Retrieved from https://www.britannica.com/biography/John-Wanamaker

Wathne, K.H., Biong, H. & Heide, J.B. (2001). Choice of supplier in embedded markets: Relationship and marketing program effects. *Journal of Marketing*, 65(2), 54–66.

Watson IV, G.F., Beck, J.T., Henderson, C.M. & Palmatier, R.W. (2015). Building, measuring, and profiting from customer loyalty. *Journal of the Academy of Marketing Science*, 43(6), 790–825.

Watson, J., Ghosh, A.P. & Trusov, M. (2018). Swayed by the numbers: The consequences of displaying product review attributes. *Journal of Marketing*, 82(6), 109–131.

Webster, F.E. & Wind, Y. (1972). A general model of organizational buying behavior. *Journal of Marketing*, 36(2), 12–19.

Wedel, M. & Kannan, P.K. (2016). Marketing analytics for data-rich environments. *Journal of Marketing*, 80(6), 97–121.

Weisstein, F., Monroe, K. & Kukar-Kinney, M. (2013). Effects of price framing on consumers' perceptions of online dynamic pricing practices. *Journal of the Academy of Marketing Science*, 41(5), 501–514.

Wernerfelt, B. (1984). A resource-based view of the firm. *Strategic Management Journal*, 5(2), 171–80.

White, T.B., Zahay, D.L., Thorbjørnsen, H. & Shavitt, S. (2006). Getting too personal: Reactance to highly personalized email solicitations. *Marketing Letters*, 19(1), 39–50.

Wien, A. & Tafesse, W. (2017). Merkebygging på Facebook. *Magma*, 4, 15–21. https://www.magma.no/merkebygging-pa-facebook

Wies, S., Bleier, A. & Edeling, A. (2023). Finding Goldilocks influencers: How follower count drives social media engagement. *Journal of Marketing*, 87(3), 383–405.

Wiles, M.A. & Danielova, A. (2009). The worth of product placement in successful films: An event study analysis. *Journal of Marketing*, 73(4), 44–63. https://doi.org/10.1509/jmkg.73.4.44

Williamson, O.E. (1985). *The Economic Institutions of Capitalism*. The Free Press.

Winkler, R., Nicas, J. & Fritz, B. (2017, 14 February). Disney severs ties with YouTube star PewDiePie after anti-Semitic posts. *Wall Street Journal*. https://www.wsj.com/articles/disney-severs-ties-with-youtube-star-pewdiepie-after-anti-semitic-posts-1487034533

Wirtz, J.G., Sparks, J.V. & Zimbres, T.M. (2018). The effect of exposure to sexual appeals in advertisements on memory, attitude, and purchase intention: A meta-analytic review. *International Journal of Advertising*, 37(2), 168–198. https://doi.org/10.1080/02650487.2017.1334996

Wolters, P.T.J. (2018). The control by and rights of the data subject under the GDPR. *Journal of Internet Law*, 22(1), 7–18.

You, Y., Vadakkepatt, G.G. & Joshi, A.M. (2015). A meta-analysis of electronic word-of-mouth elasticity. *Journal of Marketing*, 79(2), 19–39.

Zajonc, R.B. (1968). Attitudinal effects of mere exposure. *Journal of Personality and Social Psychology*, 9(2), 1–27. https://doi.org/10.1037/h0025848

Zajonc, R.B. (1980). Feeling and thinking: Preferences need no inferences. *American Psychologist*, 35(2), 151–175. https://psycnet.apa.org/doi/10.1037/0003-066X.35.2.151

Zeithaml, V.A., Berry, L.L. & Parasuraman, A. (1996). The behavioral consequences of service quality. *Journal of Marketing*, 60(2), 31–46.

Zhou, T., Lu, Y. & Wang, B. (2009). The relative importance of website design quality and service quality in determining consumers' online repurchase behavior. *Information Systems Management*, 26(4), 327–337.

Zhu, F. & Zhang, X. (M.) (2010). Impact of online consumer reviews on sales: The moderating role of product and consumer characteristics. *Journal of Marketing*, 74(2), 133–148.

Zoltners, A.A., Sinba, R. & Lorimer, S.E. (2009). *Building a Winning Sales Force: Powerful Strategies for Driving High Performance*. AMACOM.

INDEX